KEDLESTON ROAD

KNOWLEDGE CAPITAL:

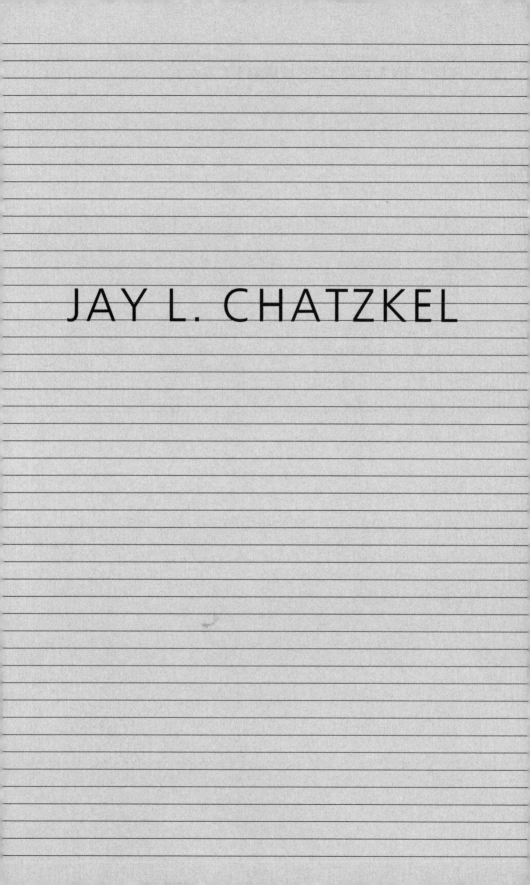

JAY L. CHATZKEL

How
Knowledge-Based
Enterprises
Really
Get Built

KNOWLEDGE *Capital:*

OXFORD
UNIVERSITY PRESS
2003

OXFORD
UNIVERSITY PRESS

Oxford   New York
Auckland   Bangkok   Buenos Aires   Cape Town   Chennai
Dar es Salaam   Delhi   Hong Kong   Istanbul   Karachi   Kolkata
Kuala Lumpur   Madrid   Melbourne   Mexico City   Mumbai   Nairobi
São Paulo   Shanghai   Taipei   Tokyo   Toronto

Library of Congress Cataloging-in-Publication Data
Chatzkel, Jay L.
Knowledge capital : how knowledge-based enterprises really get built /
Jay L. Chatzkel.
   p. cm.
Includes bibliographical references (p.) and index.
ISBN 0-19-516114-9
1. Knowledge management.   2. Executives—Interviews.   I. Title.
HD30.2 .C743 2003
658.4'038—dc21   2003001213

9 8 7 6 5 4 3 2 1

Printed in the United States of America
on acid-free paper

To my wife, Barbara,

the partner who makes me know

that all things are possible

The idea for this book began with a conversational interview with one of the foremost theoreticians and practitioners of the knowledge movement. The goal was to quickly and easily get a sense of his understandings, practices, and ideas. In short, the aim was to get a working sense of his world, how he developed his views, and the directions that he saw the field taking. I was taken by the wealth and richness of understanding that emerged in that session. I felt that by holding similar sessions with others who have shaped and led the fields of intellectual capital and knowledge management, a body of knowledge and experience would become available that would be remarkably accessible, extremely powerful, and highly useful.

This is exactly the kind of hard-won knowledge that anyone interested in the fields of intellectual capital and knowledge management could sorely use. People at conferences and those searching through books want to know how things really work and how those ideas and approaches came into being. The conversations in this book provide precisely that kind of knowledge capital: authentic, broadly embracing, clear, and dynamic.

These linked sessions reflect the major learning principles of the field, most centrally, that knowledge is not separate from people. The contributors to these chapters are remarkably candid in sharing with readers how they developed their knowledge strategies and initiatives. They are outspoken in articulating what is important to them concerning how to craft and implement strategies, as well as their views on the roles that values, learning, performance, relationships, innovation, and change play in the development of a usable knowledge environment.

One of the remarkable aspects of this book is that while all of the contributors begin from their own unique perspectives and backgrounds, as they work their way through their experiences and practices, they each move toward a convergence of understanding. As they push the limits of what their understandings allowed them to accomplish, they reexamine their premises, cross boundaries, and forge the next stage of responses. Reaching the edge of what is currently possible has thus led to the marking out of a new generation of the field.

Engineers, like Karl Wiig, are turning their mental model on its head and saying that learning and education are what we need to focus on. Hubert Saint-Onge, who is rooted in a human resources background, sees that the traditional human resources perspective has become too balkanized and obsolete and that we must reframe our efforts to focus on developing strategic capabilities. Stephen Denning, a lawyer with a strong analytic and administrative background, has discovered that storytelling, something that is experiential, often anecdotal, and highly emotional, provides exactly the springboard for knowledge sharing that people and their institutions need. These are fresh and new understandings. The value of this book is that all of these dynamic perspectives are brought directly to the reader for review. All of these views are, in a sense, works in progress. With the benefit of feedback, ever-broadening experience, and the incorporation of new ideas, these perspectives will go through additional iterations at a rapid pace. This means that all of these conversations could be significantly different three or five years from now, as people continue to experiment in constantly changing conditions. At the same time, these conversations are some of the best collections of insights and experience available to readers, and they are, simultaneously, the seeds of the new era in the knowledge field.

One of the opportunities afforded by this collection of knowledge perspectives is that readers can try them all individually in their own lives and in their organizational work. A second opportunity is that readers can take elements of any or all of these perspectives and fuse them to create their own new and unique approaches.

Readers are encouraged to bring this material into a new focus and to synthesize it to meet their needs. This book is designed as the beginning of a conversation on creating knowledge capital, rather than as a set of prepackaged prescriptions, where one size fits all and the world does not change. Please forward your questions, issues, and outcomes to the Progressive Practices website, www.progressivepractices.com, where you can share your reactions, experiments, insights, and concerns.

As in any complex, novel, and fruitful effort, this book is an outcome of many people's contributions. I would like to first acknowledge each of the contributors who have participated in these conversations. All have devoted extensive amounts of their time in making sure that these materials as fully as possible reflect their experiences and perspectives. They have shared their insights, contributed their graphics, given critical and valued feedback, and in all cases inspired me by their courage, authenticity, ability to articulate their ideas, willingness to get their hands dirty, intelligence, and devotion to their disciplines. The debt I owe them is immeasurable. Thank you to Vince Barabba, Alex Bennet, Jim Botkin, Thomas O. Davenport, Stephen Denning, Leif Edvinsson, Jac Fitz-enz, Kent Greenes, Dorothy Leonard, Jonathan Low, Brook Manville, Sharon Oriel, Göran Roos, Hubert Saint-Onge, Don Tyler, Steven Wallman, and Karl Wiig.

I would like to thank Rory Chase, my editor at the *Journal of Intellectual Capital* and the *Journal of Knowledge Management*, for encouraging and supporting these explorations. Excerpts of several of these chapters have appeared in both journals.

I would also like to acknowledge Martha Cooley of Oxford University Press for her enthusiasm about the value of this book to readers and for shepherding it through the publication process. The value of a good editor cannot be understated in moving a book from stage to stage and into publication.

Finally, I need to express boundless appreciation to my wife, Barbara Chatzkel, for her unwavering support, patience, editing, focus, and just good company throughout this extensive process.

CONTENTS:

KNOWLEDGE CAPITAL:

Why Knowledge Capital?

1

Knowledge for What?

In 1939, Robert S. Lynd in *Knowledge for What?*[1] wrote that people need to rebuild their organizations so that knowledge flows freely to create opportunities and solve problems. This view of knowledge as key for significant change is as relevant for those leading and operating enterprises today as it was then. Knowledge inputs are increasingly valuable not only in all goods and services offered by any kind of organization, but also for how that enterprise does its business day to day. The ability of an organization to effectively nurture, capture, leverage, and share its knowledge resources can be the key that provides an enterprise with its strategic power advantage in the world.

Knowledge is not detached from the people, processes, or infrastructure of an organization and its network. It is part of all of these things and progressively a more pivotal part. The ability to mobilize knowledge resources has become even more critical than the ability to control and amass physical and financial resources. As physical and financial resources have started to take on the character of commodities, the ability to capitalize on knowledge resources is becoming the creator of uniqueness and the differentiator of value.

---

[1] Robert S. Lynd, *Knowledge for What? The Place of Social Science in American Culture* (Princeton, N.J.: Princeton University Press, 1939).

When an organization develops its ability to build, access, and leverage its knowledge resources it is creating its knowledge advantage. It is learning how to most effectively bring to bear its know-how and know-what to yield substantial gains in performance so that it can achieve its strategic outcomes. By understanding the role of knowledge in the enterprise and enabling itself to use its knowledge resources for advantage, an organization is in the process of becoming a knowledge-based enterprise, able to transform its knowledge capabilities into wealth.

Creating Knowledge Capital

The ability to leverage knowledge to create value has grown significantly since the 1980s, with much of this enhanced capability tied to the rise of the disciplines of knowledge management and intellectual capital. While the two fields started from markedly different backgrounds, both have gone through several stages of development to the point that they have major areas of overlap. Enterprises can now weave together powerful strands of both intellectual capital and knowledge management to yield substantial increases in day-to-day performance *and* the related achievement of strategic outcomes.

The term *knowledge capital* is used here as a way to bridge the differences between these two disciplines. *Knowledge* is the resource and *capital* speaks to generating wealth. The central question is: How can enterprises mobilize their knowledge resources to produce wealth?

A way of looking at the knowledge capital equation is to say that intellectual capital is the stock, or content of knowledge, and knowledge management deals with the flow of knowledge. Each plays a critical role, and neither is complete by itself. Amassing sizable amounts of intellectual capital without being able to access, share, or capture value from that resource can be costly and wasteful. For example, the expense of maintaining the best know-how or keeping the richest patent portfolio can exceed the ongoing return on the value of those resources. Similarly, not developing and bringing into play the knowledge resources of staff members, whether leader or front line, marginalizes their value to the enterprise, suboptimizing knowledge capital. On the other side of the coin, focusing on investing in technologies and approaches to enable the flow of knowledge resources when their quality and relevance are barely usable to enterprise networkers is just as questionable.

As an organization remakes itself as a nurturing, leveraging, and knowledge-sharing enterprise, it starts to base its understandings, strategies, and actions on its knowledge capital and begins to be a *knowledge-based enterprise.* It cultivates usable knowledge resources and makes them readily accessible and actionable, putting itself and its people in the best position to create and capture value.

Conversations and the Building of Knowledge Capital

This volume is an integrated and structured set of interactive sessions with thought leaders and key practitioners in the fields of intellectual capital and knowledge management, which maps out how knowledge organizations *really* get built. These sessions are in the form of conversations that explore the multiple dimensions necessary for creating and implementing a knowledge-based enterprise. Each of these dimensions needs to be effectively addressed for the enterprise to make a successful transition from an activity-based organization to a knowledge-based, intelligent enterprise.

The real work of organizations is in conversations such as these. Listen to conversations in any organization, and you will find out what the enterprise takes seriously, what its strategy is, how well it is executing that strategy, what works for it, and what does not. It is in these conversations that the enterprise recreates itself every day. This is true for any type or size of enterprise, whether it is a for-profit, a not-for-profit, or a government organization.

As participants engage in these conversations, they reflect on their experiences, share understandings, and in that process create knowledge capital. The questions are starting points. In the back-and-forth, the conversations take on lives of their own, moving in the directions that most concern the participants. In doing so, they reveal how participants are continuously reexamining their own views in light of their accumulated experiences and the emerging conditions. As owners of their knowledge capital, they feel free to review new inputs and rework them as they see necessary. They are driven by their own curiosity and the need to respond to the challenges in front of them, as well as the ones that are well beyond the next hill. The conversations demonstrate the major elements of what innovative knowledge capital is about: reflecting on the past, incorporating what will make a difference in the present, and remaking oneself and the enterprise, without hesitation, for the future.

Activity-Based versus Knowledge-Based

Activity-based organizations focus on particular tasks people carry out in the course of doing their work. These activities can be any mixture of large or small, simple or complex. The important thing is that in an activity-based organization there is an unending stream of "things to do." The execution of these activities may require having the skills, processes, and resources for a mission, but there is little acknowledgment that knowledge and know-how may be the essential, even critical, inputs for a successful outcome. When the goods and services are fairly standard and practices are essentially repeatable, this might not be a significant problem. However, in our rapidly changing world, standardized outcomes are less and less valuable as conditions, requirements, technologies, and partners are in constant flux, and customer requirements are dynamically growing in complexity and variety.

The new conditions, highlighted by the advent of the Internet and globalization, have spawned the demand for rapid-response, knowledge-based enterprises. The creators of knowledge-based enterprises understand that the intangibles of knowledge and know-how are at the core of all processes. They are aware that their main role is to frame an environment that supports the access, flow, and use of knowledge. They know that rather than controlling resources, they need to facilitate the appropriate flow of the necessary knowledge resources to the right place at the right time to the right people for the right outcomes, and many of these resources are intangible. They have to have trusting relationships since employees now own the most important capital in the enterprise: the human capital.

Part and parcel of their responsibility is the building of strategic competencies that can leverage knowledge throughout the extended enterprise. The extended enterprise includes everyone inside the organization and along the supply chain and the entire customer network. The knowledge-based enterprise is uniquely suited to take advantage of the know-how that is scattered in the nooks and crannies of the organization to reach anywhere in the world, 24 hours a day. It can instantly and interactively link computer programmers in India with a project team in South Africa, a branding group in New York, and a customer in Japan, in a venue where each party takes on the role of being a co-creator of the outcome.

In essence, then, the knowledge-based enterprise is a sense-and-respond, intelligent organization, and its work is ongoing conversation, characterized by building new knowledge capital with new players, new information, new perspectives, new possibilities, and new responses to new customer needs.

Dimensions of a Knowledge Capital Strategy

Conversations involving an enterprise's knowledge capital strategy need to incorporate these dimensions:

- human
- financial
- research and development
- process
- physical and technological infrastructure
- legal
- measurement
- relationships to customers and suppliers

Each of these dimensions is addressed in the sessions that comprise this book from a firsthand perspectives, since the participants in the conversations have had to effectively deal with them in order to create viable, successful knowledge-based organizations.

Knowledge Management as a Practice Field

The advantage of carrying out these explorations using the conversations approach is that the thought leaders and practitioners are fully engaged in what matters most to them. They have experimented and often created the basic ideas and practices of their fields. They know what works and what does not, what is essential and what is hype. With them as guides, the reader gets a unique set of understandings, not only of particular points of theory and lessons learned, but also of the people who are creating these fields. The knowledge and know-how in these sessions comes from their lifelong experience and learning, giving the reader a strong sense of each participant's whole world view. The reader has the opportunity to directly experience the main points in these conversations, as well as to learn about the context, learning process, and values of the participants. The result is not only a knowledge transfer but a context transfer as well.

There is often a fine line between theory and its practice, since the development of each is such an interconnected, evolutionary process. The reality is that thought leaders partner with practitioners, who use their organizations as practice zones to build their knowledge-based enterprises. Their informed practices and learnings provide the immediate feedback that contributes so strongly to the continuous shaping and reshaping of the field.

These sessions are with many of the most outstanding creators and practitioners in the fields of knowledge management and intellectual capital. Participants were extremely candid and broad ranging in their comments. As a result, the reader will get a clear and unvarnished set of insights into what is involved in developing a knowledge-based organization.

One core lesson to be learned from these conversations is that there is no right, mechanistic, cookbook way of building a knowledge-based enterprise. Rather, there is an evolving way, one that is grounded in principles and illuminated and expanded through practice.

While all of the participants started with their own unique views, as the conversations evolved, all began to show a more common perspective and set of concerns. This led to the most remarkable outcome of the sessions: a group of indicators that, when clustered together, form the next stage of the common field of intellectual capital and knowledge management.

Who Can Use This Book

This volume has several purposes:

- *Enterprise CEOs and senior leaders* will have an easily accessible set of perspectives to help them learn what a knowledge-based enterprise is and what is involved in creating and sustaining such an organization in the twenty-first century. This understanding is critical to decision makers in any type of organization. Just as organizational leaders had to learn how to create efficient bureaucracies in the early twentieth century, they will have to learn how to become skillful in creating and managing knowledge-based enterprises in the twenty-first century.
- *Middle managers and front line staff* will find an important set of reference points and guidelines for action. In the knowledge-based enterprise, everyone is a leader and everyone is a decision maker. Autonomy replaces dependency in the knowledge-based organization. In the electronic and Internet era, there is immediate interface and feedback with customers, as well as all along the supply chain. Middle managers and front line staff are increasingly in situations where they do not have time to move up and down the hierarchy when rapid decisions and actions need to take place. They need a model where the glue that holds the knowledge-based enterprise together is made up of knowledge, communications, and values, and supported by technology. They can use these sessions to understand the behav-

iors, relationships, and knowledge capabilities they need to master in order to have a future in a knowledge-based environment.

- *Students* are the next generation of organizational leaders and need to build on the foundation of this generation's ideas and practices. The sessions give a full range of perspectives, and while several of them are academically rigorous, they are unvarnished and not at all pedantic. Rather, they are very much common sense, and, in most cases, materials can be easily shared. *Knowledge Capital* will give students a head start in alternative ways of thinking about organizations as they embark on their professional careers.

- *Practitioners* will gain direct access to many of the founders and shapers of the knowledge-based enterprise. These conversations provide insight into the concentrated experiences of the participants and systematic exploration of the major issues they are working through. Practitioners who are developing knowledge strategies for their organizations need this kind of unfiltered, accessible information. One of the most valuable aspects of *Knowledge Capital* is that practitioners can clearly see the pathways that an array of thought leaders and advanced practitioners have taken, how they have reconsidered some of their earlier stances, what they see as the essentials for effectiveness, and their views on the evolution of the field. The broader and fuller perspectives found in these sessions can save enormous amounts of time and money and put an organization on a sound footing as a knowledge-based enterprise.

A Little History

We all use knowledge every day to make a difference. It might be to leverage power, to generate wealth, or simply to get the job done. The core question is: Are we using that knowledge well or poorly?

While the question of whether we are effectively using our knowledge has become increasingly important over the last 50 years, it has been vital throughout human history. Every culture and society from our cave-dwelling ancestors onward has carried out its version of knowledge capture, sharing, and leveraging to survive and prosper.

One of the greatest achievements in the strategic use of knowledge took place in the fifteenth century when the Portuguese Prince Henry the Navigator began the process that enabled Portugal to move from being a small, unremarkable kingdom on the fringe of Europe to becoming the wealthiest trading empire in the world. At the time, Portugal was far from the centers of trade in the Mediterranean and Near East. It did not have access to the land and sea routes that would let it compete in the traditional ways. The way for it to create power and wealth was to find other, unknown pathways.

Prince Henry saw that the opportunity lay in the sea route around Africa. He began a step-by-step, collaborative national program for advancing into the unknown, a program that turned out to be a century and a half in the making. Being on the outside edge of Europe, the Portuguese were not captives of the entrenched prejudices against the new ways or new knowledge that they needed for their breakthrough. Rather, their way was to test their own limits and, over time, to forge new understandings.

To accomplish this, Prince Henry built an early version of a center for research and development. He assembled the most experienced mapmakers, seafarers, shipbuilders, and instrument makers at Sagres, in the isolated, southwest corner of Portugal. It was at Sagres that Henry began his "conversation" to build his knowledge-based enterprise. His premise was that the unknown could only be discovered by extending the boundaries of the known.

His experiments in shipbuilding produced a new ship design, the caravel, which could sail against the wind. This design gave the caravel the unique ability to not only go out on voyages of discovery, but to be able to return as well. Caravels were not designed to bring back a vast physical wealth but rather the more valuable, intangible wealth of "news." This new knowledge was continuously synthesized in Sagres and eventually became the accrued wealth of knowledge capital that produced the capacity to sail farther and farther down and then around the African coast. The outcome of the leadership, strategic thinking, courage, skills, and innovation at Sagres was the discovery of the sea route to India and then Southeast Asia, which led to a trading empire and the generation of enormous wealth for Portugal. For almost 200 years, this small but archetypal, knowledge-based enterprise, with few physical resources and limited numbers of people, became the dominant, richest trading power in the world.

Prince Henry's experiment demonstrates that in any era, in almost any conditions, the strategic power of a knowledge-based enterprise has the capacity to yield a huge difference. Our challenge is to harness our advanced technology and newly possible networked enterprises to use those same principles for outcomes that go far beyond our own expectations.

How to Use This Book

Knowledge Capital is designed from the reader's point of view. Pick the perspective that best meets your needs. You can read *Knowledge Capital* from cover to cover to get an overview of the field. You can seek out a section that emphasizes a particular set of themes. Or, you can simply turn to the end of each chapter for a summary of key learning points, each of which is more fully explored in that chapter.

The conversations are clustered by major theme or practice area and are followed by an epilogue, which anticipates what the next stage of the field will look and feel like. The major themes are

- Starting Points
- Strategic Issues
- Human Capital, Values, and Learning
- Drivers and Accounting for Intangible Wealth
- Bringing It All Together in Practice

Return to the chapters often. The different perspectives will provide ever-broader and increasingly rich insights into what is necessary for building knowledge-based enterprises to become the interactive, multidimensional entities that they need to be.

Knowledge Cluster I: Starting Points

This cluster outlines the transition to knowledge-based enterprises, the changes of perception, relationships, and behaviors required for an organization to become a knowledge-based enterprise.

2. Dorothy Leonard: Operating as a Knowledge System
The foundation for looking at the way we operate as a knowledge system enables readers to begin to see what kinds of knowledge are being brought in, what are the channels through which knowledge flows, and where we are arbitrarily shutting out various kinds of knowledge assets.

3. Jim Botkin: The Knowledge Business
A new business is emerging: the knowledge business. And there is a new organization emerging: the knowledge community. These two require a new communications or management model called knowledge management. All of these elements need to be in place for a knowledge business to work.

4. Karl Wiig: The Knowledge Movement Emerges from Its Infancy
The amount of knowledge that people are able to capture is minimal compared to what is required to run a business. The balance resides in people's heads. The challenge is to set up the environment so that there

is an understanding of knowledge needs, availability of relevant knowledge, and new ways in which people can collaborate. If you get people together and give them the understanding and freedom to act, they will act in their own interests as they see it and certainly in the organization's best interests.

Knowledge Cluster II: Strategic Issues

The goal of a knowledge initiative is to make a strategic difference. Knowledge capital strategies have a set of concepts, key reference points, and processes that an enterprise can use to navigate its knowledge efforts. An effective knowledge capital strategy will have an appropriate return on investment, align throughout the organization, be supported by staff and suppliers, and improve the value offered to customers. The chapters in this cluster examine the role of strategy in knowledge-based enterprises, suggest methodologies, and raise questions that must be answered by leaders in any serious knowledge endeavor.

5. Göran Roos: Recipes for Knowledge-Based Value Creation
Intellectual capital is the science and art of extracting the maximum value from an enterprise's resources and the way it chooses to deploy them. Business recipes combine those different resources and transform them into new and more valuable outputs. Both resource stock and flow need to be fully taken into account in the transformation process.

6. Leif Edvinsson: The Intelligent Organization
Intelligent organizations are about global intelligence, the courage to move to the next plane, the accounting for intangibles, and how to leverage knowledge recipes for effective outcomes.

7. Vince Barabba: Understanding the Enterprise as a System
The first task in a knowledge strategy is to understand that enterprises are interactive systems with different parts that interface outward with customers and interact among themselves. That is where the opportunities are. It is corporate strategy's job to forge a process to assist management in creating a strategy to implement. This involves surfacing ideas, speculating on how they will interact with the enterprise, involving management in dialogue about them, and providing the analytic tools and resources to support their implementation.

Knowledge Cluster III: Human Capital, Values, and Learning

Organizations are increasingly realizing that it is their human capital that is the source of renewal and innovation. Yet, the rules of engagement for human capital are changing. Human capital was thought to be something that an enterprise could acquire, control, directly manage, and come very close to owning. However, those in successful knowledge enterprises know that human capital can only be brought into full play in a negotiation, where the enterprise and the individual determine mutually satisfying conditions and outcomes. At the same time, the knowledge-based enterprise must redesign itself as an extended learning enterprise.

These are not simple changes, but they are doable changes. The conversations in this cluster delve into what the elements of a new framework for human capital are, the values that support that framework, and the learning structure that enables value to be both created and captured by the enterprise.

8. Jac Fitz-enz: Human Capital Is the Only Active Asset

People are the differentiating factor for an enterprise, and human effort and knowledge efforts are the real levers for achieving markedly higher performance and desired outcomes. Enterprises need to recognize that people are grabbing information, mobility, and connectivity (via the worldwide web and the Internet) and often moving faster than management. Management needs to keep up with them or else it will be dragged along behind them.

9. Thomas O. Davenport: People Are the Owners and Investors of Human Capital

People have taken charge of their human capital and how they want to invest it. Enterprises and managers need to have a strategy to optimize the return on their investment in human capital both to their employees and to the organization. At the center of this strategy is the multiparty "deal," which forms the new social contract among the individual, managers, the organization, and coworkers. The new framework involves understanding the deal, acceptance by all parties, strategic alignment, competence building, and reinforcement.

10. Don Tyler: Shared Values—The Prerequisite for Knowledge Sharing and Creation

Values plus skills equal capabilities for people and their enterprises. Values provide the meaning and motivation to learn new skills. Organizational values need to be first identified and then consistently nurtured. High levels of knowledge sharing and creation can only be sustained after meaningful relationships are established and constantly nourished. Ultimately, the challenge resides in evolving sets of values that extend across the newly networked organizations and that honor a diversity of values as part of the organization's core ethic.

11. Brook Manville: Learning in the Knowledge Era

Knowledge management is part of a broader and more integrated effort to manage and develop human capability for business performance. Managers will assess the gaps in their workforce and direct interventions. At the same time, individual workers will have the opportunity to take control of their learning, which, in turn, moves the organization to be able to achieve its goals and objectives.

Knowledge Cluster IV: Drivers and Accounting for Intangible Wealth

There has been a continuing decline in the relevance of tangible assets and earnings as predictors of stock market performance. Yet there is no decline in the needs of decision makers for transparency and understanding of market drivers in an environment where the intangibles of an enterprise are more significant than the traditional tangible ones for the operation and valuation of enterprises. These conversations delve into efforts to navigate in an environment where biases and distortions are just being sorted out and alternative methodologies for measuring intangible wealth are beginning to be formulated.

12. Jonathan Low: Value Drivers for Intangibles

Traditional measures do not provide enough detail or texture to give managers or investors the information they need. With some insight and effort, we can begin to put together a clearer picture of what is going wrong in an organization, what is going well, what could go better, and how to improve it.

13. Steven Wallman: A Level Playing Field for Intangibles

Financial reporting and disclosure systems are increasingly susceptible to not capturing important drivers of wealth production, specifically, knowledge-based assets. Recognition of intangibles is central in decisions involving capital allocation, financial reporting, appropriate disclosure, and volatility of the financial marketplace.

Knowledge Cluster V: Bringing It All Together in Practice

Practitioners are the ones who lead the transformation from activity-based enterprises to knowledge-based enterprises. They determine how the concepts and practices are introduced into the enterprise. They explore with leadership, middle management, and front line staff how each will benefit by identifying and using knowledge inputs to guide their work. They navigate the alignment of the enterprise's values, technology, strategies, structure and processes, and measures. The sessions in this cluster illustrate a number of different approaches that practitioners are using.

Think about your organization and envision how you could use these approaches to evolve it into more of a knowledge-based enterprise. Do not feel the need to copy any of their efforts in a cookie-cutter manner. They created their methodologies through a great deal of trial and error. Learn from their experiences, try out their ideas and practices, and see what will make the difference for your enterprise.

14. Hubert Saint-Onge: Creating and Implementing a Knowledge Strategy

Hubert Saint-Onge understands that the knowledge strategy of an organization must be geared toward building the capabilities and relationships that form the intangible assets of the firm. The strategy needs to take into account that intangible assets are quite different from tangible assets and need to be managed quite differently. The strategy must link supporting values that align and renew the tacit knowledge of the organization and a compatible technological infrastructure.

15. Kent Greenes: Knowledge Management Is about Change

Kent Greenes lays out the process for creating a knowledge initiative, starting with building a business case for the knowledge initiative to get the attention of a business leader and staff and finding out how the knowledge effort will make a real and personal difference in the day-to-day areas that matter most. It is their buy-in that will allow the knowledge process to have a chance to live. Greenes clearly frames key points that any practitioner must take into account to cultivate a successful knowledge enterprise.

16. Sharon Oriel: Finding "the Hook"

Sharon Oriel sees that leaders in enterprises need to think in terms of managing intellectual capital assets as structural resources. The extension of this view is to align the intellectual capital effort with the enterprise business strategy. The key, then, is to find "the hook" that shows the value of managing intellectual capital to help solve a critical issue in an organization. Once that happens, the practitioner has the license to operate.

17. Stephen Denning: The Springboard Story
Stephen Denning tried everything at the World Bank to engage people in its knowledge initiative. Nothing worked effectively until he found that through storytelling people could identify with and co-create a vision, in their own words, of what their organization could become. Stories became the springboard for sharing knowledge across the organization and eventually with the broader community of users across the world. Storytelling made the knowledge movement alive at the World Bank and, in conjunction with putting in place seven key structural elements, is the basis for it to become a knowledge-based enterprise.

18. Alex Bennet: The Knowledge-Centric Organization
Alex Bennet was in the lead position in the development of a knowledge-centric U.S. Department of the Navy. She demonstrates the role of knowledge in a twenty-first century public sector organization. A key to success for the Navy is knowledge superiority. To accomplish this meant that the Navy needed to build its basic capacities of hardware, software, and wetware. The chapter examines how knowledge is linked to and supports organizational goals. It also explores how the building blocks of a strategic vision, knowledge sharing, knowledge capture, connectivity, alignment, and metrics have been designed into the Navy's approach so that knowledge management supports the achievement of its strategic goals.

Epilogue: Convergence—Toward the Next Stage

As the series of conversations took place, a group of themes started to emerge that will shape the framework for the next stage of the knowledge field. The people involved in *Knowledge Capital* are experimentalists and continuous learners. While they carried out their work on knowledge initiatives, they reflected on their experiences and began to better grasp both the underlying dilemmas and the new sets of issues and perspectives that they saw were in need of being addressed.

Some participants whose roots were in the computer sciences have seen the limits of information technology at this stage, and they now see human learning as the key. Others, who emphasized either knowledge creation or knowledge capture, found that both are equally important in any enterprise, although there is a need to create a framework in which they can be holistically integrated and form a new knowledge value chain. In addition to that, many participants expressed the view that we are in just the initial phases of learning how to nurture and use communities of practice and metrics and how to account for intangible value in organizations. These are among the strands that are woven together in the epilogue and that become the whole cloth of the next, richer, and more reality-based phase of the knowledge movement.

Growing the Seeds

Every enterprise has within it the seeds of becoming a knowledge-based enterprise. Organizations already have extensive amounts of information, data, and measures in their various repositories. However, probably 90% of their knowledge is tacit, residing in the know-how of their staff, suppliers, and customers. The conversations that follow provide a framework and benchmarks to evaluate to what extent an enterprise is knowledge-based, what strategic capabilities it needs to cultivate to further its transformation, and how to go about doing that. The different sessions map out how to create strategies and build the vehicles, relationships, and supporting environment so that knowledge capital is easily accessed, comes freely into play, and is nurtured and leveraged to achieve gains that exceed expectations.

The currency of an enterprise is increasingly based upon its knowledge capital and its ability to mobilize its knowledge resources to respond to changing conditions. The advantage of a knowledge-based enterprise comes from it being better able to understand its resources (both intangible and tangible), its opportunities and risks, and its ability to mobilize those knowledge resources in ways that make a distinct difference.

The future will be won by enterprises that have the capabilities to out-think, out-organize, out-maneuver, and out-perform their rivals. This means enterprises must prepare themselves for continual renewal so they can go beyond the edge of what exists and create new passageways, just as Prince Henry the Navigator did over 500 years ago.

The convergence of networked enterprises, increasingly autonomous human capital, and advances in electronic collaboration technologies provides a unique, and perhaps historic, opportunity for knowledge-based enterprises to leverage their knowledge capital in ways that were never possible before. With these mentoring conversations as a stimulus and guide, embark on a voyage of discovery to find and capitalize on whole new fields of possibilities.

KNOWLEDGE
Cluster I:

This cluster sets out the parameters for what a knowledge-based enterprise is. It explores the elements of a knowledge-based enterprise, what difference it will make to become one, where and how to begin, and the role of innovation and continuous renewal in such an enterprise.

Dorothy Leonard, Jim Botkin, and Karl Wiig map out how being knowledge-based is an outlook or a perspective, as much as it is a certain kind of structure. They share their understandings that we can look at a knowledge-based enterprise as a system with various kinds of knowledge being brought in. They chart the channels through which knowledge flows and note where and how knowledge is converted into goods or service outcomes. The knowledge that is brought in and cultivated is the knowledge that is necessary for building the core capabilities of the enterprise. At the same time, knowledge-based enterprises should be aware of the hazard that, if not regularly reevaluated, core capabilities can change into inflexible core rigidities that constrain the organization.

The Continually Renewing Enterprise

Dorothy Leonard points out that a knowledge-based enterprise is in a process of constant renewal. It starts with a stock of knowledge resources that the enterprise is able to renew by recombining and fusing with other existing knowledge assets and with novel approaches to create new outcomes.

Leonard asserts that since the world is changing so rapidly we cannot really see far enough into the future to know what is in store for our enterprises. This dynamic requires that a knowledge-based enterprise and its people have a high degree of flexibility, the ability to leverage what they know, and the capacity to redeploy assets rapidly and in new directions. The enterprise needs to nurture its people so that they feel free to move about in their organization, to group and regroup in different configurations as needed, and to rework themselves and their resources in concert with their new conditions.

Knowledge Businesses, Knowledge Communities, and Knowledge Networking

Jim Botkin focuses on how knowledge is changing the ways that organizations create value as they become increasingly knowledge-based enterprises. This transition is tied to the growing reality that knowledge has become the new factor of production, one that is emerging as even more significant to the enterprise than the traditional factors of production of land, labor, and financial capital. A powerful indicator of this shift is that the use of knowledge as a factor of production is creating such a competitive advantage that its dominance allows an enterprise to redefine and transform not only itself, but its entire industry.

According to Botkin, we first have to understand that "knowledge products and smart services" are those offerings that embody learning and the capacity to create new knowledge in them. The next step is to grasp that we are dealing with creating knowledge businesses and new forms of organization, which he calls "networked knowledge communities." Keeping the knowledge offerings and knowledge communities' ecology healthy and performing at the highest levels then requires a new communications or management model that we call, in its broadest meaning, knowledge management.

In Botkin's view, in order to understand the role of knowledge in business, we have to consider that the business, the organization, and the management model are parts of a whole cloth—and look at them in the new light of being knowledge businesses, knowledge communities, and knowledge networks. This requires a shift in perception, but it also means that enterprises have to build the infrastructure that supports the flow of knowledge and educate staff, suppliers, and customers on how to operate in this knowledge-grounded environment.

Part of this change involves knowledge-based enterprises redesigning themselves using the format of communities and networks of communities. Communities allow the kind of governance that enables a company to be both centralized and decentralized at the same time. Word of new conditions and requirements can be quickly dispersed throughout the communities, with necessary responses generated to provide feedback to develop informed strategies that are executed locally. In this model, individual communities are the nodes, and all of the communities together form the network.

An important element of this model is that the individuals who make up these communities understand that they have to take responsibility for developing their personal knowledge and skill sets for their own personal success as well as the success of the enterprise. This shift in responsibility pragmatically means that each person comes to act as her own chief knowledge officer.

Different Kinds of Knowledge

Karl Wiig looks at the different kinds of knowledge that are necessary for a knowledge-based enterprise. One is the various types of personal knowledge, a second is shared knowledge, but all strands must come together to form the structural, or institutional, knowledge of the enterprise. This is a living knowledge that clusters together as people build a "synergistic orchestration environment." If the enterprise is transforming itself, people find it natural to share and collaborate, and they do that as a matter of course and culture. The shared knowledge becomes part of the culture and is owned by the organization. In that sense, the shared knowledge takes on a life of its own among the staff and is not based on any one individual's knowledge. But the challenge to the organization is that only 8–10% of the knowledge that is needed to operate the enterprise can be captured. The balance lies in people's heads. That means that the enterprise must recognize the value of its human capital and understand how to cultivate it to build the knowledge ecology, so that knowledge creation and sharing become the way it does business. The enterprise must facilitate knowledge flows, knowledge migration, and the creation of knowledge pathways. Technology is an enabler here for knowledge flows and migration, but it is only part of the necessary response.

Within the organization, working with knowledge is an ongoing process that is supported by a number of tools, systems, and procedures, but it also stimulates a different way of life in the organization.

A major role for leadership in the knowledge-based enterprise is looking to bring to bear all of the best resources and knowledge as part of daily life. This is a leadership that understands that if you get people together and give them the understanding and freedom to act, they will act in the directions that are in their own interests as they see it and certainly in the organization's best interest. An implication for the enterprise is that its knowledge effort will be built around a very small, very energetic, and visionary office, in contrast to the building of another new bureaucracy. This is a proselytizing office, as well as one that can secure the resources needed for sharing across departments. It has a flexible vision of how the knowledge management practice should be undertaken and can identify the business reasons for pursuing it. The next step for the knowledge office is to align its projects with what is on management's hotplate and to evolve its knowledge strategy.

While projects may be catalysts for transforming an organization into a knowledge enterprise, the more embracing object of concern is to be able to identify how an effective enterprise needs to behave intelligently, what that entails, and why knowledge management is important in this regard.

An Active Knowledge Network

These three chapters frame knowledge-based enterprises as open but structured systems that make usable the knowledge capacity of the enterprise. The active nurturing and deployment of this knowledge capability creates innovation and strategic advantage. Only part of this capability is the knowledge that is captured intelligence, stored for later reuse. Other components are the know-how and know-what that run through the fabric and being of the entire enterprise network.

Contributors to this cluster realize that becoming a knowledge-based enterprise involves a continuous transformation of the people *and* the enterprise. Innovation, learning, and change need to be built into all phases and processes of the enterprise network. A knowledge management or intellectual capital group can initiate and assist in the transformation, but the enterprise's leadership, workforce, strategic partners, and even customers each need to take on their counterpart roles as the network's co-creators.

Operating as a Knowledge System

2

Dorothy Leonard explores how organizations effectively build and manage knowledge. She has found that some organizations have developed a capacity for constant renewal. By fostering values and managerial systems that support key knowledge-building activities, managers in such companies continuously enhance their competitively critical core capabilities. Other organizations have not made knowledge and development important, and some are structured to undermine the creation of knowledge assets. In this conversation, Leonard discusses the perspectives, attitudes, and behaviors that are characteristic of each type.

Dorothy Leonard is the author of *Wellsprings of Knowledge*[1] and coauthor with Walter Swap of *When Sparks Fly*.[2] Both are basic books for understanding the role of how knowledge works in enterprises.

Leonard is the William J. Abernathy Professor of Business Administration and director of research at the Harvard Business School. Her major research interests and consulting expertise are in organizational innovation and technology strategy and commercialization. She has worked with a wide range of private and public sector organizations around the world in innovation-related areas.

[1] Dorothy Leonard-Barton, *Wellsprings of Knowledge: Building and Sustaining the Sources of Innovation* (Boston: Harvard Business School Press, 1995).

[2] Dorothy A. Leonard and Walter Swap, *When Sparks Fly: Igniting Creativity in Groups* (Boston: Harvard Business School Press, 1999).

Wellsprings of Knowledge

JC: *What do you mean by wellsprings of knowledge, and what are the conditions for wellspring renewal?*

DL: *Wellsprings of knowledge* refers to a constant process of renewal, that is, having enough knowledge assets that you can constantly renew them. One of the first requirements of renewal is that managers understand what the knowledge assets of their particular organization are. Then, they have to understand how to expand and leverage those assets.

Let me give you some examples. Knowledge assets can be technological. For instance, 3M has deep knowledge about great abrasives, adhesives, and coatings. We would not have a product such as masking tape were the engineers at 3M not able some time ago to be able to combine what they knew about putting paper on the back of things (for example, in sandpaper) with their knowledge of adhesives. Combining those basic knowledge assets gave them a new product.

Recently I was asked by a reporter whether a Kodak foray into using its software capability to improve underwater photography using traditional film was an unwise use of resources, because after all this was merely enhancing—using digital means to enhance analog technology. My feeling was: "No, that was extremely wise." What we do is take what we know best and combine that with what is new and exciting in the market, and often that synergy gives us a boost. So renewal can come from the fusion of existing technological knowledge assets, or it may come from simply looking at what we do best. One last example. At Harvard Business School, the core capabilities are its ability to deliver experiential learning and to provide topnotch classroom experiences. Now, we happen to be the first business school that ever delivered that experiential learning through case studies. If we were to say that all we know how to do is case studies, we would be selling short the more important basic capability of delivering experiential learning, which we now need to interpret in new ways. We need to think in terms of multimedia, electronic simulations, and distance learning. We need to incorporate new technologies into the delivery of one of our core capabilities.

We do not want to confine our definition of our knowledge assets to written case studies. We want to think about the core capability of experiential learning. If you define your competitive advantage narrowly by describing exactly how you operationalize your core capabilities today, then you will not have room for renewal. If you define them generically, then you have more room to morph, to change, and to adapt.

Perspectives That Make the Difference

JC: *What difference does it make that managers view every-day activities from the perspective of knowledge management and growth?*

DL: It makes as much difference as any other perspective or screen through which you habitually look at your activities. Let's consider the Toyota production system, which is viewed as one of the most interesting, efficient, and effective learning processes in manufacturing today. It is a very complex system that people have tried to imitate piecemeal without understanding the philosophy and viewpoint behind it. Yet, considering the manufacturing process through the lens of the Toyota production system philosophy fundamentally affects everything that a manager at Toyota does.

Let me give you an example. The purchasing manager of a particular Toyota plant set up in the United States came out of traditional U.S. manufacturing. He was accustomed to selecting suppliers on the basis of lowest *price*. Toyota taught him to look for the lowest *cost* supplier and to work with that supplier to increase its knowledge about how to hold costs down. Now, consider the difference in investment and long-term payoff in terms of partnership and cost advantage you get if you partner with a supplier with the idea in mind that you are going to transfer some knowledge assets to it about holding its costs down so that it can, in turn, reliably deliver components to you at the lowest cost. There is a big difference in mental attitude as to whether one seeks low *cost* versus low *price*. Your relationship with your suppliers is based on how much they know and how much you can help them learn.

Every little decision can be viewed from the perspective of whether it helps us learn, helps increase the knowledge assets of the expanded enterprise—which is what Toyota was doing—or whether it simply represents an expedient way to get something done for the moment, which is the way the purchasing manager had been educated in his prior job.

How We Know What We Know

JC: *How do we understand knowledge assets and the depths at which we need to operate in order to keep them as well-springs?*

DL: I think what you are asking is: "How do we know what we know?" There's both breadth and depth to knowledge assets. Much of the knowledge of any organization is held in the heads of the people. Recognizing this fact immediately causes one to ask, "How do we really treat our people and regard the people who are our employees?" Every company today would say, "Our people are our most important asset." But very few companies really treat them that way. Those that do, that have used their knowledge of their people and their knowledge assets, can turn themselves around in dire situations. I am thinking of Harley-Davidson at the moment. Rich Turlink, the retired CEO, was at the helm when that company turned itself around, and it was clear that he relied tremendously on the people in the factory to do that. In order to really understand our knowledge assets in depth, managers all the way up the line really have to understand "What do our people know?"

Let me give you a negative example. I remember being in a boardroom at a large company in the steel industry that shall remain nameless. The CEO turned to me and said that he was considering letting go (nice terminology) a group of people who were in their advanced sales department. He asked me, "What is the humane way to do that?" I asked, "What do they do?" It was clear he did not know. He turned to his henchmen, and they did not know. Nobody in that room knew what this group of people did. How could they decide, really? They had decided to fire them because it was a cost center that they did not think had any particular importance to their business, but nobody had gone to explore.

I was allowed to go find out what they did. What I discovered was that these people anticipated the need for certain kinds of products years ahead of time. For instance, there was one fellow whose geographic location and responsibility was Washington, D.C. He found out, a couple of years before it actually became law, that there was legislation making its way through the House and Senate that would require a drastic reduction in the emissions of noxious fumes from home furnaces. This meant that some caustic fumes had to be trapped in the flue. Reasoning ahead, he thought, "This means that our customers are going to be requesting much more corrosive-resistant steel in the furnaces that they produce." And, he knew that his company had some of these corrosion-resistant alloys in its nuclear division, which could be transferred over to the commercial division.

He put all of this information together and then positioned the company in the market so that it would have the requisite alloys for the furnace companies when the legislation came out. He opened up a market two years ahead of its competitors. In that one instance, he paid for the salaries of the five or six people in his group many times over. But nobody in the boardroom knew what he did.

JC: *Was he building the background for what they were doing in the foreground?*

DL: He was advanced sales, so he was anticipating the market. But nobody had stopped to ask what the group did. It turned out that these five or six people had been in the business for quite some time, and most of them were going to retire in a few years.

The other thing this company had not done, once they realized that the group was, in fact, extremely valuable, was to figure out how they were going to replace them. The lesson is to know what people do.

Motivating Knowledge Building

JC: *How can managers, and all staff for that matter, learn how to select the correct knowledge sources, understand how knowledge is accessed, how it is channeled and redirected, and fight contamination?*

DL: That is an enormous question. I am not sure that you could answer that question in a targeted fashion. It also relates to how we get people to think about their knowledge building and the importance of small decisions they make routinely in a day's work. I think if you look back at the quality movement you would find that it was a huge struggle to get anyone to think deeply about quality. W. Edwards Deming, pioneer of the quality movement, was preaching overseas before he was ever accepted as a prophet in his own country. One of the reasons was that no one was being *measured* on quality. They were being measured on output.

Measurement is tremendously important. People are smart. They respond to the incentive systems and the rewards systems that we put in place. Therefore, it is always crucial to look at how our organization is set up to reward people. If we set it up for short-term gains with no regard for the long term, then we are going to get what we deserve—which takes us back to my example of Toyota and cost versus price.

If you reward people for creating knowledge, for developing other people, and for transferring knowledge to other people, you will get a certain outcome. For instance, at Hewlett-Packard, at least historically, you could not be promoted until you had trained someone to take the place you were vacating, that is, you had to become a teacher, a mentor, in order to progress. Think what a different mentality that rule encourages. You get ahead in the organization by sharing knowledge—and *only* by sharing knowledge. This rule probably goes a long way toward explaining Hewlett-Packard's long stretch of success—although it may be faltering now—and the impact that HP alumni have had in parts of the world, such as Singapore, where the company has had a division since the 1970s.

JC: *Who develops those incentives, and how do those incentives come into being?*
DL: The founders have a tremendous influence on the value system instilled in their organization. In turn, that value system influences the way that people are motivated and rewarded. But too often, at least in the past, there has been a disconnect between the human resources department, which determines policies, and the daily activities of people in the organization who are concerned with knowledge. Often, if you ask, "Why is this not a learning organization?" you can track the lack of learning and transfer of knowledge directly to the incentive system.

JC: *It is that embedded in the organization?*
DL: It is deeply embedded in the organizational/managerial system.

JC: *What do you think of the moves to transform HR into strategic capabilities?*
DL: It is not just HR, either. The same thing has been happening throughout the organization. Take purchasing. Personnel in purchasing in many organizations used to be order takers or order writers. And as I said, if you look at the Toyota system, the purchasing people have had to become strategic thinkers. They are setting up partnerships that will affect the company's well-being for years to come.

Knowledge-Based Strategic Thinking

JC: *Is having that knowledge perspective part of being a strategic thinker?*
DL: Absolutely. If we accept the idea that we really cannot see far enough into the future to know what's coming down the pike in most of our businesses, then we have to accept that we must be flexible, we must be able to leverage what we know and deploy our assets quickly in new directions. Such agility requires an incentive and motivational system that allows people to move about in the organization, grouping and regrouping in different configurations.

Human resources is becoming recognized as a very strategic capability. Organizations that have long recognized that they were knowledge organizations, for example, consulting firms, have spent a tremendous amount of effort on recruiting and training, because from the beginning they knew that they did not have any other product beyond the knowledge their employees produced.

JC: *Their intellectual capital was their asset.*
DL: Right. So now that mentality is very gradually spreading to other companies, which are beginning to realize that many of their assets are knowledge assets.

The Tacit Dimension of Knowledge

JC: *Why is any technology advantage people-based?*
DL: Because so much technological implementation and use relies on the tacit dimensions of knowledge. If we look at the knowledge required to use technology to the best advantage, we find that a lot of it requires understanding technology's place in an overall system of delivering goods and services. That understanding often is composed of the tacit as well as the explicit dimensions of knowledge. In other words, you do not get people to use technology to the best advantage by handing them a manual. They will learn how to operate it. But the manual does not tell them how the technology can be used to the best advantage within the particular system and context in which they live and are delivering their work.

JC: *Is it the people's know-how that has to be engaged?*
DL: Yes. The machine by itself is rarely a strategic component of a core capability.

JC: *Others have said that the only active assets in an organization are the human assets, since the other assets are passive. Are you saying we have to engage the active assets to leverage all the other ones?*
DL: Yes, that's what I'm saying.

Core Capabilities versus Core Rigidities

JC: *How can core capabilities be simultaneously core rigidities, and how can that dark side be overcome?*
DL: The Western mind is very uncomfortable with a paradox, and the concept of core rigidities as the flip side of core capabilities is a paradox. It takes about seven to ten years, according to the folks who have studied expertise, to become truly expert in some field, whether it is music, chess,

operating a particular machine, writing, or whatever. Cognitive psychologists have discovered that expertise and superior competence depend less on native ability than on attention and practice. The same is true for any company or organization. The very time and attention that employees devote to developing certain core capabilities means that those core capabilities are entrenched and pervade the organization. Therefore, by definition, they are also ways of operating and looking at the world that are resistant to other forms of knowledge. For instance, if we are the very best company in the world in the knowledge of silver-halide technology, we are less likely to be the world's best in electronics, until we decide that we're going to devote some attention and practice to that field. We have recruited, rewarded, and promoted experts possessing knowledge about film; we have not attracted and retained experts in digital imaging. Therefore our core capability is simultaneously a core rigidity.

JC: *How do we overcome that?*
DL: Overcoming core rigidities is the major topic of my books, both *Wellsprings of Knowledge* and *When Sparks Fly*. The first step is to diagnose where your organizational systems lead you to screen out certain kinds of knowledge and bring in other kinds. In other words, if you look at the way that you operate as a knowledge system, you will see what kinds of knowledge are being brought in, what are the channels through which knowledge flows, and where you are closing out various kinds of knowledge assets.

JC: *Would that require a strong desire?*
DL: That goes back to the first point—that you have to know what you know in order to be able to renew it. In today's world, I do not think any of us has much choice. We have to innovate to survive, and thus we have to figure out how to constantly challenge the core rigidities in our organizations and constantly create new knowledge.

Choosing the "Right" Knowledge-Creation Activities

JC: *How do we know if we are initiating the "right"*
knowledge-creation activities?
DL: One diagnostic is benchmarking. We have to judge ourselves by the very best in our class, not just in our industry, but also anywhere in the world and in any industry in order to know how we measure up. If we are a learning organization, we are constantly measuring ourselves against the very best customers, the very best competitors, the very best organi-

zation or group in any particular function, whether it be a direct competitor of ours or not.

JC: *Do benchmarked organizations provide some referencing to help you guide your choices?*
DL: Yes. The only way you can tell whether you are initiating the right knowledge-creation activities is to measure your progress along some dimensions, and one way to measure your progress is to hold extremely high standards for a particular function, say, for logistics or for manufacturing.

Let's go back to Toyota again. If it finds that it is falling behind on the usual kinds of manufacturing measures, that throughput time or overtime is going up or productivity waning, it doesn't just try to treat the symptoms, it tries to look for the deep cause and seek the knowledge that is missing. It uses well-known manufacturing measures as indicators of when it needs to look at its system and see where it is failing.

JC: *The company is going more into profound knowledge then?*
DL: Yes. If you are really interested in the right knowledge-creation activities, you'll always be looking for the root causes of problems rather than treating the symptoms.

JC: *What are the activities that create and direct key activities into becoming core capabilities? How can managerial behaviors either build or undermine those capabilities?*
DL: The activities that I highlight in *Wellsprings* are not core capabilities in and of themselves, so they do not *become* core capabilities. They *feed* core capabilities. They bring the knowledge in that is necessary to build the capabilities.

For example, I have written quite a bit about the need in many organizations to bring in knowledge about unarticulated user needs that are unlikely to be uncovered through traditional marketing research. Empathic design[3] is one example of an underutilized activity that can bring in many more new ideas and product and service innovation possibilities than the usual marketing knowledge channels. I wrote a *Harvard Business Review* article about it in 1997, and I have written about it in *Sparks*.

Empathic design is an example of a set of nontraditional market research techniques that can augment traditional techniques—but not act as

---

[3] *Empathic design* is a set of techniques, a process of developing deep empathy for another's point of view and using that perspective to stimulate novel design concepts (*When Sparks Fly*, p. 82).

a substitute for them. Empathic design is a set of activities that brings in knowledge through new and different channels. Using this set of ethnographic techniques can help build new capabilities or enhance an existing core capability. I give a lot of examples in both the article and the book of how people have used empathic design to come up with novel ideas that could not be identified in surveys or interviews—because the users themselves were unaware of their own needs and the possibility of meeting those needs through an innovative product or service.

The activities that I enumerated in *Wellsprings* seem to be very important in renewing knowledge assets. One such activity is the ability to prototype and experiment. Another is the capability for creative problem solving, something that we wrote about quite a bit in *Sparks*. Being able to set up teams so that you have the potential for creative abrasion is an example of an activity that can enhance your innovative capacity and leverage your core capabilities in new ways.

Creative Abrasion

JC: *What is creative abrasion?*
DL: I borrowed the term from Jerry Hirshberg, formerly the president of Nissan Design International. I was calling it something else until I talked to Jerry, and I thought it was a wonderful term. *Creative abrasion* refers to the impersonal intellectual disagreement that occurs among people who bring to a problem very different perspectives, born of their tacit knowledge. Managers who deliberately hire and formulate teams of people who think differently raise the probability that team members will generate more options from which to choose. They will also disagree more with each other, and therefore the manager has to shape the debate for more light than heat—more idea generation than personal argument.

JC: *How do managers function as the gatekeepers of knowledge in organizations?*
DL: Managers function as gatekeepers because they become extremely aware of the knowledge-building or-destroying implications of anything they do. If they are educated to the perspective that they are in charge of knowledge assets just as much as they are of financial assets, they also will become aware of their own biases. We all become comfortable with certain kinds of knowledge, in part because of our personal thinking style preferences, our backgrounds, and our education—our own knowledge assets. If a manager is very well versed and comfortable with the financial measures of an organization, she may be very uncomfortable with measuring knowledge assets that are not

as easily defined and for which accounting principles have not been set up over 300 years as they have for financial measures.

Managers, consciously or unconsciously, encourage their subordinates and their colleagues to present and use certain kinds of arguments based on certain kinds of knowledge, with which these managers are comfortable. Some of us crave lots of detail; others of us prefer the big picture. Some of us are extremely comfortable being given lots of data; others want structure and closure in the knowledge shared with us.

The Role of the Manager

JC: *How are the different levels of managers important for engendering a knowledge management perspective?*

DL: I think often the firstline supervisors are the most important, and we give them the least training. They are critical. One of my colleagues, Amy Edmondson, has studied a phenomenon she calls *psychological safety*, which is the perceived ability of people in a team or group to report undesirable occurrences—failures, slip-ups, mistakes. She has studied this in a number of settings, including hospitals. She noted that even within an organization that has the same positive upper management attitude toward reporting failure and thereby correcting mistakes and setting up better systems, one finds tremendous variance among groups depending upon the behavior of the nurse leading that group. In many cases, the upper management is not the key gatekeeper of how an organization learns, but, in fact, that ability to learn and accrue knowledge, especially from mistakes or failures, is evidenced by people at the supervisory level. This is the ability to *fail forward*, as I have called it.

Time for Learning

JC: *How can you factor in the slack time for learning that is necessary for building knowledge-based enterprises?*

DL: There are two aspects of this. One is that I think a lot of knowledge management systems miss the boat because they emphasize extracting and putting knowledge into systems off-line—not while you are actually doing your work. I do not think that knowledge management systems are going to be successful until our computer systems are smart enough to capture the knowledge while we are doing our work. No one really has time to sit down to write reports or put knowledge into systems. This is why so many of the knowledge capture systems have not been successful; companies have had to assign people to become the knowledge librarians and archivists. I am sure that's tremendously useful, but I think the real breakthrough will come when we can archive potentially critical knowledge as we are working.

JC: *Is that not part of the design process of the work?*
DL: It is also part of the design process of the knowledge management system, isn't it? Point number one is, then, that we should not have to have slack time to capture knowledge from daily work. But the second point is that we do need some incubation time for creativity. I am not saying that those are totally separate. Obviously there is a lot of creativity that enters into our daily work.

Another one of my colleagues, Teresa Amabile, has found in a very extensive study something that we all have suspected: The more rushed people are and the more time pressure that people are under, the less they produce creative solutions. That may seem to be contradictory to the experience that a lot of people have today with "speed, speed, speed," innovating quickly and getting to market first, and so forth. But those two observations are not totally incompatible.

First of all, I think we will find that we are outpacing with time pressures the human capacity to be creative and to be innovative. I think the time pressures can be too extreme. On the other hand, you can have too much leisure, too. That is not a problem that we have right now.

Structured and Unstructured Learning

JC: *Chaparral Steel has a multiyear apprenticeship system,*
where an employee goes through a master learning process.
That is factored in, and it is part of the philosophy. Is that
how Chaparral is developing the knowledge it needs to be a
knowledge organization?
DL: Although those individuals do have to invest some of that time on their own, too.

JC: *Is that part of a contract that has evolved?*
DL: Yes. This relates to structured and unstructured learning. A tremendous amount of money is spent today on structured learning in organizations, and it is very important. Unfortunately, the training and education budget is often the first to be cut when there's a problem. But there is a lot of investment by companies in the training of managers, and we have all these universities that have been set up by companies.

At the same time, I would argue that actually unstructured learning is the most important learning in any organization. In *Sparks* we talk about structuring the physical organization and environment as well as the psychological environment to allow informal learning and knowledge transfer to occur. For instance, we talk in *Sparks* about how you can set up areas for unplanned communication and how critical that is to people, because so much innovation occurs at the intersection of planes of thought that have not been connected before.

JC: *Can we have the supporting elements for unstructured learning in both the design of the organization and the design of the physical spaces?*
DL: Right. You can encourage unplanned communication and allow it to happen, and we know that co-location is very valuable for that reason. We know that open doors encourage communication. That does not mean that people do not need time to have doors closed as well.

The Fractal Factor

JC: *Is this the fractals aspect of things?*
DL: Yes. I think that goes back to the issue of how any value system has to permeate the whole organization. I just gave you the example of the hospital. Even if top management has stressed learning, reporting mistakes, failing forward, and having psychological safety, if that mentality does not permeate the organization, and if every nurse's group does not agree with that and every nurse-manager does not promote that, then that attitude is not going to permeate the organization, and you are still going to have mistakes and people afraid to talk about mistakes, and therefore they will not learn.

The idea of fractals is that the value system has to permeate all the way down to the lowest managerial unit, whether that is 3 people or 13. And again, harking back to the quality movement, you know how easily quality can be undermined by factions or groups within the organization that don't really understand its criticality. Under pressure, you go back to your old routine. Or you, as an employee, respond to the most immediate stimulus—which may be your supervisor rather than the vice president, the president, the CEO, or whatever.

JC: *Did that tie into your views on homogeneity versus heterogeneity in values?*

DL: Yes. To have innovation, intellectual diversity, and heterogeneity is critical, but homogeneity in *values* is desirable because, for example, going back to Amy Edmondson's work, if you have a nurse who really is very authoritarian and does not allow or encourage people to speak up about mistakes, then that group is going to be subject to a lot of fear about mistakes and failure. The value system there is "Don't rock the boat, and don't talk about problems." The norms are "Don't admit when you have a near-miss. Let's not worry about improving the system, and let's be sure that we cover our rear ends."

You can undermine the value of an organization at many different levels. That is why it is important to have everyone understand what the overall value system of an organization is.

On the other hand, you do want heterogeneity of viewpoint, background, and perspective to the degree that you want innovation and along the dimensions in which you want innovation and creativity.

Constantly Renewing Organizations

JC: *What are the characteristics of constantly renewing organizations?*
DL: I think that the most important things we have talked about are

- valuing knowledge assets at least as much as you do financial assets,
- understanding the importance of unstructured learning and encouraging learning, and
- having a value system that supports a certain degree of risk taking and innovation.

JC: *Do you think we are moving to an adequate extent in that direction?*
DL: I think there is still a lot of debate as to how we innovate in large organizations. I think that is the next frontier. Gary Hammell would say that we need to have innovation be as much a part of the fabric of the company as any other quality. We can encourage innovation and creativity within even large organizations. I think Clayton Christensen's work suggests that many organizations are forced to spin off creative and innovative little units because they would be killed off within the large organization. Those two viewpoints are not incompatible. I think, though, that both people would argue that there is difficulty innovating within organizations, for a particular kind of innovation.

Technological innovation, as long as it serves the same market we have always served, is actually relatively easy. We know how to do that. We have extraordinarily talented engineers and scientists. It is not easy, but relatively so. When we are addressing whole new markets or whole new business plans, business models, and so on, it is quite difficult.

The Next Conversation

JC: *Is that the next conversation?*
DL: I think so. Yes. I know that the group out here is beginning to tackle the issue of what should the large corporations of the future look like. And I know that both Clay Christensen and Gary Hammell are giving a lot of thought to how we innovate within large organizations. I hope that we will find that there's a menu of ways. Some organizations will, indeed, find that one of the ways is to acquire new little companies, as Cisco does, whereas others will say we have got the people within, but they need to be spun off into a separate little organization, and we will take some equity and they'll continue to feed back to us some knowledge. And still others may find ways to organize that will allow a constant innovation within the organization without spinning it out.

Key Learning Points

- Managers need to understand what the knowledge assets of their particular organizations are. Then, they have to understand how to expand and leverage those assets.
- Renewal can come from the fusion of existing technological knowledge assets.
- If you define your competitive advantage narrowly by describing exactly how you operationalize your core capabilities today, you will not have room for renewal. If you define them generically, then you have more room to morph, to change, and to adapt.
- Every little decision can be viewed from the perspective of whether it helps us learn, helps increase the knowledge assets of the expanded enterprise.
- Measurement is tremendously important. People respond to the incentive systems and rewards systems that we put in place. If you reward people for creating knowledge and developing other people, transferring knowledge to other people, you will get a certain outcome.
- Looking at the way that we operate as a knowledge system will allow us to see what kinds of knowledge are being brought in, what are

the channels through which knowledge flows, and where we are closing out various kinds of knowledge assets.

- The only way we can tell whether we are initiating the right knowledge-creation activities is to measure our progress along some dimensions. One way to measure your progress is to hold extremely high standards for a particular function.
- If you are really interested in the right knowledge-creation activities, you'll always be looking for the root causes of problems rather than treating the symptoms.
- Managers function as gatekeepers because they become extremely aware of the knowledge-building or -destroying implications of anything they do.
- The upper management is not the only gatekeeper of how an organization learns. The ability to learn and accrue knowledge, especially from mistakes or failures, is also controlled by people at the supervisory level.
- The most important things to focus on are
  - valuing knowledge assets at least as much as we do financial assets,
  - understanding the importance of unstructured learning and encouraging learning, and
  - having a value system that supports a certain degree of risk taking and innovation.

The Knowledge Business

3

This conversation with Jim Botkin explores how knowledge is changing how organizations create value as knowledge-based enterprises. Botkin argues that the knowledge framework is actually the larger context for organizations and that e-business is actually a subset of its operations. Botkin also shares how knowledge has come to be a new factor of production in organizations, both "new economy" organizations and "old economy" legacy organizations. Even so, the acceptance of the knowledge movement is still tentative. The very name *knowledge management* still often implies information technology "applications" to key organizational visionaries and is not always well received. The controversies over nurturing knowledge communities within the framework of knowledge initiatives are also examined in this dialogue.

Botkin has an excellent perspective for delving into these issues as cofounder and president of InterClass, the International Corporate Learning Association. InterClass is a knowledge community of Fortune 500 companies seeking to improve its members' organizational learning and to enhance their knowledge assets. Since 1990, Botkin has led InterClass as it has grappled with the future of work, organizational learning, intellectual capital, virtual organizations, managing change, knowledge management, and new leadership styles. While still a senior advisor to InterClass, he has his own practice as an executive coach, focusing on leadership and life coaching.

Botkin is the author of *Smart Business: How Knowledge Communities Can Revolutionize Your Company.* He is an expert on corporate learning and knowledge and a student of the ideas and practices involved in successful innovations in legacy companies. He is also co-author of *No Limits to Learning* and *The Monster Under the Bed.*[1]

Botkin is an IC2 fellow of the University of Texas in Austin and has taught at the Harvard Graduate School of Education. His doctorate is from the Harvard Business School.

The Conversation

The Knowledge Organization and E-Business

JC: *Can you comment on how the knowledge organization, or k-organization, goes beyond e-business?*

JB: In a way, e-business, e-commerce, and the dot.com companies have become such a big deal that it obscures the fact that they are only part of the picture. Some would say e-business is basically a new business and a new business model, but I am skeptical about that. To understand the role of knowledge in business, you have to consider the business, the organization, and the management model—or the knowledge business, knowledge communities, and knowledge networking—which are, respectively, the new economy companies' basic business, organizational, and management models.

The knowledge business can go beyond dot.coms—for example, consulting companies are knowledge businesses. The larger question is: "What are knowledge products and smart services?" They are those offerings that embody learning and the capacity to create new knowledge in them. They can be Internet-based or not. My favorite example is the company in Boulder, Colorado, called Outlast Technologies. It has the patent rights to develop materials (cloth, fabric, clothing, car seats). They can weave micro phase-change materials (PCMs) into the fabric. The PCM is genetically engineered to sense cold, which makes it turn hot. When it senses hot, it starts to turn cold. That is a great example of a non–computer-based, nonelectronic, non-Internet knowledge business. Your shirt literally knows better than you do what the temperature is outside, and it adjusts itself,

[1] Stan Davis and Jim Botkin, *The Monster Under the Bed: How Business Is Mastering the Opportunity of Knowledge for Profit* (New York: Simon and Schuster, 1994); James W. Botkin, Mahdi Elmandjra, and Mircea Malitza, *No Limits to Learning: Bridging the Human Gap: A Report to the Club of Rome* (Oxford: Pergamon, 1979).

unknown to you, to a more comfortable temperature. Here's a new a biochemical process knowledge product that goes far beyond the Internet. And there are other examples of those. Some are Internet-based, and some are not.

JC: *The main thrust is that there is a larger perspective beyond e-business?*

JB: Yes. The more a product is interactive, self-customizing, capable of remembering and improving your use of it, the more it is a knowledge product. When it has these characteristics *and* is web-based, you've got double-strength knowledge. But just because it's Internet-based does not necessarily mean it's a knowledge product.

Take Nike sneakers. The new Nike sneaker has special material in the sole that when it feels I am running, it starts to stiffen up, and when I slow down it gets softer. It is interacting with me in real time. I could imagine the step further being that, as soon as they get a little microprocessor in there, I could communicate with it. I could control the stiffness or looseness of the shoe as I am running. This is the basis of a knowledge business when you are talking about products that have the ability to learn and the capacity to create new knowledge built into them.

So, the changes of the last 10 years have brought us to just the tip of the iceberg. Eventually we will realize the scope of the whole knowledge business and see that the Internet part is just a subset.

New Business Models

JC: *What will the new business models look like?*

JB: There are two aspects implicit in your question. One concerns KM—knowledge management—or what I prefer to call *knowledge networking*. Another is community. I was amazed at a recent knowledge management summit that it was not just me talking about community. A lot of people were into that field.

There is a whole new movement around the word *community*, which generates a lot of emotions. Different people feel very differently about it. We are in a situation just like 10 or 20 years ago when teams were seen as the next big thing or when quality was accepted as necessary to all companies. The next big organizational thing is going to be the community. Community allows a company to be both centralized and decentralized at the same time. Using community as your basic building block can be thought of as the new network model of organization, where the nodes are communities and a number of communities together form a network. You do not see this in very many places yet. But once you tune into the concept, you will be amazed at the number of companies that describe themselves this way.

So there is a new business emerging: the knowledge business. And there is a new organization emerging: the knowledge community. These two require a new communications or management model that we call knowledge management. So I do not see KM as the be-all and end-all, in the sense that if you do not have the other two things, you are missing part of the bigger picture.

Knowledge Management and Intellectual Capital

JC: *When you say knowledge business, do you differentiate between knowledge management and intellectual capital?*
JB: I'm not convinced that KM and IC are closely related, but my doubts may come from my own experience. We are all captives of our own experience. I learned about intellectual capital at one of our InterClass business meetings, back in the early 1990s when Leif Edvinsson and Hubert Saint-Onge were just starting to flesh out the theory of intellectual capital. At that same meeting, we had Brian Hall, who developed a 130-item questionnaire we can use to discern our own values, how they match with the organization's values, and where on the developmental scale it puts us. I found that experience terribly informative.

Thus, I associate intellectual capital with the values question. I also find the IC model of structural, human, financial, and customer capital to be a very useful device to think about our future directions and what our organizational strategy will be. For example, in which of those four areas does my company, InterClass, need more work? We have great customer capital. We have relatively normal, perhaps somewhat weak, structural capital. Our financial capital is always shaky, but then again, everybody's is. Our human capital is quite strong. The question is: "Which of these areas needs to be strengthened?" What is the proper balance?

KM, however, I do not associate with values or strategy but with communications, the capturing of best-yet practices, and sharing for reuse what's worked before. Therefore, I do not even associate IC and KM in the same ballpark. I do know, however, in speaking with some of the intellectual capital proponents, that they have felt somewhat assaulted by the knowledge management movement. There is an intellectual competition going on for "a share of mind space." Any of us can hold in our heads only one, two, or three of these things at once. If you are holding in your head the intellectual capital model, it's difficult to get your arms around the knowledge management one. And vice versa.

Visionaries and Pragmatists

JC: *Are you saying that they seem to be presented as mutually exclusive?*

JB: Each seems to appeal to a different subset of the population. I was very influenced by Geoffrey Moore's books, *Inside the Tornado* and *Crossing the Chasm*.[2] He does a wonderful job at differentiating the population, any population, into visionaries and early adopters, who are on one side of the chasm, and then market mainstream and later adopters, who are more pragmatic. Moore's point is that you need both visionaries and pragmatists, but you need them at different times in the life cycle of a product or a company. So, don't be stupid and fire all of your visionaries just when things are going great because that is when the pragmatists have their say. When you are in need of reinvention, you better be sure you have your visionaries around or you are in trouble. My experience is that there is not one but *two* chasms. The first is the one that Moore describes, which comes at the beginning of an innovation curve. The second, which is known to those who practice "built to last," comes at the end of the curve, when it's time for renewal. That's when the visionaries come back into the picture to add value.

This view gives me a lens with which I view my own role in Inter-Class—which is a bridge across the two chasms. InterClass is one of the few organizations that has both visionaries and pragmatists talking to each other and learning from one another.

JC: *That is one of the themes of your book* Smart Business. *You say we need both capabilities to carry this off.*

JB: Yes, I consciously wrote with language that is acceptable to both visionaries and pragmatists. My quick take is that the knowledge management movement has been highjacked by pragmatists prematurely. When I went to a recent meeting attended mostly by visionaries and we brought up the issue of knowledge management, it was almost shouted down: "How can you even associate those two words with each other?" Then, they would

[2] Geoffrey A. Moore, *Inside the Tornado: Marketing Strategies from Silicon Valley's Cutting Edge* (New York: Harper Collins, 1995); Geoffrey A. Moore and Regis McKenna, *Crossing the Chasm*, rev. ed. (New York: Harper Business, 2002).

look at people like me and say: "Worse yet, Botkin, you came up with the *community* word, and want to build communities. Don't you know they can only be nurtured?"

There are three options for management of communities: build them, nurture them, or just leave them alone. I could feel the emotions rising in the room: "Just leave them alone. You can't manage a community. Managing knowledge is one of the most absurd things we've ever heard of."

In my mind a movie comes on: "Oh, this is the visionaries speaking. They're fed up with pragmatic IC people thinking they can manage knowledge. The visionary response is to withdraw from or reframe the KM debate." This is how KM comes to be mostly pragmatists in contrast to IC, which is still mostly visionaries.

We can see the possible futures of IC and KM by looking back at the quality movement and reengineering. KM is more like reengineering than it is like quality, that is, it may die a premature death unless it gets on a quality trajectory. Everybody has to have quality today. It's basic to doing business. This should be where KM (or K-networking) needs to move. It just becomes part of everyone's business system.

Reengineering, on the other hand, was a movement doomed to failure by its name and the deadening images associated with its implementation. Some of my friends who were very active in the reengineering movement in the early days are now embarrassed to be associated with it. It was a great idea whose implementation somehow went astray. In the name of reengineering, many companies went through downsizing only to rehire all of the same people as consultants at higher prices. It was a shortsighted vision for something that wanted a long-term vision.

The visionaries got squeezed out of the reengineering movement, often as victims. This was partly due to the name. Imagine if it would have been called "redancing" instead of reengineering. Visionaries would have cheered and gotten into it and figured out a way to have companies grow rather than downsize.

Preparing for the New Economy

JC: *What are the key characteristics of the new economy and organizations that fit the new economy? What would it take for businesses to be better prepared for the explosion of knowledge?*

JB: Wherever possible you need to think in terms of network organizations built on communities. You need to think about your culture as being a knowledge-sharing culture. The only way to deal with the explosion of knowledge is to have lots of scouts out there in all of the different domains of your business where knowledge makes a difference. And you have to figure out a way to get the knowledge widely shared, widely understood, and widely accepted as the business purpose. A lot of words, which are usually encapsulated under the term *knowledge-sharing culture*.

JC: *So those would be the kinds of things that people need to consider for the explosion of knowledge?*
JB: Yes. I think it has a lot to do with whether your corporate culture is knowledge-friendly or not.

JC: *How can we make an old-style firm, designed for the industrial world, ready for a different world and transform it into a "smart business"? Most firms are in that category, so how do you morph?*
JB: There are only two ways to morph: either choose "restart" or "shut down." Saturn is an example of a restart. It could not morph at home in Detroit, so it moved to a greenfield (previously undeveloped site developed for commercial purposes) situation in Spring Hill, Tennessee. Some old industrial cultures are so strong that the only way I would know to get them to change would be to simply bypass them. You set up and finance a new operation outside the corporation—which is what IBM had to do to start up the PC, the famous case of the IBM skunkworks. This is what General Motors had to do to start Saturn.

The other option is a shut down. In other words, it takes a shock, or usually two shocks, in case the troops didn't get it the first time. We ought to look at shocks, such as near-bankruptcies, as blessings. Los Alamos National Laboratory had such a shock at the end of the Cold War that totally threatened its existence as a nuclear weapons laboratory. Faced with those kinds of situations, everybody said, "My God! We really have to change!"

There are a few historical cases of companies that seemed to find a "third way" between the choices of restart or shut down. IBM's successful makeover from typewriters to word processors; Motorola's successful morphing from TV sets to cell phones. These are great stories; they are miracles. A problem is that they are seldom replicable. They depended on historical circumstance, right leadership, and spectacularly flexible workforces able to learn new ways of working.

There's a possible trap here: the best and the brightest trap. Hire the cream of the crop, and they will be able to work miracles. Wrong. The best and brightest have no monopoly on miracles. Cases in point are Polaroid and Digital Equipment. Both always hired the best and the brightest.

They had huge successes in their early days. But they were not able to parlay their early successes into new economy businesses.

Leveraging Knowledge as a New Factor of Production

JC: *What do you mean when you say that companies must leverage knowledge as a new factor of production?*
JB: Key to the old economy are the classical factors of production: land, labor, and capital. And the operating model is one of scarcity. When we talk about the classical factors, we are talking about wanting to accumulate more of them. We want to have as much control over them as we can, in the sense of managerial control. Essentially, there is a fixed amount of land, labor, and capital at any one time. Until recently, we had thought that capital was scarce, and the challenge was to allocate it well.

The new economy adds knowledge as the chief factor of production, and the model changes from one of scarcity to one of abundance. Knowledge does not behave the same way as the classical factors. The more you use it, the more it grows. It's sort of like the ultimate fax machine. You get this packet of knowledge and you send it out over the fax machine. But you still have the original knowledge, even if the more you send it out, the more people know it. The more people know it, the better it becomes. The better it becomes, the more valuable it becomes.

Knowledge is a factor of production that is fundamentally different from the classical factors. This is our new economy business challenge: How do we capitalize on that? We have to learn the new rules of knowledge sharing—when to share and when to not.

We talk, for example, of the value of sharing knowledge. A lot of people will say that, but we have to take another step. In the real world, you better know when to share knowledge and when not to share knowledge. There are some things that are prohibited by law from sharing. Such cases are patents, or doctor-patient confidentiality, or lawyer-client confidentiality. The rules of the new economy are going to challenge the old economy's patent system.

JC: *Why do you find it surprising that Internet-era companies seem to be maturing with all the "ugly warts and whiskers" of the industrial heroes of yesterday?*
JB: The Microsoft case bugs me. A big inventor, Bill Gates, is on top of a pyramid and, God forbid, you should do anything against his wishes. It's almost like Ken Olson of Digital, with the whole company reading the

Ken Olson tea leaves to see what to do next. This goes back to Standard Oil, John Rockefeller, Andrew Carnegie, and the financial world. I don't see a new organizational model in Microsoft.

I have a feeling the new networked model of organizing may be as likely to come from some of the old industrial companies or industries, of which Saturn is the most exemplary, as it will be from the new software companies, computer hardware companies, and dot.coms. Sun Microsystems and Cisco are two possible leaders in this regard.

The Near-Death Experience: Is It Necessary?

JC: *Do these organizations also need to go through a "near-death" experience to see the need to transition into being knowledge-based enterprises?*

JB: You mean, are they subject to the restart-or-shut down dilemma? Yes, they are, and how it will turn out depends on learning. Learning is the active acquisition of new knowledge. Highly successful older organizations tend to acquire the two worst enemies of learning, which are monopoly and arrogance. Sound like Microsoft? When I seek new companies to join my InterClass learning community and look at some very successful brand-name companies, if they are too successful I've learned to pass them by. It's not worth trying to get them to join a knowledge community. Some places are not just open to learning from others. They will need to go through a near-death experience in order to transition to any kind of knowledge-based economy or enterprise.

JC: *What are the consequences to the economy if organizations do not go through this transition?*

JB: The consequences for each of the companies are major. They will go out of business. Royal and Underwood Typewriter thought that they were the kings of the hill back in the 1930s. So did RCA. They did not make the transition, and they went out of business. The only typewriter company that survived the onslaught of microprocessors was IBM.

But what's the impact on the economy? It will become even more of a boom-and-bust economy than we already have. Wild swings in the NAS-DAQ and Dow are evidence, and the up-and-down wild rides will likely increase.

I always was struck by Taichi Sakaiya, who says in his book *The Knowledge-Value Revolution*[3] that the knowledge economy is essentially a

[3] Taichi Sakaiya, *The Knowledge-Value Revolution; or, A History of the Future*, trans. George Fields and William Marsh (Tokyo: Kodansha, 1991).

boom-and-bust economy. Knowledge is so fluid, moving around from place to place. It shortens our time horizons, production runs, the life cycles of products and services, so we are always having to reinvent ourselves.

The two surprising industries are oil and automobiles: They have more knowledge work going on than anybody in Silicon Valley would ever admit. Good old General Motors with its OnStar system. That is leading-edge stuff. They don't get credit for it because General Motors is always the whipping boy. If you look at the automotive industry as a whole, in the United States, Europe, and Japan, there are more new things that you can define as knowledge accessories coming out on more new cars than you can believe. That begins to change the nature of the beast. It might be that the General Motorses and Fords of the world will actually undergo some very significant organizational changes.

JC: *What is a knowledge business? How can knowledge businesses transform themselves and their industries?*

JB: *Knowledge businesses* have products and services that have the abilities to create new knowledge and to learn embedded in them as natural parts of their process. To use the car case: What will we call the thing on four wheels that drives itself when your choice is to be an expert driver or a passive passenger? When I first came across that type of example, I thought, "Oh, they will have to change all the roads. There's huge infrastructure change." Someone from Sun Microsystems said, "Give me a break. I just drove for the last half hour in a car that had no driver. It was powered off the global satellite system. It can see perfectly well where you are, whether there is an obstruction in front of you or not."

This is another case of building more and more knowledge into an old product. It's going to transform the industry. You have to reframe the whole way you conceive the business you are in. If we could have new implants that took care of failing memories, would you be in the health business any more?

Where Does Knowledge Reside?

JC: *Where does the knowledge reside in different businesses, and how do you manage that knowledge?*

JB: In the old days, knowledge came out of the R&D function—people inventing new knowledge, the old scientific model. Today, it is as if the whole company has become the R&D function. Everybody is responsible for contributing to the new knowledge base. We don't rely just on R&D any more. The new model follows Nanaka's tacit to explicit and from the individual to the entire organization.[4] These are two other ways to create new knowledge. Rather than residing in just a single part of the organization, the R&D part, now it's everybody.

Somehow, companies have to capture that knowledge. If they don't capture it, it will retire and go away. High-energy nuclear physicists are on the endangered list. The people who know how to build and, even more important, how to defuse atomic weapons are retiring, and they are not being replaced by a younger generation, because no younger person in her right mind would want to be in a field known as creating nuclear weapons. If you happen to be responsible for the nuclear stockpile in the United States post–cold war, this is a big problem. Your knowledge workers are retiring and going away. You would like to capture and get down in your secure computer what it is they knew when they built them. A lot of companies have this problem. Plenty of the best workers and some of the older workforce are taking early retirement. That is an important reason for wanting to capture knowledge before it goes away.

JC: *What is your waves-to-wisdom model?*
JB: I took the model Stan Davis and I used in *Monster Under the Bed* and updated it to a new economy context, where things are waves rather than steps. The progression "data to information, knowledge to wisdom" is meant to raise the wisdom issue, which is a very real one. As the baby boomer generation matures and starts to go into elderhood, we will need to create what I call the "wisdom dialogues." Businesses are going to take seriously the question: "Where are we going, and what is the meaning of all this?"

Another way to look at it is: Is the new economy exportable? Is it global? Do you believe that the countries in Europe and Latin America are going to start dot.coming themselves to be part of the new economy? Well, they might. I think that those sorts of questions are going to become of more and more concern to more and more CEOs as they take over the CEO slots in their businesses.

Why should business start the wisdom dialogues? Well, religion and government have had their chance, now it's business as the strongest institution in society. We have had our age of religion. We have had our age of government. The age of business is with us. Businesspeople, as untrained and unsuited as they are for these big questions, will need to start engaging in them. You are going to find whole companies talking about what is

<hr>

[4] Ikujuro Nanaka, Hirotara Takeuchi, and Hiro Takeuichi, *The Knowledge-Creating Company: How Japanese Companies Create the Dynamics of Innovation* (New York: Oxford University Press, 1995).

their real impact on the environment, what is their real impact on human relations, what is their real impact on global relations, and their responsibility for worldwide economic development and elimination of poverty. It is very important that our companies take that next step.

Companies have unwittingly gone from data to information, and we still talk of the Internet as the information highway. (It is really beginning to be the road to knowledge.) Can we spawn dialogues around the next step beyond knowledge, which is wisdom?

The more the network organizational model becomes a reality, the more lots of people are going to want to participate in lots of decisions. They can only do it via the Internet. There is no way to pull together everybody in the company if they are all over the world every time a major decision comes up. I see a huge potential for community building online.

Key Dimensions of Building a Knowledge Business

JC: *What are the key dimensions of building a knowledge business? What are the roles of knowledge communities in a smart business?*

JB: One of the key tasks of building a knowledge community is to be able to do it both face to face and online. Communities mean 10 to 100 people. I know a couple of cases where they are larger. What do you do when you work with a great big company that has 100,000 to 300,000 employees? How do you give a community feeling to a company that large? The companies that figure that out are going to be triumphant, and the ones that do not figure that out will go by the wayside at some point.

JC: *Can you comment on your approach to finding knowledge in an organization and how you accomplish knowledge capture?*

JB: It applies to the three big K areas: the knowledge business, the knowledge communities, and knowledge management. The three Ms apply: How do you make them, how do you manage them, and how do you measure them? Interestingly, in the community area, you do get a lot of pushback. With communities, you can either build them, nurture them, or leave them alone. One of the questions is: "How do you make, measure, and manage knowledge communities?" The people who are on the side of "just leave them alone" get really upset.

I am generally not a measurement guy, but I think we need to move the concept of community out of the sky and bring it down to earth. If it is going to benefit large numbers of people, it is going to have to be built, measured, and managed.

Knowledge Communities

JC: *What is the difference between knowledge communities and communities of practice?*

JB: In actuality, I think there is very little difference. Knowledge community, learning community, and community of practice are essentially the same things. The only difference would be that, if you look at Etienne Wenger and Bill Snyder, they tend to be more with the communities of practice: "Just leave them alone; don't screw them up." And the knowledge community and myself tend to go more toward: "You can make them manageable. There is nothing wrong with that."

Suppose you have a great community of practice in your business, but it is practicing the exact opposite of what you are trying to achieve. What are you going to do? Just leave it alone? That does not make sense to me. There are lots of communities that I have been involved with that are doing the exact wrong things in life, and just because they are a community of practice does not mean that you should not take a hand in trying to modify their behaviors.

The notion that no community of practice is subject to management influence or change is wrong. I do think it is valuable to understand the three things you can do with community: You can nurture it, build it, or leave it alone. That is a good measure to look at any community and ask which of the three does it fall into. By build it, I mean active management. You have a group of managers that gets together and says, "We really need a community in this area. We do not have one right now. What do we need to do to get a group of people to start acting like a community? What are the environmental things, the risks, and the rewards that we need to put into place that say we would really value a community?" Nurturing is: "Here's a community of practice that already exists. It's really great; it's doing all the right things. What can we do to support it moving further than it's already doing?" The leave-it-alone is: "We have a community that is doing all the right things. This is great. Our best action is just not to do anything."

I resist saying that organic, homegrown, and sprung-up-naturally are the only communities worth their salt.

JC: *Have you seen companies that have made significant headway?*

JB: AT&T has made considerable headway. It does not make the press, but it has made headway. The World Bank has been able to institute knowledge management and sharing despite initial strong cultural resistance. Shell Exploration is another organization. I have seen big, old companies that are doing this. The question is: "Are we just seeing the tip of the iceberg? Is it the whole company?"

Learning and Knowledge Businesses

JC: *What type of learning is essential to the knowledge business?*

JB: Not enough people see the difference between maintenance and innovative learning. Most of the learning we do is just to maintain who we are in our present jobs. Very little learning is devoted to how we should do things differently, which is innovative learning, or generative learning, as Peter Senge would call it, or double-loop learning as Chris Argyris would call it. Too many people associate the way we learned in third grade as what learning is all about. It isn't. Schooling is not a good model for innovative organizational learning, which business needs.

There are bunches of companies that do this now, all the way from Saturn to any of the Big Four (Price Waterhouse Coopers, KPMG, E&Y, Deloitte & Touche). They have to. That is their business. It's not their accounting and tax advice, as nice a base as that is. It is essentially the consulting part; the more creative it is, the more successful they are.

Leadership in the Knowledge Organization

JC: *What is the nature of leadership in the knowledge organization?*

JB: It's *learning leadership* rather than the old style of *knowing leadership*. The old-style leaders know "the answer." The new type of leadership learns the answer faster than competitors. This is a fundamentally different orientation and reflects how the leader presents himself. The CEO of HP, Carly Fiorina, is a real learning leader. Another learning leader was Skip LeFauve, former CEO of Saturn.

JC: *How do these learning leaders understand their leadership roles in their organizations?*

JB: I use Gordon R. Sullivan (former U.S. Army chief of staff) here. Think of leadership as creating a future for your organization. That is how I see my role at InterClass. I try to provide a future for this community, rather than thinking that I know all the answers on the best way to go. My constant conversation with my InterClass community is: "What's next? What should we try out?" This is becoming more intense as we approach our tenth anniversary. We are trying out more new things next year than we have tried in all our ten years put together. I am trying out all sorts of stuff. I don't know which way will be right. Every time I think I do, I find somebody in my community who has a better idea. My ego isn't so deeply invested that I can't admit that somebody else thinks I am dead wrong.

JC: *Is that a form of network management that you have embarked upon?*

JB: I think so. I think of InterClass as one huge network. I am very, very aware that if I want to try out new stuff, and if I don't want to consult a good part of my network in advance, I know I am on the wrong track. They will let me know I am on the wrong track.

JC: *How do you see the manager's job in this new environment? Is it different than the chief learning officer or CEO? How do they operate? What kind of behaviors and values do they need?*

JB: Everybody in a managerial role is like a CEO. It devolves. The same pattern holds in your own community as it does in the entire company. We may not all have the responsibilities of a chief learning officer, but we all are chief learning officers. We have to be because the chief learning officer cannot do your learning for you. You are going to have to do it for yourself. A chief learning officer can help set up the environments, give the encouragement, and set up the situations for making learning more valued and materials more accessible, making the learning function prominent within the culture of the organization. But ultimately, each person is like a leader in that if you want to move a group forward, you better do your own learning.

From another context, a good learning leader does not have to wait for instructions. You have self-initiating learning all the time. You don't have to wait for instructions. You just start doing it.

Key Learning Points

- The more a product is interactive, self-customizing, capable of remembering and improving your use of it, the more it is a knowledge product. When it has these characteristics and is web-based, it has double strength.

- A new business is emerging: the knowledge business. And there is a new organization emerging: the knowledge community. These two require a new communications or management model called knowledge management. All three need to be in place.
- We need both visionaries and pragmatists, and we need them at different times in the life cycle of a product or company. Visionaries are critical when it is time for renewal.
- Knowledge has become a factor of production in organizations, although fundamentally different from the traditional factors of land, labor, and capital; the shift is from a model of scarcity to one of abundance.
- The knowledge economy is a boom-and-bust economy since knowledge is so fluid, with short time horizons, production runs, and life cycles requiring continuous reinvention.
- If you can build more and more knowledge into an old product, it will transform the industry and reframe the whole way you conceive a business.
- The R&D function has become the domain of the entire organization. Everybody is responsible for contributing to the new knowledge base.
- The new style of leadership does not know the answers; it learns the answers faster than its competitors.
- We are all chief learning officers who need to self-initiate our own learning.

The Knowledge Movement Emerges
from Its Infancy

4

Karl Wiig is one of the key developers of knowledge management theory and practice. He is chairman and CEO of the Knowledge Research Institute and the author of four books and numerous articles that have helped define the field.[1] He works extensively with client organizations to build internal knowledge management capabilities by focusing on business-related issues with senior management; tactical approaches and solutions with middle management; and hands-on methods and techniques with professional knowledge practitioners.

Wiig sees himself as a reformed "techie." He actively integrates learning, knowledge management, intellectual capital, strategy, and process into an approach that allows for the complexity that actually reflects how people and organizations operate. He explores deeply and broadly, as well as with a curiosity that is infectious. He is continuously looking to discover what the field is and what it could be about.

Wiig holds undergraduate and graduate degrees from Case Institute of Technology and was director of applied artificial intelligence and of

[1] *Expert Systems: A Manager's Guide* (Arlington, Tex.: Schema, 1990); *Knowledge Management Foundations: Thinking about Thinking—How People and Organizations Create, Represent, and Use Knowledge* (Arlington, Tex.: Schema, 1993); *Knowledge Management: The Central Management Focus for Intelligent-Acting Organizations* (Arlington, Tex.: Schema, 1994); and *Knowledge Management Methods: Practical Approaches to Managing Knowledge* (Arlington, Tex.: Schema, 1995).

systems and policy analysis at Arthur D. Little. He also served as a management consulting partner at Coopers and Lybrand. He is cofounder of the International Knowledge Management Network.

<hr/>

The Conversation

Learning and Knowledge

JC: *What is the learning challenge that knowledge workers and their organizations face as far as you see it?*

KW: This is a very comprehensive question because what we are really talking about is the learning of individuals, on one end, and the organizational learning that might take place, on the other end. Knowledge is different from information and is difficult to communicate. For example, on the personal level, learners must internalize what they understand is being communicated. After that, learners try to make sense of the received information within the context in which they find themselves. When we start looking at the whole issue of the learning challenge, we realize that we mainly have focused on the provision part of it—on communicating knowledge—but not on the reception part of it. We have been talking about sharing knowledge, about telling others what we know, but we have not really focused very much on making effective learners.

JC: *Yes, that has not really been brought up in most knowledge management conversations so far.*

KW: I guess it is not surprising because, initially, we are so focused on getting the process started. If we are in the supply-push mode, to put it that way, instead of being in the demand-pull mode, we are very concerned about how we get people to participate in knowledge sharing and how we initiate capturing knowledge, from the organizational perspective, to make it into structural knowledge. The real learning challenge is that there are a number of cultural barriers to sharing knowledge, for example, to help others, or to ask for help. In addition, many people think they are conducting knowledge management but have not yet discovered what knowledge is.

JC: *That would make it hard.*

KW: It does make it hard. It does make it very hard.

JC: *What are the implications of that?*

KW: The implications are that we are making very slick information distribution systems, computer-based and otherwise, which are available for people to access when they know they have a problem. But, of course, most people do not know they have a problem unless they have sufficient knowledge to discover that a problem exists. Providing people with knowledge or information about knowledge through the fingertips is fine, once you know which knowledge is needed and once you know what the problem is. But often you do not know what the problem is unless you are knowledgeable in advance.

Is All Knowledge the Same?

JC: *Is all knowledge the same? Or does it need to be cultivated, shared, or accessed differently inside and outside an organization?*

KW: From my perspective, there's a great difference between know-what and know-how, or in other words, between theoretical knowledge and practical knowledge. We need to look at several levels of knowledge the same way that James Brian Quinn does, in his book *Intelligent Enterprise.*[2] He has four categories. I have five. I look at vision and paradigm knowledge as the knowledge that motivates us and leads us. Through it, we see the opportunities.

Below that, we have what Quinn calls "knowledge-why." This level is more systematic schema and methodology knowledge that we may have learned in the university and learned fairly procedurally. It is knowledge of "what," how to be, how do machines work, and what the systematic part of this process that we encounter is.

On the third level, we have pragmatic decision making and factual knowledge: know-how. That, to some extent, is automated, yet it is also available for us to reason with in a conscious way. To some extent, we are now talking about personal knowledge.

The fourth level is automatic knowledge, the real working knowledge. We know it so well that it has become nonconscious and unavailable to us. That knowledge is the bulk of what we know and is the part of the iceberg that is below ocean level.

We have a fifth level, tacit subliminal knowledge, which is established when we are first introduced to a new notion or concept and start forming a beginning understanding. You might say that the tacit subliminal knowl-

[2] James Brian Quinn, *Intelligent Enterprise: A Knowledge- and Service-Based Paradigm for Industry* (New York: Free Press, 1992).

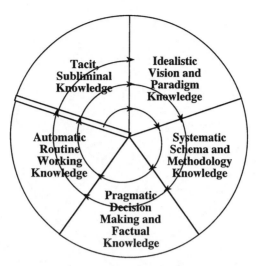

FIGURE 4.1 Levels of Knowledge Flow

edge is what started out in episodic memory. As we internalize it in our REM (rapid eye movement) sleep, at 3:00 in the morning, it is being built into these other areas, and we also develop association bridges between concepts and other mental models.

These knowledge levels are motivated by cognitive sciences research about how we learn and by experiences over several decades of working with knowledge workers ranging from novices to experts and grand masters.

Is all knowledge the same? No, all of this knowledge is not the same. That is just one dimension. There are other dimensions of knowledge. For example, when we think about knowledge that we use in business, we might have professional and craft knowledge, in contrast to enterprise navigational knowledge. People now tell me that they have found that the body of the enterprise navigational knowledge that is associated with delivering "work" is bigger than professional knowledge in most areas. That is, the larger body is enterprise navigational knowledge that consists of knowing how we work around here, who you consult with, what the systems and procedures are, and so on.

JC: *Is that the environmental, cultural knowledge?*
KW: It is knowledge of what our customers require, who the customers are, and a myriad of practical things that might take a year or two to build up before you become fully functional.

All of this might be on the personal side. We also have the need for the organization to build as much as possible of personal knowledge into structural knowledge. It is very important to share knowledge among the

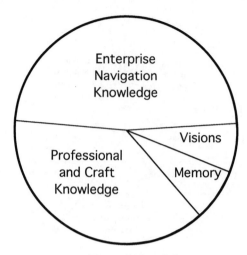

FIGURE 4.2 Types of Knowledge

people to build a "synergistic orchestration environment," where people find it natural to share, to collaborate, and do that as a matter of course and culture. The shared knowledge then becomes part of the culture and becomes owned by the organization—in the sense that it lives among the present staff, people they hire, and is not based on any one individual's knowledge. This knowledge is on the road to becoming institutional knowledge.

These days we have a strong movement to make personal knowledge become structural knowledge, in the sense that it has been captured. I think that is a very appropriate and very worthwhile set of efforts. But the amount of knowledge that people are able to capture, from what I have seen, is minimal compared to what is required to run the organization. You can obtain only a small portion—call it 8–10%—of the knowledge that required to run the organization flawlessly, knowledge that resides in people's heads.

JC: *Is that the documented knowledge that you are referring to, or is there more than that?*
KW: More than that, because, for example, engineers who design technology embed a fair bit of what they know in the technology solutions that, they create. That part of knowledge is crucial for the competitiveness of the organization. What has been missing quite frequently in that area is that, although we find explicitly what the decisions were and what the knowledge resulted in, we frequently have no idea, after the fact, what led people to make those decisions. We have a number of situations where

people have modified decisions of previous experts and ended up in hot water, because their modifications clashed with the principles that had led to the solutions in the first place. We see this in heat exchanger designs, on one end, and very sophisticated designs of advanced computer programs, on the other end. We now see efforts to capture the reasoning behind many decisions, particularly design decisions, to allow future workers to understand the context in which decisions were made, the options that were discarded, and information about blind alleys.

JC: *Depending on the ground from which they derived, their outcomes are different?*

KW: That is correct. The new solutions that were thought to be improvements on the old actually clashed with the old and became nonworkable. In software, we know this very well. It has been an eye opener to me to see it also is the case in what I consider relatively crude equipment: in a heat exchanger.

All of this is done within the organization. Then we ask: "What about sharing and accessing knowledge outside the organization?" That is a very interesting area, because then we start looking at what John Seely Brown and Paul Duguid call *networks of practices*, which are between organizations, in contrast to *communities of practice*, which are usually internal in the organization. These networks of practice have enabled, for example, the emergence of the Route #128 corridor in Boston and Silicon Valley. They are the result of the sharing of knowledge among organizations and building up a total regional capability. From that perspective, it has elevated the capability of many places in this country and abroad.

Look at Israel, for example, which is a gleaming jewel because people are working among organizations as well as within organizations, right? We have the same thing in some of the Scandinavian countries, such as Denmark, which started out with hearing aids then went into other areas of sound systems. We have an important societal phenomenon that is very powerful for wealth creation in many areas. And, of course, it is also very beneficial to the firms that find themselves in those locations.

Understanding Knowledge

JC: *What do you mean when you say that we do not understand much about knowledge?*

KW: From a personal perspective, and also later from an organizational perspective, we are discovering from recent work in the cognitive sciences a tremendous amount about how we—people—think and how we store knowledge. Ironically, we might even know less than we did before. Many of our modern thoughts on how this happens have been shattered. For example, people apparently work very differently in decision making from what was thought based on earlier laboratory experiments. We make decisions more based on intuition and associations with behavioral models and other mental models. Within the organization, a recent statement by a management pundit indicates, "We are in a blind alley to the reality of how work actually gets performed."

People at the Institute for Research on Learning are repeating again and again the fact that we do not know how people work with their brains. We do not know how work is done from a knowledge perspective in organizations. We have serious misconceptions that are obvious when people say, as I have seen on every page of one company's website, that "innovations are not made by people, they are made by organizations." When people seriously suggest that, I think, these are "keep it simple, stupid" (KISS) errors, which come from trying to make us believe that, while individuals might originate innovations, the innovations are not producing results until the organizations have accepted them and are executing them.

JC: *Is that not a split between people and the organizations they work in?*

KW: I think it is. So, we don't know much about knowledge. We know that it is vitally important, we know some of the knowledge flows, how to migrate knowledge, and how to facilitate some of the pathways. Clearly, we must realize that, even though our understanding is limited, what we do understand and the methods and techniques we have developed are already very valuable from practical enterprise performance perspectives. There is no doubt about that.

At the same time, we have more than a dozen different companies, each of which is claiming it has the answer to how to capture tacit knowledge and make it structural knowledge. None of them seem to go very deeply into mental models that people have. They essentially go to the level of operational knowledge, which is, again, the part of the iceberg that is above sea level and only accounts for a small percentage of a person's expertise—and furthermore, is mostly concrete and routine knowledge rather than the more valuable, deeper insights.

JC: *Isn't that because that is where we can most easily capture it? The level of effort required to capture that is a lot less than the level of effort to get into the interstices of the mental models.*

KW: Yes. The reality is that people use higher-level mental models, such as scripts, schemata, and metaknowledge, to deliver good work in all but routine situations.

Knowledge Maps

JC: *Does this relate to your notion of knowledge maps?*

KW: Yes, in part. The way I see knowledge maps used in many organizations is as a graphical mechanism for people to work together to make explicit work to be delivered next month and next year, associated knowledge needs, and the availability of relevant knowledge. For example, professionals and managers, shop stewards, and also people further down the line can work together to build the knowledge maps. But knowledge maps, from my perspective, are not stationary. They are forever changing. More than providing a map of knowledge needs and availability as is, it provides insights into what the mechanisms are and what things are happening and provides new ways to collaborate, making these people start thinking about what they are involved in, as individuals or as managers. The value of the knowledge map from that perspective is far greater than the value of the knowledge map as a document and a reference.

JC: *It is an indicator?*

KW: Yes, it is that. But the creation of a knowledge map is often more a discussion and thinking guide rather than a look-up document. And there is a slight difference. When I work with one version of knowledge maps, I work with people who are living the situation and who are deeply involved presently and in the future. Other knowledge maps are for people who seek information for various purposes by visiting websites and so on. And for visitors, knowledge maps might be tremendously important as reference documents.

JC: *So, knowledge maps are trying to bring to the surface the ongoing terrain and reference points and also support the ability to navigate?*

KW: That is right, but of course, it all hinges on my view of knowledge management practice as being an ongoing process, in contrast to being a system. It is an ongoing practice within the organization that is supported by a number of tools, systems, and procedures, if you will, but it is also a different way of living in the organization. Bringing in the knowledge perspective has been done so beautifully at Chaparral Steel, for example.

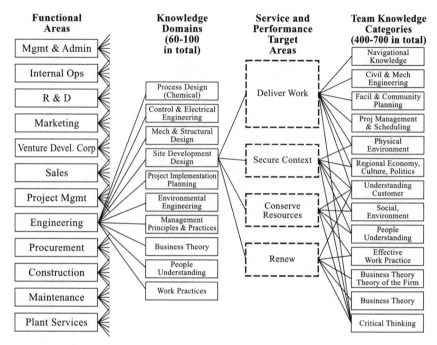

Functional Areas	Knowledge Domains (60-100 in total)	Service and Performance Target Areas	Team Knowledge Categories (400-700 in total)
Mgmt & Admin			Navigational Knowledge
Internal Ops			Civil & Mech Engineering
R & D	Process Design (Chemical)	Deliver Work	Facil & Community Planning
Marketing	Control & Electrical Engineering		Proj Management & Scheduling
Venture Devel. Corp	Mech & Structural Design		Physical Environment
Sales	Site Development Design	Secure Context	Regional Economy, Culture, Politics
Project Mgmt	Project Implementation Planning		Understanding Customer
Engineering	Environmental Engineering	Conserve Resources	Social, Environment
Procurement	Management Principles & Practices		People Understanding
Construction	Business Theory	Renew	Effective Work Practice
Maintenance	People Understanding		Business Theory Theory of the Firm
Plant Services	Work Practices		Business Theory
			Critical Thinking

FIGURE 4.3 Knowledge Management Practice as an Ongoing Process

A Correct Way to Manage

JC: *What has Chaparral Steel done that would embody what you are saying?*

KW: The company is actually concerned with making sense out of every situation, every problem, and every client situation, making sense based upon the best knowledge that it can bring to bear. Or, the best understanding is really the way that it thinks about it. Chaparral educates people in a two-year, part-time program as they come into the organization. It is part of their workday. It teaches them very broadly: everything from organizational theory, steelmaking, marketing, the theory of the firm, and so on. Chaparral gives the same education to people who come in off the farm, who will be essentially sweeping the floor, as to the people coming in with doctorates in metallurgy.

JC: *So, it is the theory of the firm?*

KW: It is the broad theory of the firm. Having given them this understanding, the employees bring their new learning to every challenge they are up against, even if it's a challenge associated with: "Do I roll this ingot that is slightly too cool, or do I send it back to reheat?" This may sound simple, but they have three or four seconds to make up their minds, taking into account: knowing who the customer is, what the day's market situation is, knowing what the energy consumption has been of the firm, and so on. This means being able to make that quick judgment and quick decision. Chaparral has actually made these types of considerations part of everybody's daily life. That is only one part. The other part of it is the whole issue of innovations.

Chaparral does not have a research department. Every team does research as it can think of what is possible to improve, which innovations are possible for equipment, operating practices, new managerial procedures, and all types of things of this nature. This also includes: "What type of knowledge do we need to put together to do this job?" This is particularly true when they have novel tasks. All of this becomes a synergistic orchestration environment, where everybody under the orchestration of the leadership understands the necessity of bringing to bear all of the best resources and knowledge as part of their daily life.

JC: *Is that how they "do their work" in a profound sense, and is that their ethos for carrying that out?*
KW: That is correct. They look at their competitive capability: what is shared among all of their people, what their people know, again, not as individuals, but what they share as a group.

JC: *Who put together this two-year program?*
KW: Dr. Gordon Forward, who is president and CEO of the organization.

JC: *Did you have a role in this?*
KW: No. My role has only been as an outside observer. I have not helped them at all with any of this. They have done this for 25 years. And, of course, they don't think of it as knowledge management.

JC: *What do they think of it as?*
KW: Just the correct way of managing.

JC: *What are their core principles? How do people get introduced to what the organization is and how they need to be and act?*
KW: The core principles are essentially that if you get people together and give them the understanding and freedom to act, they will act in the directions that are in their own interests as they see it and certainly in the organization's best interest. What they are engaged in now is quite inter-

esting. Chaparral Steel is a subsidiary of Texas Industries, which has cement plants and other basic industry operations. They are currently migrating the Chaparral company philosophy to Texas Industries, and I occasionally talk to them. I am not part of the migration process at all. I'm very curious as to how that will work, but not nearly as curious as they are themselves. Can they actually migrate the Chaparral Steel management practice into an existing organization? This is a challenge because Chaparral Steel was started in this way, and the other parts of the larger organization were not.

Beyond Knowledge Mapping

JC: *Does that get back to the knowledge map?*
KW: It goes beyond that, because Chaparral Steel does not use methods like knowledge maps, from what I can see. They do it informally. They are very concerned about what other people know in terms of collaborating, but they don't have any formal knowledge maps and they don't sit down to create knowledge maps.

JC: *When you say* knowledge map, *is that the person's understanding of the world and how he acts in it, or an organization's understanding?*
KW: That would be one type of knowledge map. There are many manifestations of knowledge maps. There are road maps of knowledge, like Chevron has. It has actually laid it out pretty much in a document that folds up like a road map. We have other types of knowledge maps that might be associative maps, that is, semantic maps. To start looking within from the organizational perspective, we need to determine the chief concepts and how they hang together, moving that set of principles from personal psychology into the organizational structure. We also might have knowledge landscape maps that take into account identification of the cultural aspects of the organization all the way down to strengths and weaknesses, opportunities and threats as related to knowledge throughout perhaps as much as 13 or 14 different dimensions. Culture is one; information quality is another; and so on. We have all of these different perspectives of what a knowledge map is. In some instances, they are very important for getting an overview of what the current situation or status is. For other reasons, they are very important because they allow people to have a "hat rack" (categorization system) to hang their observations on as they observe. With this, people can have a structure for their thinking, which they then can live with and start utilizing when they also discuss things with their peers.

Incorporating a Knowledge Management Capability

JC: *There is the question about incorporating a knowledge management capability in an organization. Is there an office of knowledge management and a chief knowledge officer? Is it part of IT (information technology)? How does someone begin to take responsibility in a healthy way in an organization to cultivate knowledge and bring it into play?*

KW: I think there has to be a visionary and a driver within the organization. It could be only a department. But, of course, hopefully it ultimately would get to the center of the organization. There are a number of tasks that I see comprehensive knowledge management requires within the organization. They include the coordinating ability and also the gathering of visions, if you will, into the concerted vision and therefore include everything from infrastructure to how we work together. That set of rules is absolutely important within the larger organizations. This leads to the necessity of having a small, benevolent knowledge management office that really has a lot of responsibilities but not necessarily any authority in telling people what to do. Maybe having a budget for task forces, but essentially it is a proselytizing office, as well as one that can secure the resources that need to be shared across several departments that they individually cannot argue for, for example, infrastructure capabilities. What have been very successful in these organizations are the models that are built around a very small, very energetic, and visionary office, in contrast to building yet a new bureaucracy. And where does it belong? I don't really know.

JC: *Is that dependent on each individual organization?*

KW: I think so. It is dependent on the organization and its traditions. But it is also dependent on where the knowledge management leadership actually hangs their hats prior to getting involved in this. Some leadership comes out of human resources, some comes out of the professional groups, such as engineering in a manufacturing firm, or if it is an insurance company, they might come from the financial management group, and so on. This leadership belongs to the class of infrequently found individuals. But all leadership offices are filled by people from that small group, so that is not new.

We have started to find out that there are different kinds of people in the world. There are those who are very competent at doing daily work, and they have their focus. On the other side of the spectrum, you have people with totally wide horizons. People ask me: "So, can you migrate people from one group to the next one up?" Sometimes you can.

Knowledge Management and Innovation

JC: *What's the relationship between innovation and knowledge management?*

KW: I don't know if innovation is an outcome of knowledge management. Knowledge management might facilitate innovation. One way of looking at innovation is that it is very closely connected with reframing. The ability to reframe is very much a function of the breadth and depth of the knowledge that is possessed by a person or by a team or, for that matter, even an organization. One thing that people at Norsk Hydro, Norway's largest manufacturing organization, are very concerned with is what they call people's, department's, and the organization's *action space*. This is similar to the box that we are taught to think outside.

When you start looking at a person's ability to reframe, that is closely connected again to this action space. The action space can be influenced by providing people with broader insight and broader understanding. Norsk Hydro is helping educate people and helping people educate themselves, as they look at it. By the way, they also have some very similar models to the Chaparral Steel model. They are trying to promote innovation. They don't quite look at innovation for the purpose of advancing the state of the art. They look at innovation as a necessary aspect of everybody's work. They look at systems, procedures, and guidelines for how to do jobs both from the 30,000-foot level and down at the ground level. They realize that Murphy's Law is very much in evidence, that things never work the way they are supposed to, and that really routine work may be a myth!

We need to have immediate innovation to deal with the reality of life. Broader knowledge, particularly broader understanding, backed up by computer systems that would give us details on how to handle various kinds of situations, allows people to innovate. From that perspective, knowledge management has a lot to contribute to daily work life innovation. Following on this is innovation for improving work situations and improving products and services, which involve both single- and double-loop learning. Chris Argyris and Donald Schon defined single- and double-loop learning,[3] with *single-loop learning* being where you're learning a specific thing and *double-loop learning* where you're learning how to learn about how to deal with it—or metalearning.

Argyris and Schon also had a third one, which they called *deutero learning*. That is when organizations learn how to carry out single-loop

---

[3] Chris Argyris and Donald A. Schon, *Theory in Practice: Increasing Professional Effectiveness* (San Francisco, Calif.: Jossey-Bass, 1992).

and double-loop learning. In other words, when the organization learns how to single-loop and double-loop learn, that is also metalearning, as I call it.

JC: *What does that let you accomplish?*
KW: That lets you teach people within the organization the principles of single-loop and the principles of double-loop learning and how to engage in each.

JC: *What's the relationship between that and innovation? How does knowledge management embody that, and how does that feed into innovation?*
KW: As you give people the ability to broaden their action space, they start seeing opportunities for dealing with novel knowledge situations. If the action space is kept broad, they can reframe, which is what you really have to do to be creative and innovative. When we start having the meta-knowledge understanding of single-loop and double-loop learning and so forth, we start to see the methodology that we might pursue to improve not only our work in the existing workplace, but to improve the workplace itself, as well as improving products and services. We can proceed rapidly from being able to handle the knowledge situation that Murphy's Law has created, and move to seeing opportunities for dealing with situations in general in a better way.

JC: *Is innovation an outflow of that?*
KW: To me, it is.

We Technologists Have It All Wrong

JC: *You were just talking about technology as an enabler for this. Oftentimes people see, or it is presented to them, that technology is the vehicle, that is, you press button B, and out will come everything you need to know.*
KW: I know. It has been so refreshing to see the book by John Seely Brown and Paul Duguid called *The Social Life of Information*.[4] Brown is a computer scientist, and one of the top-of-the-line technologists in this world. He is now saying, "We technologists have it all wrong. We have this very narrow perspective that technology is going to do it all. Whereas, in reality,

---

[4] John Seely Brown and Paul Duguid, *The Social Life of Information* (Boston: Harvard Business School Press, 2000).

all technological changes have to go through a 30-, 40-, 50-year socialization process. The socialization processes for the railroad, for the automobile, for the industrial revolution, and all of these things did not change the society as much as the society changed the technology."

JC: *Really?*
KW: Exactly. The specific technology needs to adapt to fit into the needs of people instead of adapting people to the requirements of technology. Brown says that the IT people have not yet discovered that. They are in for a rude awakening when they discover that, for example, the World Wide Web will not necessarily change people as much as people will change the World Wide Web.

JC: *Culture trumps technology?*
KW: Think about how crude our technology is now, for example, in natural language understanding, in terms of identifying what the knowledge or representation schemata should be for our knowledge bases and our ability to do automatic reasoning in one way or another. I'm saying that information technology for knowledge management is in its sixth month of pregnancy. It isn't yet born. Technologists are about to throw rotten apples at me. And, of course I used to be a techie.

JC: *So, there are still three months of gestation to go before technology can become more than a crude enabling force?*
KW: And, even at that point, it is going to be an infant. Then it has to go through childhood and then adolescence. Maybe, someday, it will emerge as a fully worthwhile player.

JC: *That is going to take a lot of explanation to the technology folks. They do not seem to sense that.*
KW: All I have to do is start pointing to all the different solutions that are being offered as the Holy Grail, and they are totally different from each other. All of these companies think that they have the best and only answer for the technological knowledge management solution. It is almost sad.

Going Deeper

JC: *Where is this all going?*
KW: I don't know where we are going. For example, one of my interest areas is natural language understanding. I do not see us being able to create neural networks for natural language understanding, having the ability to

operate with concepts in unstructured natural language documents, or being able to reason with the thinking that is behind the application, if you will, using hermeneutics to determine meanings and to understand.[5] Of course, these are the types of things that people do. When you read an engineering report that somehow pertains to what you are doing now, you are actually engaging very heavily in hermeneutics. If you look in the encyclopedia from a decade ago under "artificial intelligence," it has 20 pages on hermeneutics as a branch of epistemology.

For us actually to be able to manage knowledge content, we are talking about the mental manipulation of deeper concepts that often are hidden in the actual communication. We really are dealing with just that when we are talking about knowledge management application, or when we talk about the application of knowledge to novel situations. We are in a very difficult situation when we are talking about applying information technology to real work. Even if we are able to store these mental models somehow in appropriate representations in knowledge bases, operationalizing these mental models to fit a particular situation that we are faced with, and which does not follow the idealized pattern, requires mental gymnastics that we are not even close to realizing with our automated stuff.

JC: *Does that mean that we are in an art-and-science dialogue on this? Is there an art and a science to all of this?*
KW: Yes, if by that you mean we need to drag in people who previously have been kept out of the locker room, people with backgrounds in semantics, for example, and in all the softer areas, the understanding of poetry, and so on.

JC: *Storytellers as well?*
KW: Yes, we need to involve them.

Getting Started

JC: *If you were engaged by an organization, what would be the key knowledge management implementation issues? How can an organization go about initiating its effort on a stage-by-stage basis to deal with those issues?*
KW: What is necessary, first of all, is to have a vision of how the knowledge management practice should be undertaken, how it should proceed, and particularly what the business reasons are for pursuing it. That is one of

[5] *Hermeneutics* is the science of interpretation.

the obstacles because many organizations are really jumping into it to do knowledge management without even having a hazy vision where this should end and why this should lead to a new practice. What I am talking about is having a broad vision with a set of principles that should be flexible, far from being cast in stone. Obtaining that vision takes a little thinking and a little sleeping. In other words, you need to sleep on it a couple of nights. Determining the current situation and how it is aligned with what is on management's hotplate is the next step in bringing a successful knowledge management movement into play. I try to avoid talking about knowledge management projects or programs and things like this, but they are a necessary part of starting a knowledge management effort to create a permanent knowledge management practice.

We do need, for example, infrastructure projects. We need to have the capabilities, the building blocks, but quite frequently I find that there are obstacles associated with this. Often people are not interested or do not find any time because they don't really see how knowledge management applies to them or to the part of their organization they are working with. We also often have a fair bit of internal friction in getting some of these things off the ground, even if senior management and the visionary appointed by senior management finds it to be very, very necessary and desirable. One management team I'm working with right now is very frustrated because they see "failure is not an option." Yet, the people whom they have appointed are not really motivated to pursue this, come hell or high water.

Becoming an Intelligent/Effective Organization

JC: *They have a problem. But aren't we ultimately trying to have an organization operating intelligently? Isn't that the case?*

KW: Yes. Intelligently or, if you will, effectively. I'm starting a book with the title *Knowledge Management and the Effective Enterprise*. I'm very concerned about being able to identify for people how indeed an effective enterprise needs to behave intelligently, what that entails, and why knowledge management is important in this regard. I find that knowledge influences many of the things that we associate with desirable behavior in the intelligent enterprise. We say that in the intelligent enterprise, people, and often the enterprise itself, always do the right things in the idealized theory. But, what does it mean to always do the right thing? What do we have to understand to do the right thing? We immediately start backing into the need for looking at the implications of what to do, understanding the effects that our actions will have on all the parties involved. Suddenly, we have a relatively comprehensive need for a broad understanding.

Again, Chaparral Steel is a role model. One of the reasons it educated people to look at or to understand all of these different areas is to have people who not only understand these areas and make sense of information they are provided, but to particularly understand the implications of their actions. It is trying to make it possible for people to understand what doing the right thing is and then give them the motivation to actually do it.

JC: *One of the things that I've learned from the conversation with you is that it's not just providing knowledge to people, but the learning process of people, as they are the autonomous actors.*

KW: Until we can get some better, intelligent agents, yes. Of course we already have a fair number of very good intelligent agents, that is, payroll packages, supervisory control systems in refineries, and all of those things.

JC: *What are the conditions that you see preventing an enterprise from acting intelligently?*

KW: Politics might be one of the major ones. This is where people are not interested in promoting the success of the enterprise but in promoting their own success. There's a tremendous amount of that. There are some of these in knowledge management. I know a chief knowledge officer who says the first thing she pursues when she gets into a new situation is finding out the personal agenda of the senior people with whom she works. In some instances, she says she has to just walk away and say, "This is not going to work," because the personal agenda is overshadowing the interests of the organization to such an extent that it cannot be pursued. There are other aspects within the culture itself. If you have a very strong "not invented here" culture, coupled with a culture where people are rewarded for what they do with their personal knowledge and not rewarded for sharing knowledge with others, you might as well forget about it. We run into those. Larry Prusak and Liam Fahey's list of 11 deadly sins is just right in the middle of the target.[6]

JC: *Are we in a kind of infancy period?*

KW: Yes. I think knowledge management might actually have been born, but it isn't very old.

[6] Liam Fahey and Laurence Prusak, "The Eleven Deadliest Sins of Knowledge Management," *California Management Review: Special Issue on Knowledge and the Firm* 40, no. 3 (Spring 1998): 265–276.

JC: *Is it learning how to walk or crawl?*

KW: I think it actually is crawling. It has learned how to crawl and how to stand. And, as all children of that stage, unless the house is childproof, it wreaks havoc.

JC: *When you talk about Chaparral Steel acting intelligently, what are the keys to Chaparral Steel's effectiveness in using knowledge for successful business outcomes?*

KW: The initial key is the fact that the CEO decided that this was the way to run the organization. But having said that, what is then the key? The key is to consider each individual as being a source of very good or very intelligent-acting behavior when provided with two things: knowledge and motivation. I should add that the employees get good feedback and information about where they are, where their performance is, this day, this week, this month. As a result, they actually are able to judge, based on their knowledge, how to behave intelligently. The key is to let people be highly knowledgeable, inform them well, and then have them be motivated at the same time. Everything Chaparral has done is essentially to make these three things happen. These are key issues.

Applying across All Organizations

JC: *Do you think these principles apply universally across all types of organizations: old versus new? high-tech versus bricks and mortar? small versus large?*

KW: Let us put it this way: I don't have any competing model. So, yes, I do believe it applies everywhere. In the U.S. Army, when you send a squad out, you let its people be very knowledgeable about their ability to manage their own affairs. They are told to go "take that hill" but not how they are going to take that hill. They are given good general understanding and as much information as possible about all aspects of everything, from where the enemy is, what the enemy has, to what the supply possibilities are, to all kinds of stuff, all types of intelligence from that perspective. They are given the freedom to act, and they are motivated to do so.

We are social animals. We learn very much from one another, and we have a need to be together. We need to be able to exchange viewpoints and insight. Telecommuting in organizations will be important, yes, but not as important as the zealots portray.

As far as the dot.com companies versus the brick-and-mortar companies, I think that we are mistaken with regard to the importance of dot.coms. I do think that we actually will find that we have overblown enthusiasm in many instances. I don't think that the Internet, even with a hundred times more bandwidth—a thousand times more powerful computers—will be able to supplant the need for us to work together in other modes as well.

I think working together will be the dominant mode, and it's going to be much stronger than it is presently. E-based interactions will not be a dominant mode is perhaps what I need to say.

JC: *Will it be a component or dimension?*
KW: Yes, sure. It's got to be a very important component or dimension, but it's not going to be dominating everything, as many people see.

Evolving Views of What Matters

JC: *How have your views of knowledge management and intellectual capital changed over the past ten years? And how do you see them changing in the future? Take an opportunity to look in both directions.*
KW: Ten or twelve years ago, I really discovered the importance of thinking about intellectual capital as a separate set of entities, with the valuation of intellectual capital as part of the valuation of the corporation. That is something that I must admit I have picked up on very much and become enthusiastic about as a leg on the stool.

With regard to knowledge management in general, I started out having what I now consider a very narrow and perhaps infantile perspective on the management of knowledge. I adhered to the notion that it would be possible to automate much more work than we now think is possible to automate.

As a result of what has been discovered in the computer sciences arena, I have had to revise my opinion on how to support human beings in work situations, decision-making situations. With external knowledge led through expert networks, consulting with peers, access to knowledge-based systems, and so on, I've attained a totally different view of not only the complexity of what works entails, but also the very dynamic and very intimate relationship between knowledge and performance. I am talking here about knowledge in the forms of existing mental models and associations—what some researchers call *intuition*. They see that, on average, it takes six seconds to make a decision. But they also see that the reframing of situations also happens very fast. The framing of the decision, the framing of the premises for the decision, are very much functions of the associations that you have, and we sneak in our biases, one way or another.

Therefore, when we think about knowledge management, we are faced with a totally different set of challenges for how we make or help make people more effective than we thought about ten years ago. Also ten years ago, I had the opinion that it is possible to have people work with the "correct" knowledge for a situation.

JC: *Is that possible?*
KW: These days, I'm woefully aware of the fact that there is no such thing as "correct" *knowledge*. Diversity is what makes you robust, and we have to have the ability to deal with a number of very often conflicting informational issues to try to make sense of situations and handle them appropriately. It is very interesting that we have started to arrive at seeing, again, the intimacy of what people know and their ability to behave.

Key Learning Points

- The learning challenge for organizations is that we have focused mainly on communicating knowledge, sharing it, but have not really focused much on making effective learners.
- The amount of knowledge that an organization is able to capture (8–10%) is minimal compared to what is required to run a business. The balance resides in people's heads.
- Although we do not know much about how knowledge works in people (mental models), we do have some valuable understanding of the knowledge flow, how to migrate knowledge, and how to facilitate some of the pathways.
- Knowledge maps make explicit the work to be delivered, associated knowledge needs, and the availability of relevant knowledge, which enable new ways to collaborate and make people start thinking about what they are involved in.
- If you get people together and give them the understanding and freedom to act, they will act in the directions that are in their own interest as they see it and certainly in the organization's best interests.
- An office of knowledge management most likely needs to be a very small, energetic, visionary office. Its work is essentially proselytizing, but it also can secure resources that need to be shared across several departments for infrastructure capabilities.
- Knowledge management has been born and has learned to crawl and stand. However, as with all children of that age, unless the house is childproof, it will wreak havoc.

KNOWLEDGE
Cluster II:

f strategy come to the foreground once an organization chooses
ne a knowledge-based enterprise. Through its strategy, the en-
aligns its knowledge-based resources with its financial and physical resources and leverages them to achieve its goals.

Göran Roos, Leif Edvinsson, and Vince Barabba lay out their approaches to knowledge strategy in this cluster.

Leveraging Resources

Göran Roos starts with the premise that any organization is a system of resources that are deployed in a given structure. The question is how to mobilize to extract the maximum value from the knowledge, physical, and financial resources the enterprise has and how to deploy and transform these resources for the best outcome. Roos emphasizes that the strategy must fit the particular enterprise. He uses the intellectual capital process to identify relevant dimensions along which the strategy of the firm can be discussed. One organization may want to identify what is needed to create value. A second enterprise may be more concerned with how to deploy its resources to maximize their potential to create value. A third entity may want to track how efficient it is in transforming its resources. And a fourth organization may feel that it is doing everything right but that it is undervalued by investors and needs to demonstrate the value it is creating.

Once the enterprise determines its necessary resources, the enterprise can map how those resources need to flow through the structure to create value and capture that value. This is the value creation path. At the same time, each organization has knowledge recipes that it uses to transform resources so as to generate a desired outcome. A successful organization can navigate its value creation path to find out where and how those resources can be brought into play most effectively. Roos also discusses using topologic mapping to develop a visual picture for determining the best value creation pathways. All of these elements come together to frame the next generation of intellectual capital practices, which will allow for value accounting, that is, accounting for the totality of value of all constituent dimensions, rather than being limited to financial, transaction-based accounting.

Knowledge Recipes of Intellectual Capital

Leif Edvinsson says that we have to recast our approach to knowledge and focus on using the enterprise's structural capital (for example, its organizational capacities, including its processes, practices, networks, intellectual property, data, and innovation capabilities) as a springboard, or turbocharger, for human capital or talent. Leadership needs to understand that its role is to release its human capital and leverage it through its structural capital.

In Edvinsson's view, networks among individuals, corporations, and nations will be the conduits for the flow of intellectual capital. These are networks in motion and where intellectual capital is created. The major focus for these networks is participating in future centers that serve as meeting spaces where people can connect with each other to understand and anticipate future needs. Future centers are experimental zones that chart out those needs, determine what kinds of knowledge recipes are necessary to respond, and develop enterprise prototypes to test potential responses. By placing itself in the future, the organization can learn what it needs to reframe now. In this holistic model, the future is valued as a focus for the organization in addition to the present. This approach also serves as a counterweight to tendencies for the enterprise to become too internally focused.

The enterprise then becomes a developmental company for knowledge recipes of intellectual capital. It sheds much unnecessary, traditional administration and concentrates on a core focus of development, knowledge recipes, and continuous innovation. It creates a structural capital nexus around which human talent gathers and produces the momentum that can seize the future.

Market-Based Adaptive Enterprise

Vince Barabba grounds himself and the role of knowledge in an organization in a systems perspective. In that systems view, the enterprise strives to set itself up as a market-based adaptive enterprise, developing a balance between what the customer requests and what the company is capable of delivering. The adaptive dimension means that the organization designs product development processes to respond swiftly to changing conditions.

A consequence of using the market-based adaptive enterprise approach is that it makes the organization rethink all of its relationships and boundaries. It needs to create unprecedented alliances with other enterprises, some of which might even be competitors, to have the capabilities for a rapid response. In this approach, access becomes more important than ownership. More open access means that knowledge workers have access to what the enterprise knows as well as access to other sources that allow them to do their jobs more efficiently and effectively. Leadership's role is to create the environment in which people share what they know and have learned from others. For leadership to be able to create that environment, it must understand the principles of systems thinking. In other words, leadership must understand how people can work to optimize their own areas without lessening effectiveness in the overall system.

The process that guides the system is "listen, learn, and lead." An example of listening is when engineers and designers are connected into key events, where they can get a sense of how customers are reacting to some of their ideas. The learn part says that, if you listen, you can then decide to implement a new idea and write down the decision, clearly stating that this is the decision that was made and why. People are required to include a description of the particular things expected to occur by a specific date. And, in the lead element, people take their actions to the next stage of connections.

Barabba sees his role as making the necessary knowledge accessible to the people who need to use it to enable them to move from a market-and-sell approach to a sense-and-respond dynamic. Emphasis is placed on how to get knowledge used rather than how its contribution is measured. His fundamental premise is that the true value of knowledge or intellectual capital is in its use—not in its collection.

Through the Lens of Strategy

These contributors articulate various frameworks for strategically looking at a knowledge-based enterprise. A knowledge-based enterprise needs to find the recipes that create its value and the perspectives it can utilize to optimize and demonstrate its value. The potency of the knowledge-based enterprise lies in how it can cultivate, leverage, and capture its human capital and related intangible resources. Equally important is knowing how the enterprise can bring its future into its present. It can do so by exploring emerging needs, creating prototypes that address those needs, and then refocusing knowledge and relationships so that the enterprise can serve as a springboard for developing the talents necessary to satisfy those needs. Finally, the knowledge-based enterprise does not exist outside its environment. Incorporating the view that it is a market-based adaptive enterprise means that all parties engage in continuous sense-and-respond behaviors to recalibrate their efforts and environment to meet ever-changing conditions. The people in organizations may not be in control of the world they live in, but they are in control of how they can advantageously use a knowledge-based understanding to guide them in designing and operating the enterprise dynamically and responsively.

The Measurement Controversy

A controversial issue raised in this cluster is whether measurement in a knowledge-based enterprise is either possible or effective. Barabba and others feel that the resources of the enterprise are far better used in establishing the system of tools and structural supports for the enterprise than in amassing a questionable and potentially distorted set of measurements. In fact, Barabba believes that inappropriate measurements can be counterproductive by setting up arbitrary competitions for scarce resources, rather than collaborations that grow the resource pie, enhance performance gains, and satisfy customers.

In contrast, a number of other contributors to this volume are advocates for the development of measures that indicate performance and can guide decision makers in their choices, whether strategic or tactical. Is it wise to make the investment in measures for something as elusive and intangible as the value of knowledge flow? It may well be, but only if leadership is clear on its strategic goals, if management can determine the business issues that the knowledge effort can affect, if there is a strong collaboration ethic in the enterprise, and if adequate resources can be garnered for the effort.

While there is difficulty in developing specific metrics, there is a great demand to show the value of knowledge initiatives. In lieu of formal measuring systems, one favored proxy measure for gauging how much a knowledge initiative has made a vital difference in organizations is anecdotal stories.

Part of the problem of measurement is that the knowledge movement is, as Karl Wiig pointed out in an earlier cluster, just emerging from its infancy and has yet to fully align with and be an integral part of the way organizations do their business. As enterprises are able to more thoroughly determine how knowledge inputs make a difference in resolving important business issues and as the experiments with measurement continue, over time more reliable measurement frameworks will develop. As a start, a strategy in relation to measures is to

- review the numerous approaches to measurement discussed throughout *Knowledge Capital*;

- assess the priorities, readiness, and capabilities of the enterprise; and
- search for trial sets of measures that both demonstrate return on investment and provide indicators to be used in navigating the course of the enterprise.

Recipes for Knowledge-Based Value Creation

5

Göran Roos is continually developing some of the most advanced and yet readily usable approaches to leveraging the interrelated roles of intellectual capital and strategy in contemporary organizations. As both a thought leader and practitioner, he has made seminal contributions to the field of intellectual capital through his writings and his implementation of practical solutions.

He has created frameworks that enable making the intangible of intellectual capital understood as a very real asset to be cultivated, measured, and appropriately exploited for competitive advantage. He helps managers rethink how their strategies and practices determine and utilize the drivers for intellectual capital growth and how to rigorously evaluate and effectively use their intellectual resources throughout their enterprises to make significant differences.

He is the founder of Intellectual Capital Services (ICS), developer of its main concepts, and manager of its day-to-day operations. As a practitioner, he delivers the services of ICS to a wide variety of both private and public sector organizations around the world in a broad range of market segments. Roos holds several academic positions, and he is the author of numerous books and articles in the field of intellectual capital and strategy. He also serves on the editorial board of the *Journal of Intellectual Capital*. Roos was named one of the 13 most influential thinkers for the twenty-first century by the Spanish business magazine *Direccion y Progreso*.

The Conversation

Stock and Flow

JC: *What do you mean when you say that intellectual capital is any stock or flow under the control of the firm that contributes to the value creation of the firm?*

GR: The reason we use that statement is that we do not want to limit ourselves to predetermined structures. A given firm or organization, government department, or not-for-profit is actually a system made up of a set of resources that are deployed in a given structure. Intellectual capital is the science and art dealing with how to extract maximum value from the resources you have and the way you have chosen to deploy them.

JC: *What is the intellectual capital (IC) process and how does that relate to business recipes?*

GR: You can use many terms. Business models, business recipes, value creation models, and strategic models are common terms in the strategy literature. You can contrast two logics in this area: the financial logic and the strategic logic. The strategic logic basically says, "All right, take the strategy of a firm as a given. Within that framework, how can you ensure that you can create maximum value?" You can do so by developing the best possible effectiveness and efficiency as they relate to the deployment of the resources you have at your disposal. These resources include, for example, the competence of the people, the processes of the organization, the brands, the intellectual property, the customer relationships, supplier relationships, plant and equipment, and the working capital needed to actually generate cash, the cash that converts into market value.

The IC process is about identifying relevant dimensions along which the strategy of the firm can be discussed. Identify what the firm means when it says that it creates value. Identify the resources that the firm considers necessary to have, the ways these resources are being deployed, and compare and contrast that with the logical conclusions from the strategy.

In other words, you are talking about classic strategy theory with key success factors and key performance indicators compared, contrasted, and synthesized with a resource-based view, in the widest sense, of the firm. One of the things we need to do is to align key performance indicators that are extracted from the strategy, with the key performance indicators measuring the relevant resource transformations, thereby allowing us to create a tracking system to predict changes in our ability to create value.

The IC process (see figure 5.1) is about developing an understanding for how value is created, thereby providing an opportunity to improve the potential of creating value as well as the actual value created. For this, the IC process offers the tools necessary to actually track the value creation, and, if we wish, it can provide us with tools that allow us to value whatever it is that we do from a given beholder's point of view.

Business Recipes

JC: *And the business recipes are?*
GR: A *business recipe*, in our terms, is the specific resources and the way they are being combined in terms of transformations.

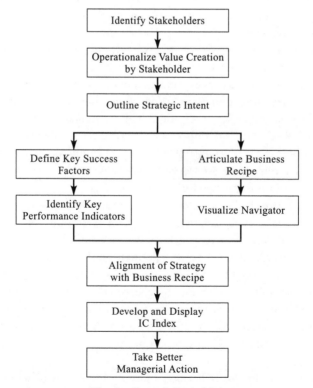

FIGURE 5.1 The Intellectual Capital Process

JC: *You take IC as a way to work that through?*

GR: The IC lens allows us to work that through, yes.

JC: *Does that relate to how you determine the value creation path in the organization?*

GR: By using the IC lens, you can determine the value creation path in the organization. Two simple examples will illustrate the point. Let's compare two companies called Company A and Company B, to be imaginative!

Both of them are consulting firms. Company A is made up of very bright people who work together in order to make money and have fun. The resources they have at their disposal in order to make some money are some working capital to keep the business going; they do not need a lot, but they need some. They probably need some miniscule physical things, like computers and the like. They need a lot of relationships with customers and other people, and they need to have an enormous amount of competence as individuals. And, as individuals, they build relationship with clients.

They make money from two transformations. They make money by converting their time to cash, which is based on their competence, so they charge a lot. And, since they have very strong personal relationships, they can charge even more than they otherwise could. So, the relationships contribute to the charging level and is the second transformation. They then reinvest some of this money into maintaining the relationships and in furthering their own competence. Now, as you notice, there is no structure, there are no processes. Every time they do something, they tend to reinvent the wheel. They are unbelievably flexible but have great problems growing because you can't train anybody here. The only way to train somebody is to take him on as an apprentice. So, this is an organization that has chosen one business recipe for advisory services.

The other firm, B, has a different view. It says, "We provide packaged solutions. We have ready solutions for you. That means that you buy from us this solution, and that is what you pay for." The company has some average people that it leverages through excellent structures to produce very good deliverables. Its processes, its systems, its brands and intellectual property allow it to use average people to provide good solutions. But what you, as a client, pay for is the solution primarily. You pay some miniscule amount for person-hours but that's not what the company makes money on because it cannot charge these average person-hours at very high rates.

This organization also builds a relationship between itself and the client's organization. So, the brand of the organization rather than the individual is important. In other words, you have three contributing transformations to cash flow here: first, a small amount from person-hour sales; second, large amounts from sales of standardized solutions; and finally, some amount from the organizational relationship (brand) that the firm has with the client organization. You then reinvest this in maintaining and strengthening relationships and in building processes, systems, and structures.

A Firm B–type organization can grow easily because it just hires some more people and leverages them through the system. On the other hand, these types of organizations are not very flexible because it takes a long time for a new idea to be converted to a standardized offering that can be leveraged through the people and relationships used by the organization.

One other aspect is that, in the first example, in Company A, if the people get run over by a bus, there is nothing left. In Company B, if the people get run over by a bus, you hire 15 or 20 or 200 new M.B.A.s and say to them, "Continue on page 47, paragraph 6," and the client will not notice the difference.

Now, if you look at these two firms from a financial perspective, in other words, the cash side—how much goes in, how much goes out, and the balance sheet—they can look exactly the same. They can have the same turnover. They can have the same margin and the same balance sheet. Then, let's go to the next level and ask clients about how satisfied they are. Even there, they can look exactly the same, with the same customer satisfaction level and same retention ratio levels.

Where they look different is when we go out even further into the intellectual capital side and talk about what type of competencies they have, and how they use them, what types of processes, structures, systems, brands, intellectual property and so on, and how they use them. In many ways, this determines their fitness to meet the unknown challenges of the future. That is where they differ. So the only way you can see the difference between these two firms and analyze the effectiveness and efficiency by which these approaches actually create value, is by taking the intellectual capital perspective.

In a navigator, the key resources are represented by circles, whose size reflects the importance of the resource. The transformation of one type of resource to another is represented by the connecting arrows whose thickness represents the importance of the transformation. In figure 5.2, the difference between Company A and Company B is immediately obvious. The reliance of Company A is reflected in the size of the human resources and the resulting transformations while in Company B, there is more reliance on the written-down processes, part of organizational capital.

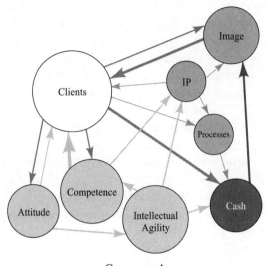

Company A

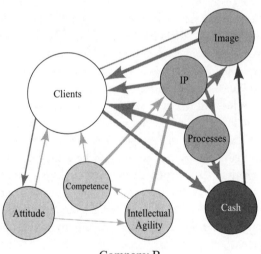

Company B

FIGURE 5.2 Transformation of Resources, Company A and Company B

The Path to Strategic Intent

JC: *Can you chart the path of how they go from strategic intent to their financials and to user benefits?*
GR: Yes, whichever is your starting point, you can chart it.

JC: *What is the link between strategy and how we use the different types of resources needed to accomplish that strategy, both the tangible resources and the intangible resources?*
GR: The first thing about strategy is to identify the wanted position. Strategy is about asking, "Where do I want to be?" The second part is: "How am I going to get there?" because you can choose different routes.

From our point of view, the difference between where you and where you want to be is called Hume's Fork, in philosophical terms. Hume was a Scottish philosopher, and Hume's Fork is the difference between what is and what ought to be. This difference will force you to perform better on your cost drivers and better on some of your value drivers (see figure 5.3). In order to perform better on these drivers, you need to execute certain activities better.

There are two ways you need to look at it. One is to look at how each individual activity can be performed better. The other is to look at how the system of activities can be performed better. This is rather like taking a top-level look at the organization as a whole, on one hand, and a tactical

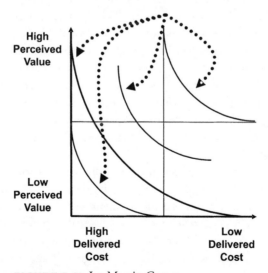

FIGURE 5.3 Iso-Margin Curves

look at improving the operation of the components, on the other. Let's look at the whole organization first.

In terms of systems of activities, we have to make a choice among three logics. Are we a value chain operator, a value shop operator, or a value network operator? A true value chain as first described by Porter is actually a very rare thing, however, some manufacturing companies work as a collection of chains assembled to look like a tree structure.

JC: *Could you define those?*
GR: A bank, for example, can be a value chain when it focuses on converting inputs to outputs. The value resides in the output, and once you have the output, you can remove the producing organization. This removal does not impact the value of the output. A bank could choose to be one of these things, in which case the focus will be on efficiency. It will look at itself as a factory that processes loans, applications, or something similar.

The value shop is a solutions provider. It's somebody who solves problems. The input is a problem. The output is a solution to that problem. A bank that does this would view itself as a financial service operator, a financial advisor, which also has the ability to provide the money. But what it would do is identify your problems, it would address those problems, it would select a solution together with you and help to implement it. It would have stringent quality controls. As part of its offering, it would probably supply you with some cash as a loan or accept some of your cash for investment.

Or, the bank could be a value network, which is basically the logic of the marketplace. The bank would say, "Well, I am solely a conduit between people who do not have money and those people who do have money." What I do is that I arrange the flow of cash between them. You can see that it would still be a bank, but it would have completely different consequences for what the bank would focus on doing well, what it would focus on doing itself versus what it would not want to do itself.

This provides a kind of strategic systems logic. It asks, "Which strategic system am I going to operate in?" Figure 5.4 illustrates the three value creation logics.

For each of these activities, there is a requirement that the activity is done well. Even if this strategic system provides you with the right activities, the next question concerns doing them well. Doing them well is the ability to transform different types of intellectual resources effectively and efficiently. For our consulting case, it boils down to transforming the knowledge that resides in the individual into good, useful solutions for the client. And, we all know that there is no correlation between how much you know and how good you are at transforming that knowledge into

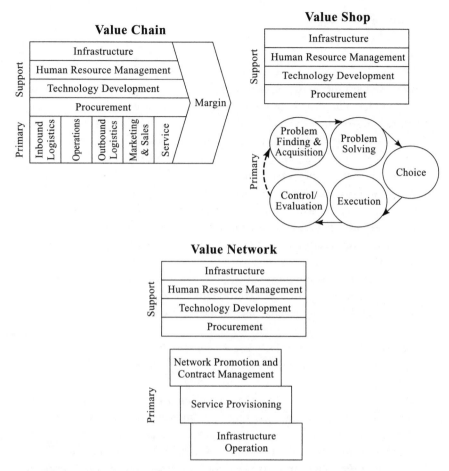

FIGURE 5.4 Three Value Creation Logics: Value Chain, Value Shop, Value Network

something useful for somebody else, because if that were the case all university professors would be millionaires, and they are not.

JC: *The number of Ph.D.s does not equate to the number of dollars in the bank account?*
GR: Correct. Rather, it is sometimes the reverse. We need to make a very important distinction between having a resource—whether it be competence, process, system, intellectual property, relationship, machines, or cash—and putting it to value-creating use, which is the ability to transform one resource into another.

Useful Knowledge

JC: *Is that useful knowledge?*

GR: This can be seen as useful knowledge, in this case, or useful processes, useful systems, or useful relationships—whatever is significant in your business model. The issue here is about identifying, for each activity, what are the starting resources, what are the finishing resources, and what are the things that impact the effectiveness and efficiency of the transformation between the two sets. That determines how good you are going to be at executing that activity well. The IC perspective here allows you to work with a strategy to identify the necessary resources and to talk about the alternative ways in which these resources can be deployed to address issues about strategic logic. The outcome is that you can change your performance on your cost drivers and value drivers in such a way that you move from where you are to where you strategically desire to be. This move would have an impacting consequence on margin, revenue, working capital, cash, taxes, acquisitions, and investments, thereby directly impacting your market value in a predictable and manageable way.

JC: *For what reasons are you typically brought into an organization, and what are the key issues you're brought in to address?*

GR: There are normally four issues that bring organizations to us. The first one is that the company feels that it is not certain about what types of resources it needs to have to be able to create value in this new e-environment. For example, I am a traditional manufacturer of paper pulp. What does the e-environment mean for me? What type of competence am I required to have? What type of processes do I need to change? What type of relationships do I need to have in order to create value in this new environment? And so on.

Here we have an issue about identifying what is needed in order to continue or commence the creation of value. Dealing with this issue also helps the organization make itself credible to the external world by showing that it has what it takes. So, it's an issue about identification and disclosure. That's the first set of issues that drives companies to us at Intellectual Capital Services.

The second issue is that they are convinced they have what it takes, but they are unsure and uncertain about how they should deploy their resources to maximize their potential to create value. One way to look at this is by saying, "I have hired all these brilliant Ph.D.s, and I have bought all these wonderful IT systems, and I have this wonderful list of contacts I can turn into customers. How do I turn this into a working business?

How do I make money out of it? You know, I'm g
e-business, and I don't want to lose money. I want to
do I do that?" This is an effectiveness issue. The qu
assure that I, as an organization, do the right thing
deploying these resources?"

We have over the last year or so been heavily in
specifically from e-related companies, and obviously, ...
back to the cash flow issues and the pressures that they are under. They
ask, "What is the strategic business model? How do we make money out
of these things? We have everything. We have the latest IT. We have the
latest this and that. We have all the bright people, but how do we make
money?" This is the second issue, and it is relevant not only in the e-world
but for organizations in general.

The third issue that drives people to us is that companies have highly
IC-dependent businesses. That is, "We are in pharmaceuticals," or "We are
in R&D," or "We are in something which is totally dependent on brands
or IP. And, we think we have a good business model. We think we have a
good deployment structure. We are good at knowing that we have the right
things. We have put it together in a good deployment structure. We are
effective, but we want to track our efficiency. Are we actually creating real
value to the level that we ought to be able to from an effectiveness perspective?" This is an efficiency question. Here, they come to us basically
for a measurement system: "How and what should we measure? How do
we combine the measurements in some meaningful way, because there's
all kinds of funny units of things, into something or other that has a
predictive power for our market value, our cash flow, or some other value-
contributing factor?"

They have normally been quite frustrated and gone through the traditional route of trying out all kinds of tools and techniques that look good
but really don't give them what they want here. That is where we have
some sophisticated offerings, depending on how sophisticated they want to
be, which allow them to measure the right things and to track their performance on these right things.

The fourth issue that drives companies to us is the question: "I do all
these things, and I think I do them well, but for some reason or other, my
observers, my beholders, my investors, whoever it may be, don't seem to
value what I do. So, how can we increase the perceived value of the organization that we have? And what are the issues at stake here?"

In summary, here are the four issues: Have we got what it takes? Are
we deploying it in an effective way? Are we efficient in putting it to use?
Are we actually creating value in the eyes of our beholders?

C: *Who is generally your client? Is your client the head of strategy, the CEO, or the head of a business unit?*

GR: There are a couple of issues there: Who are the people who contact us? Who are the people on the project? And who are the people who actually get the benefit from it?

The people who contact us tend to be one of three: either the CEO of a corporation or a business unit manager. Or, the equivalent of a chief technology officer, usually responsible for R&D or similar issues, or a human resources director.

The person who becomes the owner, or who take ownership, of the project tends to be mostly the chief financial officer. The reason for that is that when we come in, normally, he's an extremely skeptical gentleman. He is very skeptical about all this soft stuff and can't deal with it in a way he perceives to be rational. But once we have proven that the methodologies that exist in this field are as hard as the hardest version of finance, he suddenly discovers, "Oh, this is great. I can now come to grips with all those soft areas. I can now start to require them to deliver something that I can track. I can ask my HR director to deliver hard numbers on performance issues here. I want this. This is in my area of responsibility and control."

Specifically, since chief financial officers are normally targeted with maximizing the value creation of the company from all of its assets, not only the traditional ones, this is an area where they, quite rightfully, take ownership. They also tend to be quite powerful in the organization.

Who are the people who tend to benefit? In other words, what is the level at which these projects are executed? There is a methodological issue here. The first three approaches (that is, do we have what it takes? the effectiveness issue, and the efficiency issue) need to be implemented first in the largest entity in the organization with a coherent strategy and a coherent business model or business recipe, which is normally business unit level, before you can do it on the corporate level. This is because each business unit may have a different strategy and a different business recipe, and you need those as inputs in order to do it on the corporate level. The fourth, or valuation approach, tends to have the corporate level or an independent corporation as the unit of analysis.

One of the interesting issues is that there are some unexpected benefits for some in this. For example, an HR director normally finds this to be extremely appealing because usually he sits in the boardroom and talks a language that the other ones do not talk, and he cannot talk the language they talk. They talk the language in numbers. He does not or she does not. This suddenly provides him with an opportunity to do so. But the side effect is it also makes him accountable in those terms. You can be sure that the chief financial officer will make sure that they become accountable in these terms and that is normally an unexpected outcome for the HR director. The chief financial officer tends to call it a benefit.

JC: *What are the four drivers of value in an organization, and what do they relate to?*

GR: If we are to make any progress in understanding how we can turn our new view of the company to practical advantages, we will need to couple the company "engine" to its value drivers. Why are drivers of value important? These are drivers of value in the minds of customers. These are the drivers of perceived value. They are important because they impact two drivers of cash. The first driver of cash is margin and the other driver of cash is revenue. Revenue is driven by revenue drivers. These are, for example, the number of client relationships, how long they last, how much they buy every time, and how frequently they buy. But those terms are impacted by the perceived value of the customers. If you do not generate perceived value, you cannot generate revenue.

Margin is driven by your relative performers of perceived value and delivered costs, and therefore perceived value is one of the two things to drive the margin of the organization. Therefore, what we need to know in order to manage margin and revenue well is an excellent understanding of our cost drivers and an excellent understanding of our perceived value drivers. Most organizations have excellent control of the cost drivers, specifically those that work with activity-based costing. We can find sufficient cost information inside the company.

The more difficult part is to get to the value drivers outside your organization. Many organizations have not been comfortable in doing this for the reason that they have to go outside the company. And if they have done it, they have normally delegated it to some extent to marketing or some outside supplier. We have done some research in this over the years, and we have identified, first, what the value driver categories are and, second, how you can measure them. And there are some interesting insights we've gained along the way.

It turns out that there are four categories of value drivers (see figure 5.5). First, there is price, which are all the resources that the organization has to give up in return for the service or product that it gets. This can be actual money, it can be some other resource, or it can be time or anything else.

The second is functionality, which is everything objectively measurable surrounding your delivery. These are characteristics such as did it arrive on

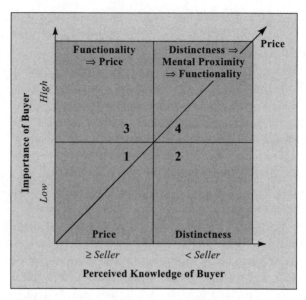

FIGURE 5.5 Situational Importance of Different Perceived Value Drive Categories

time, did it have the right color, did it do what it was supposed to do, and so on.

The third is distinctness. These are the things that generate mind share as a precursor to market share. It's things like brands, reputation, and references.

The fourth category is mental proximity. Those are the things that lower the barriers for building person-to-person trust. We can call it, if you want, shared values and beliefs.

Those are the value drivers. In a given customer group, these are not equally important, and therefore we have found that something called a natural segmentation approach is the best segmentation approach. For example, if you are a brand-dependent organization, what we found through many empirical pieces of work and also academic study is that you want to use this difference in the importance of value drivers as your segmentation criteria because that creates segments that want to have the same things to the same extent. This is something that we frequently help consumer goods companies with.

If you can identify, for each brand or brand attribute, its specific contribution to value, you will be able to see the difference between what you are doing at the present level and what doing it very well would be. Then you can identify the actual outcome in money that closing that gap would generate. That, in turn, can allow you to know the offsetting revenue against the investment that's necessary. That, by definition, allows you a very precise way of valuing brands in this area.

Business Logic

JC: *Why is it that the better a company knows its business logic, the fewer key performance indicators, or KPIs, it needs?*
GR: That's a very interesting question. We sometimes use a term called *gut feel*, which is our accumulated experience and knowledge brought to bear in a given problem situation, where we are not using articulated reasoning, but unarticulated reasoning. In other words, if we have a situation we are intimately familiar with, we need little additional information to form a gut feel, which in nine cases out of ten will be correct.

If you are in a situation where you are not familiar, you have nothing to bring to bear. Therefore, you need to form an articulated model. And, in order to do so, you need a lot of input.

Here is a case that illustrates this point. A cookie company was run by its founder, now an elderly gentleman, who had run this company for a long time. In his later days, he decided to sell the company. He sold it to a large multinational company, which put in extremely professional management. The gentleman who founded the company happened to live next door, and he was given an honorary position on the board but was really removed from the operation of the company. The new multinational owner put in all of these wonderful systems. In spite of this, at each board meeting, it seemed like the old man knew more precisely the financial position of the company than management did. And why was that? He was never in the factory. Never!

They asked him how he knew. His answer was: "Well, I know. It's obvious." Then the gentleman, unfortunately, died. At the funeral, it so happened that the CEO of the company was sitting next to the guard who staffed the entrance to the factory, and they came to talk.

The CEO asked the guard, "How did you know the founder? Why are you here?" "Well, I've known him all my life. We grew up together." And on and on. Then the guard said, "When he retired we used to chat every morning on his walk."

The CEO asked, "What did you talk about?" The guard responded, "Well, we spoke about this, that, and the other. But he always asked me the same questions." "And what were they?" asked the CEO.

"Well, he asked me how many people came to work today. He asked me how many trucks of raw material were delivered. And he asked me how many trucks of rejects were taken away. Those were the only three questions he asked me."

That was the basis for him knowing exactly what the performance of the organization was, because he had, by building the company, internalized an incredible understanding of the business. He knew that those were the only three variables that he needed to know anything about. On the other side was this extremely bright and extremely able professional manager who had not internalized the business recipe and, therefore, was depending on lots of data. But even with the data, the CEO couldn't synthesize the information in the same way as the old gentleman could.

The more you know about your business, the less data you need. But the bottom line is not zero. There's always something you need to know, but if you do not know anything, you need a lot of data. The point is: If you ask for a lot of data, you probably do not know your business very well.

JC: *What is the importance of stock and flow indicators?*
GR: Resource and transformation indicators are very important. A *resource* is something you have, and a *transformation* changes one resource into another. In order to create value, you need to be good at transformations. And there is no correlation between having a resource and being able to transform it.

To illustrate the point, consider this simple example: I hire the best accountant in the world for my company in order to minimize my tax burden, and I pay whatever salary this person wants. The person turns up Monday morning and asks, "What shall I do?" And I say, "Down in the street is my car. Your task is to wash that car eight hours a day, every day." If I, on day three (assuming that the accountant is still there), execute a competence mapping or competence inventory exercise in order to check if I have the competence of the best accountant in the firm, the answer is: "Yes, I do." Does that competence contribute to my value creation?—which, by the way, is a question never asked. And the answer is: "No, it doesn't." Here we have a resource, but we are not transforming it. Therefore, measuring what we have is no predictor of our ability to generate value. What we need to measure and track is our transformation ability.

To reiterate, the only thing you need to know about your resources is: "Do I have the necessary and sufficient amount?" That is a yes or no question. You know, from above, that more than the necessary and sufficient amount doesn't matter except that the excess is being wasted. Whereas "How good am I at transforming one into another?" is not a yes or no question. It's a continuous answer question, where you need to measure in detail the time, the amount, the effectiveness, and the effi-

ciency of this. That is why there is a big distinction betw
transformations.

Unfortunately, many organizations primarily focus o
sources, which is the least meaningful way of looking at it,
ceptually the most simple to measure. Whereas, in order to be
should focus on measuring transformation, which is the more co
one but the most useful one.

JC: *So, the flow is a transformation?*
GR: Correct.

JC: *I do not think that has been explained by other people
at that level.*
GR: I think that this is a fundamental conceptual distinction between the
stocks and the flows, the resources and transformations.

The IC Approach

JC: *What is the fundamental difference between a balanced
scorecard approach and your approach, the IC approach?*
GR: There is a fundamental difference between a scorecard approach and
the IC approach. The original scorecard-type methodology is a very old
process. I mean, in the Anglo-Saxon world, it is most well known as being
developed by Kaplan and Norton, who developed an excellent tool. The
French developed a similar scorecard approach 50 years or so back. The
scorecard in its original way was generally an exceedingly good tool. But
the French experience, over all these years, tells us that the scorecard approach tends to be a better tool for communicating things, that is, what
is important to the company, what you should focus on as a manager, and
so on, than in providing managerial support. The reason is that it is very
difficult to make a trade-off decision in a scorecard. You know, two things
go up and two stand still. Is that better than the opposite arrangement of
the two, where the second pair goes up and the first two stand still? You
don't know. It becomes a judgment issue.

The balanced scorecard allows you to identify effectively the resources
you need to do something, and it allows you to communicate well about
those resources—all of which is very important. What we tend to do, in
addition, is focus on the ability to transform one into another. We are not
primarily into the issue about a communication tool. We are into the issue
about a managerial support tool, which allows you to make trade-off decisions. Our question is: Is it better to use the competence to develop

sses, or is it better to use the competence to sell person-hours for money, or is it better to use the competence to develop relationships? The IC process can help you make these types of trade-off decisions.

JC: *Would you use both, or does the IC encompass the balanced scorecard?*

GR: We find it easier to work with organizations that have worked with a scorecard-type approach. It's easier because they have identified what they do not get from their scorecard, and therefore it allows us to give a very specific deliverable. It's also easier to work with people who have played some of those games, like Tango, because there is already awareness about relevant, from our point of view, issues.

JC: *What results have you achieved using the IC process?*

GR: By using the IC process, ICS has achieved quite substantial results. I have a presentation from CEOs and business unit managers that shows that the IC approach contributed substantially to increasing the value of the organization in the eyes of its stakeholders, to the articulation and alignment of its strategic intent, to developing a disclosure policy as it relates to different stakeholders, to providing knowledge transfer of leading-edge know-how, and to learning how to mesh and manage intangible value assets. Many of these successes have been publicized as academic cases.

I think the issue we find is that when people come to us, they expect that the benefit will be in the outcome of the work. When they leave us, they tend to say there was as much benefit in the process as there was in the outcome. In other words, all the questions that we ask in the process, all the challenging, the issues, the awareness, and the language creating become for the senior management team as valuable as the tools, techniques, and measurement systems that are left behind. We have had major impact on organizations through our work; we have contributed to enhancing the value of companies by multiples; we have contributed to changing the strategic directions of firms; and we have contributed to companies investing or divesting big parts of their business. We have made companies change the way they do things dramatically. We have contributed to companies dramatically improving market share. We have cases where, on a national basis for a very brief period of time, market shares of 20% have risen to market shares of 80% simply by understanding better how to do these things. So, we have some very dramatic, well-documented case studies illustrating the benefits that are around.

JC: *What are the components of the IC index, which is something you've created?*

GR: The IC index is something you can do on three levels. You can do it on the perfect, theoretically rigorous level, which means covering the greatest scope of things possible with the approach, and we have those offerings. One of them is known as the holistic value added (HVA) approach. This approach takes a lot of time and gives a lot of value, but few companies have the time, resources, or need to go through one of those exercises.

You could also do things on what we call a Pareto level. In this case, that is one of the IC index issues, and you can put in 20% of the effort for 80% of the outcome.

Or, you can decide to put no effort in and do it anyway. That is what we call using a tool and technique from The Heathrow Library of Management—these are the type of books you buy at an airport, which are called *You Can Be a Fool and Beat the Market* and which have all these wonderful, simplistic tools, which are not grounded in anything more than a Sunday afternoon thought.

Now, we do not operate on this third level. But, we do operate on the first and second levels. The IC index is the second-level solution to a measurement system that tracks value creation. The components of that index are primarily indicators of the relevant transformations that are of importance in your organization. They are extracted from the business model using matrix algebra techniques. They are weighted using fixed sum and binary combination matrix process approaches. They are tested using necessary and sufficiency criteria. They are then combined into an index using measurement theory. That allows you an index, a curve that tracks changes in your value creation ability. But since it is a Pareto tool, the absolute value of the index is not important. Solely, the change in the value of the index is important. Whereas on the HVA side, since it is the perfect approach, you can also talk about the absolute value of the outcome. The IC index is made up of weighted measures of transformations between resources, allowing you to predict changes in your value-creating ability.

Third-Generation IC Practices

JC: *Now, you've talked about differences among the first, second, and third generations of intellectual capital practices. What are these differences?*

GR: As research on intellectual capital progresses, one can distinguish among three generations of IC practices. There are distinct differences among the first, second, and third generations of intellectual capital practices, which roughly align with the measurement possibilities just discussed.

The first-generation practice is basically the scorecard-type practice, where the focus is on identifying resources and dealing with those. A good example of an application of a first-generation practice is Skandia, which was all about identifying what is important and disclosing whether they had it or not or to what extent, which can be extremely valuable to an organization, as such.

The second-generation practice is when you look at the transformations as well as the resources. That is where you deal with issues concerning the drivers of value being the ability to transform rather than whether you have something or not. The second generation adds and puts the emphasis on the transformations rather than the resources.

The third generation of IC practices are the ones that allow you to combine measures of different units into a totality measure that reflects the value perceived by a given observer. Those are the three generations. Their attributes are compared in figure 5.6.

We could put it this way. The classical tools are first generation, a scorecard-type tool; the second generation is a kind of IC index–type tool and navigator-type tools; and for the third generation, the only approach available at the moment is the HVA-type tools.

The HVA is built on the IC index technique developed by me and a methodology called the IVM (Inclusive value methodology) developed by

Main Criteria	Test	Financially based, EVA	1st gen. IC and BBS	2nd gen. IC (e.g., IC index)	3rd gen. IC, (e.g., HVA)
Auditable and Reliable	Data meet a standard	Yes	No	Partial	Yes
	Data address the future	Partial	Yes	Yes	Yes
Overhead and Ease of Use	Low measurement overhead	Yes	Moderate	Moderate	Moderate
	Easy to initiate and use	Yes	Yes	Moderate	Complex to initiate
Strategic Management	Allows multilevel management	Partial	Does not allow trade-offs	Yes	Yes
	Measures stock, flow, and influence	Stock	Stock	Stock and influence	Stock, flow, and influence
Shareholder Information	Provides data at all company levels	Partial	Yes	Yes	Yes

FIGURE 5.6 Criteria for Three Generations of IC Practices

a colleague, Philip M'Pherson. The building of HVA has also relied heavily on another colleague, Stephen Pike.

JC: *What is value accounting?*
GR: Value accounting is a more general approach to accounting than financial accounting, which is the more normal approach. We all know that investors take more things into account than pure cash when they invest. Some companies could argue that this is a license-to-operate issue, but that is not always the case because you may have personal preferences. For example, some people have preferences for companies that have red in their logo or companies that have little nice, cuddly animals as a logo, companies that donate lots of money to environmental issues, and so on. These are things that are not necessarily possible to use a license-to-operate approach on.

Value accounting is the collection of tools, techniques in a science that allows you to account for value with all its constituent dimensions, as opposed to just accounting for one of those constituent dimensions, which is cash. If you say to a value accountant, "I want to use your tools and techniques, but I want to limit myself to resources that are financial and additive in nature," you would get a subset of techniques known as transaction-based accounting. But if you generalize this to: "I want to deal with all resources, and all dimensions, and I want to capture the totality of value," then you need to have value accounting.

JC: *And that puts you in a different position?*
GR: A completely different position. Yes. Absolutely.

Holistic Value Added

JC: *What is the process for carrying out the holistic value added approach?*
GR: With HVA, I am looking at creating a simple structure because what I want to do is to measure the value of something. The reason why I want to do that is because I want to be able to answer one or more of three questions. I may want to know what the value of our organization is in some term or other. I also may want to know the outcome of a sensitivity analysis, so I can determine which factor has the largest impact on value where I am at the moment. And, I may want to make trade-off decisions. This would be things like: "How much cash am I willing to spend to increase my brand perception by 3% in order to be perceived as having at least the same value as I have now." I, in essence, want to achieve three

things: something approaching an absolute measure of value, sensitivity analysis, and trade-offs. And, obviously, as a consequence of that, you can have all kinds of disclosure applications.

Look at this very simplified process. The first thing you need to do is define your perspective. For example, when somebody asks, "What is my company worth?" the immediate response has to be: "From whose point of view?" This is because your company's worth will have a different value from an employee's point of view, from an investor's point of view, from a government point of view, or from management's point of view.

So, the first question is: "Who is the observer?" You need to identify one or several observers. Then, for each of these observers, you need to discover: "What is it that they want to see changed in this observed object in order for them to get more value out of it?" Next, you need to identify the object very well so you have a well-delineated object. Then, each of those things they want to see changed (normally a "motherhood and apple pie" kind of statement) needs to be broken down into attributes that are measurable, and then you need to identify the measures. You need to transform those measures into measurement space. In other words, give them a 0 to 1 nondimensional scale, by understanding what is the lowest acceptable and the highest achievable range of points, and what happens in between. You need to weight them and then to combine them using the axiomatic approach of measurement theory. There are many ways of combining two measures into one, but four approaches cover most practical situations.

As a consequence and an outcome of that, you get what we call a *value function*. We can then use that value function to achieve the three statements I made first.

Let me run through an example to make it a bit livelier. My examples are very simplistic but will give you an idea of the point. Let's assume that the observer is my wife and the object under observation is me. We ask my wife: "What would you like to see in the object? What change would you like to see in the object in order to get more value out of it?"

The answer will be mainly of the "motherhood and apple pie" type. It would be on the order of "more happiness in life." If the object displays more happiness in life, my value perception of the object goes up. Now, I can't measure happiness in life. I need to break that down into some attributes. I may now need to ask questions of the observer and break it down into actual constituent parts.

In this case, my wife may well decide to say, "Happiness in life is made up of three things: good health, disposable income, and free time." For each of those, I need to define some good measures, and then for each of the measures, there may be more than one measure for them. I may have to find out what is the lowest acceptable level, what is the highest achievable, and what happens in between, and that is normally not linear. Then, I need to talk about how relatively important they are. Next, I need to know how they combine. And, obviously they don't combine the same way in each version. If I'm asked, "How much money do I need to be paid for me to give up some free time?" I will be able to come up with an answer: $X thousand, $X hundred thousand, or $X million, and I will give up this free time.

Then, I ask myself the question: "How much money do I want now to give up my health?" That, obviously, is not for sale. So, they have completely different trade-off characteristics. They have different ways of combining together.

What we want optimally is to have total free time, total disposable income, and total health. But, we are not willing to give up total health because without health, the rest is worth nothing. On the other hand, without either free time or money, then health isn't worth a lot either in this scenario. But, we can trade off both disposable income and time. That would be all right, and we could stay at the same value level. If you notice, the whole exercise down to the last point is solely done by extracting information from the observer.

Once that information is consolidated, we go to the object and say: "Now, here is what I can do to increase your value in the eyes of your observer." In other words, you sometimes hear people making the statement: "My company is undervalued." And from this point of view, there are only three interpretations of that statement. The first is that you, as a CEO, know something about your company that if known to the investors would have increased their value perception of the company. You may have tried to communicate it but for some reason it didn't reach. It was stuck in cyberspace or something. That is alternative one. That is a communication problem.

Alternative two is the same scenario: You know something but have chosen not to tell anybody, which in most cases, if you're listed, is illegal, and we cannot help you with that.

The third one is "our problem": There is an assumption implicit in the statement that you, as the CEO, observe these indicators of your company and get to one value. The investor sees the same indicators; therefore, she must put them together in the same way as you do and must get to the same value. And that is not the case. Value, like beauty, is in the eye of the beholder. So, there has to be a realization that the same indicators give rise to different values in different observers. So the question you have to ask yourself, as a CEO, is: "If I want to maximize the market value or shareholder value of my company, what balance do I strike between performing on what I think is correct, as opposed to performing on what my investor thinks is correct?" In other words, how do I balance delivering what you want to get versus educating you into getting to my viewpoint? That is where this technique comes in.

JC: *Do you mean that it begins to be differentiated so you can make better choices?*
GR: Correct

Value Space

JC: *In the holistic value added approach, you've defined something called* value space, *and you use a multidimensional contour map to take a look at it. What is the advantage of looking at the value spaces using a multidimensional, topographic perspective?*
GR: It allows a number of things. First, it allows a clearer understanding of how value would change with different input variables. Obviously, on the Z axis, you have value, and then on the X and Y axes, you have some combination structure on that level. For example, you could have the contribution from intangibles versus contribution from tangibles to something else. Here I can see what happens if I give up 100 million units of this in order to get ten units more competence, or whatever it may be. I can ask myself: "What does that mean in my contour surface?" I can also use a shape structure to understand how sensitive my value-generation ability is. I can ask if it is very steep there, or very shallow. I can begin to ascertain whether it matters if I do something, or if it does *not* matter if I do something. Also, it allows me to project this value surface onto any of the constituent dimensions. I can project this known dimensional value onto the finances axis and say: "This is how many dollars my competence is worth," or "This is how many dollars my brand is worth." I can also point at the perceived effort that's going to be needed to move in different directions along this contour map.

JC: *You mean I will be able to gauge how much effort would be required?*
GR: Yes, I can choose my route. I can discover or create a minimum energy route to get from point A to point B.

JC: *Fascinating. What are the critical issues you see in the present and ahead in the field of intellectual capital?*

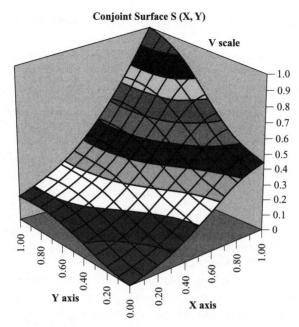

FIGURE 5.7 Value Space Topographical Map

GR: There are two ways to define the present and future in the field of intellectual capital. We can define it either as a science in its own right, in which case it faces the first hurdle of achieving a recognized standard of language. Or, we can define it as a synthesis of a number of subsciences, like finance theory, systems theory, strategy, accounting, and so on, in which case the hurdle becomes to "get" an acceptable practice. These would be practices such as: "This is how you report the values of intangibles," or "This is how you do this, and this is how you do that."

In the first scenario, it's about the academic community agreeing to a standard practice of operation. In the second scenario, it's about the practitioners, for example, the auditors, agreeing upon a standard practice of operation when it comes to the area that intellectual capital deals with. I think that would be my short answer. I have an extremely long answer but that would be my short answer.

Key Learning Points

- A given firm or organization is a system made up of a set of resources that are deployed in a given structure. Intellectual capital is the science and art of dealing with how to extract maximum value from the resources you have and the way you have chosen to deploy them.

- A business recipe is the specific resources and the way they are being combined in terms of transformations.
- Using the IC process lens, you can determine the value creation path in an organization. Where firms differ is in the types of competencies they have and how they use them, what types of processes, structures, systems, brands, IP, and so on, and how they use them. This determines a firm's fitness to meet the unknown challenges of the future.
- There is a very important distinction between having a resource—whether it be competence, process, system, intellectual property, relationship, machines, or cash—and putting it to value-creating use, which is the ability to transform one resource into another.
- Think about the IC perspective to
  - reconsider what competencies, processes, and relationships are needed for the new e-environment,
  - deploy existing resources in an effective way,
  - see better how to measure efficiencies, and
  - better create value in the eyes of stakeholders.
- Most organizations focus on their stock of resources, which is the simplest but least meaningful measure, versus focusing on measuring flows or the transformation of one resource into another, which is more complicated but more useful.
- While the balanced scorecard allows the identification of resources, which enables communication about those resources, the IC process focuses on the ability to transform resources, which enables value creation and essential trade-off decisions.
- Value accounting focuses on all constituent dimensions to capture the totality of value, as opposed to normal accounting, which focuses on one of those constituent dimensions, which is cash.
- Looking at value spaces using a contoured, topographical perspective map allows us to discover or create a minimum energy route to get from strategic point A to strategic point B.

The Intelligent Organization

6

Leif Edvinsson is a key contributor to the theory and practice of intellectual capital. In this conversation, he explores the basis for IC and the IC growth model. Edvinsson examines what creates value in the world of knowledge-based organizations and the various ways in which we will be upgrading our own knowledge base. Since understanding and focusing on intellectual capital requires a significant rethinking of what really drives value, he looks at the challenge that intellectual capital leadership has in changing its mindset so it can use the structural capital of organizations to turbocharge the capabilities of our human capital. The outcome of this is the development of truly intelligent organizations but organizations of a very different nature. These new organizations may well evolve into communities, and instead of employees, we will become citizens of those communities.

Edvinsson is the founder and CEO of UNIC (Universal Networking Intellectual Capital at www.unic.net), whose mission is to generate new insights as to what an organization's intellectual capital is, as well as how to grow, appraise, and better understand how to commercialize it. He is a catalyst for the possibilities inherent in the new era of intangible wealth. He is active in prototyping boards of directors on intellectual capital in several countries. In addition, in 2001, he was appointed to the world's first chair on intellectual capital at Lund University.

Edvinsson was formerly the corporate director of intellectual capital, the first position of its type in the world, at the Skandia Group, where many of the fundamental ideas of intellectual capital as an organizational framework were developed and put into operation. During his tenure at Skandia, he oversaw the creation of the first IC annual report.

Edvinsson is foremost a visionary of intellectual capital. He says, "The future is our home." A sense of the future underlies the in building throughout the world of a number of Future Centers, which are experimental stations to prototype how to create the organizational capital that will be the basis for creating the wealth of the new millennium.

He is the co-author, with Michael S. Malone, of a defining work in the field, *Intellectual Capital: Realizing Your Company's True Value by Finding Its Hidden Brainpower*, as well as a contributor to numerous other books and journals. His most recent book is *Corporate Longitude* (2002), which is discussed on his website, www.corporatelongitude.com. Edvinsson was recognized for his achievements when he was awarded the Brain of the Year from the Brain Trust of the United Kingdom in 1998.

In light of his work in both training and intellectual capital, Edvinsson has been a special advisor on service trade to the Swedish Ministry of Foreign Affairs. He is also special advisor to the Swedish cabinet on the effects of the new digital economy, a special advisor to the U.N. International Trade Center, and a cofounder of the Swedish Coalition of Service Industries. Edvinsson holds an M.B.A. from the University of California, Berkeley.

The Conversation

Value Creation

JC: *How does value get created in organizations and networks?*

LE: Value is created if there is a buyer or customer of the organization, that is, a buyer of the shares or a customer of the product. Actually, the value of knowledge organizations is created mainly outside the organization. The fundamental observation is that value is not created within the organization. It is created on the edge: among the context, the business community, and the organization. This means that the networks are becoming extremely important, as is the sensitivity to the surrounding world. That is also why most organizations of today are perhaps not as efficient as they could be.

JC: *When you say they are not as efficient as they could be, what does that mean?*

LE: It is that productivity is rather low. According to Paul Straussman, most of the organizations on the New York Stock Exchange are having a negative return on their knowledge capital, as he sees it. The intellectual capital growth model focuses on the enablers and drivers for future earnings potential, whether they are networks, knowledge, processes, or innovations. There are a lot of different dimensions and perspectives.

Market capital growth is related to the investor relationship dimensions, while the IC growth dimensions are related to the phases of the balanced scorecard, or rather the IC navigator, with the phases and focuses of the ones we developed for the IC process with Skandia.

Here are the major IC process phases: The first is the missionary; the second is the measurement and visualization; the third is the leadership; the fourth is the knowledge technology; the fifth is innovation; and the sixth is capitalization. All those are described in the book I wrote called *Intellectual Capital*.[1]

Market capital is the external dimension, and intellectual capital is the internal one.

JC: *And they all form the growth model?*

LE: Combined, they do. But, you should also remember that there are some organizations that do not have a market cap, like public institutions, hospitals, and so on. They could still grow their intellectual capital.

JC: *How can an old economy organization use the IC growth model to transform itself into being a new economy organization? This is what you did with Skandia. Are you doing it with other organizations now?*

LE: Yes, but I am mainly trying to add value by being a professional board member to organizations, rather than a consultant. First of all, we need to see the economics dimension rather than old economy versus new economy. It is more the same economy, but the economics has changed. In the old economy, the economics was based more on having the product as the revenue carrier. In the new economy, the intangibles or the knowledgeable person are very much the value carriers. Most of the intangibles have other logics than the tangibles. For example, the value of a computer is decreasing over time, while the value of software is increasing over time. In the same way, the value of knowledge sharing is increasing, as is the value of knowl-

---

[1] Leif Edvinsson and Michael S. Malone, *Intellectual Capital: Realizing Your Company's True Value by Finding Its Hidden Brainpower* (New York: HarperBusiness, 1997).

edge application, and so on. We are starting to see that the combined perspective of the new economy, as a new economics, is about the logic of value creation of intangibles.

That is what we were starting to refine at Skandia. The old economy was represented by the insurance, where we were selling insurance products per se. The new dimension of Skandia was that we were launching innovative financial services contracts, with a long sustainable revenue chain. That led to Skandia's growing market cap, and it was the application of the IC growth model that cultivated this.

JC: *Can you do that with any organization, if you find the right strategic intent?*
LE: Yes.

Upgrading Competencies

JC: *How did you find the right strategic intent at Skandia?*
LE: It was common sense. It is so obvious. In the old economy, we were having insurance for cars, or tables and chairs, that is, tangibles. In the new economy, we are going to see many more insurances for intangibles. It is still to come, but, for example, we developed competency insurance as an illustration of that. Competency insurance is an insurance to support you in sustaining your knowledge. There is actually a financial scheme that helps you to fund your renewal. In the old economics, you, as an employee, were regarded as a natural resource. You were hired, consumed, and eliminated. In the new economy, you have to keep updating your knowledge. The famous Moore's Law says that global knowledge is growing at roughly 100% every 18 months. The most recent forecast says that within five to ten years, we will have a global knowledge growth that will be 100% every six months.

You can imagine the difficult position that our doctors, lawyers, financial planners, and all professionals are going to be in if they do not upgrade. And who is going to fund these upgrades: the state, the company, the individuals? In the election campaign in the United States, there was much talk about funding for retirement. How about funding for knowledge upgrading, which is going to be much more critical than the funding for senior-age citizens?

JC: *Are you involved with knowledge upgrading?*
LE: Yes, in many ways. I am a part owner of a new intellectual capital university online. I am on the boards of a number of knowledge-upgrading

companies, I am working with a new brokerage firm for knowledge automation, and so on. I am also developing Future Center International as a global chain of arenas for cultivating intellectual capital.

Knowledge upgrading is so important if you have the cycle time of 100% every six months in the future. It is like going to school and getting a professional degree, which takes five to ten years in the case of a Ph.D. in medical science. Are you then updated on the latest when you come out? Or, are you well educated with the old stuff? The tendency is that you are going to be very well educated with the old stuff.

The Challenge of Intellectual Capital Leadership

JC: *What is the challenge for intellectual capital leadership?*
LE: To give you a very tangible illustration of this challenge, let's look at the following. One hundred years ago, it took four weeks to produce a telephone, and it took about four years to get a Ph.D. Today, it takes about eight seconds to make a new telephone. And it takes more than four years to become a Ph.D. If you could apply the same process of automation in the educational community as we have in industry, you would become a Ph.D. in around ten weeks.

JC: *Do humans have the capacity for that kind of intellectual growth at that rate?*
LE: Of course. If you are reading a newspaper today, like *USA Today*, you will be offered the same volume of knowledge in that newspaper that was given during a whole life for a medieval person.

JC: *When people say they are overwhelmed by new information, do they really mean that they just do not know how to handle it?*
LE: Yes.

JC: *How could they learn how to handle it?*
LE: I don't know. I am learning. That is what knowledge automation is all about. We have to start to see new angles as well as opportunities in it. The answer is not just to treat it in the way knowledge management has treated knowledge.

JC: *Do we have to recast our approach to knowledge?*
LE: Yes, challenge traditional approaches. Asking the following question: How long does it take you to change a bad tire on your car?

JC: *About a half hour to an hour for a flat tire.*

LE: Do you know that they do it in five seconds in Formula One?

JC: *Yes, they are set up for that.*

LE: Yes. You see, it is possible. Nobody would say it was possible to do it in five seconds, but they have the knowledge systems for it.

Changing the Mindset

JC: *Are you saying they use knowledge-based systems?*

LE: Of course. One of the first big challenges is the mindset. In traditional leadership, we focus on human capital. In IC leadership, you focus on the structural capital as a springboard for human capital, as a lever for giving a turbocharge to the human capital. We have to change leadership perspectives 180 degrees from human capital to structural capital. We need to release the human potential and leverage it by structural capital.

JC: *How would leadership go about doing that?*

LE: So far, leadership has done very badly on knowledge leverage. Skandia is, however, a good example (Jan R. Carendi, deputy CEO of Skandia, was named one of the world's top ten most admired knowledge leaders in the year 2000), though there are a few others as well. It is so different from management. You probably find it much more in show business. You offer the structural capital to the talent. But you cannot command. It is not command and control, it is create and communicate. It is this new c-and-c, which is about the creation of the human potential, the human talent, and then getting a turbocharge to it.

JC: *Is the turbocharge what the organization provides?*

LE: Yes. That is why the organization's capital is, by itself, structural capital. The organization is not its people. The common phrase is that the organization is its people. That is why this is a big mental challenge.

JC: *If the organization is not its people, what is the organization?*

LE: The organization is its structural capital, its networks, its databases, patents, trademarks, and so on, all intellectual properties. They are all the vehicles of the organization.

Navigation Is Movement

JC: *How does knowledge navigation allow us to realize the intellectual capital potentials in the knowledge-based economy, both now and into the future?*

LE: The navigation dimension is that it is a movement. It is a motion. That is why the phrase is: "A modern company is on the move." The old phrase is: "A modern company is its management, or maintenance." That is why old companies become prisons instead of springboards for their talent and their potential.

Intellectual capital potential is, first of all, the human potential. According to Peter Drucker, the potential of knowledge-based work is today operating on an efficiency level of only 20%. The opportunity cost is 80%, but it might be that it goes beyond 100% when you start to realize the potential of what can be done. That is emerging when you combine the 6 billion people on earth with Internet opportunities. We are going to see that US Steel, GM, or even Cisco and companies like that are far from their potential. If you multiply 6 billion brains, with the growing global Internet technologies, you can see that these organizations are not taking advantage of the 6 billion brains.

JC: *Are they are not taking advantage of their external organization or their external network?*

LE: Fifty percent of Internet users today are in the United States. There are about 300 million people in the United States, and many billions in Asia, and they today represent between 5 and 10% of Internet users. But the numbers of Internet users are growing at the rate of almost 100% every year. Within around five to eight years, the major proportion of Internet users are going to be in Asia.

The implications of that scenario are tremendous. If the value is in these networks, the capital base is going to be different. As the value base shifts, we are going to see an economy not dominated by North Americans, Europeans, or Japanese.

JC: *Is this going to require a very significant recasting of how we think about the world?*

LE: Yes. Look at the number of millionaires in Bangalore, India, and compare that with the number of millionaires in the area of Washington or Boston. There are more millionaires in Bangalore already. That is in actual numbers, not percentages. Even the servants in some of the restaurants have portfolios of value stocks, of growth companies on the Internet, and are millionaires. Challenging, isn't it? A new wealth perspective is emerging.

When the BBC did a videotape on the Skandia Future Center and my work, they labeled it *Intellectual Capital: The New Wealth of Nations.*

JC: *How does knowledge navigation allow us to realize the*
IC potential? Is it because it allows you to tap into these
networks?
LE: Yes. It is about know-who as well as know-how. As we use the term, competencies are a temporary freezing point for know-how. Capabilities of know-who are much larger than competencies. The usage of our mental capabilities is on the level of 1%. Therefore, we have to learn to use our brain capabilities much more for the future. That is another enlarging knowledge area: how to use your brain, not only your muscles.

We have training programs for athletes going to the Olympics, but do we have similar programs for brain capability training? This might be called, as done by Dana Zohar as well as Tony Buzan, *synapses flow training* to expand the mind networking. It is measured as a synapse quota, SQ, instead of the old IQ.

Intelligent Organizations

JC: *What does it take to develop intelligent organizations?*
LE: Most organizations are dumb. To acknowledge that there are intelligent organizations is an indirect or implicit recognition of where we are. Intelligent organizations are about global intelligence, the courage to move to the second curve, accounting of intangibles, and leveraging knowledge recipes as well as making meaning.

JC: *Is what you are proposing a quantum leap here? Can*
we use the IC process to make that happen?
LE: Precisely. I think that is why the IC process is the quantum leap. It is a quantum leap that includes the steps that I referred to earlier. But, it is mainly a mind shift from harvesting to nourishment, from maintenance to innovation, from human capital to the springboard of structural capital, for the benefit and honor of human talent.

JC: *Is the IC process externally oriented?*
LE: Yes, and that is why we had it in our navigator and took into account the surrounding context for the various knowledge activities.

JC: *How have you seen the IC process working to accomplish that?*

LE: It is about starting to sense the surrounding world, to have the intelligence to see what is going on. A second dimension is that you have the courage to move from the first curve to the second curve. To follow that shift, you have to have a navigational system, which is the new accounting system. Once you get that, you have got to move away from tangible products, because that is freezing your ambitions, and move more toward intangible knowledge recipes. At that point you start to realize that the organization is a very temporary one. It is just there for a few seconds. We now see click-and-go organizations where you have a relationship, like a virtual bank, or home banking, or whatever. You click in, you have a relationship, and you click out.

JC: *Who invests in click in and click out organizations?*

LE: Investors will be the stock markets and venture capitalists that realize that this is the new organizational design reality instead of factories. It needs a lot of infrastructure for that.

Cisco is a tremendous click-and-go organization, like Amazon, America Online, and so on. But the whole point is that it is click-and-go, which means that you do not need to have offices, but you do need to have technology infrastructure. It might be value networks like Verna Allee speaks about,[2] or the one we developed in Skandia AFS with more than 100,000 value-adding persons. You need to have the highways and broadband that form the infrastructure for it. But, it is a different kind of infrastructure than has historically been used for the logistics of raw materials.

Furthermore, we are starting to realize that the value dimension of raw materials and trade of goods represents a minority of the world economy today.

Value Drivers

JC: *What are the hidden value drivers of nations or regions?*

LE: One of the most influential hidden value drivers is attractiveness, which is the glue for networks and magnetism for communities. We look for what makes a nation, or a region, or a corporation attractive. Individuals

[2] Verna Allee, *The Knowledge Evolution: Building Organizational Intelligence* (Boston: Butterworth-Heinemann), 1997.

gather around that attractiveness, which means that the attractiveness is part of the structural capital. This might be the culture, the trademark, easy access of telecom lines, or whatever.

The networks among individuals, corporations, and nations are the most important dimension of IC. So, IC is not the object. IC is the flow. The multiplier function between human capital and structural capital is the flow, or the motion. If we take a human body, we can see the vibration of the cells. When we look at the cell in the microscope, we can start to see that it is not still. If it is still, it is dead. The cell is a living organism. The brain works in the same way. The networks are not frozen. They are continuously shifting. The more they are shifting, the more they grow into new synapses, and the cleverer you become.

JC: *In working with different countries, what values or value drivers exist, and how can they be cultivated?*

LE: We were quite early when we started to do that in 1995. We did it for Sweden as a prototype. Then we moved on to Israel and Denmark. Now we are doing it for the science park of telecom in Sweden. That is a little region of IC, the Mobile Valley, as it is called. Ericsson, Nokia, and the mobile Internet startups are there as well as GE, Cisco, HP, and Microsoft.

We began to see that one of the hidden value drivers is the possibility to connect with other people. A second hidden value driver is having the meeting space there, which could be the arena for gathering, which we call in our Future Center the *knowledge café*. The third value driver is the lifestyle, or living style: easy living, easy access, good climate, and so on. But first of all, it goes back to the interrelationships of people and the search for the so-called relationship efficiency.

The Quantum Leap

JC: *Can people leverage and create a quantum leap for themselves based on this, regardless of where they are?*

LE: I think so. If you look at the evolution of societies along the lines of the American railroads, we are going to see the same kind of cybercities along the telecom lines or the Internet lines. The technology infrastructure is going to create new communities or server cities. That is going, later on, to be reinforced by the political entrepreneurship, if there is political entrepreneurship enough to support that infrastructure growth for new city or urban planning.

In Sweden, for example, we have had two very interesting observations regarding this. One is that Sweden is a society with the highest capability of its citizens to read musical notes. This is an effect of basic schooling, but it also leads to a very high literacy in music. Consequently, Sweden has nowadays an outstanding number, relative to its size, of music exports, groups like ABBA, Dancing Queen, and Money-Money and shows like *Mama-Mia*.

That leads to a shift of business style. These are the early signs of the experiential economy, which is sometimes also called the *dream society*. That is to some extent related to that very basic literacy training of notes that we have in music schools in Sweden. Nowadays, we have a tremendous inflow of artists coming to Sweden to record their new music albums. It is a new type of foreign trade.

The second one is the home accessibility of the Internet, which is related to political entrepreneurship in Sweden. Swedish tax laws have given tax relief for employers to offer employees a home computer. Therefore, there was a tremendous subsidy, from a tax viewpoint, for employees to get home computers. This means that we have the highest penetration of households in the world, next to Finland, of households with PCs. That shows how public policy can reshape the landscape. That has been done since the mid-1990s.

Most of all, we need to get a new mind compass for a better linkage of the IC logic to the organic perspectives and global human potential.

Overcoming Resistances

JC: *How can companies overcome the resistances of financial analysts to incorporate intellectual capital and intangibles in their valuations?*

LE: It is a kind of opportunity cost because if you do not reveal the drivers for your financial future, you are going to be punished by a higher interest rate or by not getting the financial credit. It is a kind of self-governing system. There have been some recommendations along these lines emerging out of the report *Unseen Wealth*.[3] The financial analysts today are working on what they have. But if the companies are offering more information and insights, they have to incorporate that. I was, in 1997, a cofounder of a special rating company for intellectual capital, and we have done more

---

[3] Margaret M. Blair and Steven M. H. Wallman, *Unseen Wealth: Report of the Brookings Task Force on Intangibles* (Washington, D.C.: Brookings Institution Press, 2001).

than 100 IC ratings so far. There is, according to recent basic research, a very strong correlation between the rating of intellectual capital and future earnings and market capitalization on the stock exchange.

JC: *Do you have a methodology to determine a valuation of intellectual capital?*
LE: We have a method to visualize that value. It is based on the IC value scheme I developed during my time at Skandia. We refined it together with the scheme that is the same as Standard and Poor's so that we could get a triple A for our intellectual capital, as well as a triple A for our financial capital.

JC: *Was there some objective criteria that you began to use for that?*
LE: Yes. It is based on a rather deep analysis like Standard and Poor's, but they are so focused on the financial dimensions that they miss the other ones.

Fundamentals versus Sentiments

JC: *How do you account for the shift in emphasis from context to process at American Skandia?*
LE: It is a kind of emerging blindness. When the company grows, its efficiency focus becomes mainly on the process dimension. Then you need the navigator, or the balance scorecard, to safeguard that you do not lose perspective on the other focus areas. These are about innovation, human capital, relationships and networks, context, and so on. Then you become blind! Because you focus on one or two areas instead of the whole thing. And the most challenging is the holistic perspective with focus both on the present and on the future.

JC: *Is that where you need an intervention to get yourself a broader view?*
LE: That is why we were so extremely focused on the innovation dimension and the quest for a more intelligent enterprise.

JC: *Why do so few financial analysts have an interest in the intellectual capital perspectives? How do you get them involved?*
LE: I think that is what the IC ratings are doing. The large investors are already looking into the IC indicators. They are starting to ask for this

deeper information. The financial analysts are seeing the increasing volatility of the stock exchange. The volatility is actually based on going from fundamentals to sentiments. If you do not have fundamentals about the various intangible components, the intellectual capital, the only thing you have is sentiment.

Therefore, it is quite natural that you are going to see these evolutions coming. It is, however, hard for a financial analyst to give up what she has as a professional tradition with inertia strongly based on the long-term use of an extremely simple model.

JC: *When organizations like Dow Chemical and Shell are developing their nonfinancial reports, is that contributing to a recognition by the analysts as well?*
LE: It is a step in the right direction. But you need to have more robust mathematical information. You need to see the numbers. You need to see consistency in that kind of reporting. It should be a part of what is called the management audit of companies, which is supposed to be, by law, a part of the annual report. But usually that is not treated in depth in the annual reports of companies.

Third-Generation Intellectual Capital Accounting

JC: *What is the third generation of intellectual capital accounting?*
LE: It is focused on the IC multiplier and the weather forecasting analogy.

The first generation was the navigator, or the balanced scorecard. The second generation was the IC rating and the IC index. The third generation is when you look at the landscape of the efficiency of the IC multiplier. The IC multiplier is human capital multiplied by structural capital (HC $\times$ SC), or structural capital divided by human capital (SC $\div$ HC).

It goes back to common sense. Whereas human capital can work from 8 to 10 hours a day, structural capital can work 24 hours a day on a global scale. Consequently, the growing of a firm is about this transformation from human capital to structural capital.

The basic transformation could be visualized as a digital landscape. If you look upon the Rocky Mountains, visualized on a screen, the landscape looks quite rocky. The peak in the Rocky Mountains is when you have reached a high yield of this ratio between structural capital divided by human capital. For example, you can multiply human capital five times with an organization's structural capital, then you have a very high yield. Sometimes you have a yield that is less than one, which is a deep valley in the Rocky Mountains. The distance to travel from the deep valley up to the peak is an investment journey.

If that investment journey could be visualized, the distance could be transformed into an investment decision. Therefore, you get the forecasting accounting system versus the old first and second generation, which were ex post. This is ex ante. The one is before and the other is after, which is like weather forecasting. This is an emerging, developmental IC-accounting model.

JC: *What is the difference between what you are calling third-generation intellectual capital accounting and the version that Göran Roos does?*

LE: I collaborated with Göran Roos, and back in 1997 he was invited to experiment with Skandia to develop the IC index. This IC index is the second generation, which is on the edge between the second and the third. It is still based on data from the past, but it is a good step from the first generation, which we developed some three years ago in Skandia. What we are doing now is looking into the drivers for accounting for the future, as well as visualizing the digital landscape. The reason is that you need a clarifying pedagogical dimension and show it like a digital landscape, so you can see the complex pattern of a company like a Shell or a Skandia, with many peaks and many valleys. Consequently, if you have a very high peak, how can you get a low performing unit to reach that peak? Is it worthwhile? Then you get into this forecasting accounting for the future dimension that will be about measuring the usage of the idle IC potential.

Digital Landscape

JC: *How are you beginning to use the digital landscape to assist in IC accounting? What are the benefits of using digital landscapes?*

LE: This goes back to one of the earlier insights, which is that you have to visualize the hidden and intangible values in numbers and charts. The IC index was number-based as was the IC rating. It was charts. The navigator was a graphical landscape, but one-dimensional. The third dimension is the digital landscape, with topography flows and transformations, which we started to develop around 1999. It is very similar to the evolution of weather forecasting, which is today based on very, very complex data analysis, on a global scale, then, presented in a clarified, very simple format on CNN or whatever. Even an average person can understand whether there is going to be snow or sunshine tomorrow. The third generation of IC accounting is about complex data presented in a clarifying forecasting model, as an IC gyro or 3D approach to capture the momentum of IC.

The financial analysts are like the old bellboys, standing on the hill using the bell to say, now is a good time, now is a bad time, now it is time to invest, now it is time to sell. But the traditional analysis is not more than seeing dark clouds coming or not coming.

JC: *Does this begin to tell you what the critical points are for investments?*

LE: You can start to see the drivers and enablers for the peaks and the valleys, which makes it more possible for the leadership to focus on them. There are connections that are authentic connections.

JC: *How has your approach to measurement evolved since you first developed it at Skandia? How is it being used and with what effect?*

LE: Basically, the IC logic is the same for all types of organizations. What is interesting is that what seems to be a tremendous trigger is when you go from the measurement of the organization to the measurement of the individual. Having a personal navigator is a tremendous driver for people to see the evolution of themselves regarding networks, competencies, processes, and innovations. It seems to be a map for their personal potential as well as a strategic growth map.

This is used in Skandia. Skandia has developed a whole software system, together with Oracle, on the navigator called Dolphin, which is used by most employees in Skandia today. This could be used also in nonprofit and governmental organizations. The earlier mentioned IC rating has also been applied to schools and hospitals.

JC: *What does someone's personal profile look like?*

LE: It is the same shape as the IC navigator but applied to yourself. You have indicators for the various areas of the navigator. It is all computerized on a screen, with various starting dates, target dates, and things like that. You follow it up with an assessment.

JC: *What would be indicators for someone to know that she is doing better or not better? What is it measuring?*

LE: It could be the number of new customers visited, or number of phone calls per hour, number of emails per week, time spent on innovation, time spent on language upgrading, or time spent helping colleagues. There are a number of indicators. The whole pattern for it is the navigator, or the balance scorecard, which is profiled. The point is that you do it on an individual basis, then consolidate it on a group level, and then on up to the corporate level, thereby combining individual growth with corporate growth.

JC: *Would the individual enter the data on a regular basis so that she is responsible for her own profile?*
LE: Yes. You see the same similarity with weather forecasting, which is based on very simple observations around the world, which are aggregated, and then we see the global weather forecast. To have good relationships among all of the data, we need mapping systems. The whole globe is actually divided up into units of ten kilometers, multiplied by ten kilometers square. For each such ten-kilometer area, you get the data. You can see such an area as one, singular individual in the Skandia system among thousands of colleagues.

UNIC

JC: *What is the work of Universal Networking Intellectual Capital (UNIC)? What are its goals, and who would be involved with it?*
LE: If you spell it out by the letters, U-N-I-C (you and I see), this is the context of universal networking. The second dimension is prototyping a challenge of the common tradition that says that an organization is its people. What will happen if you take away all of the people? What is left? That is what UNIC is about. It is a prototype of a company with zero employees. So, it is a prototype like Skandia Future Center was a prototype and the accounting system was a prototype. The focus is: How do you develop an organizational structure network without employees? It is all focused on intellectual capital recipes and intellectual property. Another way to say it is that it is a very virtual corporation. An alternative way to say it is that it is a holding company for intellectual property, or intellectual capital recipes. A fourth way to say it is that UNIC is a development company for knowledge recipes of intellectual capital, which is profitizing its own existence.

JC: *How does it work with no employees?*
LE: It works very well. You get rid of a lot of the bad traditional administration. The core focus becomes the development, the knowledge recipes, and the continued innovation. It becomes the structural capital around which talents are gathering, a sort of nexus.

JC: *How does it derive its strategic orientation, And how is it maintained? Or is it just a self-organizing body on a continuous basis, a sort of complex, adaptive system?*

LE: Probably. I do not know yet. We will see. It is like these complex adaptive systems that you referred to. The point here is to experiment with its strategic focus on recipes for intellectual capital, and surrounding UNIC are a number of IC specialists in cooperation as satellites and application companies, like Future Centers International (FCI). FCI is a company focused on developing a chain of Future Centers. Another company surrounding UNIC is a company called NICE, which stands for Newly Intellectualized Capital and E-Solutions. It is a broker company for knowledge automation supplies. Surrounding UNIC are also satellite specialist companies, but it has its roots in Skandia where we developed this idea of specialists in cooperation. The Skandia model has 3% of the staff, and 97% percent is in the network. What we are doing in UNIC is saying, "Let us keep it zero, and see what is happening." So far, it has been in existence more than a year now, and it works.

JC: *How do people become members of the network?*

LE: People can be partners, associates, or members. Part of the challenge is how you develop a language or taxonomy for this new type of knowledge association. It is probably more "citizenship" than subscription. It is more of a community than a corporation. But there are a lot of interesting observations you start to do when you work on this question about subscription versus membership, or citizenship, and community versus corporation. What kind of balance sheet do you have for a community? Is it the same as the old balance sheet, or is it another one?

Participants at this point are specialists in various dimensions of intellectual capital, persons with an interest in collaborating, who are adding probably more than they are getting for the moment. The profit-and-loss statement is with the individual citizen, not with the consolidated network, that is, a kind of lateral value accounting.

The Future Is Our Home

JC: *You say that the future is our home. What are Future Centers, and what do they allow organizations and nations to do? How are both companies and countries using them?*

LE: The notion that the future is our home goes back to the understanding that it is a motion forward, from imperfect to future. And the Future

Center is an arena that allows organizations and nations to experiment with not products but organizational capital. The multiplier between human capital and structural capital is actually the organizational capital. So, how do you run rapid, small, prototype experiments on organizational capital? Most organizations do it full scale, in real time, which means that they have to prepare tremendously. They have union negotiations and so on to allow them to make the organizational changes. The Future Center is an off-site lab for future organizational capital where you can run experiments on the complex intangible and tacit dimensions of the organizational capital.

That is what we started to do at Skandia. It is an arena where you are inviting the business context. If you think about how most firms today are organized, they are like fortresses. You go in, you have security checks, and so on. How do you think that the future enters into those organizations? In slow motion. The security system is blocking out the future. But you do not open up the organization because you have so much confidentiality. You need a separate arena, as a space for experiments, and that is what the Future Center is about. It is a small-scale outside arena for testing new approaches.

JC: *Who comes up with the approaches that will be tested?*
LE: The people who go there. It could be future teams, discovery teams, revolutionary teams, or combined teams from internal and external sources. It could be, as we developed at Skandia, teams from different generations and different cultures. It is across-the-border collaboration. It is a transparency across the organizational fences, across generations, across cultures, and across jurisdictions. It is also a search for the new association recipes of organizational capital.

For the moment, we are experimenting with a Future Center startup in Norway, one in Denmark, and one in Israel. We are also starting to focus on special niches, like a Future Center for health. These communities are electronic as well as physical. The Danish one is sketched as a boat, a mobile organizational hub, a combination of a boat and a tent. The Norwegian one is located in the neighborhood of a cathedral. The Israeli one, I do not know quite yet what it is going to be.

The founders shape these, together with the architect. In Israel, they said that it should be the artist of the Guggenheim Museum in Bilbao. What you will start to see is that the Future Center becomes an icon for another message. If you go back, looking at paintings of 200 years ago, it used to be that you had factories as the icons of wealth. Recently, we have had the corporate architecture of large glass buildings. The Future Center

is also a part of this evolution of another corporate architec?
edge community architecture, like the Guggenheim Mus?

Momentum

JC: *Can you discuss the concept of momentum and why it is significant?*

LE: It is around this little edge, like the California phrase: "If you are not on your edge, you take up too much space." This is the momentum. You cannot balance on the edge. If you stop, you usually fall off. You have to move a little bit. It is a gyro exercise where you are balancing in a lot of dimensions.

Most organizations are firms. *Firm* comes from Italian and grew up at the same time as the accounting system. It is *firmamente*. The theory of the firm is *firmamente*, which means that you freeze it. You capture the moment, but you do not capture the momentum. It should be the opposite of capture the moment, seize the day. Instead, it needs to become "seize the future."

The momentum is the movement, the motion. That is why the accounting system should show the navigation as an IC gyro. That is why the individual navigator shows whether you are growing or not. That is why the traditional headquarters is a fortress instead of a springboard. The organizational capital should be a springboard for human ingenuity and talents; it should not be a *firmamente*.

Key Learning Points

- In the IC growth model, the focus is on the enablers and drivers for future earnings potential, whether they are networks, knowledge, processes, or innovations.
- It is more or less the same economy, but the economics has changed. In the old economy, the economics was based more on having the product as the revenue carrier. In the new economy, the intangibles or the knowledgeable person are very much the value carrier.
- In traditional leadership, we focus on human capital. In IC leadership, we focus on the structural capital as a springboard for human capital, as a lever for giving a turbocharge to the human capital.

- The organization is its structural capital, its networks, databases, patents, trademarks, and so on, intellectual properties. They are all vehicles of the organization.
- Most organizations are dumb. Intelligent organizations are about global intelligence, the courage to move to the second curve, accounting for intangibles, leveraging knowledge recipes, and making meaning.
- Intellectual capital is the multiplier function between human capital and structural capital; it is the flow, or the motion.
- The growing of the firm is about the transformation from human capital to structural capital. Look at your organization as if it were a digital landscape topographical map to see where you have a high-yield or can improve a low-yield IC utilization.

VINCE BARABBA:

Understanding the Enterprise as a System

7

Vince Barabba is the general manager of General Motors's corporate strategy and knowledge development and is also responsible for overseeing GM's new business development network.

Barabba has been a part of an extensive, long-term effort to infuse a systems thinking approach into how problems are perceived and dealt with at General Motors. He sees that not embracing this approach has been the cause of endemic problems in organizations and that recognizing the systems phenomenon permits us to reconceptualize the complex, significant, and unprecedented issues we face. Barabba draws upon the work of Peter Drucker, Russell Ackoff, C. West Churchman, and W. Edwards Deming to frame his systems view.

The contribution that Barabba makes is that he has come to understand the role of knowledge in an organization from that system's perspective. Knowledge of the system and how it operates is even more critical than knowledge of the particular parts of the system. In developing this view, Barabba offers a balance between the whole and its parts that is still nascent in knowledge management and intellectual capital thus far. In a related way, Barabba sees the value of knowledge in its use rather than valuing the collection of knowledge per se.

Prior to coming to GM, he held positions at Eastman Kodak and Xerox and twice served as director of the U.S. Bureau of the Census, the only person to be appointed to that position by presidents from different political parties. He served as president of the American Statistical Association, U.S. representative to the Population Commission of the United Nations, and chair of the National Research Council panel that reviewed the statistical program of the National Center for Education Statistics. He has served on the board of trustees for the American Institutes for Research and the National Opinion Research Center. He is the author of *Meeting of the Minds* (1995) and co-author of *Hearing the Voice of the Market* (1991) and *The 1980 Census: Policy Making amid Turbulence* (1983).[1]

The Conversation

Market-Based Adaptive Enterprise

JC: *What are the characteristics of a market-based adaptive enterprise, and how is General Motors moving to achieve the vision of such an enterprise?*

VB: A *market-based adaptive enterprise* is an organization that understands its purpose in the broader system within which it functions. It continually challenges the assumptions that underlie that role and adapts or changes that role, as conditions in the environment require.

This approach requires the intensive internal education of the members of our workforce—helping them see more clearly the overall role GM plays in the marketplace and in society. During our recent Global Leadership Conference, our CEO, Rick Wagoner, led a dialogue with more than 3,500 executives based on the Root Learning Maps process. This process involves developing a visual representation of (1) the environment in which we are working, and (2) how our developing strategy positions us to be a leader.

A market-based adaptive enterprise must also effectively use technical, business, and market intelligence. This is accomplished by designing intelligence systems based on what we need to know in our decision-making processes.

The use of market or customer intelligence has been at the heart of significant discussions at General Motors going back to the early 1930s.

[1] Vincent. P. Barabba, *Meeting of the Minds: Creating the Market-Based Enterprise* (Boston: Harvard Business School Press, 1995); Vincent P. Barabba et al., *Hearing the Voice of the Market: Competitive Advantage through Creative Use of Market Information* (Boston: Harvard Business School Press, 1991); Ian I. Mitroff, Richard O. Mason, and Vincent P. Barabba, *The 1980 Census, Policymaking amid Turbulence* (Lexington, Mass.: Lexington Books, 1983).

The basic question hasn't changed: "Is the market capable of articulating what it really wants, or must the enterprise bring forward things that it knows it can do that the market is not capable of articulating?" The problem has been, both in the past and to some degree today, that people address the issue as if the answer must go one way or the other. We call this the "tyranny of or." The question is framed in such a way as to suggest that you must either rely on consumer input *or* move forward with company-initiated innovation. In truth, it is possible to effectively do one *and* the other. Conducted properly, the opportunity provided by the "and" approach has resulted in greater benefits for GM and its customers.

The perspective that says customers cannot tell us what to do has, at times, led us to believe that we must get ahead of customer preferences and then convince them that we know what they really want. There is, as some might expect, evidence that supports that perspective. There is, however, also evidence that demonstrates that customers are more than capable of telling us what they want.

In fact, as early as the 1930s, Buck Weaver, GM's first director of consumer research, set about finding out what customers really wanted. I have a chart in my office that shows all of the features GM added to vehicles, as well as things that were changed or improved, based on customer feedback. These were features like air conditioning, automatic transmissions, longer bumpers, rubber pads on pedals, and a greater emphasis on safety. In the years from 1932 to 1937, Weaver identified 170 such improvements, all in the name of serving the customer in ways in which the customer wanted to be served.

In my book *Meeting of the Minds*, I describe some of this research from the 1930s, in which customers fairly well articulated the needs for a minivan and had ideas for things such as sunroofs and pneumatic bumpers. These were all things that were not on the market until many years later.

For possibly the first time in automotive history, Weaver recognized the importance of looking beyond what the company's engineers were already working on. Rather than simply relying on existing market conditions, he used market research to gain insight into what might occur. In this way, GM's engineers could be better prepared to respond, if and when the possible changes came to be.

One of Weaver's techniques for helping people imagine future vehicles is particularly interesting. He would provide a simple worksheet and ask individuals to sketch suggestions for design changes. He was generally looking for ideas to enhance or change current designs, but what he got often went far beyond that.

My favorite is the first drawing we've found of the concept of the minivan, from back in 1932. There's no reason to believe that the person

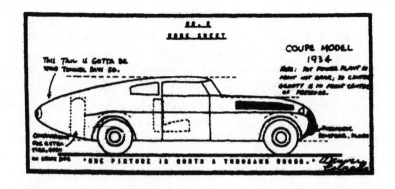

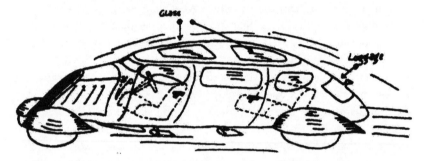

Source: General Motors Corp., "Streamlining from the Customer Viewpoint," *The Proving Ground of Public Opinion*, December 1, 1932. Reprinted by permission.

FIGURE 7.1 Customer Ideas for Car Features, 1930s

who drew this was telling us: "Design this car." More likely, he was describing needs. First, better vision. (See how the driver's position is far forward?) Second, a rear engine, because in those days, the engine produced a great deal of heat and odor. And finally, "French doors," which would improve entry and access.

So this is one approach—asking customers what they want. It is equally important to remember that many available concepts and technologies are not easy to understand. Technology is moving at such a rate that we must take some risk and ask: "What is the underlying need out there? Can we offer solutions to problems that are not yet clear in the customer's mind? Solutions that—if customers were aware of them—would allow us to provide better products and services?" For example, we know that customers care about privacy, individual choice, and saving time and energy. If you ask them how well these needs are being addressed, they would say, "Not very." These customers are not directly asking for mobile commu-

Source: General Motors Corp., "Streamlining from the Customer Viewpoint," *The Proving Ground of Public Opinion*, December 1, 1932. Reprinted by permission.

FIGURE 7.2 Customer Ideas for Minivans, 1930s

nications, but mobile communications, when properly administered, could address those needs for privacy, individual choice, and saving time and money—needs that are not easily articulated by customers.

This balance between customer requests and company offerings is why we call this the market-*based* adaptive enterprise. We use the term *based*, rather than *driven* or *focused*, because it is not one or the other. Rather, we are interested in a combination of what the market asks for directly and what we are capable of delivering.

We are seeking decisions *based* on what the market is talking about. We could, for example, have a situation where there is something the market wants, but we are not capable of delivering it. It is also possible that we have a better solution in mind, and therefore we are going to take the risk that our solution, even though it may meet with some resistance, will eventually win out over more easily accepted ideas.

The term *adaptive* is equally important. It reflects the realization that things are moving so fast today that we can no longer operate as we did in the old days, when we said, "Let's go find out what the market wants.

Let's look at that closely. Let's find out what we can deliver, and then deliver it. And then, customers will come." By the time you have gone through that process, something else has happened.

Instead, you need product development processes that can respond quickly to changing conditions. We must learn how to adapt to change a lot faster than we have in the past.

Moving from Control to Access

JC: *How are you moving at General Motors to achieve that vision? Do you need to define* enterprise *as well to understand that?*

VB: That is the other part of this dilemma. We recently joined, as a founding member, the Internet Home Alliance. You might say, "What is GM doing in an Internet Home Alliance?" And, we could respond with: "There's a garage in most homes, isn't there?" But that is not the reason. Think about customer needs, such as time and energy, and then say to yourself, "When I'm in my vehicle, wouldn't I like to know what's going on in my home?" If the alarm goes off in my home, then I want to know about it just as soon as my neighbors do, no matter where I am. When I hit the remote garage door opener to get into my garage, I should also be able to disengage my alarm system, turn on the lights, and perhaps even adjust the heating or cooling system in my home.

From a safety and security point of view, the protocols and the capability of our mobile communications services are truly outstanding. But we also must address the question of why the customer has two security systems: one works on the house and the other works on the car. A customer would say, "I want one, if possible, and if the one you provide is better than the combination of the two, that tells me that you really are listening to me and providing products and services that are in my best interest."

From that perspective, our management has had to rethink the boundaries of the General Motors enterprise. We now know that, as an enterprise, we are going to find ourselves in alliance with companies that (1) we never would have thought we would be in alliance with, and (2) we might have competed with. If we can get the companies in related industries to agree on standards and protocols, the industry itself gets bigger and—although we might not increase our share—we open ourselves to new products and services that allow us to better serve the customer overall.

In many cases, we find it easier to create alliances with companies than to buy them. For example, we have excellent alliances with Suzuki, Isuzu, Fiat, and Fuji Heavy Industries (fundamentally, the Subaru brand). We have observed that when others attempt to buy vehicle companies, it sometimes creates far more turmoil and conflict than if alliances were developed instead. Our goal is to gain access to and share the creative talent of these companies. Do we need to own them to do that? Not necessarily. Most of the people involved in those organizations feel strongly about the companies that they helped create. Our position has been: "You don't have to sell us the entire firm, but we'd like to create an alliance with you. We think that what we bring and what you bring creates something more than the sum of our two parts." When we do that, we find ourselves extending our capabilities.

JC: *Do you mean that you are moving from control to access?*
VB: The word *control* is a troublesome term in the world of systems thinking. In reality, in today's fast-paced world, the best you can hope for is the opportunity to influence others—primarily through leadership.

We have learned to be a lot more flexible and adaptive in our willingness to do business with potential partners and alliances. We make sure that we understand both what we want to do and what the market has been able to articulate that it wants. Sometimes this leads us to uncover an unarticulated need which, when fulfilled, will provide significant competitive advantage. We need to continually remind ourselves that we are dealing with a moving target. Anybody who says they have precisely defined future customer requirements is either in a very simple business or is about to be out of that business.

JC: *How does the market-based adaptive system put knowledge to work in an organization, and what is the role of GM's leadership in this?*
VB: In this model, the role of GM leadership is everything. For a knowledge system to work effectively, we need to ensure that GM employees have access to what GM knows and how to get access to what GM doesn't know to allow them to do their jobs more efficiently and effectively.

GM leadership must create an environment where people share what they know and what they have learned with others. At the same time, people are continually (and actively) seeking that knowledge which they need to help them do their work more effectively. For this to happen, leaders must promote the right sort of environment by asking: "What did you learn from others before starting this project?" and "How has what you have learned impacted others in the company?"

One of the difficulties I have with some of the practitioners in the knowledge management consulting practice is their belief that we need to lock in on a set of specifications regarding what we need to know. My experience has been that locking in on specifications is a major limiting factor. At GM, we tend to find that the ideas we started out with are improved dramatically the closer we get to implementing them. Although the principles underlying our strategy have held from when we started out in 1991, we are doing things quite differently in 2001. The more we try to set specifications and then hard-wire systems around what we specify, the less capable we are going to be to adapt to changing conditions.

Leadership's role, in my mind, is to understand the principles of systemic thinking. That means constantly looking at the system in which somebody's specific decisions operate and continually asking the question: "Am I asking people to be more efficient in what they are doing and, perhaps, optimizing at their unit level at the expense of improving the effectiveness of the total system?" Our management is really coming to grips with that, but it is hard work. We are such a large enterprise, and our footprint is not only very global, but it also reaches quite extensively into people's everyday lives. Although we are best known for the vehicles we make, we are also a very large financial institution. We place mortgages and insurance, buy and sell houses, and are one of the largest commercial lenders around. Because of that pervasive contact with different markets and different kinds of customers, we need to understand how the parts of our enterprise interact and how to use that interaction to provide the greatest value to our customers.

I would say that the kind of emerging knowledge that is becoming most valuable to the enterprise is learning to understand GM as a system, more so than any specific piece of knowledge about any one of our activities. That does not mean that the latter is unimportant. While it is absolutely necessary, specific knowledge is insufficient on its own.

JC: *How do you diffuse that knowledge across the organization?*

VB: We fundamentally attempt to describe the enterprise from the customer and societal perspectives. We have to look at how people spend their time and how they allocate resources in their daily lives. Then we say to ourselves: "Where does the GM enterprise interact with those consumer activities?" In developing that understanding, we came to realize that we are capable of affecting approximately 20–40% of some customers' disposable income. We deal with people's mortgages and the value of their homes. We also deal with their vehicles and transportation costs, and now we are starting to affect a good deal of people's communications costs related to information and entertainment. When we step back to look at all of that, we find ourselves saying: "That's quite a bit different than I expected."

How do all of these parts interact? Looking at the specific parts, we could have said: "We're going to optimize the car-making business. We're going to make sure that we get as much profit out of that as we can." But, as we came to understand the customer's deeper requirements and needs, we realized that our greatest asset is the number of customers we have. We saw that if we increased our services to each customer in these other areas, first, that would be more beneficial to the customers, and second, we could grow our business more. We have started to understand that we should figure out not only how to get more people in our vehicles, but how to generate more revenue per customer as subscribers to our services.

A Systemic Approach

JC: *This sounds like you've greatly expanded your definition of the enterprise. But if it has no real boundaries, what constitutes the enterprise, and what is beyond it?*

VB: To address that issue, we need a deeper understanding of systemic thinking—an approach that takes more of its cues from the realm of synthesis and systems thinking and is not limited to the realm of analysis and management. As Russ Ackoff explains it:

- A system is any entity, conceptual or physical, that consists of interdependent parts.
- A system is a whole that cannot be divided into independent parts.
- The performance of the whole cannot be taken to be the sum of the performances of its parts.
- Success is the product of the interactions of the parts.

To be successful in today's world, you need to know a lot more than just what your customers express in terms of their articulated needs. You also need to understand their unarticulated needs and ensure that your employees—or members of any organization—have access to what the organization knows that will allow them to do their job in meeting these articulated and unarticulated needs more effectively. In addition, the communities around us have to know enough about our goals and practices to consider us an enterprise worth supporting.

Any enterprise is a system first and foremost. Optimizing at the wrong level can sometimes hinder the effectiveness of the overall system. Various independent parts of the organization, which often operate as silos, must communicate with one another for the enterprise to thrive. In this context, it becomes clear that the role of the manager of the system is to manage the interactions of the parts and not to manage the parts taken separately—in other words, to consider the *extended* enterprise.

As we become more systemic in our thinking, we must consider the larger system beyond the enterprise itself, where the stakeholders of the enterprise are all of those individuals or entities that can affect or be affected by the decisions of the enterprise. This includes:

- The customer, which includes both consumers and individuals in the distribution system who accept products from the enterprise.
- The community, which is made up of consumers in a societal context, the government interests that attempt to represent them, the special interest groups that carry strong views on specific issues, and the competition for customer and community attention and resources.
- The enterprise, which (in addition to itself) includes everything that delivers the products and services to the customer and community: employees, suppliers, investors, and so forth.

As this is a system of interacting parts, the stakeholders in the extended enterprise must deal simultaneously with each other's interests, seeking synergy from their relationships. If the total value of that relationship is greater than the sum of stakeholders' individual contributions, the relationship will flourish. If its value is equal to or less than the sum of the individual contributions, the relationship will and should fail.

Of course, among the three groups, some dissonance is to be expected. Customers, the community, and the enterprise itself have different voices,

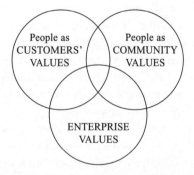

FIGURE 7.3 The Extended Enterprise as a System

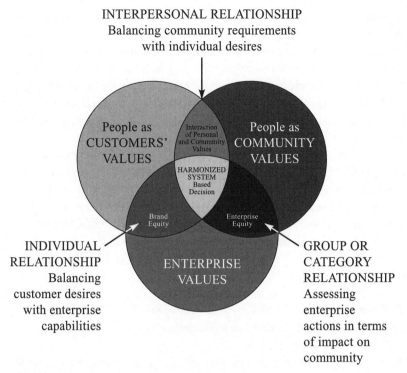

INTERPERSONAL RELATIONSHIP
Balancing community requirements
with individual desires

People as
CUSTOMERS'
VALUES

Interaction
of Personal
and Community
Values

People as
COMMUNITY
VALUES

HARMONIZED
SYSTEM
Based
Decision

Brand
Equity

Enterprise
Equity

INDIVIDUAL
RELATIONSHIP
Balancing
customer desires
with enterprise
capabilities

ENTERPRISE
VALUES

GROUP OR
CATEGORY
RELATIONSHIP
Assessing
enterprise
actions in terms
of impact on
community

FIGURE 7.4 A System of Interacting Interests

and they often conflict. But in their interaction is where we find the greatest opportunity. In figure 7.4, if customers are seen as one circle and the enterprise is another circle, it is in the overlap area—the interaction zone—where we build brand equity.

An enterprise making laundry detergent, for example, might find that customers want a "whiter than white" wash, which the enterprise knows it can provide by using phosphate-based detergents, while the community—which includes customers, government regulators, and interested organizations—wants "cleaner than clean" public waters, which are compromised by the introduction of phosphates. Meanwhile, the enterprise—the shareholders and the employees—wants to produce a customer-satisfying and profitable product that is compatible with its sense of environmental responsibility. Needless to say, there are plenty of opportunities for agreement and conflict among these different groups.

JC: *Is that the kind of conversation that is taking place at the headquarters level, at the business unit level, and down throughout the field?*

VB: This is what leadership is all about. I mentioned earlier that we held a management conference last year for 3,500 executives. This conference was attended by the people who are responsible for not only managing but leading the enterprise. We spent the first part of the conference discussing how the market in which we operate is changing. We also addressed who the players are who can either be affected by us or can affect us. And we talked about what we can bring to this complex environment, as well as our opportunities for growth.

A systemic understanding of the whole issue surfaced in that discussion. Our CEO then outlined the business plan, explaining that we have to extend our relationship with each of our customers. That is how we are going to grow the enterprise. We then asked the executives at each of the 350 tables to discuss how they could implement this concept within their units.

The issue here is finding ways to manage each of the parts so they interact with each other to create an outcome that is greater than the sum of the parts.

JC: *What is the difference between a systemic approach to learning and adaptation and the conventional approach to managing the use of knowledge?*

VB: A systemic approach requires that you first understand the nature of the whole enterprise—its purpose, its character, and its interactions within the larger environment, including the marketplace and society.

By first understanding GM's purpose in this larger context, we set the frame for thinking about the major work processes that can help accomplish that purpose. The purpose and processes then provide the framework for thinking about how to organize what we know in a taxonomy that reinforces our understanding of the whole. We have all been trained to break a problem into its most essential parts. We try to understand each of the parts because we think that will make it easier to understand the larger problem.

In the industrial age, where the simple machine metaphor dominated, that was a good model for learning how to fix things. But that model is not adequate for today's problems. The world in which we operate is better characterized as more of a molecular structure, where everything interacts and changes based on the environment in which it is framed. In this view, as soon as we break something apart, we lose some of the value. Instead, we need to emphasize the interaction of the parts. Admittedly, that is a heck of a lot easier to say than it is to do.

The systemic approach requires that we learn how to do things that will still employ an analytic approach, but understand the analytic approach in the context of synthesis—of bringing things together and observing how we can get more out of their interaction than just through understanding the parts by themselves. Given that most of us have been trained, and rewarded, to focus on the analysis of the parts, this is very hard stuff to learn. It takes a strong commitment on the part of management to communicate the importance of doing both analysis and synthesis, rather than one at the expense of the other.

JC: *How is GM leadership indicating that they are grasping this?*

VB: We saw it in the interactive exercise at the Global Executive Conference I described. We laid out, in almost a game format, some 350 tables of 10 executives each, with a senior executive trained in this discussion process, and had them think through how all of these things interacted. We said, "Here is one way in which you could look at GM as a system of interacting parts," and then had everyone work through what that meant. Our CEO then said, "I wanted you to see what the executive team has been going through in thinking about this strategy. Let me now outline the business case for you." He then went up to a whiteboard with a big camera on it and sketched out a business design that showed the interaction of the main elements of GM. That has an incredible impact on an enterprise that is used to having parts not only stand alone, but sometimes even compete with each other.

We built in enough time in the design of this exercise to pilot the use of these drawings in different parts of the world before the meeting. In that way, we found what it would take to make sure they would be interpreted globally as they were intended, rather than missing some nuance from a cultural, language, or metaphorical perspective. The feedback during these dry runs enriched the actual outcome greatly.

JC: *How are you challenging the "success-breeds-failure" syndrome of General Motors, a company that has been the standard setter in its field?*

VB: This issue is at the core of Peter Drucker's great dictum that the greatest problem you can give to your enemy is 40 years of success. But we have not had 40 years of success. In fact, as we go back and look at what we thought was success, back in the 1950s and 1960s, it really was the beginning of the decline of this enterprise, which had been perceived as the hallmark of corporate activity. There are very few people in our enterprise today who would say we have been successful. I think we recognize that we have done things that were not in the best interest of the institution as an enterprise and that we are in the process of recovering from that.

Your question is important, and it should also be addressed to companies like Cisco and Amazon.com, which are, at least until recently, being seen as successful enterprises.

Acting as One Company

JC: *You think then that GM has unlearned a lot of the premises that it was operating on and is ready to learn freshly?*

VB: In the old days, people in the Chevrolet division were rewarded by how many transactions the division completed. Even if those transactions resulted in a sale taken from Pontiac, they were treated the same way as if they were taken from the sale of a Ford. We have had to undo all that, to undo a reward system that did not consider contributions to the interaction of the parts of the enterprise.

One of the four prime cultural initiatives that our CEO established is that we will Act as One Company. That is a big change from the past. Since he has been driving this message home, we see far less of the internal warfare that we had in the past.

JC: *What role have you played in that?*

VB: GM made a decision a while back that those who will implement the strategy will also develop it. That means my job, as the general manager of corporate strategy, is to create a process that assists the management of the enterprise in creating the strategy that they will implement. Our group surfaces new ideas, speculates how they interact with the enterprise, and creates dialogues with our management around new ways of thinking about them. In addition to that, we have a group whose job it is—when ideas are developed and need to be implemented—to provide the decision and analytic tool sets and resources to help those ideas get started. The group is made up of bright, young people who aspire to be consultants but do not necessarily like the working environment and lifestyle of consulting. In our setting, they finish the projects they start and do not travel extensively.

Listening, Learning, and Leading

JC: *You talk about listening, learning, and leading as operating principles. What do you mean by that?*

VB: This relates back to being market-based. Some people say, "You have to listen before you start." Other people support the "ready-fire-aim" approach, or "fire-ready-aim," which means: put a shot out there, see if you are close to the mark, then adjust. Others take the position that you have to learn before you make any decision.

We have found that all three elements are important, but it does not matter where you start. What is important is to do all three things. If you ignore any of them, you do so at your own risk.

JC: *Whom do you involve in the listen, learn, lead process, and how do you see them working to become one with that?*
VB: We try to involve everyone. One thing that is very good about the new technology is that it makes it a lot easier to engage people. We used to rely on product clinics, but we always had the problem of having to bring product concepts out to customers to gauge their reactions. Engineers and designers did not necessarily have time to go on these trips, but they were the ones who most needed the information provided in the clinics. When they stayed back, they were limited by the market research community's ability to translate what customers said into terms that were meaningful to the engineers and designers. Now when we run a product clinic, we feed the video right back to the technical center in real time. Engineers and designers observe the clinic while it is going on without having to make the trip and can ask questions based on what they see and hear directly.

This makes it easier for people to be engaged in the listening part, which is where they actually get to sense how customers are reacting to some of their ideas. The learn part says that after you listen, if you decide to implement a new idea, you should write down the decision, clearly stating that this is the decision that was made and why. This statement should include a description of the particular things you expect to occur by a specific date. Our learning and adaptation process (adapted from Russell Ackoff's learning and adaptation model) requires that, at that certain date, you go back and compare the actual results to the expected results.

In the past, people did that, but with the intention of determining whether somebody was a good performer or not. They were not necessarily interested in learning from the decision. That report card approach is less prevalent today. Not that delivering on a promise is not important. What is more important is that we learn from the decision. So, we do not simply ask what was the decision you made; we ask why you made it. We do not ask whether you missed; we ask why the plan missed.

In reflecting on that "why," we may find out that this really was a good decision, but that something unexpected occurred, or the person who made the decision and those who were supposed to implement it did not share the same expectations. We then go back and try to understand why things either happened or did not happen, and build what we find into a knowledge base of learning.

The introduction of the Chevrolet Camaro offers an excellent example. We designed the product launch, in part, around the movie *Days of Thunder* with Tom Cruise, where he was driving in a NASCAR vehicle, a Chevy Camaro. We set up a massive promotional campaign tied to the movie's opening date, which was when we expected the vehicle to debut. Because of production problems, the vehicle came out after the movie opened and after all the promotional money had been spent. We had great expectations and generated great anticipation among the people for whom this vehicle was developed. Everything was there except the product. If we just went back and looked at the results, we could have said, "That promotion did not work very well." As it turns out, it had nothing to do with the promotion. It was the fact that the product did not show up on time. That is the learn part.

The lead was the decision to say: "I'm going to tie the promotion of this vehicle to something that we think will be attractive to the market for which the vehicle was developed."

Listen, learn, lead are not necessarily sequential. It is just that all three have to be there, interacting with one another.

Idealized Design

JC: *How do you use thinking in terms of idealized design and looking at strategic issues backward to help create a knowledge-based organization?*

VB: Idealized design and strategy are ways to formulate what we want or need to be. This is part of the imperative, from a systems perspective, to understand our role in the larger system. That then provides an organizing framework for what we currently know and where we need to learn and adapt.

Russ Ackoff has had great influence on us in this area. We draw extensively on his ideas in our work. Ackoff takes the position that the question is not: "What do you think you could do?" but rather "If you could do anything you wanted, what would you do today?" Once you have articulated that, then you find that most of the barriers that you thought would prohibit you from doing that are more easily overcome. This relates to creating a knowledge-based organization in that you are not going to start with just the base of knowledge that you currently have. The idealized design approach drives you to find out what it is you need to know to move beyond your current point of view.

It is not: "Let's get all the facts together and then analyze the facts and then decide what we can do." Rather, start with: "This what I want to do. If I could do whatever I wanted to, this is what I would do." Instead of asking, "Now, why can't I?" We have learned to ask, "What is the closest approximation that we can have now?" This kind of question focuses on possibilities rather than obstacles.

Although this is not how things are thought about universally at GM, it is the process that we are infusing into the organization. We saw it in action when we were trying to figure out how to install the OnStar mobile communication system in new vehicles. If you know anything about the automotive vehicle development process, even when you are the best in the world at it, it still takes a long time. One of the things that drives this is an intensive validation process we go through to ensure the safety of our vehicles and to meet regulatory requirements. Since that was the case, we first said we would install OnStar at the dealership as an after-sale item. We knew that this would, unfortunately, drive the price up dramatically, but we didn't see any other option. And the higher the price, the less likely the demand, so therefore the less likely this new product was going to be sold in large volumes. As a result, we kept asking: "Why not install it at the factory and drive the price down?"

The counterargument was: "Not everybody will want it. Why install OnStar in cars where it won't be used?"

But then we asked, "What are we trying to accomplish?" Our answer was that we were trying to get each of our customers to *have* this capability. We could then get a revenue stream from the vehicle for as long as it is on the road, not just at the time of transaction. In discussing the issue with the engineers who believed, based on past practices, they could not do this, we positioned the argument as: "If we can't do this, we are never going to get that revenue stream, and therefore we're going to be locked into the margins that we get at the time of transaction forever." Nobody liked that.

We then asked them, "If we could do whatever you wanted today, how would we install this on the vehicle?" They said, "You do this, this, and this." And, we said, "Well, why can't we do that?" And they responded, "Because you'd have to skip over some steps." When we asked, "What steps would be skipped?" we discovered that they were applying the rules of hardware development to the application of software development. Since the changes needed to factory install OnStar primarily centered around software development and application, the engineers were able to develop a faster validation process, as long as we did not mess with the airbag, the brakes, and the emission system, which have rigorous safety and emission requirements.

Over time, they sat down and realized that the amount and type of revenue that would be generated by making OnStar a factory-installed product was worth the extra effort and was best for the enterprise overall.

The message was that everyone involved benefits if the enterprise benefits. As a result, the reward structure has been redesigned to reflect this larger institutional reality. If we are going to act as one company, then *we* have to figure out a way to do this. And, they figured out a way of doing it without compromising any safety or emission regulations.

We install OnStar at the factory in a large proportion of our cars. While everybody else is scrambling and trying to figure out a strategy for mobile communications, we have signed up more than 2 million subscribers and have become the standard bearer for this type of service.

Part of this involved changing the bonuses for executives, so that they are now based on how well the company does. There are rewards within that, but if the company does not meet its objectives, the amount to be shared based on individual performance is reduced.

The Knowledge Network

JC: *How does the Knowledge Network operate at General Motors? What is its purpose, and what do you consider the biggest challenge that it faces?*

VB: The Knowledge Network is not so much an organization as it is an idea, an idea that reflects a commitment to creating an environment (be it the organizational behavior, individual practices, work processes, or information systems) that ensures all GM employees have access to what the company knows that will help them do their jobs more effectively. It is more of a virtual organization that is made up of people with similar interests, which disseminates information tied to eventual decisions. You could not find it on the organization chart. I see two big challenges: (1) how to instill a responsibility within all people to think about who else in the company could benefit from understanding what they have learned and proactively sharing that learning, and (2) how to accelerate our commitment to doing work in a similar fashion across all regions and thereby increase our capability to rapidly learn and change across the globe.

In many ways, the concept is still in startup mode. We have demonstration projects that are working reasonably well, but it is not universally applied across the board yet. This is because the enterprise itself is going through tremendous change. We only have so much time, so much money, and so much capability. Further, at GM, we really have to prove the merit of what we are talking about before it is universally accepted. If we try to do it across the enterprise without that acceptance, it is unlikely to be successfully adopted. Our strategy has been to find places where the principles apply and then to grow from those experiences.

JC: *How do people become involved in the Knowledge Network?*

VB: Again, listen, learn, and lead comes into play. People become involved by setting up the means to inquire (seek out, listen, and learn) before starting new initiatives. They also are finding ways to lead or communicate to others what they are doing in the likelihood it can help them do their jobs more effectively. We communicate the things we are working on through day-to-day contact. Given that our currently allocated resources are fully being used, we have to figure out ways in which we can extend ourselves into the center of the organization.

One example of how this is working is in what we are learning in the vehicle development process. The people who have worked on that project—which has included creating the basis for providing background on decisions that have been made and how well they have turned out—are sharing that knowledge with people who are working on different projects. The operating groups have begun saying that this was very beneficial and that they want to do more of it.

JC: *Who is involved with the Knowledge Network?*

VB: Everybody, both internally and externally. As we move from the make-and-sell model to the sense-and-respond model, we realize it absolutely requires the engagement of the supplier community as well.

JC: *How do you connect all of the individual networks and activities that exist in the enterprise?*

VB: At this point, it is all done through people. There is some discussion going on of an architecture, which would be a very thin client[2] that would go out to these deeper silos of knowledge throughout the enterprise and be able to pull that information together.

We spent some time looking at Cisco. We explored how it communicates and how the web is fundamentally how it does business and extends

[2] Clients are PCs or workstations on which users run applications. Servers are powerful computers or processes dedicated to managing disc drives. In client/server applications, a client is designed to be especially small so that the bulk of the data processing occurs on the server. A thin client is a network computers without a disc drive, whereas a fat client includes a disc drive.

to its suppliers and customers. Cisco is probably the exemplary enterprise that actually uses knowledge in the everyday operations of the enterprise. What is particularly striking with Cisco is that everything is available. It actually publishes on its Web site the bugs that are in its software so that its customers are aware of them. It has found that some of the customers have created solutions for these bugs, which they are more than willing to share. The customers are saying, "You folks are really honest. Not too many people are willing to admit that they made a mistake. You not only are willing to admit it, but you show us where it is."

When we visited there, the head of Cisco's HR program said, "We found that some of our competitors' systems engineers were getting into the site to find out what these problems were so they could use them in selling against us. Some of our people thought we were paying too heavy a price and should stop this, but we felt it was the right thing to do."

Here is what I understand that Cisco did. The company knew when a customer was on. If you were not a customer and you were getting into the site, looking at these pages that had the bugs listed, a banner would pop up and say, "Hi, welcome to Cisco. Would you like to come to work for us?"

The HR director said, "When you think about it, wouldn't you want to hire people who were sensitive enough to hear about something and then smart enough to try to do something about it?" The firm is so web-related that it fundamentally recruits on the web as well.

Leveraging Knowledge across the Organization

JC: *Is the same approach to leveraging knowledge used across all of the different GM organizations and divisions?*
VB: No. We have gone to places that are receptive to the notion of change. Our strategy is to go where you can get something done and then let the word pass from there. We believe in using word-of-mouth as our marketing mechanism. At GM, if you want to spread an idea, demonstrate how good it is. Once people hear about something that actually works, they are more likely to ask for it.

JC: *Did you augment the word-of-mouth? Do you have materials that are available or a website that people go to where you have things like "discoveries of the week" or a "things that really work for us" type of thing?*
VB: Word-of-mouth is mostly spread by going to particular venues inside the company and talking about it. We have the beginning of web pages that people can come to, and they are having an initial positive effect.

JC: *How do you know where these opportunities are, or how do people know to get in touch with you to assist them?*

VB: We have brought together a diverse group of people who have worked in various parts of the company. People have been talking about spiderweb networks and similar approaches. The people we have selected have maintained their ties with the parts of the company they originated from. We use the concept of *weak ties*, where there are people inside of groups who are connected to the group, but who also have ties to other groups. It is those ties to other groups that effect the dissemination of information. Our people really are well tied into other areas. Also, after some time, many of the people in our group go back to their areas (or sometimes to new areas) with a better understanding of the enterprise and the new tools that are now available. When they run into an issue, they know how to address it and where to come for additional help if they need it.

I see new technology coming along that is going to address this interconnectivity need. A lot of it is going to be based on Internet and web technology, and we are getting much better at that inside the enterprise. When I look at what Cisco has done, then I know it can be done.

Dialogue Decision Process

JC: *What processes does GM use to make sure it is using the knowledge network for the desired effect?*

VB: One of these processes is called the *dialogue decision process*. The principles of that process are (1) make sure you have agreement on what the problem is, and make sure that those who will have to allocate resources agree that you have correctly identified the problem; (2) make sure you have identified alternative ways of addressing the problem; (3) each alternative must receive a fair hearing and analysis; and (4) try to find a solution that comes out of this analysis that is better than any of the alternatives that has been analyzed.

We do not always call this process the dialogue decision process. Many units have developed their own versions, but they go through many of the same steps. It works better because it is their process and not ordered by someone on the corporate staff. That was an important thing for us to learn.

We've also found that, depending on the problem, you do not have to go through all of the steps. I'm glad to say that if you walked into a meeting today and somebody came up with a wild idea as an alternative, rather than getting thrown out or challenged as being too wild, someone would say, "That really sounds like a test-well alternative. You ought to sink that and see if there's anything that that we could learn." At that point, we know that the principle got across, not the specific tools.

The shift is how people are thinking about these things, and how they are relating to innovation. That is more important than if they follow the steps of a particular tool, which is why I run into problems with people who say, "I have the tool that is going to solve your problem."

JC: *How do you make the learnings from the learning and adaptation support system available to anyone in the organization who needs them?*

VB: Not everybody in the organization gets equal access to everything. The basic principle is "need to know." But, that is a lot easier to say than it is to determine. Getting the right level of understanding about this issue at the beginning is a requirement if we want people to be open and honest with us. This is where a cultural divide takes place. Some people say, "We cannot make this information available to anybody who wants to see it, because we cannot afford to let this sensitive information fall into the wrong hands." The price we sometimes pay for that position is that people tend to be less open. If you don't trust me, why should I trust you?

We have others who are willing to let information be shared in order to gain the advantage of getting into richer discussions. Right now, we are at the stage of working within units, such as the vehicle development process unit, so their team and the other vehicle development team get access to all of the information, but that information is not broadly shared throughout the entire enterprise.

We tend to operate on much more of a need-to-know basis. And we do it most of the time for the right reasons. We sometimes do it because we're hung up on the impression that "people are going to judge me on the outcome of the decision that was made" rather than a thorough analysis of why the decision turned out the way that it did.

The Measurement Quandary

JC: *How do you know you are succeeding in your knowledge efforts? Have you developed any measures or indicators that help you and your colleagues navigate and improve your performance?*

VB: One perspective that has really impressed me is in the work of C. West Churchman, who was one of Russell Ackoff's colleagues. Churchman said, "The value of knowledge is in its use, not its collection. It is how the user reacts to the collection that really matters." My concern is the potential unintended consequences of attempting to determine the extent to which intellectual capital contributed to the outcome.

Here is an illustration of what concerns me. Suppose that I go to you and say, "Jay, you're a decision maker. I have some really great tools and information, which are ways of helping you make better decisions, like helping you to listen, learn, and lead." And you say, "Vince, that's really good, let's do it." You then go through the process that we propose, putting all your energy and resources into the effort. You like the process, and you see very positive outcomes based on the decisions you have made. A year or two later, I come back and say, "Jay, I've been really thinking about this, and I would say that 33% of the value that you've generated is directly related to the input that I have made to your decision process, and I would like to take some credit for the successful programs you have developed."

My guess is that you would first say, "Vince, how did you come up with 33%? And, by the way, how do you sort this stuff out? I believe the activity was successful because of how I implemented this so-called intellectual capital that you claim you created. Isn't that more important than what you've provided?" I think at that point I would say, "Jay, I'm sorry I raised this issue. I don't want to ruin my relationship with you by trying to create a metric that allows me to get credit for contributing to what you've done."

I believe that the support we provide, as a knowledge and decision support organization, cannot be accurately assessed by looking at any particular project by itself. We need to look at the contribution to the larger system within which many of the decisions we supported were made. When GM's leadership can see that the number of times we have repeated the same mistake is significantly reduced, then we are making headway. When we see that GM is able to adapt more quickly to changing environmental conditions, then we are making headway. When we are proactively experimenting and learning new things that take us into a leadership role in the marketplace, then we are making headway.

JC: *How do you work through your quandary there?*
VB: If one of the reasons we needed to "measure" intellectual capital is to demonstrate to management the value of my group's contribution, I would go to my customers in the operating groups and I would say, "The president of North American operations is questioning my budget. He thinks we're spending more money than we should. Would you go and explain to him how valuable you see our support being so that he understands that some of the success that you have been generating is based on the work that we've done?"

My belief is that most of our internal customers would say, "Yes, I'd be happy to do that on your behalf." If the value of information is that it is used, then I always trade off ensuring its use rather than trying to demonstrate its value.

Although I do not deny the need to gauge the value, I question the value of trying to actually put a precise metric around it. Frankly, I do not know how to develop the metric to the point where I have comfort that, first, it is reflecting what actually happened, and second, it does not spoil the relationship with the people who we support in making decisions.

Some, of course, want to put a valuation of intellectual capital in the annual report, and they have figured out ways of creating such a metric. I am not sure there is a way of portraying the value of intellectual assets as being worth "this much" and then attempting to book that amount. Are we capable of creating such a metric? With sufficient time and resources, I'm sure we could create a number. My problem is that I do not know how to make it real.

Would you say that Cisco's stock value is a function of its relationships with its customers, or is it a function of its estimated intellectual capital? If we ever asked John Chambers what he would rate as Cisco's intellectual capital, my guess is he would say, "It's the company. It's how we operate. It's how we think." He would be able to sort out the inputs from the outputs very well and probably be able to tell us how Cisco operates to create intellectual capital. He would tell us how it takes advantage of what it knows, which is really where the value comes into being. And, I'm sure he would say the manner in which the company does business is no less valuable in a depressed stock market than it is when the market is very high.

In the scheme of things, given all the other things that need to be done, I would focus on how we get knowledge used rather than how we measure its contribution. The true value of knowledge (read: intellectual capital) is in its use—not its collection.

Success in Shifting to Sense-and-Respond

JC: *How is GM transitioning from the make-and-sell to the sense-and-respond paradigm?*

VB: A good example of our moving to sense-and-respond is that we have created an order-to-delivery mechanism, that is, we are going to change the proportion of vehicles sold to the point where a higher percentage of our vehicles will be ordered by customers rather than bought off the lot. As we do that, we must start thinking about what our service capacities are and how we provide those services, based on customer preferences.

Customers will not have to buy the whole thing. They can buy that portion of the services they want. This is also where an Internet presence will be very significant. All of this is part of our moving toward the sense-and-respond model.

JC: *On a 1–10 scale, if you put General Motors, say, ten years ago, in 1990, and General Motors in the year 2000, how much of a shift has occurred?*

VB: Given that we almost went into bankruptcy ten years ago, we can easily say we were a 1. Today, we are well on the other side of 5. That is a very solid achievement. More important, everything that we have accomplished up until now has provided us greater understanding and positioned us to be great—again!

Key Learning Points

- A market-based adaptive enterprise combines what the market asks for directly with what the business is capable of delivering.
- Understand the enterprise as a system. Look at the different parts of the enterprise to see where they interface with customers and interact among themselves. That is where the opportunities are.
- Undo rewards and other systems that no longer contribute to the best outcome of the enterprise system.
- Corporate strategy's job is to forge a process to assist management in creating a strategy they will implement. This means surfacing new ideas, speculating how they will interact with the enterprise, involving management in a dialogue on them, and providing decision and analytic tools and resources to help in implementation.
- Listening, learning, leading means listening before starting an action, clearly stating and revisiting decisions to learn their value over time, and leading by actively linking actions to those choices.
- Forging a knowledge network creates an environment where all stakeholders have access to what they need to do their jobs effectively.
- Start the knowledge initiative in places that are receptive to the notion of change.
- The value of knowledge is in its use, not in its collection.
- The measure that matters is the extent that we proactively experiment and learn new things that take us into a leadership role in the marketplace.

Human Capital, Values,
and Learning

KNOWLEDGE
Cluster III:

People are the source of the ideas and actions that grow organizations. Yet the role of people and human capital has been changing in a fundamental way over the last several decades. Until recently, institutions have been the dominant part of the equation. As long as human inputs into wealth were seen as commodities, then people were interchangeable, one for another. Their contributions were marginal to the profits and practices of the enterprise. As much as leadership proclaimed, "Our people are our most important resource," very few organizations actually mobilized their people and human capital as a coherent knowledge factor to achieve strategic outcomes.

A major challenge for knowledge-based enterprises is to engage and cultivate their networks of human capital. In this era, the human capital that supports the organization is only partially a group of direct employees. In fact, as time goes on, many organizations will operate with a core group of strategic leadership and then engage human capital on an as-needed basis. The era where benign bureaucracies hired people to have jobs for life has come to an end. Instead, people will work in a number of organizations during their working lives and may have multiple engagements with a number of companies at the same time. People will increasingly begin to see themselves as *companies of one*, where they are responsible for their learning, their personal growth strategies, the quality of their relationships, and their work environment. As a result, a growing proportion of the people working with enterprises will be independent contractors, outsourced from other organizations, members of organizations with whom the enterprise has alliances, or come from the ranks of the enterprise's own suppliers.

Instead of managing monolithic, hierarchical organizations, leadership in knowledge-based enterprises is beginning to see that it is managing or leading networks of resources, including human capital resources. The implications of this are broad and varied. The enterprise needs to effectively come to grips with the questions of who owns the intellectual capital of the enterprise, who is responsible for the development and ongoing education of the people working with the organization, and how it is going to mobilize diverse and autonomous individuals in a sustained and focused way.

Participants in this cluster of conversations raise these critical questions and lay the groundwork for establishing the kinds of frameworks, practices, and relationships that are necessary for any enterprise to successfully navigate this new human capital landscape.

Human Capital: The Only Active Capital

Jac Fitz-enz sees that organizations are nothing more than an extension of human thought and action, which makes human capital the only active capital. Financial and physical resources are important, but they cannot be transformed without the lever of human capital. The input of human capital grows in value and is becoming the differentiator for organizations. Therefore, enterprises must recalibrate to see how that input operates and bring it into balance with all of the other elements, including long-term basic strategy, positioning in the market, and the alignment of culture and systems to achieve exceptional outcomes. However, this is not a static situation. There is a power shift. As people begin to be better able to autonomously gather information, achieve mobility, and initiate connectivity, they are redefining the role and value of their human capital. As a result, they are making new demands on management for more satisfying kinds of relationships, working conditions, and compensation.

Management has to, in a sense, catch up with its workforce and respond with increasing flexibility to obtain the kinds of capabilities and commitments it needs to succeed. This is a major reversal for management, which is used to being able to dictate the terms of employment. Regardless, it is a necessity. Enterprise leadership must come to know better what human capital it needs, not just for today, but also for tomorrow and the day after. It must understand how to rapidly acquire, compensate, grow, and retain it so that it can positively affect its business performance and operating objectives. The corollary is that it must change its orientation and its basic systems to be at the lead of the knowledge-based enterprise reality. Managing the knowledge and human capital for continuous learning, sharing, and connecting as human beings, while giving people space to think and rewarding them for their performance and contributions needs to be part of the daily practice of everyone, from leadership to the frontline of the enterprise. If it is an add-on or special program, it will fall significantly short of its promise or fail.

Changing the Equation: The New Social Contract

Thomas O. Davenport provides another dimension to the human capital equation. Simply put, Davenport says that people now see that they are the owners of their human capital. They are no longer just sets of hired hands, detached from people with brains and experience. The task of leadership in the knowledge-based enterprise is to have a business strategy that takes into account that people see themselves as workers-as-investors. In this collaborative relationship, the enterprise must be clear about its aims as it negotiates with its individual workforce members, who are seeking equity for their investment. In this changed equation, the enterprise needs a return of performance and outcome from its investment, and members of the workforce need the financial, social, and physical conditions and learning opportunities that will garner their commitment. The new social contract requires not just a new perspective on the part of enterprise leadership, it also mandates that the rest of management and front line supervisors grasp this and act on this new understanding. Front line supervisors, importantly, will take on the new and very significant role of negotiating "the deal," that is, the customized contracts with workforce members. They must make sure that the conditions are there to support success and make sure that all parties get the return on investment that they seek. This demands new sets of skills on the part of everyone involved. The benefit to all parties is significant. Developing these capabilities creates a platform for high-level, measurable performance, which will allow the knowledge-based enterprise to effectively compete in its market.

Human Capital, Values Alignment, and Outcomes

Don Tyler discusses how shared values function as the glue holding the knowledge-based enterprise together. Shared values allow networked organizations to share knowledge easily, act cogently and coherently, and be in alignment. Shared values set up the context and environment for sharing knowledge. If the values are in alignment, the actions and communications will also be in alignment. One of the first tasks of the leadership of an enterprise is to identify the core values of the organization, values that a diverse workforce can identify with, link with, and support. Not only do shared values provide a common ground for communications and action, they also are critical for any necessary reframing of the organization.

Different sets of people in an enterprise may have different clusters of values. The leadership may have one cluster, midlevel management another, and the front line a third. Depending on its goals and market requirements, one organization may need just a minimum of shared values to achieve a desired level of performance, while another organization may need a much more collaborative, self-initiating environment to accomplish its ends. Each enterprise needs to assess its goals and see if its core values will support and sustain it in reaching its goals. It can then target certain values to nurture that will allow it to transition.

An organization may not need perfect values alignment, but it will need values alignment appropriate to its ends. These values must be the authentic values held by the enterprise and its people. Values provide a set of common reference points that can be used as criteria for decision making and serve as enablers for deployment. The trust that comes from shared values breeds viable, long-term relationships throughout the network of customers and suppliers as well. When there is a divergence from the values framework, the enterprise becomes vulnerable as its channels begin to corrode. Incompatible or token values, like wallpaper pasted over a fractured wall, do not work when there is the least amount of stress.

Learning in the Knowledge Era

Brook Manville explores the convergence of knowledge management and learning as part of the evolution toward something larger and different, which he calls "human capital management." Human capital management is a broader and more integrated effort to manage and develop human capabilities to achieve significantly higher levels of business performance. Manville traces the emergence of knowledge management from its focus on capturing, storing, and codifying explicit knowledge to a much more dynamic field that began including tacit knowledge and then whole networks of people who are continuously learning to respond to changing conditions in their enterprise and world.

Moving to develop and deploy knowledge and people in the most effective way and to facilitate the flow of knowledge across organizations requires not just technology. It also involves building capabilities in strategy and leadership development, changing organizational design and structure, nurturing a host of informal organizations, and shaping a set of management, financial, and quality processes that are in concert and able to constantly adjust to new conditions. This means moving toward organizations that are capable of systematic transformation.

To Manville, these knowledge-based enterprises are moving away from the static "wars of position" stance and toward being engaged in a "wars of capabilities" business model. In the "wars of capabilities" environment, people and organizations have to be able to rapidly create and execute strategy in a volatile and changeable marketplace. Learning, both organization-wide and personal, and managing knowledge are fundamental in this perspective. Learning here is learning for use and learning that is just-in-time. It is learning in a business context where knowledge is immediately applicable to specific goals and aligned with the strategy of the organization. This involves establishment of learning management systems across the extended enterprise that enable its users to map its knowledge, analyze its knowledge gaps, and then provide managed learning to close those gaps. The human capital management approach gives managers, as well as workers, the opportunity to take control of the learning, resources, systems, and processes they need to achieve the goals of the enterprise.

A Framework for Performance

Much of what is discussed in these conversations deals with performance. As they have evolved, knowledge management and intellectual capital have dealt with many technical, knowledge resource, and organizational design issues. The knowledge movement is now on the verge of grappling with performance issues. In the end, it may be performance, more than any other factor, that makes the difference for an enterprise.

The contributors in this cluster lay the groundwork to take on matters of performance. By exploring the basic factors that have led to a know-how-based, performance-oriented social contract, the contributors show how an enterprise can deal with the related roles of knowledge, skill sets, responsibilities, win-win outcomes, and relationships, which form the underpinnings of the new social contract. This, in turn, will require knowledge-based enterprises to rework their relationships, values, structural arrangements, and incentives to formulate a performance framework that allows the accomplishment of strategic enterprise goals.

Human Capital Is the Only Active Asset

8

In this conversation, Jac Fitz-enz examines the leveraging role of human capital in organizations. He views that human capital is the only capital that is active. Without human capital, nothing can happen in organizations. He demonstrates that we can measure the value of human capital and the return on investment of human capital. This is important to develop the set of measures that balances human and financial factors. This balance is the hallmark of effective organizations. Fitz-enz also warns that human capital, intellectual capital, and knowledge management are in danger of failing unless they become integrated into the way organizations do their business.

Fitz-enz is an internationally recognized authority on human resource management. He pioneered human capital benchmarking and performance measurement. Among his accomplishments is a landmark study of the connection among service, quality, and productivity.

Fitz-enz founded Saratoga Institute in 1977 and was its chairman until 2002. Saratoga Institute publishes the world's largest database of human capital measurements, the "Human Capital Benchmarking" Report, which covers more than 900 companies. He has authored five books on human capital management. His most recent book is *The ROI of Human Capital.*[1]

[1] Jac Fitz-enz, *The ROI of Human Capital: Measuring the Economic Value of Employee Performance* (New York: AMACOM, 2000).

Fitz-enz received a doctorate in communications from the University of Southern California.

The Conversation

Fundamental Factors

JC: *Why is a balanced focus on the interaction of human capital and financial outcomes the leading reason for long-term financial success?*

JF: My view is that balance is a fundamental issue of nature. Remember from high school biology the process of homeostasis, wherein every living organism strives to stay in balance? Since organizations are nothing more than an extension of human thought and action, it makes sense that an organization should be in balance also. I was not thinking about this when we first did the research, but it turns out that top performing companies always focus on balancing human and financial issues.

Homeostasis in organizations is a fundamental truism of top performers as I originally reported in *The 8 Practices of Exceptional Companies.*[2] But there is a downside potential to homeostasis as well. That is, we can spend so much time on analyzing and balancing that we stagnate an organization, putting it into analysis paralysis. Like anything else, we can overdo it. Given that as the potential downside, it is still an absolute fundamental for long-term success.

In the short term, you can do anything, practically speaking, including unethical acts, such as breaking the law, and make money. That is not what I am talking about. I am focusing on how we build an institution that we can be proud of, that can be successful, can be a contributor to the community, can make money for the stockholders, and so forth, for the next hundred years. If that's what we are looking for, . . . if we want to build that kind of institution, then balance is absolutely fundamental. I do not think we can achieve our goals without it.

JC: *What are some companies that you think achieve that? Or use it as their principle?*

JF: Hewlett-Packard, Federal Express, and Motorola did it well for a long time, as well as a lot of smaller companies you've never heard of. We

---

[2] Jac Fitz-enz, *The 8 Practices of Exceptional Companies: How Great Organizations Make the Most of Their Human Assets* (New York: AMACOM, 1997).

researched a thousand companies over five years and came up with this finding.

JC: *Was this an intentional effort at balancing, or did it just accidentally work out based on the people's intuition?*
JF: We studied these companies in both their human and financial performance over a five-year period. We pulled out the top 10% of those, and in doing our report, found by accident that there were eight factors that were typical of these companies that were not typical of the other 90%. Now, it is not a total exclusivity. It is a predominance or a general lack of performance.

JC: *And balance is one of these eight factors?*
JF: Balance is one of the three fundamentals. The other two are long-term commitment to a basic strategy, a positioning in the market, if you will, and a positioning in the community and an alignment of culture and systems. This was an intentional effort on the part of the companies to do this.

Human Capital Value Added

JC: *What is Saratoga Institute, and what is the set of macro human and financial metrics that Saratoga Institute is using? What have you learned by using them?*
JF: As founder of Saratoga Institute, I have been involved in the issue of measuring the effectiveness of people, quantitatively, for more than 20 years. Since 1985, we've been publishing an annual report that tracks over a hundred different variables. Those go from macros like revenue per full-time employee (FTE), down to micros, such as the time to fill jobs. The objective of all this is to provide benchmark data by industry, company size, geographic region, and growth rate, so that on any particular measure you could compare yourself to somebody else in one of those categories. We will do this in the United States with more than 900 companies this year. We also work with another 1,000 companies in about a dozen countries in Europe, South America, Australia, Africa, and Latin America.

The core of our business is doing this kind of research, publishing principally benchmark data. We also do some publication of best practices.

The more important macro measures include some that we have coined ourselves and some that are fairly traditional. We call the new ones *human capital value added*. That is a function of teasing out of the profit of the company that which is attributable to people. The formula very simply is revenue minus all expenses, except for human expense, which is pay and benefits, divided by FTEs. That gives an adjusted profit for human effort, per employee. That is better than revenue per employee because that is just a gross measure, and we do not know what caused it. By using our new formula, we can tell how much value added came from human effort.

There's a corollary measure called *human capital ROI*, or return on investment, where we use the same formula. In this case, though, the divisor is pay and benefit costs. The result here is a ratio that, for every dollar spent on pay and benefits, there is a certain amount of profitability. To illustrate: We can get a ratio of $1.00 to $2.00 or $1.00 to $1.40, or whatever it might be. Those are two fundamentals that we have used now for a half dozen years.

Another more common measure is compensation as a percentage of revenue. That tells us what our cost is for people to generate that amount of money. If we extend that by adding in contingent labor, we call it TLC, or total labor cost. We can divide that into revenue and give ourselves another figure, which now accounts for the money spent on contingents. Since contingent labor is somewhere in the high teens and 20% of total labor, it is certainly a significant factor that we cannot ignore. We cannot just talk about people on payroll any more.

This is true everywhere, but more or less in some places, of course. We are facing a shortage of labor everywhere. Because of that, organizations are having to be more flexible in the way that they employ people, part-time people, temporary workers of all types, and contract workers. The reality is that the contingent factor is getting more and more significant. We cannot ignore it.

JC: *Is the change in organization structure also increasing that, in addition to the labor shortage?*
JF: Absolutely. Management is also trying to be more flexible, trying to keep down the core labor force and use contingent contractors more, so that they can be in and out much faster and reduce costs.

But there is another measure that can be used that is atypical, which is turnover by length of service. This tells an organization at what point in someone's career it is prone to losing that individual.

Everybody thinks that organizations tend to lose people mostly in the first year or two, and on average that is correct. It is true that more people leave or are terminated in their first year of employment than at any other point for a variety of reasons, both individual and organizational. Beyond that, we have learned that there are points in a person's career when they are what we would call more vulnerable or susceptible to leaving the organization. Those points tend to come at somewhere around two to three years, again around the five-year time frame, and again around eight to nine years.

We believe that the underlying reason for this is that people begin a job and for a while they get a certain amount of reward and satisfaction as well as frustration from the organization they are working in. When a call comes, they see an ad, or a neighbor talks about a new job, there are specific points where they begin to wonder if they have made a good decision to stay where they are. They may start to become frustrated because they didn't get the promotion that they had anticipated getting when they came 18 months ago or two years ago. These natural points are when a call from the headhunter comes or as a result of some other stimulus, which means people are more likely to consider it than they would otherwise. It is useful to have that kind of information to know what percentage of your people or which individuals are reaching those points, and then you can go do something preventive about it.

If I know that you've been here now four years and you are reaching this zone, I can sit down with you and assure you that we really value you and want you here. I can say, "Let's talk about your career," and so on, so that you understand that you are an important person to us and not just a cipher sitting in a corner somewhere. Then, if you get the call from the recruiter, you are less likely to take that call, or consider the first offer that comes along, than if you have been here for four or five years and nobody has talked to you. It happens in organizations all the time that people do not even get a performance review, even professional people. Several times in my career, I have been in an organization for a couple of years and did not get a performance review. I just got a salary increase, or whatever. It became clear to me that I was not an important individual. That is why something like turnover by length of service is useful to know.

JC: *Is this even more significant in our era, when the value equation is changing from the value in an organization being its physical capital to one where an increasing percentage of it is human capital and intangibles?*
JF: Of course. People are clearly the key issue these days. I think almost everybody agrees with that. There are still some hardheaded manufacturing people who think that the way you solve everything is by another turret lathe or stamping mill, and you do not worry too much about training people beyond just the basics of how to run the machine. But those people are clearly the dinosaurs who are going away—not as fast as they ought to, but they are going away faster.

People, particularly in the service industries and the so-called new economy companies, are clearly recognizing that people are the differentiating factor, that human effort is the real lever, that knowledge effort is the lever.

The Four Areas of Human Capital

JC: *What are the characteristics of the four human capital areas of acquiring, maintaining, developing, and retaining? Where and when do they touch operating units? This gets to how things actually work.*

JF: A number of years ago, we began to think of people as being assets. I always have to put in a qualifier. I am not denigrating the humanity of people by using these terms. I am just trying to create a new lexicon or vernacular for understanding and analyzing human effort. Part of this is because for so long we have talked about people only from the soft side of things, such as satisfaction and motivation. That way, we are only going to get limited attention from businesspeople who have to deal with numbers.

I often quote Lord Kelvin about how important it is to measure things. The simple point is: We have to be able to use a language that businesspeople use if we want to impress them. That will be the language of numbers and hard data. That is what got us toward thinking about people as human assets. This was before the term *human capital* came along. If we think of an asset, what we have to do with an asset is we have to first acquire it by buying it, leasing it, or whatever. Once we have it, we have got to maintain it. If it is a machine, we have got to oil it, do preventive maintenance, and so forth. With people, we have to pay them, provide benefits and other types of support. We have to retain assets, that is, keep them. In the case of a machine, we have to keep the machine if we want to continue to turn out the widgets. The same thing is true with people. We have got to keep people, to retain talent. One thing that is unique is development, because only people can be developed. Machines cannot be developed. We could say we could develop a computer by putting in a faster card. That is true. But, that's not developing the computer. That is making it a new machine. The key issue is that people are developable and machines are not. Those are the four things that we have to do to manage a human asset. The four are fundamental to managing that asset. We, then, have to apply these by assigning the human assets, the people, to jobs, and then by supervising their performance.

The way they touch the operating part of the organization is that if we change the way we do any of those four things, we are most likely going to change the operation of the unit that we are talking about. If we are in the human resource department, for example, and servicing one of the operating units of the company, such as the customer service department, we might get a requisition from the customer service manager that we need to hire a couple of customer service representatives. If we come up with a strategy, a methodology, or a tactic that helps us hire better-quality people faster and cheaper and then pass those people on to the customer service manager, that has to have a positive effect on customer service performance.

The caveat is that the customer service manager has to be a good manager. If she is an idiot, then putting good people under her does not help. We always have to say, "All other things being equal." Assuming that we have good operating systems, good supervision, and all the rest, if we do a better job of putting those assets in better, faster, and cheaper, by definition we have to get better performance out of that business unit.

A simple example would be: If the customer service manager loses a couple of customer service reps, there will be no one on the phones to pick up calls. If there's a large volume of calls, the other customer service reps will not be able to handle them. As a result, they are going to lose contact with some customers, or they're going to delay customers who are sitting on the line. We have all called and gotten the message: "We're experiencing an exceedingly high volume of calls right now, and the wait time on your call is going to be . . . two minutes, four minutes, five minutes, whatever." If that is beyond our tolerance level, we leave. If we have a choice, we call a competitor, or we say, "I'm never going to do business with this company again." That decision is a function of the inability to fill that job properly. That is how acquisition issues affect the retention of a customer.

We can trace other things the same way. We can talk about developing people, training them how to be good customer service reps so they do a good job with retaining the customer, making the customer happier, and maybe even selling the customer something else when the customer didn't call to buy anything. Because we had a very well trained and empathic customer service rep, we end up not only saving the customer but also penetrating the account deeper by selling something else. That is how the action of acquiring, compensating, growing, and retaining human assets, or human capital, affects business performance and the operating objectives.

This is not done in a vacuum although, quite often, people in staff departments act as though they are in a vacuum. They just do their process without a great conception of how they are connected to the business.

Here's a story that hits right on the spot for this. I gave a talk a couple of years ago in the morning, just before lunch. I sat down at a table where a woman was already seated. We began a conversation. I said, "Where do you work?" She said she worked at a company that is involved in the space program, in satellites, communications, and things like that. She said, "We just won this big new contract from the government, but I'm not really sure what it's about. It has nothing to do with communications." Just then, three other people from the same company sat down at the table, and she turned to one of them and asked, "Mary, what is this new program covering?" The woman said, "I don't know. I try to stay out of the company." That person is not doing human asset management. That person is processing something, but she has no connection to what's going on in the company, because she doesn't want one. She is never going to have any kind of positive effect. She is only going to have a hidden negative effect on the company. That is what I mean by having an effect on the operations.

JC: *What would that be in the human capital areas: maintaining or developing?*
JF: She was in acquisitions. She was in staffing.

What we have got to do with a people like that is show them how their work affects the operations of the company. This assumes the people are positive and not drones of some sort. We could show them the effect that their work can have on the company and how that's good for other employees, if they happen to be humanistic, or how it is good for profitability, if they happen to be financially oriented. Then we are going to win them over, and they are going to get engaged.

The company, for whatever reason, did not engage this person. I do not know if it was her nature or if something inside the company just got her disgusted and frustrated at some point in her career, and she said, "Forget it. I'm just going to come to work and do what I do, and I'm not going to engage in the company."

JC: *Does this lead people to make a choice that they're just going to do their tasks?*
JF: Suppose you go to your boss and say, "I've got a good idea." If that person says, "No, not now," or "Don't worry about it. I'll take care of it. Just go back and do your work," we do not have to have that happen many times before we get alienated. Millions of people have been alienated from their companies. The big challenge is getting people back, winning their hearts back.

The Power Shift

JC: *What is the effect on human capital of putting mobility and information in the hands of people?*

JF: There is a power shift going on, and it is never going to go back to what it was. A lot of people are now grabbing information, grabbing mobility and connectivity through the web and the Internet. The inmates are taking over the asylum. Management in many cases doesn't even know it, or if they do know it, they are trying to stop it. That is the great irony. Management, on one hand, is trying to engage people. On the other hand, when people do get engaged, management starts putting up barriers and says, "Do not do this, do not do that. You cannot do this, our policy is that."

There was a company that said all individual web pages must be approved by corporate communications. This means that if we want to put up our own little web page on our desktop for the company, we have got to send it in to corporate, and they have to approve what is in there. This is ridiculous.

What do people do? They subvert it, of course. If people want to communicate, they are going to communicate, no matter what you do. If you imprison them, they are going to tap on the walls. They are going to communicate because they have to communicate. To try to stop that is absolutely futile. It is already too late. You cannot stop it. As long as the economy remains viable at all, people are going to communicate. They are going to go off and do things, and they are not going to tell you about it. From management's standpoint, you better get with them. Otherwise, they are just going to drag you along behind.

As far as communities of practice, can we say, "OK, the community of practice now for this particular topic is Joe, Frank, Mary, Larry, Jay, Jack, Ellen, and nobody else." That is ridiculous. People in companies set up a community of practice, and they exclude certain people from it. If you happen to know someone who is a good person and they don't put him in this community of practice, you just drop out of the community of practice. You may go to the meetings, but you do not contribute the real stuff any more. You and that excluded person go off and have a cup of coffee and that is where you really get something. You cannot stop people from communicating with the people they want to communicate with. That is what is happening.

Silicon Valley is a community of practice. Those people know to whom they want talk here. They will voluntarily talk to whomever they want to talk to. One way or another, they're going to communicate, and they are not going to be restrained by anybody.

JC: *What is the role of human capital in making a quantum leap?*

JF: In order to make quantum leaps, you have got to engage the imagination of human beings.

I define a quantum leap as more than incremental improvement like we get from reengineering or quality circles. A quantum leap is launching a great new innovation, a great change in the organization that significantly affects margins or new products, but it is a major change in the organization—a positive change in products, finance, processes, systems, or whatever.

I think about it in terms of changing the systems and processes to achieve this new goal that is significantly higher than you might have expected it to be. For example, I've seen many cases where the CEO has said, "Next year, we are going to double profit and revenue."

The CEO of Zurich Financial said, "It's taken us 110 years to get X-billions of dollars in sales. We're going to double that in the next three years." That is a quantum leap. In order to do that, you have to engage the totality of the human being. You're not going to get it by putting new machines in place. That will not produce a quantum leap. You've got to, by definition, leap this great chasm, and figuring out how to do that is a human function. Even improving technology will not do that for you. Taking typewriters away and giving PCs to everybody does not yield a quantum leap. It gives you an incremental improvement in productivity.

Quantum leaps come from the imagination of human beings who can see what is possible. To quote Robert Kennedy: "Some people look at things and ask, 'Why?' I look at things and ask, 'Why not?' " That is a human issue. A machine never asks that question. A machine just does whatever it does.

That is why human capital is the key issue. Human capital is the one thing that can look three or five years ahead. It is the one thing that can drive the change in redesigning systems. Human capital is the only asset that is not passive. Human capital is the only active asset there is.

I am looking at a lot of capital equipment sitting here in my office, none of it is moving. It is going to sit here until it rots, unless I pick it up and use it. It is a depreciating asset.

Growing the ROI of Human Capital

JC: *What do you mean by saying that the ROI, the return on investment, of human capital will be astronomical in companies that learn how to turn on the information- and*

intelligence-gathering capability that lies dormant in most
employees?

JF: I think everybody has agreed that we are using a very small amount of our human potential. We have heard quotes that we only use 2 or 4% of our brainpower. We can move that to a higher level. We are using an extremely small percentage of the human potential of our workforce. It is not only their brainpower but also their imaginations, their energy, and so on.

A company that can more fully engage that human capability is going to get a much bigger return on that investment and achieve things that it cannot possibly achieve now by not engaging more of that capability. By simply teaching people, setting up a culture where people can learn and grow, and supporting people psychologically, emotionally, and physically, we engage people more completely and draw out of them more of their capability. Because of that, they now perform at a much higher level. If we roll that up to the top, until we make all the connections from human motivation, skill development, and commitment up through the operating organization to the enterprise goals, we will start to get quantum leaps simply because we have used more capability.

It is like stepping on the gas of your car. If you drive along at 20 miles an hour, then that is what you get out of your car. But if you step on the gas, if you engage the power of that motor and that fuel more completely, when you accelerate you get to where you're going faster.

You can say that is not a good analogy. Ok, then, go from low-octane to high-octane fuel, or something like that, but you get the point. The more that we can engage the potentiality of anything, the better return we are going to get out of it. Beyond task skill levels, I think we do a pretty poor job of tapping the experience and the motivation of the workforce. Therefore, we get a suboptimal amount of leverage from each individual.

We do a really poor job of communicating. Communication has always been a great interest to me; my doctorate is in communication. I find it is one of the things we do the worst. We do not talk to people. We do not tell them the truth. We hold back things that we think they can't handle. We think people cannot handle bad information, so we are not going to tell them things are not looking good. That is ridiculous. People go home every night and handle bad information. They can handle bad news at work, too.

By being inconsistent with people in our communication, we put up another barrier. Another thing we found in the eight practices was that total, massive communication was the hallmark of the top performing companies. They told everything to everybody all the time, except illegal and trade secrets information. Given that, we know that communication is a critical factor.

Communication is all about engaging the potentiality of people. The potential is there; we are not engaging it, even though we ask for it. On the one hand, we ask for it, and on the other hand, we put up systems that do not allow it. We also lie to people. A nicer way of saying it is that we do not tell them the whole truth. We talk out of both sides of our mouths. Sometimes it is not by design. It is through ignorance. We do not realize we are doing it, because we have not had some good models in the past.

JC: *What are models in the present, and possibly in the past, that people can take a look at?*
JF: The simplest model is just tell the truth. Be open, honest, and humble. Say to people, "Here's what's going on. This is the good news. This is the bad news."

Listen to them when they talk to you. Do not try to cover things up. In the book I am writing now, there is a man who has for a number of years defended something inside the organization which everybody knew was an issue and a problem. Yet, every time the topic was brought up, he would defend it. Everybody would sit back and roll their eyes. Finally, one day, he did something about it. By then, his credibility had suffered irrevocably because people had despised his not telling the truth: "He knows as well as we do that this is an issue, and he's trying to snow us. That does not work. We are not stupid."

Let us say that you are talking to Einstein or any other great intellect, and he poses a question to you. Would you try to lie to him? Of course not. Well, you've got to consider that everybody in the company is an Einstein, in a way.

JC: *That would recast things enormously.*
JF: I am sitting here looking at a poster of Einstein I've had on the wall for years and years and years, and so I always think about him and what would it be like to deal with that kind of person, and I try to project that.

Are We Prepared for the Future?

JC: *How can you tell if we are being prepared for the future, and what indicators show that we are being prepared?*
JF: There are macro and micro things and more direct and less direct, but here's a sampling, in no particular order of priority. One that we talk about is called *readiness*. It is nothing more than the depth chart of the company

or succession planning of the company. In all critical positions, do we have somebody ready to take over if that person drops dead or quits tomorrow? That is a readiness index. If we have 200 critical positions in this company, how many of them are we one-deep or two-deep in? If we're not, that's a problem for the future, because tomorrow some of those people are going to leave for whatever reason. If we do not have the ability to replace them immediately, by definition, we have a problem.

We can also look at rates of voluntary turnover. That tells us that, if we don't stem this, if it's too high, we are not going to be prepared for the future. We can look at statements of commitment to the vision of the company and commitment to staying in the company. Most companies conduct employee attitude surveys and ask, "Do you think that you'll be here three years from now?" The person says "yes" or "no," whatever. That's fine. However, the issue is: Are you going to do anything while you are here? Are you committed while you are here? A person says, "I'm going to stay here because I cannot think of another job," or "I'm going to stay here until my kids graduate from high school," or "I'm going to stay here until I have enough money to buy a new car." That has nothing to do with what I'm going to do while I'm here.

Commitment is not only staying. Commitment is buying into the vision and having the energy to support it. You can track those kinds of things through surveys. We can look at whether we have competencies in what looks like the things we are going to need in the future. Are we prepared to evolve from analog to digital, from metal to composite plastics, from chemistry to electronics? If we're beginning to see changes in the technology of our industry, are we starting to build competencies for that, or are we going to wait until the last minute and then pay an exorbitant amount of money for people who have that competency?

We can look at competence levels. We can look at job satisfaction levels, because they are predictors of turnover. We can look at how we are using contingent workers. If we do some benchmarking of ourselves against the competition, we can see whether or not we are using contingent workers more or less effectively than we might be. That has a bearing on the future, because if we are not using contingent workers at all or if we are using them to a very high degree, that has a lot to say about how well prepared we are for tomorrow.

We can look at something as simple as the mix of exempt to nonexempt people in a given function. Exempts are professionals and managers. These are the people who do not get overtime. Nonexempts are laborers, clerical staff, and administrative people. A good example of this is a staff department like a human resource department. If we have a high level of nonexempts to exempts, for example, a high level of clerical and a smaller amount or percentage of professional people, it tells us this is a transaction department, a paper-pushing department. If we reverse that, and have 70% professionals in here and only 30% clerical, that means we have probably outsourced the transaction activities, and we are more of a strategic or advisory function now. That tells us what you can expect out of that group. We then lay that against what we want in the future and design that kind of a mix for the future.

JC: *How have you found that these indicators are useful in organizations, in the sense that people navigate their organizations based upon them?*
JF: Perhaps 15–25% of the companies in the country use these.

JC: *Are these the ones that are moving toward quantum leaps?*
JF: Yes. They are thinking about the future. How can we do a quantum leap if we think about the past? Looking at last month's financials is not going to help us with a quantum leap.

The nature of financial accounting is to look internally at the past. That does not help us get ahead. It just tells us what we did yesterday.

Enabling People to Build Tomorrow

JC: *How do we enable people in organizations to be the builders of the organizations of tomorrow?*
JF: First of all, delegate. That is not new. A lot of this stuff is old, things we have talked about for 20, 30, and 40 years and have not done very well or have done sporadically. Delegate power. Delegate authority. Delegate decision-making. Delegate the allocation of resources. Let people lower down decide what resources they need; give bigger budget allowances or discretion where they do not have to literally sign 17 forms to get a pencil. There are many cases where people have had to sign multiple forms to get very small things. That is not going to make it.

Demand and encourage innovation. Set up systems that encourage it, as well as systems that reward it. Set up systems where you learn from failures. So, if I go out and I try something and it doesn't work, I do not bury it and I do not tell anybody about it so then tomorrow you go out and do the same thing that does not work.

We need to celebrate our failures, in a sense, and acknowledge them and talk about them. We need to say, "We really set ourselves properly, we thought, to do this, and yet it didn't work. But this is why it didn't work. It is an error we made, something we did not consider. It was an unforeseen event that came out of the blue, but we learned from that so that next time around we can expand our knowledge of how to do something."

Celebrate is probably the wrong word. *Recognize* is a better term. We need to celebrate the successes and recognize the failures, not try to bury the failures.

JC: *How much slack do you think you need to build into the system so that you're encouraging the kind of experimentation that allows for the element of innovation to flourish?*

JF: We have to build in a lot more slack than we are comfortable with now. As someone who has run a company for a couple of decades, I intellectually agree with all of this, but pragmatically I have got to make a profit and all the rest. I am a little reticent to let too much rope out. On the other hand, if I do not have the courage to do that and I do not have the belief in my people to do that, then I am going to suboptimize them. I am not going to take advantage of their potentiality. We have to reach our level of discomfort in terms of delegation.

JC: *What do you think of the 3M approach, which has about 5–10% of its people's time allocated for them to go off, where they have spaces set up in their buildings where people can just go off and think about things and experiment.*

JF: That is one of the best-structured examples. I am sure that when someone leaves that little sanctuary, they don't stop thinking innovatively.

JC: *How does this slack work in places like Silicon Valley, where the pressures to produce are enormous? How does an organization encourage people to take time to be innovative, to create the "new, new thing"?*

JF: I think that is it. It is an integrated thing. It is not a place where we say, "Ok, for the next hour, I'm going to go think." We have got to be thinking all the time: when we are driving to work, driving home, heading for the bathroom, in the lunchroom, and doing our jobs. The question is: What do we, as management, have to do to help you accomplish that? How can we relieve some stress? How can we give you tools, processes, space, and time so that we engage you? It is good to set aside 10%, because you are going to get more than 10%. But we have to encourage that as a modus operandi.

Process Management and Human Capital

JC: *How do you see the relationship between process management and human capital management?*

JF: *Process management* is how you do something. *Human capital management* is who is doing it. That is the differentiator. It is how versus who. Clearly, we have to engage the human capital to change the process. The differentiating factor is: Who is doing what? It is the human activity versus the structured process or system. It is getting work done.

JC: *Is that a matrix?*

JF: No. I look at it more like fuel or energy. Let us use as an example an assembly line, where you spend $300 million to build an assembly plant. You design in certain processes of moving raw material through there into a finished product. That is the process. Everything is defined. Engineers have laid it out and put the equipment, materials, and all the rest in place. Then we come to the human capital: the person who flips the switch, who turns the plant on, monitors it, makes sure that if a machines starts to overheat, someone is there to recognize what is happening and *do* something about it. We have not yet invented total organizations where we do not have to have a human being involved. Robots still require human maintenance. They are not totally self-serving. There is always a human element. That is what human capital is. Human capital is the force, the who that designs the process, keeps it going, and in many cases is actively engaged in it.

JC: *How can we find the effect, the human capital effect on organizational processes? How do you know what difference it makes?*

JF: We may never get to a point where we can prove that something happened as a result of human intervention unless it's a very simple, obvious, and visible single activity. In a complex organization, we cannot prove anything and that includes salesmanship or anything else. There are too many variables impacting the organization at all times. All we can ever do is set up something where we can see some kind of correlation that this and that are working together to achieve X. We would like to be able to demonstrate this over time, considering all variables that impacted this process that we're aware of, which are all the major issues. Then we will be able to say that what happened was largely or not largely due to human effort. That is possible to do. We have been doing it for years in individual cases and in larger situations. A classic example is that we can take a sales force, give them sales training, and give them equipment like a PC with a modem where they can key into inventory when they are sitting in front of the customer. Then, we can see what happens with our sales. If sales go up, we can say it was a combination of these two things: We trained people on how to be better salespeople, and we gave them access to inventory information so that they could answer the questions of the customer on the spot.

The sales force is able to say to the customer, "Yes, we have this," or "We'll have it for you in time or partly in time," or, by using salesmanship methods, convince them that they can get the rest of it maybe a day later, but it will be Ok.

The combination of the equipment and the human skill created a higher level of sales. Can you say that 82% of it was because of human skill and 18% equipment? No. You never can prove that, because they are too interlocked. Just as somebody asked, "How do you separate the eggs from the milk in a cake?" It is pretty difficult.

Catalysts for the New Economy

JC: *What are the contribution of technology and the contribution of human capital to an outcome? In terms of the new economy, what are the catalysts? Is the new economy a different economy based on these different understandings?*
JF: The economy is certainly different than it was before because of many different things, such as technology, globalization, emerging requirements that did not exist before, and the fact that anybody can be in the market today from anywhere in the world. It is a different market than it was. In addition, the speed of connectivity has also certainly changed the marketplace.

I think that because conditions have changed, people have also changed. We can see it in customer requirements. Customer service demands are now much higher than they have ever been. Customer expectations are higher because customers see that it is possible for a well-functioning company to serve them better than it could ten years ago, when it did not have the technology behind it.

What is the human capital dimension of this change? The answer goes back to the basics. It is always going to be human capital, because human capital makes all of the decisions. Machines don't make the decisions, no matter how well they're programmed. Somebody has to teach them how to make the decisions. Somebody has to program the internal learning of a machine if we want to say that machines learn and grow.

But machines are just a pile of metal and plastic until a human being puts them together and writes the program, the intelligence. The human being put the intelligence into the initial program. It was not a computer that did it. The fundamental is that it is always human activity that drives everything. Machines do not drive anything except in the direction in which people push them.

JC: *What are some examples of organizations that manage their human capital with systematic and proven evaluation methods? What difference has it made for them to do that?*

JF: First, it is a good business fundamental to maintain a basic set of key performance indicators, which are both financial and human. This is not rocket science. We set up indicators of what it is we are looking for. We have already decided ahead of time that a move in this indicator affects the movement of another indicator. It might be in either direction. A human change can affect financials or a financial change can affect humans. The point is: You have to make some decision as to what the key performance indicators are for your organization, and the balance cannot be solely financial. This is shown in the work that is being done by the Brookings Institution and others that financial systems are not adequate today, and we need to recognize the valuation of intangibles.

We need a balance of key performance indicators and need to look at those indicators periodically (daily, weekly, monthly, quarterly, annually). The next step is augmenting that with project measurement. The major intellectual capital subdivisions can reside in any major project. We monitor that project, setting performance expectations on the front end. Here we note what it is we want as a result of making this investment. Then we see what we got on the back end and what it was that caused it.

Did we get what we wanted? Was it because of human issues? Was it because of financial issues? Was it because of structural issues? Was it because of customer issues? What drove it? If we have a basic set of key performance indicators and augment them periodically with project management measures and learning from both of those, then we can begin to get a payoff from all of this. The payoffs are that we can more effectively communicate performance expectations; understand what happened; understand the results of any activity; compare our results with any standards that we set internally or with benchmarks from outside; identify the gaps between what we expected and what we got; equitably and efficiently recognize and reward performance; and do better resource allocation because we know where we are getting our best ROI.

These are a half dozen different ways that that kind of measurement will pay off. What it does for us in the longer term is develop a good deal of credibility internally among individuals and helps make better return-on-investment decisions.

JC: *Are there any organizations that are doing this better than others?*

JF: Sure. It is the ones who are better long-term performers. Go back to *Built to Last*[3] or to my book *The 8 Practices*. These are the General Electrics that have for decades outperformed the rest of the market. We will find these characteristic kinds of things taking place in them. They all have key performance indicators that are balanced.

The Next Five to Ten Years

JC: *Where do you see the field of human capital going over the next five to ten years?*

JF: People and knowledge are clearly the critical factors of the future. It is not land, capital, and equipment any longer. It is people and knowledge/information. It is all the soft stuff. That is the driver. If we have got that in place, people will pick the right kind of hard assets that they need to manage.

The issue to me is whether human capital management and the whole field of intellectual capital, knowledge management, and so on as it goes forward will make connections to the business. We shouldn't start a department that goes off and does knowledge management, intellectual capital management, or human capital management. If we do that, we end up with what happened to organizational development (OD). OD was the big thing that came out in the 1960s when I first got involved in so-called personnel work. Good things came out of the National Training Lab (NTL) but it never got connected to the business. It never got measured. Business said, "That's fine. That's nice. We'll send somebody to NTL, but then we're going to go back to business."

We have got to recognize that what drives all of this is business. Business provides the capital. Business provides the rewards. Business provides the direction. Otherwise, we are operating in a vacuum. We have got to get it out of a department. We have got to make it part of the culture. If it were up to me, I would kill all of these intellectual capital departments, knowledge management departments, chief knowledge officers, and all of that. I would get them integrated into the way we're doing business on a day-to-day basis. That can be done.

[3] James C. Collins and Jerry I. Porras, *Built to Last: Successful Habits of Visionary Companies* (New York: HarperCollins, 1994).

JC: *How would you do that?*

JF: First of all, I would have to be the CEO, or be delegated her power. I would have to have the power, because we are talking about a fundamental shift in the way an organization is going to be run. I have got to create a culture where all of these things that we've been talking about are just the way we operate. We do not even talk about it any more because it is so endemic in everything we do that it is part of our decision-making process. In this process we are balanced in the way we do things. We look at the human and financial deals; we make long-term commitments; and so on. It becomes totally ingrained in everything we do. When we teach basic supervision, we don't talk about knowledge management or intellectual capital. We talk about how people and information have to come together in order to achieve organizational goals more effectively. That is knowledge management. That is human capital management. Get the damn labels off of it and talk about what it means to achieve our goals as a business organization.

Learning, sharing, active communication, connecting as human beings, giving space to people to think, and rewarding them for that is what we have to make active and stop putting labels on it. That is where the future is. I am afraid knowledge management is going to go in the same direction as OD. It's going to get a CKO, and he is going to build a system that puts out newsletters and things like that. The result will be that everybody is going to say, "Yes, yes, yes. Now let's go back to work." I would hate to see that happen.

Key Learning Points

- Well-balanced values, long-term commitment to a basic strategy, positioning in the market, positioning in the community, and alignment of culture and systems are key factors for companies with high human and financial capital performance.
- We are increasingly recognizing that people are the differentiating factor for organizations, that human effort and knowledge effort are the real levers.
- The four human capital areas of acquiring, maintaining, developing, and retaining people as assets touch on and affect every operation of an organization in measurable ways.
- There is an irreversible power shift going on in which people are now grabbing information, mobility, and connectivity through the web and the Internet. From management's standpoint, you better get with them. Otherwise, they are going to drag you along behind.

- To make a quantum leap in an organization, you have got to engage the imagination and totality of the human being.
- Human capital is the only active asset. Human capital is the one thing that can look three to five years ahead and drive the change in redesigning systems.
- Enable people to be builders of the organization of tomorrow by delegating power, authority, decision making, and allocation of resources, by demanding and encouraging innovation, and by recognizing both successes and failures.
- The key issue is whether human capital management and the whole field of intellectual capital, knowledge management, and so on will make connections to the business. Otherwise, all will become marginal by operating in a vacuum.

People Are the Owners and Investors
of Human Capital

9

Thomas Davenport is a principal in Towers Perrin's Organization and Employee Research Practice in San Francisco. He provides counsel on human capital strategy, change management, organizational effectiveness, and business strategy to clients in the service, financial, retail, manufacturing, and public sectors.

He has made a major contribution to the field by recognizing that the evolution of the new economy requires managers to think of people as owners and investors of their human capital, an asset they invest in the organizations where they work. This metaphor extends beyond the conventional thinking that people themselves are assets controlled by organizations.

Davenport focuses much of his attention on helping clients improve the people-focused elements of business strategy implementation. He is the author of the book *Human Capital: What It Is and Why People Invest It*, published by Jossey-Bass in 1999. Among the topics he covers is the challenge of attracting, retaining, and engaging workers in a fast-paced, turbulent environment.

Davenport asserts that people must update and upgrade the way they negotiate their investment of personal, intangible equity with institutions. People must use the worker-as-investor metaphor and recognize the realities of their human capital ownership and what the return on their investment of their human capital needs to be.

Organizations that perceive this change can seize an opportunity to collaborate with their workforce to improve individual and organizational performance. Doing so requires, however, that these organizations produce a return on the human capital invested by employees. Return on human capital investment is the foundation of the relationship between individual and organization. Can managers make this leap? Some already have, in organizations like Cisco Systems and Charles Schwab.

Davenport's comments on human capital management have been quoted in such publications as *Fortune, Harvard Management Update,* and *Human Capital Strategies & News.* He has appeared on CNN and made presentations to such groups as the Conference Board, the Wharton School Center for Human Resources, and the American Gas Association. His articles have appeared in *Across the Board, Management Review,* and other general management and strategy publications.

The Conversation

Workers as Capital Owners and Investors

JC: *Why do we need to start thinking of workers not as human capital, but rather as human capital owners and investors? What are the major implications of this shift in understanding?*

TD: What we are really talking about here is a change in our thinking, a change that reflects itself in a new metaphor. If we think back to the big downsizing events of the early 1990s, we remember that CEOs talked about people as costs. When organizations were downsizing, what we read about in the business press was: "We're cutting costs, and that means we're cutting staff. Therefore, people must be costs."

It's almost as though the transformation of people from cost to asset occurred overnight in the mid-1990s. Unemployment had dropped dramatically. The economy was in an upswing. Consumers were generally confident. Prices were under control. Inflation was down. It seemed as though CEOs all over North America got out of bed one morning and said, "Holy Toledo, people aren't costs any more. We need them to survive. By golly, they must be assets."

For insightful senior managers, the thinking has evolved yet another step. They recognize that employees aren't assets. Assets are passive. Assets depreciate over time. Assets are under the full control of the organization. People have none of these characteristics.

To recognize that people are human capital owners and investors is to recognize that much of the control over the employment relationship has shifted from the organization to the individual. Employees come to work every Monday morning and decide how much of their intellectual, emotional, and physical resources to invest in a business. They can withdraw all or part of that investment at almost any time. They can move it to a different organization, or change the employment relationship, or change the terms of their implicit contract with much greater flexibility than we saw a decade or so ago. Human capital is a movable asset, and people—not organizations—control its movement.

ROI$_w$

JC: *What are the implications of that?*

TD: From the standpoint of the individual, the implication is: "I have to do a much better job than I used to do of looking out for myself. I own my human capital, and nobody else is going to see to it that I've done a good job of building and investing that asset."

I define *human capital* broadly as ability, which I put into several subcategories. Knowledge, skill, and talent are the terms I use most. Things people can learn constitute *knowledge*, which is bits of information and insight one can gather. *Skill* is what people have when they develop the refined ability to apply what they know. *Talent* comprises inborn or intrinsic abilities. Take the total of those elements and multiply it by effort and you have *invested human capital*.

Viewing people as human capital investors also requires us to understand that human capital investors—like financial investors—require a return on their investment. We might refer to the return on human capital investment as ROI$_w$, the return on investment in work. You can categorize the return on investment in work in any number of ways, but I favor four specific categories: intrinsic job fulfillment, opportunity for growth and advancement, recognition for accomplishments, and financial rewards.

When people receive a high return on their investment, they are likely to continue investing and to build their investable human capital. Companies that provide a rich array of returns on human capital investment can expect employees to contribute generously of their human capital to the success of the business.

JC: *Who has the main responsibility for building human capital: employees or companies?*

TD: When it comes to building their human capital, employees have heard a single message for the better part of the last decade. Companies are fond of telling people, "You're in charge of your career. You're in charge of your learning. It's your responsibility to take the initiative. We as an organization will help you by providing some pathways and resources, but we want you to take the initiative."

Many companies create a dilemma for themselves in the way they try to manage their expenditures on training. They try to focus their training investments on a few key areas that contribute directly to employees' abilities to do narrowly defined jobs better. Indeed, classic human capital theory says organizations should pay for training only when it helps an individual build some element of knowledge or skill that benefits the company directly.

But this theory rests too much on a narrow view of the benefits of learning. The reason is that the training, or more broadly, learning opportunities convey a triple benefit. First, learning certainly helps the organization by building elements of human capital that help people do their jobs better. Better-qualified employees produce more for their companies. Second, by helping people increase knowledge and skills, learning enhances the human capital that employees have to invest in generating ROI_w for themselves. As the individual endowment of human capital grows, so does the potential for earning a high return. Third, learning opportunities are enjoyable and gratifying in their own right. Jean Piaget, the famous child psychologist, was one of the first to point out that people simply enjoy learning. Thus, the chance to learn brings a kind of intrinsic fulfillment that is, merely of itself, a form of return on human capital investment. Companies that scrimp on training or focus learning opportunities too much on specific tasks required by today's jobs might miss some or even all of these benefits.

Everyone a Manager

JC: *What difference does it make that we are moving to a situation where everyone will manage something, but nobody will only manage, and where we all need to know things to succeed?*

TD: One of the main implications of this notion of widespread management responsibility is that the necessity to make decisions about resource allocation, service delivery, and even competitive strategy no longer rests solely with people who have "manager" in their titles. For one thing, the world simply moves too fast for a few people to make all the decisions quickly enough. Plus, as a legacy of the downsizing of the early 1990s, we simply have fewer managers per employee than we otherwise might. The remaining managers can't do all of the managerial tasks required.

Another issue is that technology and more sophisticated information management and knowledge management mean that people know things and get information that was previously in the hands of managers only. All of this produces a situation in which nonmanagement employees have the information required to make decisions, and organizations need them to do so.

It is remarkable how freely people communicate between the top and the bottom of the organization through email these days. Prior to email, an individual's chance of getting a message directly to the chief executive of a company was close to nil. Now, in many organizations, people have a pretty high probability that the CEO will look at their messages and may even generate a personal response.

Some CEOs have taken it on themselves to keep open that line of communication. Dave Pottruck (co-CEO of Charles Schwab) is one whom I know. If you send Dave an email, you will get a response. There are other CEOs who act the same way. People have the kind of access to top management leaders that used to be restricted to formally designated managers.

JC: *Pottruck has made a very extensive, special effort to cultivate leadership across the organization. He is quite impressive in his collaboration among his peers.*
TD: He definitely has a collaborative style with other senior executives. He believes that whether his organization succeeds or fails depends on how individual people within the company either are, or are not, committed to the organization and engaged in their work. Granted, Charles Schwab has had its share of financial challenges in since 2000 or so, but I believe the basic philosophy of valuing people still pertains.

I know CEOs who would say in their private moments, "You know, it's really just five guys who run this company. As far as all of the employees are concerned, I hope they do a good job, I hope they care. But, at the end of the day, however irksome turnover is, it's these five guys who make all of the decisions that matter around here." Broad-scale employee commitment and engagement are to them just hollow words.

Enlightened CEOs not only don't think that way, they don't act that way, don't measure that way, and don't behave in ways that deny the importance of line employees. Pottruck is acting in a way that bespeaks a different metaphor. Whether he realizes it or not, he treats people as owners and investors of the human capital that is his organization's most valuable asset. And this is key—human capital is the asset; the people who own it are not.

The Right Opportunities

JC: *Do enlightened CEOs have to be involved with everybody?*

TD: In an increasingly democratic workplace, there's nobody in the organization who does not want to be committed and engaged, given the opportunity. If we do the research, and look back over just about every kind of labor market we have had, from downsizing to tight labor markets, we find that somewhere between two-thirds and three-quarters of the workforce at any given time will say, "If I have the right opportunities, I want to stay where I am. I want to stay with one company for a long time, if it provides me with a reason to become committed and engaged."

Turnover happens when companies fail to provide those opportunities, fail to provide an attractive return on investment in work. CEOs will moan and groan about the current generation of workers, how people are less loyal and less dedicated than the workforce used to be. Certainly attitudes do evolve, but day in and day out, from one labor market to the next, people would rather stay where they are, build the human capital they need, and continue to reinvest it if the company can give them a continuum of opportunity.

Sometimes when I'm talking about human capital, people will say: "Isn't it really just knowledge workers, or the few strategically critical people who we ought to be thinking about?" In response, I give the example of a busboy in a restaurant. The busboy starts the first day, and all he knows is that he's supposed to clean the dishes off and take them into the kitchen. But suppose that one day the busboy has an epiphany about the contribution he can make to the organization. His epiphany leads him to think: "If I break fewer dishes, the cost of running this place goes down and profit goes up. If I clean the tables more quickly, the turnover through the evening—the dining hours—will be higher. We'll get more people in and out, and we can get more revenue. If I smile and I'm more polite to people, they'll have a better experience in my restaurant, and they'll come back and they'll mention it to their friends."

These kinds of realizations can be encouraged in every employee in every organization. Now the restaurant has a busboy who cares, who understands his contribution, who understands how his investment of effort, personality, and insight benefits the restaurant.

It is the restaurant owner's and manager's responsibility to make sure that when the busboy makes that investment, he gets a return on his investment. This return, as we said earlier, can come in terms of higher financial reward—perhaps even profit sharing and the like—and also in the form of recognition for a job well done and intrinsic satisfaction from having really contributed. When I use that example, people say, "Oh well, I guess it isn't just knowledge workers, or the critical few people in R&D or out in the field selling. We'll be better off if everybody is committed and engaged."

Factors in Motivation

JC: *We were just talking about the return on human capital investment, which you defined earlier. Don't most organizations concentrate on the financial aspects of ROI$_w$?*

TD: Companies tend to concentrate on the financial parts, because that is where the human resource department is focused to a large extent. I do not mean to be bashing HR staff in this discussion. They have an important role to play in the management and husbanding of human capital, but human resources functions are inclined to think a lot about the formulaic or programmatic elements of return on investment. On the one hand, these are not trivial. Employees are naturally very concerned about how they are paid and how their health benefits work, which are very important. But there's also a whole intangible, nonfinancial side that's also very important.

Another way to think about this is that the compensation and benefits side is the ante companies need merely to get into the game. No organization can hope to hire good people without being at parity with the competition. That means the organization must offer a financial reward package that the individual views as fair relative to what other companies are providing. Employees will define a fair level as the amount that others with similar human capital and a similar level of performance will receive from a current or prospective employer. As was shown by researchers like Frederick Hertzberg in the 1950s and 1960s, once an organization reaches a level of fairness in its financial rewards, those elements of ROI$_w$ no longer figure as prominently in the individual's motivation. Below the perceived fairness level, inadequate financial rewards are demotivators, but above the fairness line, they cease to be the most critical factors in the motivation calculus. If the organization wants to win in the marketplace by having more-engaged people with higher-quality human capital, then it must concentrate on the nonfinancial elements of the return on human capital investment. Market-level compensation is needed to play, but the opportunity to win comes from other ROI_w elements.

JC: *In other words, you can't ignore the basics.*

TD: An organization must have a foundation of fair financial compensation so that it can get the people focused on the intangible aspects. And those intangible aspects are controlled largely by the first-line manager. That's why managers are so important in all of this. The real needed-to-win elements of return on human capital investment come from the local manager.

Leveraging the System

JC: *So managers play a critical role in leveraging the system?*

TD: Yes, absolutely. In fact, managers have four critical roles that I have observed in the whole human capital development and investment process. The first critical thing a manager does is to negotiate the deal, the psychological contract between employee and organization. It is the manager who sits down with the employee, however formally or informally, and says, "Here's what we as an organization, and I as a manager of this unit, want from you in terms of human capital investment. And, here's what we're proposing to deliver to you as a return on that investment."

The employee sitting on the other side of the table says, "Ok, here's the human capital I have to invest, and here's what I want in terms of my return on that investment." Crafting that deal is the first critical thing that the manager has to do. It begins with the very first contact between an employment candidate and the hiring manager. That contract may evolve as time goes on in many different ways as employees build human capital, as organizations change strategy, and as people's life events take place. The implicit contract is always on the table.

JC: *What are the other three roles?*

TD: The second role of a manager in a human capital world is advising people; in effect, the manager is a human capital investment counselor. This is the ongoing process of helping people do their own investment planning. This role involves answering questions such as: "How can I as an employee grow my human capital endowment? What kinds of projects will pay me the highest returns? Which projects are cooler, which have greater visibility in the company, which will help me learn the most, which have the highest risk? What forms of human capital will have the highest value in this company today, tomorrow, or a year from now?" While people are in control of their own human capital investment, it does not mean they cannot seek advice, and a manager can be an important advisor.

The third role is the manager as the direct provider of some elements of the ROI_w. Recognition of employee performance is one of the most important of those. Informal recognition is incredibly important to people. People may like getting the plaque, may want to be employee of the month, might feel good seeing their names mentioned in the newsletter, but they really value it when the manager takes them aside and says, "You did a really great job on that project," or when the manager says in front of the team, "She was a real superstar on that last project. It couldn't have been done without her." That has incredible value to people. And it is free. It is a return on human capital investment, and it has virtually no price tag from the company's perspective.

The fourth manager role is what I call risk management. If I'm an owner/investor of my own human capital, I must manage the risk involved in investing my human capital, just as I must manage risk in my financial portfolio. In some economic climates, like the downsizings that occurred several times in the 1990s, we would define *human capital risk* as the potential loss of a job. But the definition of risk has expanded. In the early twenty-first century, we must also define risk as the potential devaluation of human capital, failing to learn something that keeps the employee on an equal intellectual footing with peers and competitors.

To manage their human capital risk, people need objective, up-to-date information on the future investment landscape within the organization. They want managers who can answer questions such as: "Are we likely to make a major strategic shift in the next 18 months? Does the manager of Project A have a reputation for successful completion? If I take Project A and it fails, how much am I hurt by that?"

Customizing the Deal

JC: *What is the significance of choice and flexibility in the new model of human capital?*
TD: What every individual ultimately cares about is her own deal. On an intellectual level, an employee may be curious about your deal or mine, and she certainly cares about parity. But, at the end of the day, the only deal they really focus on is their own, and they want to feel that the deal is customized for them. People realize, for example, that the organization's compensation structure for any position is largely predetermined. Certainly benefit plans, retirement plans, 401(k) plans, and the like are largely ad-

ministratively defined. But a whole lot of that nonfinancial ROI$_w$ we talked about earlier is up to the manager to deliver. If I am a smart manager, I know how to create an environment for an individual employee that makes it feel like each person has a flexible, customized deal.

We sometimes get into debates with clients who say, "We can't afford to have a different deal for everyone. It would be an administrative nightmare." I like to use a different metaphor here. I call it the "tootsie roll pop" structure of rewards. Tootsie roll pop candy comes in a variety of flavors, but all flavors have the same chocolate center. The chocolate center is analogous to the structural elements of return on investment in work, the elements that are essentially the same for everyone. But the outside coating comes in many different flavors. You can have grape, raspberry, orange, chocolate. This outside coating is like the nonfinancial reward elements, things like choice of projects, flexible learning opportunities, choice of work location, and control over work schedule. These can vary a lot from one person to the next, even if all of the administratively controlled ROI$_w$ elements are fundamentally the same for similarly situated employees. There are a lot of things that really make a difference day to day that the manager can individualize.

JC: *Are we really talking here about menu choices?*
TD: You can think of it as a menu, a form of total flex, if you will. In the compensation and benefits world, flexible benefits have been around for quite a while, and many large organizations have them. Why not have total flexibility? Why not even have flexibility in compensation, letting people make trade-offs between elements of fixed and variable pay? Why not, wherever possible, give every person the opportunity to define his own deal to the maximum extent?

Achieving Strategic Goals

JC: *What role does human capital have in achieving strategic goals? If everybody has choices and flexibility, how do you make it work optimally for all stakeholders?*
TD: We always need to start with an organization's strategic goals or, more precisely, with business unit strategic goals. A *business unit* is a part of an organization that produces a coherent set of product or service offerings focused on a market and faces off against a more or less identifiable group of competitors. Business units are where we need to look for competitive advantage in the classic terms of product differentiation, cost efficiency, or niche focus.

When a business unit defines the focus of its prospective competitive advantage, management then needs to figure out what organizational capabilities are required to be successful. The question would be: What do we have to be good at if we're going to win in this particular marketplace with this particular line of business? One critical capability for most organizations is the effective acquisition, growth, and retention of human capital. Thus, we can typically define human capital management as a necessary collective ability of the business.

As an organization formulates its list of critical capabilities, management usually discovers that people play a key role in many capabilities. Take, for example, an organization capability called *product development and introduction*, defined as the business unit's collective ability to develop great new products quickly and get them to market ahead of competitors. It's not hard to see how having creative, knowledgeable, energetic people is critical to building the product development and introduction capability. In fact, look down the whole list of a business unit's required capabilities, and you will see just how important people—owners and investors of human capital—really are. An organization must have creative product developers, insightful market researchers, and tenacious salespeople. In short, the organization needs a whole series of human capital owners whose abilities and behaviors allow them to figure out what the market wants, develop an offering quickly, and get it out there.

Human Capital: The Only Active Capital

JC: *One of our other contributors, Jac Fitz-enz, says that human capital is the only active capital; everything else is passive. Do you agree?*

TD: I like to quote one of my colleagues. He says that all forms of capital except human capital are inert. All other assets are effectively dormant until acted upon by human capital. Human capital is itself an asset, and it's also the catalyst for other assets to become valuable.

Cisco Systems is an example of a company that realizes the several levels of value associated with human capital. Cisco went through a series of acquisitions, multiple dozens over the last decade. On the one hand, Cisco's strategy was based on its need to acquire the manifestations of human capital investment: patents, ideas, products, and concepts. On the other hand, it also wanted to acquire the human capital needed to continue innovating.

This strategy means that a key organizational capability for Cisco was the integration of acquired organizations, and it became very, very good at it. It can get the fruits of smart people's brains by making an acquisition, but to keep those brains and keep them engaged, that is the real challenge. Cisco has done both well.

Cisco comes to mind for another reason. In 2001, Cisco Systems bowed to economic pressure and laid off 6,000 workers. The organization offered the employees an interesting choice, however: leave the company with six months' severance, or maintain an affiliation with Cisco by staying on the payroll at one-third salary and working full time for a not-for-profit. Something like 80 employees chose the not-for-profit opportunity. They preserved their connection with Cisco and made their reentry into the organization an easier prospect in the future. Eighty people doesn't sound like a lot, but the mere existence of this kind of opportunity says Cisco values human capital and wants to preserve a relationship with people who have what the company needs.

JC: *The company demonstrated that their employees are important to it. It is a human values equation. It thinks that you are an important part of its space, and it is going to take the time to show that, not just in some showy ways, but in a way that is really serious.*

TD: Here is another example. In the early part of 1999, the stock market trading volume became huge, regularly hitting more than a billion shares daily on the major exchanges. This upsurge made for some heavy workloads for people working in the securities industry. At Charles Schwab, they referred to this phenomenon as *market storm*. People at Schwab were going crazy. They were working intensely and getting burned out. One of the things the company did was to open the cafeteria to all employees, providing free meals. The message was: "You people are working seven days a week, 24 hours a day. The food's free. We know you'd like to be home with your families, and we'd like you to be there too, but we know you're not in many cases, so the least we can do is make your working life as easy as possible."

The cafeteria stayed open and free for a long time while people got the market storm under control. It probably added up to a fairly high cost, but here is a case where Dave Pottruck and his peers said: "If people are not committed, engaged, and working hard to serve this unprecedented transaction volume, we're not going to get through this." He backed up his belief in the importance of people in a tangible way.

JC: *Are there any other characteristics of the psychological contract between individuals and organizations to add to that?*

TD: The important point is that the psychological contract is multidirectional. The back-and-forth vectors run among at least three points: individual, manager, and organization. A key form of commitment focuses on how I feel about my peers, teammates, coworkers. They figure into the deal as well. In effect, this adds a fourth party to the crafting and delivery of the deal.

Turning Raw Intelligence into Information Capital

JC: *Companies like Cisco and Charles Schwab clearly depend on the discretionary efforts of smart people. How does an organization turn the raw stuff of intelligence into information capital?*

TD: Here is how I like to think about it. At the root of the intellectual capital tree lie data, bits of knowledge. We transform data into information by acting on it. We then add other data so that we can begin to notice patterns and glean insights. We format data and report it to add another modicum of value. When we begin to notice relationships among data elements and highlight these by the way we format and report, we have taken data and made information out of it.

By adding analysis, looking for root causes and trends, and drawing conclusions, we then transform information into intelligence. And, if we then take intelligence, sort through what really matters to the organization, and distribute it to people who can really use it, we have created organizational intelligence.

We can build distributed intelligence into the planning process, and we can require it to be part of the decision-making calculus. The result is that we have created information capital. With information capital, we start winning in the marketplace, because we have made sure that more of our employees know more about the marketplace than do our competitors. When an organization transforms intelligence into information capital, it has created a real asset.

The Six Factors of "the Deal"

JC: *How does the organization create the environment that encourages the human capital contribution?*

TD: The core of it is the return on investment in work. This goes back to the psychological contract, or "the deal." That is the single most critical element, but making the most of the deal requires a framework of supporting factors. I have identified six factors that make up this framework in which the deal between individual and organization works best for both parties.

JC: *What are the six factors?*

TD: One is *understanding*. Organization and individual must both understand, first of all, that an implicit deal exists. Both parties must know what is expected of each. The deal may not be written, but it must be understood. That means it has to be spoken and discussed. This goes back to the manager's role in negotiation. When people understand their deal and the organization understands the deal that's on the table, then the return on human capital investment has more power.

Second, both parties must *accept* the deal. Each must believe that the deal is fair, something each can live with. Company and employee must both believe that what each receives from the arrangement is commensurate with the investment each is expected to make.

The third factor is *strategic alignment*. Each employee must be able to say, "I know what they want from me, and I also know why they want it. I know where we're headed as an organization and why my contribution is important."

These first three elements form the context for maximum human capital investment.

The fourth element in the deal framework is a consistent focus on *competence building*. This means that the growth opportunity, the opportunity to get smarter and better, and to learn consistently is first among equals among the elements of return on human capital investment. Organizations that are truly focused on competency building, on increasing people's human capital, enjoy a multiplier on the ROI_w they generate.

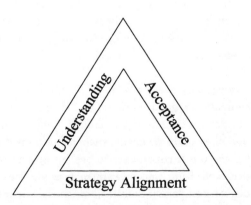

FIGURE 9.1 The Framework for Human Capital Investment

Framework factor number five is *autonomy*. The work environment in which companies expect people to invest human capital must be rich in opportunities for autonomous work. Autonomy means self-governance, and it's different from empowerment. When I hear "empowerment," I always think of a manager with a sack full of power. The manager reaches into his sack, and he hands little bits of power to people and says, "I hereby empower you. I own the power, I'm the manager, and I'm magnanimously choosing to give some of it to you." This is very much a one-way, unilateral hand-off.

Autonomy is different. Autonomy is present when the manager doesn't merely dole out power to employees. Instead, the manager says to employees: "You've got the power to begin with. You've got the human capital I want. You're free, within some reasonable bounds that we'll agree on, to invest it in ways that benefit you and the company. You are self-governing in this. Now go forth and do your job, using the knowledge and skills that you have, and tell me when you're done."

That can sound like a disingenuous point of view, I realize, because some jobs lend themselves to greater autonomy than others. We don't want the busboy deciding to juggle the cups to entertain the guests. Nevertheless, the busboy and the restaurant manager must explicitly discuss and agree upon the degree to which the busboy can be autonomous. They might agree that he should not juggle cups because that is dangerous and he's probably not competent to do it, but he can make many autonomous decisions about how he's going to bus the tables.

The other thing about empowerment is that it can also be destructive when either managers or employees think that empowerment is always advisable, or always guarantees success. After all, it doesn't help to empower a 98-pound middle linebacker. If a person does not possess the human capital to succeed in a job, all the empowerment in the world will not create success. Self-governance gives us a choice, but it also gives us the responsibility to make sure that individuals have the information and knowledge to make an intelligent choice (for instance, to decide to be a tennis player rather than a middle linebacker).

JC: *Is there an authenticity question here?*
TD: Yes, authenticity is a good word for it. To me, *authenticity* means consistently reinforcing the building of human capital where it matters most. This notion of *reinforcement* is the sixth factor in the deal framework. Reinforcement is the direct connection among investment of human capital, performance, and ROI_w received. The most obvious examples are performance-focused compensation plans, which help reinforce the connection. The important caveat is that, whether the reinforcing reward is

financial or nonfinancial, it must be delivered in a system that employees consider just. People believe justice is present when two requirements are met. First, the administrative procedures for distributing rewards must be consistent for everyone all the time, free from manager self-interest, and conducted openly. Second, each individual must believe that what he received from the application of those procedures fairly reflected his contribution and performance. In other words, everyone must receive what he thinks is deserved.

Those are the six factors that make up the deal-delivery framework. Organizations must ensure full understanding of the deal, ensure that it is accepted by all parties, and ensure that employees know how mutual adherence to the deal supports strategic success for the organization. Beyond that, companies must focus on building competence, creating an environment characterized by autonomy, and reinforcing the elements of the exchange.

When I lay out these points, people sometimes ask me, "How can a manager pay attention to all of those six factors and still find time to manage?" My answer is: "If she is effectively working on all six elements, she is managing."

Commitment and Engagement

JC: *Would you like to comment about anything else concerning how important levels of effort, commitment, and engagement are in the human capital initiative?*
TD: I want to make sure people differentiate between commitment and engagement. Commitment is an organizational phenomenon. *Commitment*

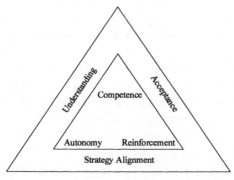

FIGURE 9.2 The Expanded Human Capital Investment Framework

is defined as how the employee feels about the organization, the bond the employee perceives between himself and the company. In contrast, people's feelings about their jobs—are the jobs interesting, challenging, rewarding, important?—is *engagement*.

If you think about these two concepts, it sheds light on some of the people management problems we find in places like Silicon Valley. Many companies in the Valley offer engaging, stimulating jobs at the frontier of innovation. Those same companies, however, have trouble building commitment in their workforces. Part of the problem is that managers often don't realize that commitment comes in several forms.

JC: *What kinds of commitment are there?*

TD: The kind that managers recognize most readily is *programmatic commitment*, which leads people to stay with organizations simply because they can't afford to leave. Stock options that take years to vest, pension plans that are not portable, retention bonuses that aren't payable for a year— these are the ties that bind for people who are programmatically committed. If I tell you: "Jay, if you stay for a year, I'll give you a big bonus," your predisposition to stay for a year may be very high. You may be very unhappy during that year, you may not care about the success of the company, you may not work very hard, but you'll stick around. Retention programs are often very good ways to solicit high levels of commitment from very unhappy people.

JC: *Do you mean golden handcuffs?*

TD: Golden handcuffs are a classic example. There is some research that suggests that high programmatic commitment has at best no correlation— and may have a negative correlation—with discretionary effort on the job.

The next form of commitment is *loyalty-based commitment*. It involves how I feel about my peers, my team in general, the people with whom I have contact every day. In effect, loyalty-based commitment depends on a sense of obligation to the organization. Unlike programmatic commitment, there is a relationship between loyalty-based commitment and motivation to perform.

The highest level of commitment, which is the one that people want to reach and organizations want them to achieve, is called *attitudinal commitment*. People who have attitudinal commitment identify with, are involved in, and enjoy membership in the organization. Attitudinal commitment has a strong correlation with individual willingness to invest discretionary effort to perform well.

In the Silicon Valley example, people are often highly engaged in their work, they love their high-tech projects, but they don't give a darn where

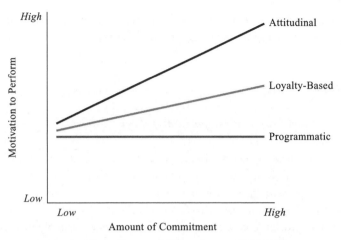

FIGURE 9.3 Three Forms of Commitment Yield Different Performance Levels

they do it. They may say, "If you don't let me bring my dog to work, or if I don't like the way my teammate looked at me, or if I question the company's last strategic move, I'll just pick up my project—and maybe my whole project team—and drive down the freeway to work for another company." These people are highly engaged, but not at all committed.

What companies obviously want is both high commitment and engagement. Commitment without engagement means loyalty without energy. Engagement without commitment means energy without a long-term focus. Projects get done, but there's no continuum of human capital investment and ROI_w that the company and the individual can count on. Organizations that fret about turnover usually think only about commitment. They worry about how to get people to stay there. They ought to be thinking about how they can get people to stay there *and* continue to invest the highest possible levels of human capital. Regardless of whether labor markets are down or up, companies must find ways to build both commitment and engagement among their critical contributors.

JC: *Aren't you really talking about increasing job satisfaction?*

TD: That's a great question. In fact, what I'm talking about is precisely *not* job satisfaction. In trying to link rewards with performance, managers often focus their attention on job satisfaction. They reason that, if job satisfaction goes up, so will performance. Actually, psychologists have had a difficult time finding a causal link running from job satisfaction to performance. The key does turn out to be rewards, but the causation runs the other way.

Satisfaction does not engender performance. Performance, reinforced through the mechanism of rewards, produces satisfaction.

What We All Want

JC: *Does all this mean that everyone wants the same things out of work?*

TD: As we've been saying, what all of us really care about is our own individual deal. This implies that two people in similar jobs may want very different things from their work experiences.

It's helpful to remember that not all of the elements of return on investment in work are created equal. Earlier, we noted the obvious point that some rewards are financial, while others are not. But there's a more subtle way to think about how rewards differ. Some are fundamentally transactional: They come from an arm's-length exchange between the company and the individual. Some form of agreement—formal or informal—governs how these rewards are administered. Relational ROI_w depends—intuitively enough—on relationships. It is less tangible, less contractual, more implicit, and more dependent on interactions among the people in an organization. Either form of reward may come in an organizational context, if a broad set of formal or informal rules influences reward distribution, or in a narrower job context, if working as a group isn't instrumental to getting a particular reward.

Pay and benefits form the hard-dollar part of a worker's return on human capital investment. They fall on the transactional part of the continuum. Referring back to some earlier points, they engender programmatic commitment. Incentive payments often focus more on individual job performance, but are nevertheless transactional.

Below the horizontal line are the more relational ROI_w elements. Some result from specific job performance—like informal recognition—while others come within an organizational context, like advancement up the organizational ladder. Consistent with what we said earlier, the real power to encourage engagement and to strengthen commitment lies with the factors below the horizontal axis.

The Business Strategy Imperative

JC: *Any final thoughts?*

TD: The deal between individual and organization is incredibly important. It establishes the reciprocal exchange that reflects what each part wants and

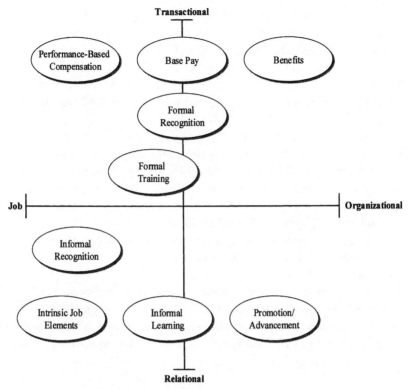

FIGURE 9.4 Factors Influencing Reward Distribution

what each has to offer in trade. But this isn't just nice-to-know HR-speak. Human capital investment takes place in a strategic, performance-focused context. Ultimately, neither party benefits if the organization doesn't achieve competitive success. That's why an organization's efforts to define and deliver a deal that increases engagement and commitment isn't just an HR requirement, it's a business strategy imperative.

Key Learning Points

- People are the owners and investors of their human capital. Human capital is a movable asset, and people—not organizations—control its movement.
- All forms of capital except human capital are inert.
- Human capital can be defined as knowledge, skills, and talent. The total of those elements multiplied by level of effort results in invested human capital.

- The return on human capital investment is ROI_w or the return on investment in work. ROI_w can be seen as having four specific categories: intrinsic job fulfillment, opportunity for growth and advancement, recognition for accomplishments, and financial rewards.

- When people receive a high return on their investment, they are likely to continue investing and to build their investable human capital.

- What every individual ultimately cares about is her own deal.

- A good manager knows how to create an environment in which each person feels that he has a flexible, customized deal.

- Six factors make up the framework of the deal: understanding the deal, acceptance by all parties, strategic alignment, competence building, autonomy, and reinforcement.

- Commitment without engagement means loyalty without energy. Engagement without commitment means energy without long-term focus.

- Job satisfaction does not engender performance. Performance, reinforced through the mechanism of rewards, produces satisfaction.

- An organization's efforts to define and deliver a deal that increases engagement and commitment is not just an HR requirement, it is a business strategy imperative.

Shared Values—The Prerequisite for
Knowledge Sharing and Creation

10

The role of values in knowledge generation and transfer is often over-looked and underappreciated. An organization's underlying values will either support or disrupt its effectiveness in achieving its goals. If the leadership acts from one set of values, the middle management from another, and the line workers from a third set of values, the dissonance in values will undermine the best-intentioned and-financed effort. While technology and methodology are enablers as well, it is how the values align in an enterprise that will determine if knowledge is shared and used for desired outcomes. This is as true in a small, single-site organization as it is in global, extended enterprises.

Don Tyler is an outstanding practitioner in values alignment. He works with client organizations to integrate their cultures and values into their leadership and business strategies. He is well versed both in the instruments for discerning the actual values at work in an organization—versus the stated ones—and in developing and implementing strategies for organizational transformation. He knows that one size does not fit all. The values have to fit the purpose of the organization.

Despite the accelerated movement toward global collaboration, the values of one culture cannot readily supersede another. People in one part of an organization or location may not feel that the values framework of the larger enterprise is significant or appropriate to their local domain. The loss of effectiveness, creativity, and efficiency may be great in these cases, but the cause may be little noticed. The values statements may be on the office walls but may not be embraced by the relevant stakeholders.

Tyler discusses how the array of values can be identified and the path of change to bring about alignment. This may involve the reality that different sets of values may need to be recognized and respected in the same enterprise. This recognition can provide a new perspective for getting beyond the either-or dominant model to one where diverse value sets can be the bases for innovation and even greater opportunity.

Tyler is a consultant with the Catalyst Consulting Team, where he works with organizations to create cultures around a core set of values. Based on his approach, he assists high-tech companies to attract and retain employees, provides executive coaching, and conducts organization-wide values audits that aid in redefining leadership competencies and organizational processes that sustain corporate value.

Tyler works internationally to implement dispersed-teams effectiveness training and global best practices.

The Conversation

Knowledge as a Social Construct

JC: *How is knowledge a social construct that emerges through interactions?*
DT: The power of information and the power to create new knowledge come from being able to leverage it and move it around among people. The magical part of it all is that it is not like the other commodities where if I have it and I give it to you, I lose it. Many different authors have talked about the notion that if I have it and I give it to you, then we both have it, and we can both work with it. The only way to make that happen is through interactions. That does not have to be face to face, but it means you have got to have people sharing with people at some level. Without that social context, the need for knowledge management is not there because it is all inside your head and only you can work with it. Knowledge management comes to the fore when you have to relate it to other people.

JC: *Are you saying that sharing with other people makes it a meaningful dimension?*
DT: Without that, there is no opportunity for the sharing of ideas, which creates new knowledge and new applications for existing knowledge. I tend

not to think about it so much as sharing knowledge but more as creating meaning as we are interacting. Powerful conversations are created when people ask questions. Inquiry is far more important to creating knowledge than advocacy. We can both advocate positions as well as put them in a knowledge repository, and that is interesting and useful. But when we get into a dialogue, we inquire more deeply into "What did you mean?" Then, we rapidly create new connections and insights. In that sense, knowledge management is usefully explored from the perspective of relationships rather than from the viewpoint of stocks of static information alone.

The Role of Shared Values in Knowledge

JC: *Why are values key to relationships in knowledge transfer?*
DT: I use a simple formula which is: values + skills = capabilities. By that I mean, the values provide the meaning and the motivation (the willingness) to learn new skills (new abilities). Without both of those in play—values and skills—people rarely sustain the new skills in stressful situations because the inner motivation to do so (the values component) is missing or weak.

An example may help to make the point. Think about a time when you were most motivated to learn something new. No one likely had to tell you to do it or to practice hard. The reason was likely that you highly valued the new capability and were self-motivated to learn. Alternatively, think about a time when you were required to learn a new skill and didn't see the value of it. Learning probably occurred but required an external source of motivation (likely a parent or teacher standing nearby and providing the encouragement).

JC: *Does that work in the same ways with different cultures in other countries around the world, and how does that affect how knowledge is used, in reference to the impediments or the opportunities for knowledge sharing?*
DT: Yes and no. Values create meaning for all of us, but the interpretation of what people mean by a given value and how they prioritize it can be very different, leading to the opportunity to misunderstand each other and to mistakes in sharing knowledge.

Asian cultures, for example, are built on values of duty, and Western society, especially in the United States, is a culture built on individual rights. These are opposite sides of the same coin. Western society is very proud of our tradition about individual rights. The flipside of that coin is duty and responsibility to the whole, to the community, or to the society. When you put that into context in an organization, the whole concept of responsibility and loyalty starts to take on a very different frame.

JC: *To what extent do shared values have to be embraced to ensure success in a knowledge management initiative?*
DT: I believe that high levels of knowledge sharing and creation will only be sustained after meaningful relationships are established and constantly nourished. The link here, for me, is that relationships are built most effectively on shared values. Working interdependently, for example, requires that we develop trust in our relationships before we can truly engage in sharing the most important parts of ourselves and our unique knowledge. Without deeper relationships, we will likely only share superficial knowledge.

JC: *Would shared values make the difference in that communication?*
DT: Yes, shared values or shared meaning. So often when we talk about values, we talk about very big constructs. I think it is important to break values down into their finest element before you can understand and say, "Ah, I see the difference between what you mean by trust, or what I mean by teamwork, or what somebody else means by collaboration," for example. Until you get to some shared definitions, you really have not got very much and can actually be fooled by it. Getting to commonly agreed-on behaviors to express the values is also important, so that we can hold each other accountable to walking the talk.

Values Choices and Effective Knowledge Transfer

JC: *How do people's values choices enable or disable knowledge transfer in an organization?*
DT: I will try to explain that. In most organizations I consult with, people are stressed or worried about their security. When we are threatened, it is a common reaction to be cautious, withhold information, and protect ourselves from embarrassment.

If we try to understand why people do not share the real knowledge, we find that most commonly they are in a fairly defensive mode and pretending to cooperate but really holding back, being fear-driven, and so on. In these instances, we are likely operating from values of competition, self-preservation, or self-worth. At the same time, we may espouse values of self-actualization, synergy, and collaboration. To be ready to engage in real knowledge sharing, we need values underpinning our behavior such as trust, empathy, and collaboration.

In our consulting practice, we have done a lot of measurement of numerous organizations. We find that an organization might display a set of values on the wall, but the employees have very different values when measured in our audit.

How the employees prioritize values can be radically different. Depending on whether their values priorities are at all close, we will have real gaps when it is time to share really powerful knowledge.

Our values create the frame of how we see ourselves, of what we value most. If we can get to understanding that, most of the time, the values that people are holding behind the scenes in their conversations are different, then we can surface those and move them to be common, and we will have a much richer conversation.

Human Capital: The Glue of the Knowledge Enterprise

JC: *What is the role of human capital, in your view, in a knowledge enterprise?*

DT: A knowledge enterprise is all about interactions among people. I like very much Hubert Saint-Onge's model of looking at human, structural, and customer capital. Human capital is the glue that holds them together, and human relationships are built on shared values. We have heard over and over again in organizations that the key knowledge is in people's heads. It kind of moves around with them as opposed to residing in the organization. This knowledge actually resides in the people in the organization. In that sense, human capital is absolutely central to the whole and holds the other two pieces together.

JC: *Is human capital, in your view, what people know and have control over?*

DT: I think we can get leverage on human capital to the extent that we can get people to share it and actually interact. It is in interaction that they generate knowledge. I think we each have control of our own human capital, but our human capital is not very valuable to the organization until we get in and play with each other. That is where the shared values come in and are important.

JC: *How do we find out what the workforce, the management, and customers actually value?*

DT: That can be actually pretty straightforward. There are three methodologies that we use. With the workforce, one method is to simply measure the values using an online instrument that asks people multiple-choice questions against a whole matrix of values possibilities and determine what the highest priorities of values are.

The second way is to listen to their conversations. We can collect stories across the organization and from its customers. In one organization, we trained workers to conduct 400 interviews with people, collecting stories of the great moments when that organization was doing amazing things, and then we did a content analysis of those stories. Embedded in the stories were all of the key values, the best values, as it were, of that organization, and we were able to roll those forward and understand what values were important just by listening to people's stories and the repeating patterns in those stories.

On the customer side, the same methodology is straightforward as well. Interviewing customers and asking them about their experiences with organizations will surface the value proposition from those customers and their reasons that they really wanted to do business with you.

Again, since values are carried in our language, we can code those conversations against the values and do a content analysis of the predominant values that repeat over and over again, which actually underpin or drive people's buying decisions.

JC: *Which people do you have to talk to, or communicate with, to get a useful picture of what they value?*

DT: I am amazed at how holographic organizations are. The traditional view is that you have to talk to a lot of customers at a lot of different levels. That has not been my experience. My experience is that the repeating patterns emerge very early in the data.

Companies typically organize their customer base into levels, including their "platinum" accounts, or "gold" accounts, or whatever they call them. Dealing with a few of those and a few of each of the different customer segments, we have pretty quickly identified the pattern. Our view is that we have been able to do as few as 20 or 30 customer interviews in large organizations and come back with suggestive data that say, "Here's where the customers are really hot." A lot of that will depend on how complex one's business is. If you are selling many, many different products, then you will have more explorations.

Our experience is, though, that people buy very much based on the brand and what the company stands for. The brand and the emotional connection to that brand have got a lot to do with why people do business with the organization. That's where the shared values are held. The company brand is its external values promise to the marketplace.

JC: *If you can tap into that, you will get a pretty good sense?*

DT: Absolutely. In a couple of other instances, we actually asked customers to anonymously fill out the values survey, which was the same survey that was being used by the employees, so that we could map the customer values directly to the employee values. That is possible as well, although that is a lot more intrusive.

Much more commonly, it is getting stories and then doing a content analysis of those stories with a good values model behind it that will surface the repeating pattern.

People Telling Their Stories

JC: *And you find that customers are fairly open to putting in the time involved in that?*

DT: People love to tell their stories, and these do not have to be long, long interviews. You can do these in 10 or 15 minutes and collect a couple of stories from people.

Ideally, what you want to pick up is the stories when they have had amazing experiences with the company. You do not want to go into a problem-solving mindset that says, "Let's find all the things this company does wrong." What we are looking for are the times when the company really exceeded people's expectations and did wonderful stuff. That is the point where we are getting the aspirational values, that is: "What do we really want this company to be all about?" We are getting a hold of the future. That is more useful from a values point of view than kind of rummaging around and looking for problems.

Stories have become really a hot issue and wonderfully so. What they do is they integrate a number of values in clusters. It is effortless to tell those stories. The great stories become kind of mythologies. A lot of what we did at one high-tech company was sharing with their employees some of the mythological stories, which are probably stretched and not fully true any more, but the essence of them is still true. Some of the early founder stories from when they first got started are still floating around in that organization.

Alignment in a Networked Organization

JC: *How does values alignment work in a networked or virtual organization?*

DT: Values become even more important. In traditional organizations, things like trust and similar values were kind of interesting and, I suppose, important, but they could be almost seen as luxuries. There was a hierarchy, pyramid, and a command-and-control structure, which was a way of keeping everybody organized and dutiful to the hierarchy. In a network of virtual organizations, the only glue that is going to hold people together is whether they choose to work together.

As far as people working collaboratively across a real virtual organization, I find people find each other and create these networks out of shared values. They do not come in and say, "Gee, you have the same values as me." But somehow, these networks form in sort of an organic way.

When we go and measure shared values in a networked or virtual organization, they are as shared as in a traditional organization and sometimes more so.

If a bunch of people are interested in something, they have a number of shared values, and the level of values alignment is remarkably high. Such a group wants to be together and gets energized from each other. They somehow have found each other. They probably also found the field of study they are in partly out of some shared values, as well. They did not create the shared values. The shared values created the group.

JC: *How would this work in an organization with a very large contingency workforce?*

DT: That is problematic, quite frankly, especially if the organization deals with its contingency workforce in the traditional way where it sees them as fringe players, second-class citizens, or kind of the flexible part that can get lopped off as soon as business conditions change.

I think you would not get shared values except at the most basic common level of respect, making a living, and doing a nine-to-five job. If the contingency workforce model is run as just another cheaper version of the old sweatshop, it is not going to work. You will not get values alignment in that situation. The biggest single reason would be structural. Think about a contingency workforce that you want to have operate in a collaborative, highly teaming capacity; you want them to be very agile, flexible, and all the kinds of words we use all the time these days. Then put them on piecework, on commission, or in a compensation system that really does not drive toward collaboration. These compensation systems drive toward individual performance and accountability or short-term transactions, as opposed to longer term because each operates as a whole, distinct set of rewards. You will get what you measure.

My point on the contingency workforce is: If we want them to really operate out of our best shared values, we have to work hard on the structural elements of how we pay them, and so on.

JC: *There are organizations that are supplying significant, highly skilled contingency staff to, for example, IT companies. Would they have a similar set of problems or issues?*
DT: I believe they will. What will happen, and maybe it is not a bad thing, is that the glue, or the shared values, will be around people-to-people or people-to-work, not people-to-organization, or it will be to the immediate team or the people with whom they work, so that we will not get any sense of continuity or longevity. The larger organization will not matter to them. It is just a vessel for them to operate in.

What Do People Align With?

JC: *Will what primarily counts to people be their relationship to a project or customer?*
DT: I have seen a number of organizations like that, where the value bond is to the customer, the project, and the team and not at all to the organization. People tend to align themselves and find themselves in teams where they will get very aligned to their customers but not to the host organization.

JC: *This is going to be a growing issue. I expect that organizations are going to have to take a proactive stance to establish their values system vis-à-vis the contingency workforce.*
DT: I quite agree with you. They are going to fight upstream on that. The organization will not matter to that contingency workforce. I just do not think they are going to care.

I think there is a generational difference there. Look at a lot of Gen Xers versus a lot of the Silent Generation. When we measure the values of people in Gen X, it is far more about growth, development, learning, self-actualization, and personal values as opposed to what I would call organizational values of profitability, competition, and so on.

The immediate connection is not to the organizational values. The concern is for the personal values. With the Silent Generation, it is often the other way around. The reality is that we have older people from one generation running organizations, who believe that supporting the organization's values is really important, and we have got a contingency workforce from another generation saying, "What's really important is my growth and development, my career, getting exciting, interesting work. It's got nothing much to do with the organizational values. It's got to do with how I grow myself. The organization is just kind of where I play that out."

Leveraging Values-Based Relationships

JC: *So, the organization has to design a response system to make it work for them?*
DT: Right. I still believe there is a huge number of people who believe that values, like loyalty, are very important. What they have not got is a mechanism to connect that loyalty to the organization, so it goes to loyalty to the work or to the team or to something else, but that loyalty value is still there. The organization just is not able to leverage it and take advantage of it, because it does not structure it the right way to do that. When companies set themselves up in a transient or transactional relationship with their contingency workforce, that is what they are going to get back.

JC: *What do you mean by a values-based relationship continuum?*
DT: I believe values are developmental. If you look at a lot of the authors in the whole area, Maslow, for example, the hierarchy goes from self-preservation up to self-actualization, and so forth.

We have built on the early authors, expanded their concept of how values develop, and linked them to an organizational framework of how organizations deal with customer relationships. We have said, "Customer relationships develop along a logical continuum, and these stages in the continuum are nested in each other." It begins with some very basic values around survival, for example, the values of how the organization looks after itself, preserves its security, and things of that sort. It builds on that foundation of basic values.

The next stage in the customer relationship would be building toward how we achieve the quantity of results that is needed. That is how we actually are productive, efficient, responsible, and so on. Building on quantity, most organizations have moved past that and added quality to quantity. It is not an either-or choice. It's a both-and choice. That is another stage of the continuum. We have chosen to look at the way customer relationships evolve and then build a continuum of values: how we do the quantity of transactions with customers; how we add quality to that dimension; how we actually put the customer at the center of things by moving to a service orientation; how we partner with customers and share risk; how we generate new knowledge with customers; and, in fact, how we create communities with customers.

That continuum can be mapped. There are specific value clusters that will be relevant at each stage of the continuum. People in an organization will have values all the way along this continuum of measurement. The key issue is: How do they prioritize them? Are they prioritizing their values, the ones that are most important to them, at the level that will support the quantity or quality orientation of the relationship, or prioritizing the values at a level that will say, "Let's support a partnering or knowledge-sharing relationship with our customers"? Those are radically different values orientations.

JC: *Are there any examples of companies that have gotten to that point?*

DT: Certainly, lots of individuals and teams have gotten to that point. I have not yet seen a large organization align its values fully around the customer relationship it is seeking.

But, I have seen lots of examples where executive teams and management teams have a tremendous convergence on the values orientations that they hold. Typically, we hope that that is something that will inspire people and move them up the continuum.

Customer Relationship Continuum						
Foundation	**Quantity**	**Quality**	**Service**	**Co-Creation**	**Integration**	**Navigation**
Respected Member	Successful at Market Transactions	Craftsmanship in Every Product and Service	Anticipating Customer's Needs	Partnering, Risking, and Creating for a Better Future	Innovative New Synergy	Stewardship, Transformation, Sustainability
Customer Relationship Continuum Values (Sample)						
Respect	Achievement	Consistency	Service	Creation	Interdependence	Transformation
Membership	Efficiency	Realism	Empathy	Cooperation	Complementarity	Trusteeship
Communication	Economical	Quality	Commerce	Envisioning	Development	Sustainability
Fairness	Working	Consideration	Adaptability	Knowledgeable	Innovation	Pluralism

FIGURE 10.1 Values-Based Customer Relationship Continuum

The Price of Nonalignment

JC: *What are the implications when the values of the work-force, management, and customers are not aligned?*

DT: To me, the biggest single implication is that they do not understand each other. They talk the same words but put totally different meanings to them. For example, a management team that is oriented around the values of partnering, knowledge sharing, and creating community talks to its workforce about teamwork, for example, or about ethics and account-ability. What they mean and what the other person hears can be totally different, depending on whether they have a shared values orientation. They will use the same words but what teamwork will mean to one person and what teamwork will mean to somebody else will be hugely different; what ethics or accountability means to one person and the others is just as different; and what support means to one person or the other will vary appreciably, as well. Figure 10.2 shows how my own values map to the overall values of a client organization in the framework of the customer relationship continuum.

As you can see, their whole model of what leadership means to the management team is radically different from mine. On the surface, they espouse partnerships and transforming the industry, but their values pro-file supports a very different proposition—meeting the standards quality expected by best practices and being a follower, not an innovator, in new business models. They hired me to put a stretch in how they see cus-tomer relationships and to create the tension to grow into a collabora-tive relationship with their customers rather than a relationship built

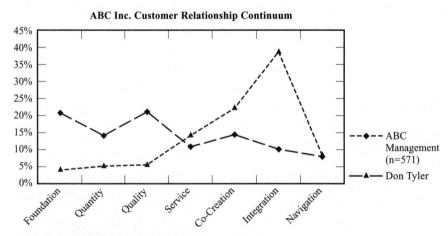

FIGURE 10.2 Customer Relationship Continuum

mostly on delivering quality products that meet the standards of the industry.

JC: *What effect does that have in an organization?*

DT: I have seen both ends of that effect. I have seen leaders and managers being very frustrated and saying, "Why don't these people get it? Why don't they operate collaboratively, blah, blah, blah?"

And, I've seen people in the workforce say, "Those managers are not grounded. They don't understand my reality. They don't understand what work and life are like here as part of the organization. They talk about things that are kind of pie in the sky or abstract and aspirational perhaps but just not real."

There tends to be no emotional connection among those people. They are far apart on the values continuum. Without a common values frame, they are unlikely to do much meaningful knowledge sharing.

The Values Alignment Process

JC: *If I wanted to change things and noticed there was divergence among values in our organization, what would be the steps in the values alignment process?*

DT: The first and foremost thing in the values alignment process is understanding what the organization's intent is and what is its vision, its mission, and what it is that it is trying to accomplish, because since all of the particular values profiles on the continuum can be positive, it really depends on your intent. If I am trying to become the low-cost provider of widgets, I want a certain values profile. In that context, I want a production mentality, cost effectiveness, long production runs, and so on. I am going to want a very different values profile to be reinforced in my organization than if I am in an organization that is dealing with a high level of ambiguity, with all sorts of uncertainty, strategic alliances, partnerships, and working globally. I want a very different value set for this different array.

The first step in the alignment process is to get real clarity on what the purpose or the longer-term reason for the organization to exist is really all about.

The second step is to get some data and to do some measurement. We tend to measure three points. We do values measurement of the people in the organization, of the customers, and of business practices. We bring all those data together and look for gaps and discrepancies around that triangle of employees, customers, and business practices.

JC: *What do you do after you perceive those discrepancies?*

DT: We then begin a consensus process within the organization to decide which of those gaps are critical and getting in the way of business performance. When we typically work with organizations on values alignment, the key step is to get data to validate where we are against the espoused vision for the organization.

The second step is identifying where all that stuff fits together: What are the gaps and discrepancies? We then map those to our values continuum.

The next step is to reach a consensus to decide how much stretch we want to put in this organization. We need to determine where we want to go with this. We need to ask where the edge is and how far we want to push it to sort of create some dynamic tension to grow the organization.

The last step is to put in place an ongoing measurement feedback system as part of the corporate scorecard.

That is a very high level of steps to values alignment. If we get more granular about it, very often one of the earliest things we do is an educational process. We find that we want to build ownership early in the process. By that I mean creating a team of people with both the external consultant and the internal change agent and educating them in the whole methodology. This sets the organization up to transfer knowledge as we are doing the project.

Typical teams that we have worked with include the corporate communications people, the organizational development people, people from marketing, the customer interface, and people at the executive level who are actually running business units.

Strengthening Values Alignment

JC: *What actions can an organization take to strengthen the alignment of its individuals, teams, and systems?*

DT: Perhaps the most basic level of action is getting managers and leaders to model the values. I think modeling the new values is perhaps the key leadership competency that we need to reinforce. Leaders always live in fishbowls, and when we are trying to bring something like values into an organization, we will face all sorts of cynicism and confusion about whether it is just stuff on the wall, or if it has been seen before, or if it sounds great but nobody really behaves in that way.

The most powerful thing is when leaders can stand up and demonstrate a tangible difference in their behavior and commit to doing that.

Getting leaders to do that is a coaching exercise, and getting them developmental feedback on how they are impacting other people is a critical part. We often create 360 degree–type measurement tools that are values-based so that they can get that necessary information and self-correct, rather than have the feedback come from an external perspective where they are being beaten about the head and shoulders and being told that they should change their values. Values alignment is essentially an inside-out thing. It can't be imposed from outside, however well intentioned you may be.

JC: *Do you give them environmental cues that this will*
make a difference, that is, show them it is worth it for them
to do it?

DT: No. The first steps are usually inside the organization. We find that early comparisons to best practices outside only reinforce a follower mentality. The first and foremost step is getting leaders to behave differently. Second, it is taking key business practices that are potentially getting in the way of people doing their jobs and making tangible changes to them. The orientation of new employees is absolutely critical in that: the recruitment processes; the compensation processes; and sometimes key policies, like the employee code of conduct, for example. That last is a classic one where there are embedded structural barriers to people operating in support of these values.

Some of these practices are well intentioned but can very much get in the way. An organization's employee code of conduct can be just dripping with paternalism and risk aversion and suffering for having been written by a committee. Then the leadership says, at the same time, "We want you to be collaborative, risk taking, agile, and so on." Then they have untold numbers of documents that are cover-your-butt documents. This does not cut it. As long as those kinds of documents stay in place, people realize, "Oh, what it's really about here is—." And, all the words about the value shifts you are trying to make are just lost on them.

Developing Performance Metrics

JC: *What are some performance metrics and values align-*
ment measures that are good to use on a corporate scorecard?

DT: Many of our clients use employee attitude surveys and climate surveys. Adding some tracking questions to those kinds of surveys over time creates an even more powerful metric. We now can track not just the values per se but whether we are actually behaving and whether people perceive we are seeing tangible evidence of people living according to the values.

We have had organizations—and Clarica, where Hubert Saint-Onge provides the leadership is a great example—which have actually built a rolling audit. They have taken the values survey and on a repeating basis have a sampling of people fill out the survey. By doing this, they are able to track over time whether in fact people are shifting their values and priorities directionally toward the aspired values of the company or not. The basic metric of actually doing repeating measuring is wonderful if you can get it.

The next level would be a measure with tracking questions in your climate survey, and it has a metric. The third one is more granular, and if you are doing policy and procedure reviews, how many of your policies and procedures have actually been put through a filter of looking at their alignment with the values and then been changed is another metric.

I have not seen anybody yet get really good measures of whether the customers believe that the company is making this kind of shift or not. That would be ground breaking.

Aligning Knowledge Strategies with Business Strategy

JC: *Why do values alignment and knowledge strategies depend on the overall business strategy?*
DT: One of the things that alarms me as much about knowledge strategies as it does about values work is that they need to be connected to what the business is all about. I do not see a lot of that, quite frankly.

Knowledge management is absolutely the crossroads, but it has not got much credibility of being on the change agenda. It is still arguing about terms and definitions, many years into its debut. If I go into a startup, it's not that they do not need knowledge management, but they throw up at even the thought of it. They do not even want to talk about it. They think it is dead. It is not relevant. They have moved on. It is not that it is not really important stuff, but it has not been able to demonstrate any direct connection to the business strategy.

Some of these companies do not even have a business model. They are still trying to struggle with that. The point is, though, they just cannot see an immediate tangible benefit that plays out in helping make different choices in their businesses quickly. If they can't see that from either the values or the knowledge management strategies, those fields become just kind of interesting diversions, and they will not go there.

JC: *Knowledge is managed one way or another in organizations, regardless of what is officially called "knowledge management," and it is either managed well or it's managed poorly. That is true in any entity or among any people. So how do they deal with it? If they do not want to deal with knowledge management, they are dealing with the phenomenon somehow. What do they think they're doing?*

DT: It is amazing to me that in many cases they think they can blow through with speed. There is such an obsession with speed in the new economy. I understand why it is there, yet they just think, "Well, that's old stuff, and we just need to move on." They do not deal with it. I do not think that is sustainable in the long term.

My point is: If they cannot see immediately that knowledge management or values can be used as criteria for this, that values can be used, for example, as criteria for decision making, or that knowledge management can give them a way of looking forward and anticipating things—as if it were simply looking backward and sort of like an old accounting model that is archiving everything we used to do—they will not operate with them. They will suffer from that, but they will not turn to a traditional knowledge management kind of architecture as a solution.

JC: *Are there any organizations that have aligned new values, knowledge management, and business strategy?*

DT: I have yet to see one that has got the whole thing together. A lot of times, the initiatives are operating separately within the organization. I was kind of stunned at one of the conferences I was speaking at to see that it was a rarity to have the knowledge management people, the learning people, and the culture change people all working together. They were working separately in their organizations, all with the best of intentions to drive their agenda forward, but not doing it collaboratively. They are all stovepiping, still working their turf.

A lot of the knowledge management skills are still embedded in IT systems. That is great. We need systems. But if you ask them, "Well, how much time do you spend with the learning people, and how much time do you spend with the people involved with what drives business strategy or culture change in the organization?" they will tell me, "Yes, those initiatives are going on also in our organization, and I'm aware of them but I'm not a part of them."

That is more common right now. When I see that they really did get it together, it is more by chance than intention.

Aligning Values in Global Enterprises

JC: *What new challenges are there in values alignment*
when you get into the arena of a global enterprise?
DT: The first one is the whole notion that people put different meanings to the same words in different cultures. What I am seeing right now in organizations is that well-meaning North American organizations with real clarity in their values are laying them on globally. They come in and say, "This is what we're all about. It's wonderful. It's great." Essentially, they are trying to sell values to people in other cultures, and it does not work.

They are not coming in and saying, "Let me really understand what the values are that operate here and how we can integrate those into our organization," and expecting some diversity in some of those values in order to leverage the different operations they have around the globe.

This lack of outreach leads to a dilution of effectiveness. I remember a most telling comment from an Asian manager at a large global technology company. I asked him, "What do you think of these values that have been put on the wall here? What does it mean to you, and how do you relate them to your Asian culture?" His answer was typically Asian: "Well, they're very general." That's all he said, and it was kind of like, "They're OK. I can put any meaning I want to them and as long as I work hard and am fast and we're getting the results that they want right now, it's OK." But he clearly didn't feel connected at a values level nor that his unique culture was being leveraged by the organization for competitive advantage in his part of the world.

The point is: It was not anywhere close to his meaning system. It was just what it was. It was not bad stuff, but it did not particularly have any great meaning to it. He was able to put a boundary around that. Now, the company loses massively if that is where it leaves things. It is not getting the best of that person at all. What it is getting is somebody who is going along and doing what he needs to do. He may even have many shared values with the organization, but there is not a meaningful dialogue going on about those values or a way to use them to create customer or stakeholder value.

JC: *Explain the benefits of having those values emerge, or*
surface.
DT: We need to emerge them and then see if we can leverage some of those differences. It starts from shared values, but that is only the beginning. Where it should go ultimately is that we become able to extensively understand the differences, and in that richness of understanding we get the next level of innovation or the next level of creativity. We need to move

it so that in the end, it is not about everybody having to have all the same values. It gets people saying, "You know, we really need to get to some shared values and some shared understanding of what they mean."

That is a really important first step. Why? Because it is necessary that we have enough in common that we can trust each other to really listen to the differences, work the differences, and reinforce them.

Ultimately, it is in that diversity that we get the greatest strength, not by making everybody the same. It is a conundrum because we want to start from shared values, but the goal of alignment is not to drive everybody to just be absolutely the same. It is to get a foundation so that we can actually leverage the diversity that we have in our organization.

JC: *Are people picking up on the fact that they are partners in this from whatever direction or dimension they are coming from? Are people realizing that they can be actors versus being acted upon, that they could make a contribution along with everybody else to create this diversity that you are referring to?*

DT: I do not see them feeling that they can influence back yet, which tells me we are still in a hierarchical system with kind of a head office and a branch plant mentality. I do not see that happening much yet in the companies where I have worked.

Emerging Issues

JC: *Is the emergence of global organizations and the Internet the major issue you see in the future, or are there other issues?*

DT: Reciprocity and mutual learning back and forth among various cultures are the kinds of things that will very much be the issues.

At one level, when I talk to managers in the United States as well as in other countries, they know the issue is there. They know that they are suboptimizing on that kind of thing. But they are still at that intellectual level of knowing it is an issue. It is not hurting enough yet for them to do something about it. I do not see them really driving to get that to happen. There is an awful lot more need to get everyone on board and agreeing on things. The reason for getting some minimal agreement is so that we can actually start to learn from each other.

JC: *Is that the key issue that is going to play out in the next years, or are there other issues of equal or more significance?*

DT: Getting the global organizations to work as a network, rather than just as big organizations that sort of smother the globe, as it were, is key. They are still replicating the same old model of being centered somewhere. They are either centric in Germany, in North America, or in some other place as opposed to actually trying to operate as a network or organization. So, we really are still operating with the old frame of what the organization's all about. There still is a center somewhere, and it all drives to that center as opposed to making use of the multiple centers all over the place, where they play off each other.

From a values point of view, the next level is moving to diversity rather than moving to sameness.

Key Learning Points

- Values + skills = capabilities. Values provide the meaning and the motivation (the willingness) to learn new skills (new abilities).
- People espouse certain values and are often unaware of the gap between espoused values and values in action. Measurement makes this discrepancy explicit and creates the structural tension to unfreeze and begin a conscious choice process to align with stated values.
- High levels of knowledge sharing and creation will only be sustained after meaningful relationships are established and consistently nourished. Those relationships are built most effectively on shared values. Without deeper relationships, we will likely only share superficial knowledge.
- The company brand is its external values promise to the marketplace.
- In a network of virtual organizations, the only glue that is going to hold people together is whether they share meaning (values) and choose to work together. People find each other and create networks out of shared values. The group does not create the shared values. The shared values create the group.
- The lack of alignment of the values of senior management, middle management, and the larger workforce creates significant communications, implementation, and productivity issues.
- The foremost thing in the values alignment process is understanding that the values in action create the world view or mental model of the business and precede and predict its ability and willingness to align around vision and strategy, not the other way around. Since all of the particular values profiles on the continuum can be positive,

the values alignment effort needs to be keyed to the organization's business model or strategy.

- The most basic level of leadership is getting managers and leaders to model the values.
- Knowledge management will only be relevant to organizations when it can demonstrate a clear connection to the organization's business strategy. It needs to be able to be used as a criterion for decision making and as a way to look forward to and anticipate changing conditions.
- The goal is not to have everyone have the same values but rather to develop a small core group of shared values and a shared understanding of what those values mean.

Learning in the Knowledge Era

11

Brook Manville is chief learning officer and customer evangelist at Saba Software, a leading provider of human capital development and management solutions. Saba provides a platform of Internet-enabled tools and applications for managing learning, skill development, and human capital development more generally. At Saba, Manville is responsible for its research programs, its own learning programs and processes, and a variety of external programs related to the development of Saba's knowledge and customer relationships.

In this session, Manville discusses the evolution of knowledge management and the trends emerging beyond what he sees as our current plateau. One such trend is the convergence of knowledge management and learning. Another is the expansion of the traditional domain of knowledge management to encompass the broader management of human capital and also the embrace of the extended enterprise, which includes partners, suppliers, and customers.

Manville stresses that linking learning to performance will be central to success in the next era of knowledge-based enterprises. He also touches on other convergences, the application of complex adaptive systems thinking, and the balance between so-called top-down and bottom-up approaches to knowledge processes in the new organization.

Brook Manville was trained as a historian and began his career as a college professor. He later became a business technology analyst for CBS.

Through a series of positions and projects over the last 20-some years, he has linked technology, communications, and education to offer what has become a unique and sought-after perspective.

Prior to coming to Saba, Manville was a partner at McKinsey & Company, specializing in organizational development and knowledge-related strategy, and consulted to Fortune 500 companies in these areas. He helped lead McKinsey's original knowledge management program and became McKinsey's first director of knowledge management, as well as its CIO between 1991 and 1994.

He is the author of numerous pioneering articles on organizational learning and knowledge management and has been frequently profiled for his work in these domains. He has also co-authored (with Josiah Ober) *A Company of Citizens: What the World's First Democracy Teaches Leaders about Creating Great Organizations.*[1]

The Conversation

The Evolution of Knowledge Management

JC: *You have worked as a practitioner and written a lot about knowledge management for almost a decade. As you think about the evolution of that discipline, what stage would you say we are now in?*

BM: I think knowledge management has come to a sort of plateau, and in many ways, I think the S curve of innovation that it represents is coming to an end. It's timely for you to be publishing this book, because it is a good moment to reflect on what it has been and where it's going. I see knowledge management (KM), on the one hand, becoming institutionalized as a sort of process-driven function in companies, but on the other hand, evolving into something bigger and different, which I'll call *human capital management* or something similar. Its strategic trajectory is really toward the latter. The new S curve will be about knowledge management as part of a broader and more integrated effort to manage and develop human capabilities for business performance. I don't mean to say knowledge management is a fad that is dying away—rather, its core ideas and innovations will increasingly make sense in a larger context, and

[1] Brook Manville and Josiah Ober, *A Company of Citizens: What the World's First Democracy Teaches Leaders about Creating Great Organizations* (Boston: Harvard Business School Press, 2003).

it may well lose its identity, at least in name. But I don't see that as a problem.

JC: *Let me unpack this a little. What would you say are the most workable approaches to knowledge management in today's organization?*

BM: Here again, given the evolution going on, you have to begin with the definitional problem. What exactly do we want to mean when we say *knowledge management?* There are lots of good things going on in any company called KM, and then there are some unproductive things, perhaps wrongly named as knowledge management. And then there are other strategies, processes, and programs that are not called KM but probably should be.

I take a relatively holistic point of view and tend to include lots of different aspects of human and organizational development and management under the umbrella of KM. One area that early on became identified with KM is measuring intellectual capital and intellectual assets—the economic or financial dimension. It is an important part of the mix and will continue to be so: Measuring is a big part of managing. Without tools, metrics, and processes, a lot of this just remains in the realm of theory. I think we are still early in the game about how to do this, and a lot more work needs to be done.

Another classic dimension that became identified early on with knowledge management was the organizational process of capturing, storing, and sharing codified knowledge. Most people today still understand this as the heartland of KM—collecting and structuring valuable pieces of information in a centralized database—along with customer information, research reports, engineering specs, patent descriptions, and making it easy for other people to access and leverage all these data. Along with this process comes all the related processes and activities of search and retrieval technologies, converting tacit knowledge into explicit, rewards and systems for sharing, and so on. It tends to be heavily technological in its manifestation for most people, though I think it is really about much more than technology, even in the so-called classic form.

Once we get beyond these two realms, we start to get more interpretive—meaning that not everybody would consider some of the other things I'll mention to be knowledge management—but that is only because the term has come to mean for most people the more narrow type, the processes of intellectual capital measurement and sharing via databases. But increasingly there are other domains that are part of the discipline.

First is the whole domain of people networks and communities, particularly communities of practice—the development of communities of practitioners who work together and feel some obligation to one another to help develop a domain of knowledge. This could be, for example, Java engineers at a software company or the guys who build brakes in the so-called tech clubs at Chrysler. Probably in this category we ought to include storytelling, developmental change programs, and rituals, the kind of organizational anthropology that learning organization practitioners, like Peter Senge, pursue. There is such a bias in the discipline historically toward technology and measurement that these "softer" dimensions are often seen as unrelated, or at least separate disciplines. In my view, that's a mistake.

There are also all the other kinds of learning, whether it is traditional training or individual or group development. Here we can include coaching, mentoring, leadership development, team dynamics, performance management, and so on. Finally, we should arguably also include staffing and other forms of people development: moving people around to build their capability and transfer their expertise. Even recruiting and collaboration with suppliers, partners, and customers might be included.

If we are talking about how we develop and deploy knowledge and people in the most effective way, as well as how we facilitate knowledge flows across the organization, we are going to touch technology, strategy, leadership development, organization structure, organization design, informal organization, and all of the processes and structures, including financial accounting, management processes, and quality processes.

So, at the outer limit, one might ask, "How is knowledge management any different than management itself in a modern organization?" As a broad interpreter and generalist, I think it's a fair question. In the knowledge-based organization—increasingly, every organization today—all management must take account of and be informed by a knowledge perspective. But I do think knowledge management is a subset of management more generally. For example, corporate facilities, cash management, and looking after servers and routers are *not* knowledge management, and knowledge management is clearly different than—though it is increasingly a component of—overall business unit or corporate strategy and its implementation. But KM broadly defined is a sizable subset of all management in that its focus is anything that builds the organizational capability of an entity through the development of individual people and their skills, experience, and knowledge.

Each of the several domains I have mentioned has developed their own workable approaches and practices for improving capability. The trick is to think about how to orchestrate them and make them all work together—and not see them in isolation as management processes that have little to do with one another, as has traditionally been the case.

Stages of Knowledge Management

JC: *You've included a lot under the umbrella of knowledge management. How did you come to define it that way? Can you talk about the evolution of the discipline in terms of the stages it has passed through, and how it's come to be what you describe?*

BM: My perspective is built on a synthesis looking back on lots of different trends that I see as interrelated. Thinking about stages of development of KM is helpful in framing the day-to-day choices we must make in the field.

The first stage, which we could call the *zero stage*, was probably in the 1980s, when there was tremendous investment in technology and, particularly, in networks and network infrastructure. Everybody began to realize that by connecting parts of the organization through computers and network technology, there would be opportunities for information management, as it was called, and thus improved management of knowledge. I don't think a lot of people were talking about knowledge management in those days, but the infrastructure for what then came to be KM was being established during that time. Putting in the roads and the bridges was part of the zero phase. Also during the 1980s, academic economists starting working on intangible assets and value creation in the theory of the firm— but nobody in business was really doing anything about it. So perhaps we should also call that part of the zero phase, that is, laying the conceptual framework.

Next, toward the end of the 1980s, we saw the birth of things like information engineering and the less-inflated, simpler notion that any organization can manage the information of its people and processes in a more strategic way, thanks to technology. By the late 1980s, there was a lot of emphasis on setting up repositories of codified knowledge, directories of experts, databases of documents, databases of knowledge assets, and so on. It was also the period of simple expert systems that, in the extreme, were called "artificial intelligence."

In the end, however, it was always about codified information; there was little realization and little or no effort made to tap into the dynamic and tacit knowledge of people nor to make the connection between human development and knowledge management. Still, in its time, it was a very radical idea that within an organization we could go to one place, a virtual place perhaps, a database, or just a well-run library and find all the kinds of things that we would want to know about our customers, the research of our organization, or about the past work that we had done for customers. As globalization accelerated and companies became larger and more dispersed, they were challenged to keep up with what they collectively knew—and basic knowledge management processes, using the new network and database technologies, were invented to address the challenges.

At about the same time, people started to realize the value of best practices and best-practices benchmarking. This was partly driven by the quality movement—with all the competitive challenge from places like Japan—and partly by reengineering, which was another competitive response to the major cost, time, and productivity efficiencies in globalizing markets. Best practices required some process of codification, a sustained process of understanding what was a best practice and what was the metric of a best practice. It involved collection, structuring, metrics, and measurement and helped build awareness that the organization could learn from itself and learn from other organizations. Not surprisingly, it was during this time one started to hear the phrase the *learning organization*.

The next phase of evolution should probably be dated in the mid-1990s. By then, there was a growing realization that all of this codified information, information management, technology-enhanced databases, search software, and that kind of thing were fine, but there was another whole world of *tacit knowledge*, as it came to be labeled. This was the knowledge in people that was not easily codified or captured by a computer network and was not easy to document for best practices or benchmarking.

At about the same time, and consistent with the whole notion of unseen and difficult-to-codify knowledge, we start to witness the rise of intellectual capital accounting. The question was: "How do we in some way take account of all of these intangible assets?" People such as Leif Edvinsson at Skandia and others started to say, "We should track things, like the age of our people, their years of education, and the amount of customer relationships they each have. These are all intangible assets that need to be part of an accounting system." As I mentioned before, academic economists had been thinking about this for some time, but it was not until the mid-1990s that companies really tried to translate the theory into practice.

In the same general period, there were certain organizational development approaches that also came to the fore, focusing on how to unlock the knowledge in people. There was a lot of research into change and change processes, learning processes, and communities of practice. The communities of practice approach holds that it is through communities of practitioners—whose work together creates learning and meaning in the workplace for the practicing members—that tacit knowledge is developed, shared, reinforced, and translated into competencies for organizational capability.

The community practice practitioners and theorists—John Seely Brown, Ikujiro Nonaka, Bill Snyder of Social Capital Group, Etienne Wenger of the Institute for Research on Learning, and many others—were complemented by an expanding population of consultants, team builders, and organizational development people who made a lot of progress in transforming organizations through structured learning and empowerment processes, tapping into the knowledge and experience of people in the workplace to improve their own and the collective performance. During the late 1990s, more radical extensions of this kind of thinking and practice evolved with organizational development approaches based on biological metaphors, chaos theory, scenario planning, theatrical role playing, and the like. Meanwhile, technology continued to evolve with the boom of the Internet, the development of intranets, and the cross-boundary management of knowledge and information-integrating intranets, extranets, and the worldwide web. Sophisticated technology solutions also evolved with the development of supply chain management, customer relationship management (CRM) systems, and e-HR applications, such as talent markets, recruiting/staffing systems, and now integrated human capital management systems (like that of my company, Saba), which track skills, competencies, and experience; help assess gaps; and link learning and performance.

Again, much of this may not be considered knowledge management. Rather, what has been going on is a steady evolution of different approaches to leveraging human knowledge and capabilities as the knowledge revolution advances. It's not very neat to have to think about all of these different things, but unless you embrace the complexity and evolution, you end up talking about KM as a sort of museum piece of the 1990s.

Knowledge Management and Strategy

JC: *How does the evolution you describe fit with the evolution of business strategy?*

BM: We can see a few obvious connections. One is the whole notion of "competing on core competencies" started by Gary Hamel and others who revolutionized strategic thinking—away from the "war of position" to the "war of capabilities." Once we have competencies as the core of success (or failure), we are fast led to the techniques, processes, and technologies to build and leverage those competencies. A related stream of thought is the whole notion of strategy-as-hustle or strategy-as-execution, which is the idea that in the increasingly volatile and changeable market spaces of the new economy, success depends on movement, change, and adaptation—

not on structural advantage or long-term planning. Organizational learning is fundamental to making change happen, so if strategy is hustle and change, managing knowledge is fundamental.

JC: *You have written that knowledge-based strategies begin with strategy itself and not knowledge or learning-based programs. Say a bit more about that.*

BM: The basic assertion is that the only real value of learning or knowledge management is when it moves the needle for performance. Strategy is about how to win; performance is the measure of success. Too many knowledge and learning programs have been launched because it is a fad or just generally seen as a good thing.

With the globalization and hypercompetition of the knowledge economy, there is an increased premium on performance in all domains. So much of learning and knowledge management has been fueled by carrying over the underlying assumptions of traditional schooling—that learning for its own sake is a good thing. Although I never want to be on the record as saying learning is not a good thing for its own sake, it is different when you are operating in an organizational context that has a particular purpose and set of goals to achieve. The world of work is application; the world of schooling is building the fundamentals of knowledge and learning how to learn.

When you are young and in kindergarten, or third grade, or even ninth grade, there are things that you definitely have to learn in order to acquire the skills to be a productive member of society, but you are also left with a fair amount of open-endedness and a lack of immediate application—mostly by design, in fact. There are many good outcomes from, say, reading *King Lear* or studying the Civil War, and they are going to differ from person to person. This is liberal education in its classical sense. You are learning in order to acquire certain skills, foundational information, ways to think about a problem or an issue, and you are building awareness generally of how to learn. That is different than in the business context, where learning will be applied to very specific goals, aligned with the strategy of the organization, whether it is a for-profit or not-for-profit organization.

The old-fashioned training organization was kind of like the school. A lot of the thinking was: "It's good for people to learn, and it is up to them to figure out how to link it to the strategy of the organization." The problem with that is a lot of people could not make the link, or the application was so removed from the training that the lessons and knowledge were lost. From a learning theory standpoint, we know that retention levels are terribly low if you are not applying it back on the job as soon as you learn it.

One of the reasons that knowledge management emerged and grew is that it filled this void of just-in-time learning. For a long time, training organizations were really offering just-in-case learning: "Someday, you are going to be a manager, so we're going to put you through a managerial program." Those programs by design were removed from day-to-day needs and based on the same kind of thinking from our school days, that is, "Someday you will be glad you read *King Lear*." But today, organizations have less and less time for just-in-case learning. The competitive demands and the immediacy of the challenges require more and more just-in-time learning. So, not surprisingly, knowledge management, training, learning, and performance management are all processes that are converging.

"Pull," "Push," and Centralization versus Decentralization

JC: *Does this tie in with your ideas about the superior power of "pull" for knowledge management as opposed to centralized "push"?*

BM: Yes, certainly. Learning effectiveness is driven by its immediate application. Does it satisfy a need that is a real need of the learner, and does it satisfy a need that is directly linked to performance outcome? Is it also just in time and in the context of the necessary application? Because if it is, it will be much more powerfully learned. All of that suggests the effectiveness of pull, that is, you are being driven by your own internal motivation to succeed: "I, the learner, need to know this in order to do this job today and achieve this kind of performance goal." It is a much more powerful engine of learning in terms of motivation, prioritization, and delivery than to have some central entity, in most cases out of the swim of the business needs, saying, "I, sitting in my ivory tower, think this would be good for you to know—and I'm going to broadcast this out to you." Mostly, this material does not get used, and people do not understand the context and are very frustrated. Not surprisingly, this approach just burns the political capital of central staff groups.

That is not to say there should be no central staff dedicated to knowledge and learning processes. At their best, they play a role of coordinating, cataloging, and generally providing and maintaining the necessary infrastructure for the internal and external "markets"—the "buyers" and "sellers" of learning and knowledge—to connect with one another.

Where Are We Headed?

JC: *Given your perspectives, and your story of knowledge management's evolution and apparent plateau, where do you think things are headed?*

BM: I see two streams of the next generation, which are still forming. They are complementary and probably will find some convergence in their own right in the future. To oversimplify, one is about top-down, integrated human capital management, and the second is about bottom-up, self-organizing systems.

The first picks up on a couple of things we have been talking about. It reflects the strategic vision of my current company, Saba Software, but I think we are not alone in seeing this new paradigm. It is composed of several elements that build on the progress of knowledge management and learning theory over the last few years. The first point is that organizations need to provide tools and processes to more directly link learning, knowledge development, and knowledge sharing to specific business goals and needed organizational capabilities.

We talk about so-called managed learning, which involves cataloging and aligning knowledge assets—codified training programs, communities, experts, or whatever—and making more explicit connections between those and specific competencies or skills gaps of both the individual and the organization. The new learning management systems provide an infrastructure to do that, both within organizations and across the boundaries of the extended enterprise. They utilize maps, tools, catalogs, assessment tools, and analytics to assess knowledge gaps and then provide managed learning to close the gaps. With this kind of infrastructure, managers can assess the gaps of their workforce, direct specific interventions, and at the same time, knowledge workers can take control of their own learning and work toward specific goals and objectives that are either prescribed or recommended.

In addition, the new infrastructure will increasingly go beyond simple learning management. It will also provide the tools and processes for creating and managing knowledge content—for example, turning a Power-Point presentation into a training course—as well as for manipulating content, particularly in the form of parsing it into individual knowledge chunks and recombining those as needed for different applications. The infrastructure will also integrate tools for live collaboration and both synchronous and asynchronous discussion and problem solving. It will further provide tools and processes for managing performance in terms of setting goals and cascading them across the organization. The Saba vision further includes the integration of processes for staffing and deploying people across an extended enterprise—on the premise that managing knowledge is not only about learning and information transfer, but also literally the moving around and deployment of people with knowledge so that the right expertise is brought to bear and new expertise is built through on-the-job experience.

This is a much broader and more holistic approach to managing knowledge in an organization: integrating learning, performance, content manipulation and manufacture, and resource deployment. It further provides for understanding that the true arena for all of this is not just the core organization but also one's suppliers, partners, and even customers. Creating this kind of context and enabling it through new highly sophisticated and integrated infrastructure is a huge step beyond most knowledge management, which is an intranet, a catalog of documents, or some other fragmented but well-intended effort.

Bringing all of the knowledge management and human resources pieces together—now also including the systems and processes of such things as supply chains, demand chains, or CRM systems—is an obvious next step of evolution. It is still early in the game—Saba has many customers who are using our infrastructure and building a context with this kind of vision—but it is a huge transformational change and is not something that any organization achieves overnight.

JC: *What about the other theme you mentioned, that of bottom-up, self-organizing systems?*
BM: Since the mid-1990s, various practitioners and theorists have been working on and talking about modeling organizations as if they are biological or otherwise natural systems. We also hear about chaos and complexity theory, the basic idea of which is that organizations cannot be artificially optimized but must rather strive for continuous adaptation, with the struggle for adaptation or "fitness" achieved through the apparently random, but actually implicitly wise actions of thousands of independent agents within the system. Through simple rules and trial-and-error, the collective organization constantly evolves toward some kind of successful equilibrium and ongoing survivability.

The implication of all of this is that knowledge management may not be at all about creating specific approaches and processes to improve an organization's learning and application, but rather may be about creating the right kind of context and freedom to let all of the individual agents in the system find their own way and adapt dynamically to the business challenges. One technical link into the theory of knowledge management is about so-called tagging—the labels or identifiers that the individual agents use to identify themselves and improve their chances of connecting with other agents within the system for innovation and adaptation. I've written elsewhere about how knowledge management classification schemes might be reconceived as "tagging processes,"[2] embedded in self-organizing knowledge communities within a system. There are numerous other discussions of these kinds of themes found in Margaret Wheatley's work, with Chris Meyer and "swarm intelligence," and in complex adaptive models discussed by Stuart Kauffman of the Sante Fe Institute.[3]

I think one can broadly talk about two main schools of thought about knowledge management and the like. The first is a sort of engineering approach, the idea that managers can put in place tools, systems, processes, and infrastructure that can move the organization to predictable and measurable goals. The second is a sort of gardening approach, the idea that managers at most are creating context, environment, and nourishment for people to do the right thing, but that the outcomes are much less predictable and can only be influenced so far by managers. Human capital management is more the first, engineering, and self-organizing systems are obviously more the second, gardening.

As always, I think the next truth will lie somewhere in the middle. We will increasingly see both increased managerial intervention—new tools, new infrastructure, new systems—and at the same time a greater embrace within those new contexts of self-organizing, individual-empowering, culture- and values-driven approaches. Human capital can be managed to better outcomes—but only so far. At the same time, to forgo all forms of traditional management, and just let full freedom reign in the hopes of self-organizing success, is also unlikely. Instead we will see an ongoing synthesis between engineering and gardening. This will be the anomalous but unstoppable convergence between management by design and design through experience. We will also see a similar convergence between top-down, manager-led and bottom-up, learner-led practices. Every organization will have to find the balance between learning from the past and learning from the present—and, again, workers learning from leaders and learning from one another.

[2] *Knowledge Management Review* (May–June 1999): 26ff.

[3] See Margaret J. Wheatley, *Leadership and the New Science: Learning about Organization from the Orderly Universe* (San Francisco, Calif.: Berrett-Koehler, 1992); Stan Davis and Christopher Meyer, *Blur: The Speed of Change in the Connected Economy* (New York: Warner, 1998); and Stuart A. Kauffman, *Investigations* (New York: Oxford University Press, 2000).

- Knowledge management will be part of a broader and more integrated effort to manage and develop human capability for business performance.

- Not everything that is called knowledge management is knowledge management, and many things that are not usually included in what is considered knowledge management are legitimately part of the discipline.

- KM, broadly defined, is a sizable subset of all management since its focus is anything that builds organizational capability through the development of individual people and their skills, experience, and knowledge.

- Knowledge management has evolved through a number of stages. In the 1980s emphasis was on infrastructure foundations for codifying commonly stored information. The early 1990s saw the inclusion of benchmarking, incorporating intangibles, intellectual capital accounting, and tacit knowledge. And, in the late 1990s, softer elements such as communities of practice and storytelling began to emerge, along with the technological capability to undertake customer relationship and human capital management.

- When enterprises shift from strategies based on wars of position to wars of capabilities and are defined by the new idea of strategy-as-hustle, organizational learning and knowledge management become fundamental to achieving successful outcomes.

- In the business context, learning for any type of organization will be applied to very specific goals, aligned with organizational strategy, and will be just-in-time (as opposed to just-in-case) learning.

- In the new learning structure, managers can assess the gaps in their workforce, direct specific interventions, and at the same time allow individual workers to take control of their learning and work toward specific organizational goals and objectives.

- The next phase of knowledge management will bring together a gardening approach, emphasizing the creation of the right context and freedom to let all individual agents in the system find their own way, adapting dynamically to business challenges, along with the more traditional engineering approach.

*Drivers and Accounting
for Intangible Wealth*

KNOWLEDGE
Cluster IV:

The need to effectively value an enterprise is an increasing challenge, as intangible assets become an ever greater proportion of organizational wealth. At the same time, more complex transactions have made tracking the value creation path less obvious and more difficult. While the traditional accounting system served organizations and investors well when conditions were relatively stable and assets were primarily physical, the changes in the economy since the 1980s have brought about a significantly more volatile state of affairs. Our age of the Internet is characterized by the ability to shift or cultivate massive amounts of intangible assets rapidly and with almost no transaction costs. This is a basic transformation in the economy and requires meeting the colossal challenge of carrying out a fundamental shift in the methods of valuation and accounting.

The value of the intangible assets of an enterprise is just beginning to be understood. The growth in the value of intellectual property, human capital capabilities, business methodologies and processes, and other intangible assets is a major element in the decision to acquire or merge organizations. Yet there are currently few ways to commonly, sensibly, and credibly account for these soft assets. Changes in acceptable accounting practices will require that intangible value, which up until now has been covered by the industrial-era term *goodwill*, be accurately defined and reported on regularly. Since goodwill can account for a high proportion of the value of an enterprise, this is a very significant shift.

Accounting is ultimately not just a matter of measurement and valuation. It is also the basis for decision making. The ability to evolve a credible, understandable valuation framework is necessary internally to guide important enterprise choices. Reliable accounting is equally necessary for investors, government, and other stakeholders who need trustworthy measures to determine investment, economic, fiscal, and tax policies.

We are at a point where the traditional accounting system has not been transformed to reliably reflect the new economic realities. Jonathan Low and Steven Wallman map out reference points for knowledge-based enterprises that stakeholders need to proactively consider in order to minimize distortions, understand the drivers for intangible wealth production, and grasp the essentials central to effective decision making as the next framework is just beginning to emerge.

What Drives Enterprise Value?

Jonathan Low notes that, since the 1980s, there has been a decline in the relevance of assets and earnings as predictors of stock market performance. In fact, portfolio managers have said that a minimum of 35–

40% of their portfolio allocation decisions are based on nonfinancial information. Since stock market performance is an increasingly important measure of value by which companies can grow globally, it is important to go beyond the traditional balance sheet and income statement measures to understand what drives equity pricing and perceived value in organizations.

Low and his associates developed an index of nine core drivers that correlated with accounting performance. These factors are innovation, management, employees, quality, environment, alliances, brand, technology, and the customer. They found that while traditional financial measures could explain a certain amount of market performance, the nonfinancial measures gave a reliable set of indicators for the balance of the company value. Additionally, it is important to note that these nonfinancial aspects are not measured or reported in any ongoing and regular way.

One implication of the significance of these drivers is that, if the enterprise does a better job of identifying and managing these factors, it increases its chances of improving its market value. Another implication is that, if managers understand the intangible sources of value and work at nurturing these sources in the enterprise, they will be more effective at creating value in their organizations. A corollary of that premise is that the enterprise can revise its own measurement framework, how it formulates and executes its business model, acquisition and marketing strategies, rewards and recognition efforts, and even the basis for how it presents itself to the world to be in accord with a more reality-based value creation and capture path.

A Level Playing Field for an "Intangible" Era

Steven Wallman believes that the financial reporting and disclosure system is increasingly susceptible to not capturing important drivers of wealth production, especially when it comes to knowledge-based assets. These assets are increasingly important as drivers of wealth production in both companies that are seen as traditional and physical asset–based and those that are seen as new economy entities, which are primarily based in intangible assets. Since reliable financial reporting and disclosure are fundamental to decisions for efficiently allocating capital resources, there is a need to update the generally accepted accounting principles to reflect the changes in the economy and the way businesses operate. For example, an enterprise could invest in a website or intranet, and under current accounting practices, that investment is seen as a cost. The same organization could purchase a piece of land or machinery, and that would be reported as an asset, one with a very different amortization rate. Similar questions and biases can exist concerning investment in human capital or core business processes.

The variability in these considerations affects decisions, such as whether an enterprise that has more intangible assets than tangible assets will get loans from banks. These decisions may be critical for the development of the enterprise. This inequity makes it potentially difficult for those in the enterprise, as well as investors, to make sense of what is of value and what is necessary to create wealth.

Wallman sees that some studies, such as *Unseen Wealth* undertaken by the Brookings Institution (with Margaret M. Blair; Washington, D.C.: Brookings Institution Press, 2001), have put on the table the intangible wealth issues that touch all areas of the enterprise. The question at hand is what is necessary so that there is a level playing field, regardless of the configuration of assets an organization is cultivating.

Shaping a Reliable Financial Framework

As the contributors to this cluster point out, it is in everyone's interests to develop a working, transparent, and more understandable framework for determining how value is created and how it is reported and disclosed. Managers, the extended enterprise network, investors, and regulatory bodies need a more informed and reliable basis for their decisions as the value of intangible assets grows proportionally in knowledge-based enterprises. The demand for a more broadly reliable value model will only become greater.

Although transitioning to a revised value framework is a complex and difficult process, new approaches to value are gradually coming into existence, and experiments are under way that are contributing to the formation of more indicative value frameworks. As these prototype efforts take shape around the world, practitioners are getting a grasp on different aspects of the value problem. Over the next number of years, these efforts will yield the essential elements of a new value network. These conversations discuss significant parts of that exploratory process.

12

In this conversation, Jonathan Low explores issues that form a perspective and a set of principles for operating in our intangible assets, knowledge-based economy. His research has given him cutting-edge insights as well as a basis for assessing intangibles, which make up the bulk of wealth in the new economy. He discusses how decisions are based on nonfinancial information, the major recent changes in the world's wealth, the nine factors of value and how they work in different types of organizations, and trends that will be shaping the next phase of our era.

Jonathan Low is senior fellow at Cap Gemini Ernst & Young's Center for Business Innovation (CBI), a research and development business focused on identifying emerging trends and creating related solutions. He is the leader of CBI's performance measurement initiative, which is concentrated primarily on the valuation of intangibles, including intellectual capital, organizational transitions, interenterprise collaborations, and other sources of value in the new economy.

Under Low's leadership, the CBI performance measurement initiative has produced four major reports and several ancillary documents. The major studies include *Measures That Matter* (1997), *Success Factors in the IPO Transformation Process* (1999), *Decisions That Matter* (2000), and *The Value Creation Index* (2001). He and his colleagues have worked with clients ranging from the largest Global 500 corporations to startups in the United States and Europe to assist them in realizing the potential benefits of this research.

Low has also organized and hosted an annual conference entitled *Measuring the Future*. He copublished, with the Organization for Economic Cooperation and Development (OECD), *Enterprise Value in the Knowledge Economy: Measuring Performance in the Age of Intangibles* (1998). Jonathan Low is the co-author, with Pam Cohen Kalafut, of *Invisible Advantage*, published by Perseus Press (2002).

The Conversation

How to Assess Intangibles

JC: *What is the changing understanding of the role of intangibles in organizations?*
JL: We tend to refer to intangibles not as assets or liabilities but simply as intangibles because we don't think that the balance sheet reference is particularly helpful. You can probably get into a month-long debate about whether brand is an asset or a liability because brand is in effect a promise to a consumer that technically makes it a liability. But rather than saying that, the important underlying issue is that there has been an approximately 20-year decline in the relevance of assets and earnings as predictors of stock market performance.

We are in a global economy in which equities are the currency. To the extent that market value or stock market performance is an increasingly important measure of value by which companies are able to both expand and operate globally, we need to do a better job of understanding what drives equity prices. If traditional balance sheet and income statement measures are not doing it, we need to understand what is. What we have done, and what a large number of people around the globe are doing both in academia and in the business world, is to try to do a better job of determining both quantitatively and qualitatively what is driving value in organizations.

Rather than audit, what we need to talk about is: How does one assess intangibles? There are two things that have to be done. First of all, we have to look at the gaps between what executives believe are the factors that are driving value in their organizations, and what organizations are actually measuring and disclosing.

Decisions Are Based on Nonfinancial Information

JC: *Is there a gap between perception and reality?*

JL: Right. We also need to look at some very hard numbers, which fortunately, many people are doing primarily in Europe and the United States, but also to some degree in Asia and South America. Then, we need to try to get a grip on what the underlying nature of these relationships is. When I am referring to "we," here, I am speaking of Cap Gemini Ernst & Young's Center for Business Innovation in Cambridge, Massachusetts, where I am leading our effort. We have, through a series of four studies now, tried to address both of those approaches.

In our *Measures That Matter* and IPO research, we first surveyed institutional investors to understand what they felt were the important factors in determining value. The most surprising thing we learned from that analysis was that the degree to which securities analysts refer to nonfinancial measures, or nonfinancial factors, determines the accuracy or correlates with the accuracy of their quarterly and annual financial projections. That was a very interesting finding.

Second, portfolio managers told us, in no uncertain terms, that, at a minimum, 35–40% of their portfolio allocation decisions were based on nonfinancial information. In other words, this was information that was not formally measured and disclosed by the subject company. As a result, we determined that there is a huge market for this information. Further, this information is helping to determine market value since the people who, in most of the Western industrialized world, control about 70–80% of a typical corporation's equity are basing their decisions, to a large measure, on nonfinancial information.

JC: *Was that a shock when it actually came out in black and white?*

JL: Absolutely. Then, we decided as a second step to focus on a specific aspect of the financial universe to see how this might affect that market. We focused on the initial public offering market in the United States. We looked at every company that had gone public between 1986 and 1997. By eliminating penny stocks, real estate investment trusts, and other outliers, we came up with a universe of about 500 companies. We surveyed those firms and got an astonishing 20% response rate from the CEOs and CFOs of those companies.

We asked them to tell us whether they thought their IPO had been successful, highly successful, or unsuccessful. Then, to get into greater detail, we asked why that was the case. We took their self-reported performance and looked at how their stocks had done. We found that they had been very honest and accurate. We discovered that there was an extremely tight correlation between how they felt they'd done and how the market determined how they'd done.

We derived a couple of really interesting learnings from that. About 50% of the companies that went public in that period failed to ever maintain or exceed the price at which they went public. More broadly speaking, we could argue that they failed to add value for their shareholders after they went public. We then looked at what were the statistically significant differentiating factors between the 50% that added value and the 50% that failed to add value. We found that the only statistically significant factors that could be uncovered were, in fact, nonfinancial. These factors were ones that were not mandatory to disclose in any financial reports.

JC: *Would not that have substantial implications?*
JL: Exactly. We found that the single most significant factor in determining addition of value or subtraction of value for shareholders in an IPO situation was the alignment of employee interests with corporate strategy. That, in simplest terms, frequently means: To what degree do your employees have stock options?

Massive Wealth Creation

JC: *Is it for the financial linkage/interest linkage more than the value?*
JL: No. It is an interesting finding in and of itself. We can look at what happened in the dot.com revolution and say that we had arguably created more wealth in the last three years than had been created for the entire human race in the preceding 300 years. That, to a large measure, was done because the stock option, among other financial mechanisms, harnessed and gave incentive to bright individuals to donate or invest their intellectual and human capital in the strategy and the enterprise. This was a very powerful motivator. What makes it even more interesting, however, is that when you then look at companies like Microsoft, Sun, and some of the other big technology companies, you have a lot of midlevel and even lower-level employees who are extremely wealthy. These are people who can, in the Microsoft phrase, "call in rich" whenever they want to, as opposed to calling in sick. This remains true for some companies, despite the economic downturn of 2000–2002.

So, how do you keep those people motivated? How do you keep them coming to work? Of course, the way you do that is by going back to the alignment metaphor, by giving them interesting problems to work on, a stimulating environment in which to work, and pleasant and intelligent colleagues with whom to do that work. Here, we get into a whole host of issues that cannot be captured on a balance sheet or an income statement.

The point is that we are creating significant value in our economy that we can correlate with financial metrics, that is based on previously described soft measures. It is, therefore, important that we do a better job of understanding what those measures are.

As a third step, in partnership with two professors at the Wharton School of Business, Dave Larcker and Chris Ittner, and with support from *Forbes ASAP* magazine, we decided to see if we could create an index or a model by which we could really bring this down to the grittiest level and understand what the drivers of value are in organizations. We called it the Value Creation Index. We came up with drivers of value that had been identified by experts and referred to in both academic and business literature. We then went on the web, to libraries, and to research institutions. We tried to determine for which of these drivers we could get information.

We had a total list of upward of 50 drivers. However, we found nine that were particularly significant. These were ones that were cross-referenced by others and for which there was actually public data. From that, we were able to create this index and then to correlate that index with accounting performance. We determined, using purely statistical sampling techniques, that there was an extremely strong correlation between these nonfinancial measures and financial value.

JC: *When you say* financial value, *how would you know that exists?*

JL: Well, you would look at market value, stock value, for instance. In the case of durable and nondurable manufacturers, we looked at the extent to which these nine factors correlated with the market value of the companies. We discovered there was a correlation of about 50%. In other words, you could explain about 50% of Proctor & Gamble's market value by looking at these nine nonfinancial aspects, which are not measured or reported in any regular fashion.

When we went to dot.com companies, we found that these intangible drivers could explain about 90% of their market value. This may explain the degree of the collapse, but the key thing here is that this value is independent of their financial performance. In the case of the old economy companies, about 50% can be explained by traditional financial measures, but about 50% can be explained by these other factors.

The Nine Factors of Value

JC: *Were you actually developing another equation?*

JL: Yes. The nine factors are innovation, management, employees, quality, environment, alliances, brand, technology, and the customer. We wrote about this in the article "Introducing the New Value Creation Index" in the *Forbes ASAP* April 3, 2000, edition.

The interesting thing is that some of these were high in importance, and some were relatively low. In the old economy companies, the top three were innovation, management, and employees.

In a traditional accounting fashion, how do you capture *innovation*? What does that mean? What does *management* mean? What does *employee* mean? There's really no way of describing that.

I can tell you that each of those drivers had several component pieces. For instance, in the case of innovation, the publicly available data we looked at, which are crude indicators, are number of patents, research and development expenditures, the *Fortune* magazine innovation score, and patent importance. We were able to determine patent importance because some patents are referred to by other patents, and so we can actually determine a score for patent importance.

For management, there are CEO reputation scores, which Burson-Marsteller has put together. *Industry Week* magazine has a Best Managed Companies list. *Worth* magazine has a 50 Best CEOs list. There are all kinds of mainstream business press assessments, which have done a great job of determining management capability or what constitutes good management.

What this tells us is that, if you do a better job of identifying and then managing the factors that help determine your market value, you can presumably improve your market value. We are not saying that there is causality, but we are saying that there is a correlation and that it is something that managers really need to start looking at.

The third piece of our effort was to really try to understand intangible sources of value and put some specific factors together to create the building blocks or stepping-stones, so if managers want to understand how their companies create value and improve the way they do so, they could begin to do that.

JC: *Are you going to take a look at these longitudinally, as well as by groupings, over time?*

JL: Yes, we are. But that is going to be a long-term project, because it is difficult to get this information.

JC: *Might the value of the drivers change for different components over time?*

JL: Absolutely. In fact, the drivers themselves will probably change.

Discovering the Gaps

JC: *Do you think that even the components of the equation might be different five years from now?*

JL: Our philosophy is that this is a narrative process, that what we have presently is purely a baseline. It is not an enduring 500-year model that will stand all tests of time.

People really need to be open-minded about this. That is why we resist the connection with traditional accounting methodology, because by definition that has to be vetted and tested, and it is as much a political process as it is a financial process. There are so many people who have so much invested in each of those measures that it is a siege, a battle, to get anyone to change.

Our point is that it is important for investors to understand how value is created, and it is important for managers to understand that and to communicate that to investors. Also, that it is in their self-interest, on both hands, to provide more information to all parties so they can do a better job of figuring that out. It has all sorts of implications for cost of capital, for capital allocation, and, ultimately, for the strength of the global economy.

As a final piece of this, we recently completed a study which we called *Decisions That Matter*. It started out as an experiment on our part. We put a survey on the web to see what kind of response we would get. We asked respondents to tell us the degree to which they thought that the drivers of value in their companies were actually the drivers that their management and compensation systems valued. Although we understand that this was not a scientific sample, since we heard back from self-selected respondents, we feel it is a good snapshot, a starting point.

Eighty percent of them said that there was a huge gap between what actually drove value for their organization and what the organization measured and compensated. Forty-three percent said that the gap was vast. Referring back to the IPO study results, where the key determinant between success and failure, or value addition versus value subtraction, is an IPO's alignment, then think about this gap analysis and decisions that matter. The troubling thing we have is that we are creating tremendous cynicism and lack of alignment in organizations. Managers are saying, "I know this doesn't matter, but it's what I'm compensated for, so that's what I'm going to manage toward. I'm going to stop caring. I'm not going to worry about it. I'm going to play the game."

Subsequently, we did a couple of other things. We were invited to speak at a *Forbes* conference a couple of months later. They have an audience response system, where someone asks a question and everyone in the audience uses a remote hand-held device to give a response automatically. The audience was composed primarily of CEOs. We expected to get creamed since these are the people who create these systems. We thought, "They are going to think everything is honky-dory." In fact, they were a lot more honest than that. Seventy percent of them said, "Yep. There is a big gap between what we measure and reward and what actually drives value."

We then asked, "How can you permit this to go on? You are presumably the people who control this." They said, "It's not up to us. It's Wall Street, and this is what the Wall Street people want."

JC: *Were they saying, "Blame the analysts"?*
JL: They were acknowledging the fact that there is this vast political web that has created the current system, and they don't want to be the only ones to fight it. They feel (and we should recognize that CEO tenure dropped by half in the 1990s), "Why should we stick our necks out to reform the global disclosure system?"

This points to the problem that we have. We did a follow-up study and came up with very interesting results. We looked primarily at the financial services industry. We tried to determine the nature of this gap. We asked them to tell us more about this gap. They came up with about 10 or 11 drivers, which are quite similar to the ones we described in the Value Creation Index. We asked them to rate those in order of importance, and not surprisingly, customer is number one, quality is number two, and operational efficiency is number three—that sort of thing.

Then we measured the gaps. What is interesting is that the largest gaps involved the measures that are most important. The largest gap between what drives value and what the company actually captures is the customer. How can that be? If serving the customer is the ultimate purpose of your organization, how can it be that that's where you have the biggest gap between what matters and what your organization is actually measuring?

Gap number two was employees. We say we are in a period which we are calling a war for talent, yet it was clear from this research that there's a tremendous gap between what we need to know about our employees, what they care about, and what we're actually measuring and rewarding. And, what a surprise, turnover is so high! In effect, we're flying blind.

With the exception of financial information, where in effect the survey respondents were saying that they have more information than they need, they said that there's a gap in every single category. We then looked at the components of the gap.

JC: *Who were the respondents in this case?*

JL: The respondents were a couple of hundred executives in large global financial service companies.

We looked at how they used this information. We looked at three categories. One was identifying opportunities, the second was evaluating capital investments, and the third was evaluating managerial performance. We found that there were significant gaps in all three areas. Interestingly, the biggest gaps were in the customer and employee areas. Closely tied for the third and fourth position were quality and alliances.

It has been 15 years since we have been saying quality is job one and bowing in the direction of quality. Yet, here were all of these executives saying that they have huge gaps in understanding whether they're delivering quality or not. And in alliances, which is a newer but extremely important measure, particularly in the dot.com/e-commerce world, there is also clearly a huge dearth of information about how we're doing. Look at the available data. Most mergers or acquisitions, say upward of 65–75% of them, fail. By looking at the fact that information like this is so poor, we can begin to get a clearer picture of what's going wrong in the economy, what we need to know, and what we need to focus on.

The point is that, with some insight and effort, we can begin to put together a clearer picture of what is going wrong, what might be going wrong, what is going well, what could go better, and how to improve it. This is crucial information, because the traditional measures simply do not provide enough detail or enough texture to give managers or investors the information they need.

We are now trying to drill even deeper and look at specific industries in the case of value creation. With regard to the IPO study, we are initiating a follow-up to see if, in the three years of the dot.com revolution, the same things still apply. We want to see if the failure rate is still 50% and if the differentiators between success and failure are the same for those three years as they were for the preceding ten years. That will be very interesting. That will be done through Cap Gemini Ernst & Young.

Drivers for Nondurable and Service Organizations

JC: *Have you explored the drivers in nondurable or service organizations?*

JL: Yes. We used the nondurable manufacturing companies as our proxy for the service world. It was statistically hard to get specific service industry data. But, if you look at our nondurable list, we have Time Warner, Proctor & Gamble, Johnson & Johnson, and Coca-Cola. We have a lot of companies where the value of what they're marketing and selling is more important than the value of what they're manufacturing.

The notion of bundling is that if you're selling a product, you need to be selling a service, and if you're selling a service, you have to have a product attached to it or in support of it. We feel we've at least got a good beginning on that. It is interesting to look at the difference between what we are valuing in those kinds of companies and what we're valuing in the e-commerce world. We discovered that the drivers in the e-commerce world are different to some degree. E-commerce's top three drivers are alliances, innovation, and what is called in the dot.com world, *eyes* or *number of page views*. Two other drivers are not particularly valuable: brand and minutes per page, or what is popularly known as *stickiness*.

We feel that if had we come out with these findings in the fall of 1999 or even as much as six months earlier, we would probably have been derided for "not getting it." But if we look at what's happened in the stock market and what happened in the 1999 post-Christmas season, we know the increasing pressure on business-to-consumer companies in the dot.com arena. What we found is that they misspent their money because they misunderstood how value is being created. In this specific case, we have an indication that if measures like this, which are not based on traditional financial reporting, were widely available, investors might have understood far sooner which companies were going to do well and which were not.

We know that alliances are the most important value driver category in this survey. As we gain more experience in e-commerce, this may change, but for the moment this is what this tells us. Innovation and "eyes" are the next most important.

What do we mean by alliances? *Alliances* are what create the ability to leverage your network or your web of commercial contacts to help create value. It is what drives customers toward you. It is also what helps you create value by providing more information about your product, by providing more products or services that are not otherwise readily available, and so on.

Innovation is not just about new products and services. It is also about your business model. It is about innovation in how you manage. Ask yourself, "How hierarchical are we? How flat is our organization? How aligned with our corporate strategy do our employees feel?" Innovation covers that sort of thing.

When we look at eyes, that says we need a raw volume of attention. But what has been interesting for the last year is that we have heard a lot about stickiness. *Stickiness* is the notion that if you can just get people to spend more time on your website, you are creating value. It turns out that that is utterly false. In fact, stickiness may be the worst thing that you can have. Because what stickiness may mean is that people are having trouble entering their credit card number.

Or, even worse, you made a mistake, you hit the wrong button, and you do not want to buy something, and you cannot figure out how to erase it. Then you call up the technical support center, and you get the recording that says, "Someone will be with you in 14 minutes." The result is that you give up in disgust. Stickiness is, in fact, not a useful measure of value.

In the dot.com universe, there was too much focus on these high-level measures. Nobody with retail experience was saying, "What's our conversion rate? We have page views, and we are measuring the number of minutes people are spending at our website, but how many people are actually, then, buying something?" It turns out that the conversion rate from page views to purchase is about 1.5%, which is like saying, if you're Macy's, if only 1.5% of the people who walk into your store buy something, you're in tough shape. And that's what's happening here: The conversion rate is 1.5%.

We also had many egregious stories about companies with no revenues, let alone no profits, buying advertising during the Super Bowl, because they were "creating brand." When we looked at why brand was relatively low as a value driver, it was because brand is not about advertising. *Brand* is a promise to the customer. In this case, why are customers shopping on the Internet? Because it is supposed to be easier and possibly less expensive. If you're not delivering on that promise and people are calling you in a panic on December 15 and saying, "I need you to send this toy to my nephew in Dubuque. I'm willing to pay the additional charges for Federal Express," and then it turns out the item never gets there, you are destroying brand value. Brand is really more much about supply chain and about operational efficiency than it is about clever advertising using gerbils.

I argue that brand on the Internet is really also dependent upon your alliances. If how you got to the site was through AOL, Amazon, Yahoo, or some other well-recognized name, in effect, the implicit assumption is that they have done some vetting for you, that they are not going to permit anyone to be part of that network unless they have some assurance that that entity is going to be able to deliver.

Can You Deliver? How Do You Create Value?

JC: *Is this a wholesomeness or trust factor?*

JL: Yes. But it is far more important than that. Could anyone tell me the difference between Petstore.com and Pets.com and Petopia.com? Ultimately it came down to: "How quickly can I get access to them, and can they deliver what I want?" It was not about their advertising, or their logo, or the look and feel of their website.

Our point is that this is not information that you can find by looking at the company's annual report. It is not information that you can get from the SEC filings. We have a population of consumers who are more educated, arguably more intelligent, better informed than any population of consumers in the history of the world. And they demand that information. They are going to make very quick judgments based on their self-confidence about their ability to navigate in this economy as to who is delivering service and who is not. The result is that you, as a manager or an investor in management, need to understand those drivers and who is doing the best job of leveraging those drivers.

JC: *Have you gotten to the point of proposing that organizations develop a supplemental statement?*

JL: Not in a formal way. We've worked pretty closely with Skandia. It is important to keep in mind that Skandia has created supplemental intellectual capital reports out of self-interest. That is what we're saying to all of our clients.

We are not trying to change the global accounting system, or trying to convince the SEC or the International Association of Securities Commissioners that they should change the accounting rules. What we are saying is that you, as management, need to understand how you're creating value. We then say that you need to communicate that to your various clients and customer groups, whether they be investors or people who are actually buying your products and services. Why? Because that is how you're going to get your stock price up. If what you are telling people makes sense, they will then make judgments about how smart you are, how good a manager you are, and if you really understand the business.

JC: *Have people started to take what you're saying to heart and act on it?*

JL: Yes. Most of the evidence is anecdotal at this point, but one important indicator is that the volume of people doing research in this area has exploded. Virtually everyone in the Big Four firms and most of our major competitors are doing research or have invested substantially in work focused around creating value.

A second indicator is that when we started this, we would go to a client. Usually the CEO or members of the board were interested because they were interested in strategic issues. By and large, the CFOs felt threatened, because there was an implicit accusation that they had not been doing their jobs and that we were saying, "You missed something." Even though we weren't trying to present it as that, we were saying that between computerization and globalization, we just know a lot more than we knew when you got out of business school and started working your way up. This reaction pattern was true until about 1999. There was a dramatic shift in the space of about three months. We went from having quite emotional arguments with CFOs—who said that the net present value of future cash flows was all that had ever mattered, did matter, and ever would matter—to suddenly having them impatiently telling us, "Yes, yes, yes. We get it. Now tell us how to do it."

I think what drove that was largely the dot.com revolution in the capital markets. Now CFOs of 100-year-old companies with 50,000 employees scattered around the globe were suddenly finding that they had a lower market cap than companies with three employees, most of whose assets were metallic piercings in their bodies. They were trying to figure out: How could this be?

Who Is Thinking in Terms of Intellectual Capital?

JC: *Was it that their world no longer made complete sense?*
JL: That created a significant change of mind. Since then, what we've found is that people really do want to try to understand how to better manage their organizations and how to communicate the ways that they are creating significant value for shareholders, for employees, for customers, for all their other stakeholders.

JC: *Are there some companies or sectors that are picking this*
up more than others at this point? What are the tendencies,
the trends?
JL: I think there are companies that are what I would call *intangible dependent,* that have by necessity picked this up. Part of that was driven by experience. There has been a lot of interest in EVA (economic value added). It turns out that EVA, unless it is finely tuned to a certain extent, discriminates against companies that require significant amounts of R&D, because

ultimately the best way to perform in EVA is to starve the denominator, that is, to just stop investing.

The implication is that life science and pharmaceutical companies, telecom and entertainment companies are really negatively impacted by using EVA. It is no surprise that Coca-Cola was the EVA icon for a decade because its R&D was done in 1899. All it has to do is crank it out. What was left to do is create a market. I do not want to take anything away from an extremely well managed company, but that is the reality.

We are looking as well at who else is being hurt by the current focus on shareholder value. We began to determine who are most interested and most focused on demonstrating how they're creating shareholder value. We have gotten away from the conglomerate structure. We are now in the intensely focused business model phase of the economy. I suspect that will swing back again at some point as the dot.coms and NASDAQ continue to falter and people look for ways to manage their earnings. In fact, one might argue that the AOL/Time Warner merger is the first shot in that battle.

Convergence

JC: *Do you agree with those who say that by 2005 both sides are going to converge, and everybody is going to be an e-business or be in big trouble?*

JL: Yes. There is some interesting commentary. If we look back 80–100 years and see what happened in the stock market in the 1920s, it exploded because of the introduction of two new technologies: One was electricity and the other was the internal combustion engine. Companies had vice presidents for electricity or vice presidents for automobiles, just as today we have vice presidents for e-commerce or vice presidents for management information systems. I would agree completely on the idea of convergence. We are going to look back on this era and laugh because the Internet will be so deeply suffused within the business model that it will be second nature.

JC: *Are the people most affected, the ones who are bleeding the most, are they the ones who are most picking up on what you're talking about?*

JL: I do not think that's true in all cases. There are some companies that really are forward looking and are trying to figure this out. General Electric's well-publicized focus on the Internet is an example of that. But, necessity drives people to try to figure out how they're creating value. So, to some extent, it is the people who perceive that they are most threatened who are doing the most in this area. Let's look at any converging industry, and I will mention three: financial services, life sciences, oil and gas. There are tremendous changes going on with all of these. And, to some degree, they are all trying to figure out what they should do about it.

Telecom is another one. They are trying to find out how they recover, what does all of this mean, how do they begin to figure out how they are part of a global network, and where do their revenues come from? It is increasingly evident that the revenue potential from data is going to far exceed the revenue potential from voice, and yet when will that happen? Or, are they organized to deal with that potential versus the drop in revenues in the present?

JC: *That takes a lot of thinking through.*
JL: Forgetting about the collapse of the sector as a whole, just look at one aspect of what's happened since 2000 in Europe. Telecom Italia was undergoing a hostile acquisition by Olivetti. It turned to Deutsche Telekom, and that deal fell apart not because of any economic or business reasons, but because of traditional, age-old, cultural fears about selling out your telecom business to another country.

We have Sweden and Norway, which are trying to combine their telecom companies, and that deal falls apart because there's been a history of enmity that goes back two centuries between Norway and Sweden. More recently, Spain and the Netherlands tried to combine their telecom companies. That deal also fell apart, because the Spanish government fears the Dutch government will retain an interest. It is very interesting.

The Culture Factor

JC: *Does that mean we have to overcome 500 years of history?*
JL: Exactly. We have got the whole globalization issue, the technology issue, and then we have got this squishy, not well understood soft stuff, which really has to do with national boundaries, culture, and identity, which are sinking vastly valuable economic combinations.

JC: *How does that relate back to what you were exploring?*
JL: It relates directly. What we are saying is that if we were looking at Telecom Italia or Deutsche Telekom from a traditional economist's, accountant's, or banker's standpoint, we would say, "Here are the benefits of the deal, and here are the potential problems with the deal. Obviously, this

deal makes tremendous sense economically, and therefore, anyone who opposes it is a fool." And, in effect, we saw three major combinations just like that, with winning financial characteristics, which all fell apart because of things that are not captured on a balance sheet or income statement. That is why we are saying we have to do a better job with intangibles.

JC: *Are the things that may have contributed to the dissolution of those deals the factors of innovation or alliance or whatever else you have been studying?*

JL: I would say that it is very much about alliances because to some degree we're really talking about alliances and combining cultures. We are also looking specifically at things like employees, management, and very fundamental issues. We are asking: "How is this going to affect me? Am I giving up a huge source of jobs, of income of national value?"

The understanding is that one's telecom company is one's connection to the global economy. The concern is: "Do I really want control of that entity to be in the hands of someone who's not of my country or race?" What is that? That is not a balance sheet or income statement item. It may not be specifically the kind of value driver that we have identified, but as I said before, we just had a baseline here. The more that we look at industries or specific companies, the more we find different value drivers, and the more we study this, the more we will find the relevant value drivers.

JC: *You continue to identify what the drivers are and which are the nonfinancial and financial drivers for each set of conditions. Does this tie in with your work with the Brookings Institution's study of intangible values,* Unseen Wealth?

JL: Very much so. Brookings undertook a study to try to understand intangible sources of value. My former colleague Tony Siesfeld and I cochaired a subgroup of that task force looking at strategic and organizational issues. The focus of the overall study was to try to understand what companies were doing or perceived they should be doing and what government, particularly the U.S. government, should be doing about this. Were there any effects on value, on capital allocation, on global economic indicators that should be addressed?

Where we ended up in the overall Brookings study was that our understanding of this set of issues is still pretty plastic, still in formation. While there are probably some people who are benefiting from asymmetries or misallocations of value, we do not know enough to know what we should be doing differently. If we made a bunch of sweeping regulatory changes, we'd probably end up hurting some people and helping some other people, but it would all balance out because we don't really know that well who's being hurt and helped now.

An area where there did appear to be agreement is that the United States has kind of a singular approach to intellectual property, particularly patents, licenses, and copyrights, and that we need to get more in tune with the global network for those items. What we view as pirating, other cultures and countries do not. Our sense was that we are only hurting ourselves and losing current and future value by not getting better aligned with the global system.

We found that, within companies and as a country, government can play a convening role or an analytical role by trying to gather more information and to understand these forces. Government can play the role of a referee. It needs to do that because value is being created, companies are being bought and sold, individuals are being affected by these issues, and we know very little about them. Who better than the U.S. government, through Bureau of Labor Statistics or all of the other government statistics organizations, to try to figure this out? That is where we ended up. We did not come up with any significant public policies that we thought were interfering with companies' efforts to rethink their intangibles. We did find there was a great lack of knowledge and a hunger for knowledge and that hunger should be addressed.

Global Explorations of Principles and Standards

JC: *The Brookings study set up a platform for this kind of conversation in the United States. The only other similar effort had taken place in Denmark. Are there other such studies under way?*
JL: The Organization for Economic Cooperation and Development (OECD) is now taking this on. The OECD is primarily European but basically comprises the 29 or 30 largest economies. Korea, Japan, Mexico, Canada, and the United States are in the OECD, but I do not think any other Latin countries are in it. The OECD has begun working on what I think will emerge as a set of principles regarding the measurement and disclosure of intangibles.

JC: *Is what you're doing through the studies we discussed earlier being taken into account by the OECD?*
JL: Yes. It has always been open to our work. It was just a question of understanding the various levers. There was a small group that was hopeful that it could come up with "a model for measuring and disclosing intan-

gibles," which it would copyright or patent and then become insanely rich as a result. The group had to be convinced that no one was going to rally behind its vision of how this should be done. This was not purely for economic reasons but just because we do not know enough yet.

JC: *How does a new focus on investments and intangibles, especially human intangibles and intellectual capital, affect public policy?*

JL: I do not think it is going to have any immediate effect on public policies. I expect that people will keep an eye on a couple of issues. One might argue that having such a vast investment in intangibles, invisible to the public's statistical and recordkeeping set, may be creating the so-called productivity paradox, that the GDP and productivity numbers may in fact be lower than they should be. The economy is in effect stronger than it might otherwise appear because we do not have a better understanding of these issues.

JC: *To what extent is the new reality or the new economy understood—or is it a new economy anyway?*

JL: That is exactly the point. That is probably the most important public policy issue. There are related issues about how, on an individual level, income is treated; what constitutes income in the traditional sense; how people are compensated given the widespread interest in equity, options, and related instruments; and also what effect that has ultimately for taxing authorities.

The Future of Intangible Asset Measurement

JC: *What is the future of intangible assets measurement, and how will that affect the shape, structure, operations, and relationships of organizations?*

JL: I think there's actually a reasonably simple and comprehensive answer to this. That is, the world is going to be increasingly transparent, or the economy will be increasingly transparent. The differentiator will not be what you know, it will be how you act on what you know.

JC: *Does knowledge then really begin to mean usable knowledge?*

JL: Right. The ability to execute a strategy becomes far more important, say, than the quality of a strategy.

There have been many new companies formed which had great ideas. The great concepts and the research they had done on the potential market and how to serve that market were excellent. I anticipate that what we will find is that the companies that were able to execute their plan versus the companies that had the most brilliant plan ultimately prevailed or will prevail.

JC: *Is that what seems to be the message that's being heard out there?*
JL: Exactly. That argues for two things. First, it argues that brilliance in the historical form of closely guarded business secrets or strategic information is not as valuable. This suggests that there's less value in protecting information and more value in sharing information because by sharing the information, you interest more people in what you are doing.

The second significant implication beyond transparency is the permeable organization, the organization that derives value from alliances, not from its linear "we do it all from taking the iron out of the ground to producing the car that comes out the other end" approach.

JC: *What do you think is the role of shared values in that?*
JL: That is going to be tremendously important because if you are incapable of determining what your shared values are, you are going to be incapable of creating the appropriate alliances. In the end, you are going to be completely incapable of making those alliances work.

JC: *Does the work you are involved in create the ground for the next 30 or 40 years?*
JL: We will see what happens. In the meantime, we are pleased with the response we're getting, and we are going to continue working in this area. Hopefully, we will be able to continue to provide some interesting insights.

Key Learning Points

■ There has been an approximately 20-year decline in the relevance of assets and earnings as predictors of stock market performance. Securities analysts and portfolio managers refer extensively to nonfinancial factors to determine the accuracy of their quarterly and annual financial projections and to make their portfolio allocation decisions.

- We have arguably created more wealth in the last three years than had been created for the entire human race in the preceding 300 years. That, to a large measure, happened because the stock option, among other financial mechanisms, harnessed and gave incentive to bright individuals to donate or invest their intellectual and human capital in the strategy and the enterprise.
- The Value Creation Index uses nine drivers to understand the creation of value in organizations: innovation, management, employees, quality, environment, alliances, brand, technology, and the customer. These nonfinancial measures explain about 50% of the market value in most companies and about 90% of the market value in dot.com companies.
- In old-economy companies, the top three factors were innovation, management, and employees. In e-commerce companies, the top three factors are innovation, alliances, and "eyes."
- Most managers and executives feel that there is a huge gap between what actually drives value for their organization and what the organization measures and compensates. This creates tremendous cynicism and lack of alignment in organizations.
- With some insight and effort, we can begin to put together a clearer picture of what is going wrong in an organization, what is going well, what could go better, and how to improve it. Traditional measures do not provide enough detail or texture to give managers or investors the information they need.
- The dot.com revolution in the capital markets created a significant change in the acceptance of the value of intangibles as traditional CFOs tried to figure out how tiny companies could have far higher market caps than their companies did.
- Even though we have been able to deal with such issues as globalization and technology, we do not really understand the intangible "stuff" of national boundaries, culture, and identity, which can readily sink vastly valuable economic combinations.

A Level Playing Field for Intangibles

13

Steven Wallman is a recognized authority on securities markets and the challenge of revising financial reporting to account for the new drivers of wealth production. He is the founder and chief executive officer of FOLIO*fn*, an innovative financial services and brokerage firm, a senior fellow of the Brookings Institution, and a former commissioner of the U.S. Securities and Exchange Commission (SEC).

As an SEC commissioner from 1994 to 1997, Wallman organized the first symposium addressing the increasing role of intangible assets in the changing economy and the related need to make financial statements reflect this significant shift in business and financial activities. After leaving the SEC, he co-chaired the Brookings Institution study on intangibles that resulted in the report *Unseen Wealth*.[1] The report serves as a foundation piece for legitimitizing intangible assets as a vital issue worthy of study and resolution. The report explored the public policy implications of the growing level of intangible assets in the U.S. economy and made recommendations on a number of specific issues.

Intangibles, such as intellectual capital, research and development, brand names, and human capital have not been recognized as having value but are traditionally seen as expenses. Wallman advocates a core

[1] Margaret M. Blair and Steven M. H. Wallman, *Unseen Wealth: Report of the Brookings Task Force on Intangibles* (Washington D.C.: Brookings Institution Press, 2001).

change in the understanding and treatment of intangible resources to re-solve the disparities that have resulted from the existing framework of valuation. He sees this as essential for the efficient and effective valuation of companies and even of whole sectors of an economy. Without this change, he feels it will be difficult to realistically appraise the value of a business's activities and assets and to make the appropriately informed re-source allocation decisions.

Transparency and intercomparability are two essential tests of a relia-ble reporting system. A transformed system will satisfactorily acknowl-edge the value of intangible as well as physical and financial resources.

The conversation with Wallman explores how an understanding of intangibles is critical to investors, institutions, and governments. He gives a number of examples of circumstances in which current accounting practices do not take into account how intangible wealth is created, and he demonstrates the need for the continuing review, study, and reconcili-ation of the changing economic value landscape.

The Conversation

Financial Reporting, Intangibles, and a Changing Economy

JC: *You codirected the Brookings Institution study* Unseen Wealth: Report of the Brookings Task Force on Intangi-bles. *What was the rationale for establishing the study, and what do you hope to accomplish with it?*

SW: The genesis for the Brookings study came from several sources. One was the effort I commenced in 1995–1996 while I was at the SEC to study the source, value, and impact of intangibles with regard to financial re-porting and changes in the economy. The genesis for that came from my increasingly firm belief (back then, only a hunch and a suspicion) that the U.S. financial reporting and disclosure system was increasingly susceptible to not capturing certain important drivers of wealth production, basically knowledge-based assets or intangible assets. Moreover, these assets are in-creasingly important as the drivers of wealth production in both traditional-economy companies and in what is now referred to as new-economy com-panies. Any such potential deficiency, of course, requires study and correction as our system of financial reporting and disclosure is the foun-dation for providing information to investors and others, which results in an efficient allocation of capital resources in this country. To the extent that the system is still premised on generally accepted accounting principles derived from the standpoint of a bricks-and-mortar economy, it needs to be updated to reflect changes in the economy and the way businesses operate.

Just look at the juxtaposition of new-economy companies with older companies. An easy example is Amazon versus a more bricks-and-mortar-oriented bookstore like Barnes & Noble. In Amazon's financial statements, all of its efforts aimed at creating a brand by building a website, engaging in a significant amount of marketing, and, by contrast, not spending money on bricks and mortar, big stores, and other more tangible and permanent kinds of things is, under current accounting, an expense. But, if Amazon's advertising and brand-building efforts were focused on building bricks-and-mortar stores, then most of those costs would be capitalized and amortized instead. So, Barnes & Noble's store-building efforts result in assets on its balance sheet and lower upfront expenses as compared to Amazon, which instead shows no assets on its balance sheet but high expenses during this brand-building period. Consequently, if you were to take traditional measures of price-to-earnings, book-to-earnings, or almost any other traditional measure, Amazon, at least at the initial stages while it's growing and building, looks horrible relative to companies engaged in more traditional activities.

On the other hand, Amazon will receive a great gift and advantage as it switches its strategy and operates on the other side of the cusp, if you will. It will have expensed a lot of the things already that its bricks-and-mortar competitors will have to continue to charge against income as a periodic amortization expense. In the future, Amazon's numbers, all things otherwise being equal, will look better than those of a company engaged in a more traditional bricks-and-mortar strategy. With the current rise and fall of the new-economy sector, it is important to recognize that this is not now and never was a debate about whose business model is better. It was and is a concern that the information needed to evaluate those business models—both old and new—on a basis relative to each other and to their peers, is increasingly hard to find.

The disparity in how we account for things, based on whether the underlying drivers of wealth production are tangible or intangible, struck me as increasingly obvious and increasingly creating a problem as to the transparency of financial statements. Transparency of financial statements is important so people both can understand the financial statement presentation of a company and be able to compare across companies and sectors. Financial statements, simply put, need to make sense, and they need to reflect business and financial activities—not artificial constructs.

The simple truth is that increasingly they are not making as much sense as we wish they would. It is harder and harder to compare company to company and sector to sector.

In 1995–1996, we studied these issues at the SEC and held the first SEC symposium on these kinds of questions. That symposium was controversial at the time, both inside and outside the commission. There were some who believed that there were no real issues worthy of study, and others who believed that simply studying the issue might exacerbate the problem because any solutions would contribute to, not resolve, the issue, and raising the problem would simultaneously erode public confidence in the current system. Still others were concerned that any changes would be mandated, involve significant additional costs imposed on preparers, and would not add much to solving the stated concerns. Finally, some thought the current system with its opaqueness was fine as it encouraged or forced investors to rely more on analysts who were presumably in a better position to discern the true financial position of a company because they had more tools and time than the ordinary investor could deploy. But the dominant view, again both within and outside the commission, was that this is a very important issue that has to be discussed and studied, and over time solutions need to be found.

We held a day and a half symposium, which was quite well attended. Joe Stiglitz, the chairman of the president's Council of Economic Advisors, spoke, as did Secretary Robert Reich from the Department of Labor and a number of other stellar scholars and leaders in the field and surrounding fields. The symposium created a lot of thought and interest in the academic community and elsewhere on these issues. Professor Baruch Lev, one of the best known academic accounting researchers with a global reputation, created a center at the Sterns School at New York University devoted to the study of intangibles, based in part on being able to indicate that there is continuing interest at high levels of government on these issues. I personally was able to continue to promote this from my position at the commission and encouraged additional study of these matters.

Unseen Wealth

JC: *How are you now involved with these issues?*
SW: At the Brookings Institution, there were a number of others who reviewed these kinds of issues from time to time and saw their importance both to the new economy and also more generally to the issues of capital allocation, financial reporting, appropriate disclosure, volatility of the financial marketplace, and related matters of public policy concern. When

I left the SEC and joined the Brookings Institution as a fellow, I presented the topic of the study of intangibles as one matter that would merit further review. It was viewed by the appropriate people at the Institution as important and worth doing. Margaret Blair, who was a senior fellow at the Brookings Institution and is now a professor at Georgetown University Law School, also volunteered to work on this and became my co-chair to commence a study (*Unseen Wealth*, which has now been released by Brookings) of these issues. We started from that base to assemble both the financial support for this work and the intellectual patronage to participate in the study activities. And, we then went from there.

JC: *What are the goals of the study? What would the outcomes be if you could will them into existence?*
SW: There are a couple. The original 1995–1996 efforts of the Commission were focused on trying to get the message out that there is an issue here, that it is an issue worthy of consideration, discussion, debate, and eventually of solution—to the extent that there are "solutions" or resolutions to these kinds of problems. It succeeded in getting out the message that this is worthy of discussion, started the debate, and began the long process of trying to make things better—in other words, it began the process of coming up with solutions.

The SEC effort itself did not, of course, prescribe detailed policy solutions. It was really designed to raise the profile of the issue so that people would start to think about it. The Brookings effort, by contrast, was really designed more toward starting to focus on and isolate some of the particular issues from the Brookings perspective of public policy.

The task that was originally set was both narrower and broader than that of the SEC symposium. It was not as broad as some of the discussions at the symposium, which focused on how to improve financial reporting and disclosure generally in this area. Yet it was broader in that, although it focused explicitly and solely on intangible assets, as opposed to all of the drivers of wealth production in companies, it focused on intangibles from a number of different perspectives, with financial reporting and disclosure being only one such perspective. Moreover, our focus was not on how we take new productivity stemming from improving drivers of wealth and distribute them better, more fairly, or more equally in society nor did it address the issue of whether we should distribute them differently. For this purpose and study, important issues such as the "digital divide" were not included.

The study was more focused on the biases for and against certain intangible assets stemming from systemic or government actions that might not even be recognized. We might conclude as a society that the bias is justified or even desirable, but we need first to recognize that it is there and apply policy analysis to determine if it should be maintained or whether it was even intentional. Some biases, for example, may favor the creation or promotion of intangible assets. Some may oppose that. Some may just be biases in the sense that they neither always work for or against something, they just disturb the way it otherwise would be. The financial reporting that I discussed earlier is an example of a bias that is both good and bad, depending on what period in a product or company life cycle one is reviewing. Depending upon the life cycle of Amazon, for example, and what it decides to do next, there could be a financial reporting result that Amazon might say, "This is great." Or, Amazon might say, "This is horrible." For example, if the market suddenly concludes that a company needs to have reportable profits in order to be financed, then the new-economy companies that do not have the capability of showing profits early on are going to be in trouble. All of a sudden, there is a significant adverse change in the prospects for an entire sector—as it relates to the newer startups in that sector—based very much on our current financial accounting system, specifically as it relates to intangible assets.

By contrast, those new-economy companies that had already invested when times were better in web sites and advertising and that are now ready to exploit that effort, where they don't have to spend such sums going forward will be benefited. Instead of amortizing that $1 billion, $2 billion, or $5 billion worth of investment, which would be a drag on earnings for the next 20 years, they have already got it behind them, so they are able to show higher levels of profits from now on than would be the case where the investments were principally in bricks and mortar. This is due to the fact that the current accounting system has the tendency to distort the relative juxtaposition of income and expense from the way one would normally see it in bricks-and-mortar companies to the way one sees it in dot.com companies. Now, that is just a bias and that may help the new economy or it might hurt the new economy, depending upon what the market thinks at the time and depending upon the life stage of the companies at the time. It could be good or bad from a particular company or investor's standpoint depending on a whole host of factors, but it is clearly a bias that needs to be recognized and one that I think needs to be addressed.

Our task was to identify where there are distortions and biases: regardless of whether they are for, against, or sometimes one and sometimes the other, depending on external circumstances. We then attempted to determine if there were solutions we could suggest that would eliminate those biases. That was the underlying rationale for the study: to find solutions that do in fact create a level playing field, so one kind of asset and driver of wealth production—intangibles—is not being discriminated for or against. Then the private sector, endowed with the ability to allocate resources (based on the views of millions of people deciding for themselves where they think the next great investment will be and at what value), can be expected to make those decisions efficiently and on its own, free from artificial pressures that bias that decision. That was our fundamental premise.

The goals of the study transcended that, though, and aspired toward a more efficient capital allocation and investment environment. We also cared about, for example, issues in the intellectual property arena. Questions were posed, including, for example, whether the business method patent is a great and beneficial development, or not.

The Impact of the Internet

JC: *How does viewing business methods as intangible assets affect the resource allocation equation?*
SW: Business methods are intangibles. And we have got a new vehicle in the Internet, a new means to create new business methods. What the Internet has done is create a whole new platform for thinking of all sorts of new things and new businesses. That is a pretty tremendous and effective underlying paradigm shift.

JC: *A new ballgame?*
SW: Yes. It's truly remarkable. It has opened up the world for a whole new set of thinking about what it is that one wants to allow to be patented and patentable and has created lots of interesting policy questions. One is: "Do we want to separate out business method patents from all others?" We can say, "Yes, a new business method may be novel and unique, but we're just afraid of where this goes over time and therefore we think they should have a shorter life or something else." I've got my personal views on that, and others have their personal views on it. But it is an interesting set of questions that needs examination. The current examination, which is to take the old law and simply make believe there isn't any paradigmatic change, make believe everything is simply an incremental little change and that we can just simply have the evolutionary aspects of the common law dictating what the new answers are, is, I think, not as useful as it once was when the world was changing a little bit more slowly.

Brookings Task Force Issue Areas

JC: *You've also gotten into a bunch of other areas. What were the other task forces, and what were the issues they were raising?*

SW: There were a number that were doing a variety of different things. One was the intellectual property task force that discussed some of the issues noted above. Another was the accounting task force, whose work I have also mentioned already. A third task force tackled the issue of human resources and human capital, which had a broad and somewhat amorphous agenda to think about a variety of issues, including whether or not, for example, Social Security taxes are a tax on labor versus a tax on capital. For example, take the case of a company that purchased a machine to do the same thing that an employee did, and the employer has to pay the same dollar amount to do the same unit of work. In one instance, he also has to pay an extra tax, which is the Social Security employer contribution. If we are trying to promote full employment, why would one want to impose a disincentive on hiring a person with an extra tax burden on the employer (that arises just because the company is an employer), as opposed to having a differential tax burden that may be on profits or something else and that does not impose a tax on labor? These and other issues like that, in terms of workplace practices and so on, were being looked at by that group. One concern was that there is a deduction for employer education that is job-related, but not for employer education that is not job-related. If you can take employees and marginally improve their productivity through education so they only can do a little bit more than what they have been able to do, then there is an incentive to do that with a deduction. But to take an extreme example from the movies, if an employer provided someone who is currently a janitor the chance to obtain a Ph.D. in math, where he can really do something wildly different, then the employer would ordinarily not receive a deduction. It is those kinds of disparities that this task force spent some time reviewing.

JC: *Yes, there is wetware (brainware), as well as software and hardware, that needs to be taken into account in the creation of intangible value.*

SW: But, we can obviously continue this analysis and get into an entire issue of deductibility of education and other expenses and a whole review of the tax code. We had another task force involved with organizational processes and methodologies. This related to process management, process methodologies, valuation within a company of intangible assets, and things of that nature. Again, the task force had a broad-based agenda. Still another task force reviewed the ability of companies to finance intangible assets, which are not easily collateralized, and to obtain other forms of capital. What we found was that there is a good deal of anecdotal information that suggests that banks won't provide loans to companies that do not have tangible assets as collateral. But we could not find a significant amount of solid research to conclude whether or not that's true.

The study has been released, and all of the conclusions and findings are available for public consumption. The study does not answer all of the questions in the area of intangibles. In fact, it hardly answers any. But it does lay out some very interesting policy prescriptions that should provide a useful framework for research in this area; it does present a compelling argument for the government, including the SEC and others, to address a number of the issues we discussed here; and it does prove the point that this is an area crying out for further review, study, and resolution given its continuing and increasing importance to our society.

Key Learning Points

- Financial reporting and disclosure systems are increasingly susceptible to not capturing important drivers of wealth production, specifically knowledge-based intangible assets, and need to be updated.
- Building brands, websites, and other intangible wealth is accounted for as an expense, instead of being recognized as creating value.
- Financial statements need to make sense and reflect business and financial activities, not artificial constructs, otherwise it is harder to compare company to company and sector to sector.
- Recognition of intangibles is important in decisions involving capital allocation, financial reporting, appropriate disclosure, volatility of the financial marketplace, and related issues of public concern.
- There are distortions and biases, both for and against particular intangible assets, stemming from systems and governmental actions, some of which may be unintentional, but all of which need to be understood and adjusted.
- Current accounting has a tendency to distort the relationship between income and expense for new-economy enterprises more than for bricks-and-mortar companies.
- The goal is a more efficient capital allocation and investment environment. To do this requires the establishment of a level playing field.
- The Internet has created a new platform for new business methods, which are intangible assets that can now be patented.

- The Brookings Institution study on intangibles, *Unseen Wealth*, explored and made recommendations in a number of areas in which disparities in policy affect practices in valuation, taxation, human capital, intellectual property, and related issues. The report was a major step toward addressing issues of intangibles not only in the United States but globally as well.

KNOWLEDGE

Bringing It All Together in Practice

Cluster V:

Good practitioners bring together the ideas, practices, and experiences that will make the difference in their target situations. They continuously experiment with their approaches to find out what works best and what does not. Although they build on their experiences, they are not comfortable in resting on past achievements, since each new day and every new circumstance requires them to craft a new and unique response. The test is not how brilliant their ideas are nor how much in the way of resources they can bring to bear, but whether their approach works to produce desired performance outcomes.

Over time, by creating responses and experimenting in a wide variety of circumstances, they create a body of work. In that process, they articulate their tacit knowledge and share it with others, either as partners in their efforts or while serving as mentors to nurture a knowledge perspective with colleagues.

Knowledge management and intellectual capital have produced a variety of outstanding practitioners who have created the field afresh in their organizations. Some started by forging an enterprise view and implementing multiyear knowledge strategies. Others began by searching out opportunities where a knowledge intervention would solve a business problem and yield impressive gains. Still others, out of sheer desperation, have created new ways to leverage enterprise knowledge for surprising and unprecedented responses to core organizational dilemmas.

The conversations with practitioners Hubert Saint-Onge, Kent Greenes, Sharon Oriel, Stephen Denning, and Alex Bennet demonstrate that a broad range of approaches can create high-level outcomes, providing that principles are sound and practices are imaginative, insightful, contactful, thorough, and grounded in reality. They illustrate that, depending on conditions, resources, and capabilities, there are multiple ways to shape a knowledge perspective that can successfully recast how an enterprise works and how it interacts with the world. The practitioners recognize that they are operating in a dynamically changing field and that there is no single right way to proceed. More than anything else, they have found that thoughtful, continuous experimentation is the key. The contributors also show that by keying their work to sound principles, practitioners can build a ground of experience, a knowledge base, significant results, viable relationships, and the trust that is vital for knowledge initiatives to succeed. The convergence of this array of elements, over time, feeds into the emergence of the organization as a knowledge-based enterprise.

Building Strategic Capabilities

Hubert Saint-Onge developed and implemented a multiyear comprehensive knowledge capital strategy during which the market value of Clarica, a Canadian investment and insurance firm, went from $2.1 billion to more than $7.1 billion. As senior vice president for strategic capabilities, he was instrumental in leveraging the firm's business growth through the systematic application of knowledge management and learning organization principles.

Saint-Onge emphasizes the strategic integration of business plans with people management systems, using technology architecture and organizational infrastructure. With his team, Saint-Onge worked to bring people and technology together in a new organizational configuration. A fundamental element that enabled success was the establishment of an initiative to define the enterprise's values and vision. The core shared values of the enterprise and its workforce enabled knowledge to flow easily throughout the enterprise. At the same time, these shared values of stewardship, partnership, and innovation allowed Clarica to renew its organizational culture in alignment with its strategic framework.

A key thrust of Saint-Onge's effort is the creation of a knowledge-based environment, where technology and culture support all members of the enterprise in seeing themselves as autonomous "businesses of one." The goal is for people to act in their own enlightened self-interest, with a full understanding of their impact on the organization. The use of communities of practice, supported by technology, facilitates the flow of knowledge throughout the enterprise, enabling all staff to readily access the best knowledge of the enterprise as they carry out their work.

KM = Change

Kent Greenes says that knowledge management is about change. The knowledge management process requires leadership commitment to deal with the knowledge issues that make a significant difference in the enterprise. With leadership setting direction, people throughout the enterprise carry out the knowledge management initiatives. This process for change weaves a top-down and bottom-up approach that aligns and creates the process and knowledge-based performance improvements that move the enterprise toward its desired future.

Greenes believes we are at a point where people have learned that merely relabeling document management and other information technologies as knowledge management is not the answer. Rather, it will be hands-on, experienced knowledge management practitioners who will be shaping the next stage of the field. He works to have all stakeholders see direct performance outcomes that benefit themselves and, by doing so, come to benefit the organization. Greenes views that knowledge is personal, and he works to have people involved on an intimate basis, with relationships that are built on trust becoming as important as the actual knowledge that is generated and shared.

The gains from this approach come not from high technology but from helping people to learn before, during, and after actions and to apply their learning on the job. Greenes does not preclude the value of technology but knows that knowledge management will not be primarily technology-driven if it is to work. During the knowledge-building process, people create a wealth of know-how that the enterprise is able to capture and harvest, knowledge that adds even more value as it is reused and adapted by others across the enterprise.

Shifting to an Enterprise Perspective

Sharon Oriel tells of the evolutionary journey of intellectual capital management at Dow Chemical. Dow shifted in the 1950s from its early focus on managing its inventions to its current thrust of managing and thinking of patents as intangible assets with the potential to create value for the enterprise. The next generation is expanding the range of its intellectual capital management efforts to incorporate all of the intangible value tied to its people, processes, customers, suppliers, and external relationships.

The key to Dow's effort is finding "the hook" to get its businesses to use its emerging intellectual capital approach. Practitioners do their homework on a problem in the business and demonstrate to the business managers, in their own language, that they could show significant value by solving that core problem using their intellectual capital approach. The value to the business units have ranged from saving millions of dollars in budget to increasing sales, having successful outcomes in litigation, or whatever made a substantial difference to the business owner. Finding the hook, translating the intellectual approach into corporate terms, and then picking up corporate support have been crucial to success. The success of these efforts has led to a shift in understanding intellectual capital management at Dow from a narrower technical perspective to a more embracing and powerful business perspective.

Over time, success in formative efforts paved the way for Dow to see that its intellectual capital initiatives were at the core of it being able to leverage a sustainable competitive advantage throughout the enterprise. Part of nurturing the intellectual capital capability has been the development of a multilevel career pathway for intellectual capital managers, who work in their business units but who also cycle through Dow's Tech Center to update and enhance their skills. This continuing learning revitalizes the enterprise-wide intellectual capital network and surfaces best practices so that they can ripple through the whole network to give the organization its cutting edge.

Storytelling as a Springboard to a Knowledge-Sharing Enterprise

Stephen Denning took on the task of transitioning the World Bank from a traditional lending organization into one where its collective and networked know-how has become a central pillar and resource in its fight against poverty around the world.

Denning realized that the real knowledge resource at the World Bank was the extensive know-how that its people had cultivated over a half century of existence. The challenge was how to share that know-how in a systematic fashion so that the World Bank would become a much more relevant, exciting, and effective enterprise.

Even though that vision of the World Bank as a knowledge-sharing organization was adopted, the means to accomplish that vision were elusive. Denning and his team found that conventional approaches to knowledge management were not geared to rapidly and broadly transforming the 10,000-member staff of the bank into an active network of knowledge sharers. Storytelling was the one thing they found that sparked the necessary enthusiasm and engagement for people to autonomously share knowledge, and that one thing was completely counterintuitive to the rational, analytic way of knowing in which both Denning and the bank were grounded.

After extensive experimentation, Denning and his staff developed an approach to telling stories that centered on how someone or some group brought about a remarkable and unexpected change in an otherwise difficult or intractable situation. The story was used as a springboard to bring listeners into whole new ways of thinking and acting. The stories of these phenomena sparked listeners to say, "If those folks could do it there, we could do something very similar to that here." In this way, storytelling became the vehicle for people to be engaged in co-creating the vision of what the World Bank could become.

Although storytelling has been the process for developing the knowledge capacity at the World Bank, seven elements of a knowledge infrastructure had to be put in place to support the knowledge-sharing effort. These were a knowledge-sharing strategy; a small but focused knowledge organization to spearhead the change across the organization; a budget; changing incentives to support knowledge sharing; building communities; providing technology to make know-how easily available; and measures gauging how well things were transforming.

The complete story of the World Bank's transformation has yet to be completely written, but with storytelling as its engine and the core of a transforming infrastructure coming into place, knowledge sharing has become enmeshed as a way of doing business throughout both the internal and external relationships of the bank.

Knowledge Superiority: The Ultimate Strategic Advantage

Alex Bennet led the development of the U.S. Navy's enterprise-wide knowledge-centric organization (KCO) effort. While the U.S. Navy has an enormous investment in ships, aircraft, and supporting technologies to operate globally, it has come to understand that it will be its knowledge superiority that will provide the advantage in its ability to carry out its mission.

Part of the strategy for a knowledge-enabled navy is to build on the high degree of social capital that is in some ways unique to its branch of the armed services. Having its people rotate every two to three years throughout the vast navy system, often in life-threatening situations at sea, breeds a sense of team and builds networks for life. One result is that navy personnel know that no single person is a complete resource unto him or her self. This fluidity of movement and the experiences of high interreliance serve to offset the tendencies of stovepiping in navy organizations and to open opportunities for knowledge sharing across the enterprise. Using this social capital as a background and supporting it with essential technologies and learning tools, the navy is developing a system of nodes where relevant information is captured and where a context is provided for that information. Knowledge flow is being facilitated through communities that are being created across the diverse navy organizations.

In essence, the navy has embarked on a journey to implement strategies that facilitate the creation and sharing of knowledge to enable effective and agile decision making. This notion of knowledge management emphasizes a small *k* and a small *m* as a means to achieve enterprise goals.

Craft the Shoe That Fits Your Enterprise

All of the conversations in this cluster explore a variety of approaches to building knowledge-based enterprises. Although each practitioner discusses operating in a unique set of conditions, all of their work reflects a related set of operating principles. And each practitioner provides an array of valuable insights and lessons on what to look for and what is possible.

An experiment for readers to consider is to overlay these different approaches on an organization that might be considering transforming itself into a knowledge-based enterprise. That creates an opportunity to see which characteristics of each of these approaches is applicable at the various stages of development of the organization. For example, in some cases, an enterprise leader may want a basic, coherent change in the organization. In other cases, where an organization may not be ready for a large-scale initiative, capitalizing on specific business opportunities may be the way the knowledge team can gain its license to operate. Regardless of unique conditions, the need to ground the knowledge initiative in a knowledge-related business strategy cuts across all of these approaches.

As the stages of the knowledge capital process unfold, readers can compare what is happening in the transitioning enterprise with what went on in the organizations discussed in these conversations. By drawing from these conversations, readers can build their own practice fields and develop a working familiarity with the key learnings of the practitioners in these chapters and the preceding knowledge clusters. In that way, readers can put their new knowledge to work as synthesizers and participants in discovering the next generation of knowledge capital and knowledge-based enterprises.

HUBERT SAINT-ONGE:
Creating and Implementing a
Knowledge Strategy

14

In this conversation, Hubert Saint-Onge delves into the perspectives, experiences, policies, and practices of one of the shapers of emerging knowledge-based enterprises. For more than a decade, Saint-Onge has been refining a model known as the Knowledge Assets Framework for the strategic integration of business plans with people management systems, using technology architecture and organizational infrastructure. Saint-Onge was formerly senior vice president for strategic capabilities at Clarica Life Insurance Company.

Clarica is a Canadian-based financial services firm offering a wide range of life and health insurance, saving and retirement products, and other financial services. One of the key elements of Saint-Onge's mandate at Clarica was to facilitate the leveraging of the firm's business through the systematic application of knowledge management and learning organization principles.

With his team, Saint-Onge developed a comprehensive strategy for building capability through knowledge. This led to the implementation of a sociotechnical approach, where people and technology were brought together in a new organizational configuration. In addition, he led an in-depth exercise to define the values and vision of Clarica to renew the development of the organizational culture in alignment with the strategic framework of the firm.

Saint-Onge is currently executive in residence at the Centre for Business, Entrepreneurship and Technology (CBET) at the University of Waterloo. He also serves as the chief executive officer of Konverge and Know, a firm that implements integrated knowledge strategies based on optimizing business processes and technology solutions.

Saint-Onge was previously vice president of learning organization and leadership development for the Canadian Imperial Bank of Commerce (CIBC).

He is a member of the editorial advisory board of the *Journal of Intellectual Capital* and co-author, with Debra Wallace, of *Leveraging Communities of Practice for Strategic Advantage*, published by Butterworth-Heinemann.

The Conversation

Ingredients of a Knowledge Strategy

JC: *What do you see as the similarities and differences between intellectual capital and knowledge management?*

HS-O: Intellectual capital, to me, is about the management of intangible assets. We know that these assets now represent the largest share of the value of most firms and that we need to manage those assets actively in order to optimize the performance of organizations in their respective marketplaces. The stocks that comprise these assets are made up of the individual capabilities of the members of the firm (we call that human capital), the organizational capabilities (we call that structural capital), and customer relationships (customer capital). These three stocks are connected and grow based on the exchange of knowledge among the individuals, the organization, and the customer. The knowledge strategy of an organization is geared to build the capabilities and the relationships that form the intangible assets of the firm. The growth of the intangible assets in turn determines the economic performance of the firm. As such, the intellectual capital framework is a representation of the stocks of intangible assets, while knowledge is the electrical current that runs among these assets to grow the human, structural, and customer capital. So there is a clear distinction in my mind between intellectual capital and what we mean by knowledge, or knowledge strategy.

JC: *Do you see any overlaps in the different roles of each in your knowledge organization?*

HS-O: As we evolve toward knowledge-driven organizations, I foresee very different roles emerging. For one thing, I question the typical configuration where we have separate mandates for IT, human resources, marketing, and strategic planning. I believe that this traditional organizational structure no longer works.

For instance, segregating the customer and the member of the organization into marketing and human resources is a rather ineffective way of defining accountability. In the knowledge era, we have found there is increasing evidence of a very high correlation between the quality of customer relationships and the extent to which members of the organization have a sense of ownership for the value created as a result of interacting with that customer. So, these are two groups of people, the customers and the members, who exchange knowledge and transact together with the commitment to create value for one another. There should be convergence in the way we understand and manage people, both members and customers. Yet, we ask two different organizational structures to ensure that their needs are met. These separate organizational pockets, with different mandates and preoccupations, cause the organization to lose the level of coherence required to optimize both the human and customer capital involved. In the industrial era, when the value created by intangible assets counted for a lot less, this lack of coherence was not as costly. As we enter the knowledge era, with the key competitive advantage coming in large part from intangible assets, we can no longer afford these organizational disconnects.

The same problem exists, for instance, with human resources and IT. A more significant part of the IT mandate now is about increasing our information technology, which will be required to bring forward a knowledge yield from transactions. This knowledge yield depends a great deal on the way the technology infrastructure is shaped to enhance the performance of people and the organization as a whole. This cannot be achieved without people management processes designed to access the levels of interdependence and collaboration required for people to exchange knowledge. Increasingly, people management will play a key role in leveraging the technology infrastructure to its full potential. This is why splitting the IT and HR mandates will become more and more problematic for organizations.

Now that 80% of the value of most firms is in their intangible assets, this balkanized configuration also makes it much more difficult to strategically plan for the development of the capabilities and relationships that form these assets. This is why I believe that we will continue to see the emergence of new structures and roles to shape organizational configurations, which will bring greater convergence between individual and organizational capabilities in order to build customer relationships.

JC: *A lot of people are asking whether knowledge management is just a superficial fad consisting of placing old wine in new bottles, or whether it is a genuinely new way of looking at how the organization creates value.*

HS-O: I believe that the knowledge approach offers a new window on the organization, a new perspective from which to look at the organization. It is a perspective that is made that much more relevant by the knowledge-intensive business environment, which has transformed the rules of the game. Intangible assets are quite different in nature from tangible assets and need to be managed quite differently. The real big difference is that tangible assets are by definition scarce, whereas intangible assets are by definition abundant.

Accordingly, when it comes to the management of intangible assets, we will need to adopt an approach that is less controlling in nature and takes more of a systems view of the organization. This is also why the knowledge capital framework places such importance on the interdependence among individual, structural, and customer capital.

JC: *Why did you move away from the term* intellectual capital *and move toward the term* knowledge capital?

HS-O: I am first and foremost an internal practitioner. I'm entrenched in the day-to-day work of my organization. Once you have understood the perspective offered by the knowledge capital model, it offers a wonderful way of explaining how we are trying to create value in the organization. So, I tend to refer to the model quite often. What I found quite fast was that many people in my organization had a negative reaction to the term *intellectual capital.* They tend to reject the term *intellectual,* in my view, because they see it as either elitist or beyond their understanding. I have found that people naturally value knowledge and are more receptive to the term *knowledge capital* to represent intangible assets.

Evolutionary Organizations

JC: *What is an evolutionary organization, or EVO?*

HS-O: The *evolutionary organization* fundamentally moves at the same pace as the market in which it operates. It does not build a deficit with its environment. What tends to happen with organizations is that they assume a pattern of evolution that is slower than what is happening in the marketplace. As a result of this mounting deficit, the performance of these organizations unavoidably starts to deteriorate. This often continues until business leaders declare a crisis situation. This is generally when organizations enter a restructuring phase designed to quickly recapture lost ground. Although made necessary by the lack of proactive and timely managerial action, these periods of organizational life tend to be as a rule rather wasteful and dysfunctional. This is when, typically, a whole lot of people get thrown out of the organization. Not only is it hurtful to people who are often the most dedicated members of the organization, but it often leads to rather costly decisions. Promising new ideas, assets, or income streams are often made part of these ritual sacrifices. Some organizations will actually go as far as scheduling these exercises every three years or so, in a way institutionalizing progress by fits and starts. This becomes the equivalent of subscribing to dysfunction.

To the contrary, the evolutionary organization detects patterns in the marketplace as they emerge. It also responds to these new patterns in a proactive manner. As a result, there is no accumulated lag time between marketplace changes and the reactions of the enterprise. So the just-in-time evolution of the enterprise vis-à-vis the marketplace is really what we mean by the evolutionary organization.

JC: *What are the characteristics that would begin to dominate in an EVO?*
HS-O: An EVO has made the shift from a make-and-sell predominant logic to sense-and-respond logic. It builds in the ability to respond fast to changes in its business environment. Learning mechanisms are built into the way it functions: debriefs on action taken, learning- and scenario-based planning processes, knowledge depositories, communities of practice, support for team and individual learning.

An EVO has no hesitation to experiment and to learn from both successes and failures. It is an organization that has the ability to adapt and change without creating a high level of static and distrust. Its knowledge strategy becomes the engine of real-time learning. As a result, the second time the organization encounters an issue in the marketplace, it knows how to deal with it effectively. There are no pegs that are restraining the organization from adapting in real time to what is happening both within and around it.

The evolutionary organization constantly debunks the collective mindsets or organizational mindsets that form boundaries around its ability to see new patterns and adapt rapidly to them. These collective mindsets are the pegs that are keeping the organization from evolving fast enough.

People and organizations develop strong beliefs through experience. The experience that created the beliefs in the first place has long ago lost all relevance but they remain, guiding decisions and forming boundaries on the level of performance. This is the key challenge with tacit knowledge: We need the basic rules it gives us in order to function effectively, but the assumptions underlying these rules might be wrong because they are based on past experience which is no longer applicable. The evolutionary organization has the capability to renew the assumptions or collective mindsets that form its tacit knowledge and to marshal explicit knowledge through the lenses of up-dated perspectives.

JC: *Is that how you see Clarica evolving?*
HS-O: A lot of my work has been around questioning things that are taken for granted, assumptions that the management team too often sees as proven facts as opposed to perceptions that were true at one point but that no longer fit the reality of the business environment. We need to renew and develop capabilities much faster than in the past.

Our focus has to be not on preserving the means that are more familiar to us but on the ultimate goal of building customer relationships. We achieve this only if we strive at every step to provide superior customer-perceived value in the marketplace. This is only possible if we look at the marketplace not from the manufacturer's perspective but from the perspective of the customer. We need to bring the customer perspective to every activity in order to demonstrate our brand promise and to respond effectively as new trends emerge.

At Clarica, part of my work as a coach to the organization is to point out where we might be taking for granted an obsolete set of beliefs and to question them with a combination of respect and courage. This role does not always lead to winning popularity contests, but it's now accepted by many of my colleagues as making a worthwhile contribution.

From Human Resources to Strategic Capabilities

JC: *Why is a traditional human resources approach no longer satisfactory?*
HS-O: Just as organizations have tended to focus on products rather than customers, the traditional human resources function focuses on its tools. As a result, the function generally is rather balkanized based on the categories of tools: compensation, training and development, recruitment and staffing. This compartmentalization has contributed to creating functions that have tended to ossify over time.

The problem is that, by and large, HR functions are not configured to deliver on the requirements of the knowledge-driven organization. These expectations are very different from what the organization needed when

HR adopted its current configuration. I firmly believe that the new configuration has to be focused on the development of the capabilities that will ensure that the organization meets its strategic goals. *Capability* is the link between strategy and performance. This is why at Clarica we have moved away from the human resources configuration and developed what we call strategic capabilities to embody this new configuration. This new mandate takes into account the need to bring greater convergence to the management of intangible assets. It focuses on leveraging organizational learning and knowledge.

JC: *What gains will be made by transforming HR into Strategic Capabilities?*

HS-O: The key contribution is to equip the organization to perform at its best in a fast-moving, knowledge-intensive business environment. The new function takes on the role of ensuring that knowledge and learning become an inherent part of effective business leadership throughout the enterprise. It ensures the development of an organizational context geared to self-initiative and interdependence. It provides the platform for accelerating learning at the individual, team, and organizational levels. It ensures that the organization has the capabilities that allow us to develop the customer relationships we target at a strategic level. The main benefit of this new contribution is to catalyze the organization to move faster with coherence and clear purpose.

The reality is always more accurately described in shades of gray, but I unabashedly put forward the case for changing human resources in black-and-white terms in order to jolt my colleagues into considering a different approach. Even then, it has to be done with respect because there is always a sense of betrayal involved in asking people to change an approach they have identified with for so long.

Knowledge Strategy

JC: *What is the role of knowledge strategy within Strategic Capabilities?*

HS-O: The knowledge strategy provides the framework within which we place new initiatives aimed at leveraging our intangible assets. It gives a context for growing those intangible assets through the exchange of knowledge, both within the organization and outside the organization with our business partners and with our customers. It points to what we are trying to achieve and how we will get there. It outlines the processes, the tools, and the infrastructure required for knowledge to flow effectively in a way that accelerates the development of capabilities. It delineates a phased approach, which takes into account the absorption capacity of the organization.

As the first phase of our strategy, a great deal of emphasis was placed on putting in place the technological infrastructure. There's no point talking about the exchange of knowledge unless the technological infrastructure is in place. Parallel to this work, we undertook an in-depth review of the values that shape our organizational culture in order to align and renew the tacit knowledge of the organization. Our next phase was to develop the management processes that support the exchange of explicit knowledge within the organization. Our focus in this regard was to develop an approach for teams to self-organize around complex and highly purposed tasks that required the participation of members from different units. We also at that time facilitated the development of several communities of practice. We have a very active and highly developed intranet, which integrates knowledge and learning and has become an inherent part of how work gets done on a day-to-day basis. These are the key elements of our knowledge strategy.

JC: *Who is involved in the knowledge strategy and in what kinds of ways?*
HS-O: Clarica has 7,500 members: 4,500 are staff members and 3,000 exclusive agents. I can't think of anyone in the company who is not involved in the knowledge strategy in one way or another. The members of the knowledge team within the strategic capabilities unit are probably most intensely involved. This strategic capabilities unit is made up of the head of our organizational capabilities practice, the head of the individual capabilities practice, and the head of the knowledge team. This team is responsible for the implementation of the knowledge strategy, including giving shape to the intranet, facilitating the formation of communities of practice, and supporting different business groups in the implementation of knowledge initiatives.

Externally, we have been able to form partnerships with a number of excellent organizations. Because we have been identified as pioneers in this area, a number of people have taken an interest in partnering with us on various aspects of our knowledge strategy. For instance, we are proud to have joined forces with Buckman Labs on key technology projects. We have also worked to develop aspects of our knowledge strategy with Motorola. We have greatly benefited from these and a number of other business partnerships. It is clear to us that the knowledge strategy requires a level of expertise and resources that our company alone cannot access. These business partnerships have allowed us to achieve what would otherwise not have been possible.

Our agents are self-employed, selling our products in communities across Canada. Although it has admittedly been more difficult to involve them, it is clear that we will not have realized the full potential of the knowledge strategy until we have reached them in a more meaningful manner. Despite our best efforts to date, we have not been as successful as we would like to be in bringing them to be active participants in communities of practice. We have made only modest progress in this direction. As we reinforce our partnership with agents, we need to give them better access to the knowledge and support of the organization. As well, the organization has to tap more meaningfully into their knowledge of the marketplace.

Knowledge and Learning

JC: *How does knowledge relate to learning in your organization?*

HS-O: We have completely integrated knowledge and learning. As a result, we are well on our way to eliminating in-class training. All learning support from across the firm is now integrated and delivered through our intranet, Clarica Connects. So when I speak of knowledge, I really include knowledge and learning. When our members put in an inquiry on the search string in Clarica Connects, they have access to everything in the organization that deals with this issue. It is available in the forms of documents, processes, and procedures that have been documented, any book or report, all communities of practice, and all learning programs either interactively on the web or on paper. Our knowledge strategy represents the foundation of our approach to learning.

JC: *What other managerial practices are impacted?*

HS-O: The knowledge strategy has impacted most managerial practices in one way or another. One of the most noticeable changes has to do with communication and meetings. We are running a multisite organization where the expertise needed to resolve problems is dispersed across the enterprise in different geographic locations. In this context, it has become increasingly important to leverage the time that our members have to spend in meetings to coordinate and align their efforts. We are achieving this by making a distinction between the explicit—or factual—knowledge required to address an issue and the context or tacit knowledge needed to resolve the issue with coherence.

We are not the only organization that has difficulties in lining up meetings. They have to be lined up well in advance to accommodate everyone's schedule. The person-to-person interaction is costly, and it is difficult to access because people as a rule take part in many different projects and teams. This factor alone can have a significant impact on our efficiency and the timeliness of our responses. As a result, we now treat face-to-face meetings as a scarce commodity that must be spent in the most leveraged manner for everyone involved. Our technology infrastructure and interactive multimedia are a lot more effective at conveying explicit knowledge than meetings. This is why those who organize meetings make sure the relevant explicit knowledge is distributed through the technology infrastructure and that the time spent in meetings focuses on how to interpret the information, make sense of it, and apply it in the specific context where it is required.

JC: *How does the knowledge strategy interface with other factors, for example, IT?*

HS-O: The knowledge strategy includes the shaping of the technology infrastructure in a manner that supports the exchange of knowledge. We often speak of the need to adopt a sociotechnical approach for the development of knowledge tools. We need the expertise of our colleagues in IT to help us select and shape the technology solutions, but this work cannot take place in isolation from the intent of the knowledge strategy, our culture, and the way people work either individually or in teams. Knowledge initiatives rely heavily on technology to ensure that the transactions involved in exchanging knowledge have greater benefits than costs for those involved. Ease of transacting is a key factor in the utilization of the technology vessels that are provided for this purpose. This is why the knowledge team encompasses a virtual team of IT professionals who ensure that the sociotechnical dimensions are reconciled for greatest impact.

Measuring Effectiveness

JC: *You say that stories and anecdotes are currently the best measures for the success and effectiveness of the knowledge strategy. What are some examples of stories, and how can you tell if they are effective?*

HS-O: Yes, we have found that this is the best way to describe specific instances where the knowledge approach has contributed to the achievement of business objectives. The story that describes most vividly the power of knowledge is about how we approached the acquisition of MetLife's operations in Canada. When we considered the prospect of making this acquisition, we were aware that a number of other bidders would be keenly interested as well. This was just at the time when significant resources were dedicated to transforming the company from a mutual ownership to a stock company.

It was clear that, in order to be successful, we needed to involve as few resources as possible for the shortest period of time possible. Speed was of the essence. The first bidder to complete the due diligence process and to indicate a possible price range would likely get to the negotiating table. Within two or three days, as many as 150 people were formed in 16 teams, each covering a component of the deal. From the start, they were linked by a common knowledge database where they filed their findings, identified issues, and asked questions.

At any given point in time, every individual on these teams knew what was going on with all those who were participating in the exercise. Things were moving fast. In fact, there was very little time for managerial intervention. People were identifying the issues, finding solutions by building on one another's ideas, and moving on to the next thing. There was no need for managerial coordination because everybody was aware of what everybody else was working on. We completed the due diligence process and the business planning process for the integration in record time. This demonstrated the strength of this approach single-handedly.

The quality of the preparatory work was such that the negotiations were concluded in a fraction of the time it was expected to take. The end result is that we were able to acquire a company 50% of our size at a price that represented good value for us. In addition, the thoroughness of the way in which the issues were recorded in the due diligence process gave a decisive advantage to our people involved in the negotiation process. Clarica's negotiators often found that they knew more about the business being acquired than their counterparts on the other side of the table. All told, the focus and teamwork supported by the knowledge strategy gave us a decisive advantage in speed and agility. We have since been able to replicate the same approach for another acquisition with equal success. It was a great deal easier this time: For the most part, we only had to duplicate the processes and the templates that had been developed in the preceding acquisition.

JC: *Can these stories replace measurement in providing a solid rationale?*

HS-O: It would be a lot easier for all of us if we could in fact measure the impact of the knowledge strategy on the bottom line. We have yet to be able to be this definitive. I am aware of research that has been done on specific, more peripheral knowledge projects, but I have not seen any research that quantifies the impact of a comprehensive strategy such as ours. In the case of the MetLife acquisition, we said, "Let's assume that the acquisition of MetLife will generate an average of $40 million in net income over the next ten years. Let's then assume that the advantage that was provided by the knowledge approach in the due diligence, negotiation, and integration process accounted for 10% of the business results associated with this acquisition." This would mean that the $4 million a year in net income potentially generated by this approach would more than warrant an investment of $500,000 per year over the next ten years. This would represent a ROE of 800% from this transaction alone.

The problem is that nobody is ever going to truly believe this logic if they think that a knowledge strategy is useless in the first place. These people will probably say, "Well, we could have probably done just as well in the good old-fashioned way." I am convinced this is not the case but, in the end, it is my view against theirs.

We are all aware of all sorts of so-called proxy measurements being cobbled together to make up a business case. To tell you the truth, I have yet to see solid impact assessments in this field. In the meantime, the more I measure, the more I find that managers will only believe their own perceptions of the impact. Often, business leaders only insist on measurement to ensure accountability. This is the bottom line. What is fascinating to me is that whenever I present a new initiative, I am asked unmistakably how we will measure the impact. Meanwhile, old, pointless processes can stay in place forever, and no one will ever be asked to measure those. It has to do with resistance to change, I believe.

Realigning Values

JC: *What are the values shifts you see as necessary at Clarica or any other organization? How do you accomplish the necessary values realignments, and what indicators do you look for in that transition?*

HS-O: The main shift is to move from an entitlement culture characterized by dependence to a culture based on self-initiative and interdependence. In an organization where entitlement prevails, people use the organization as a shelter for the big bad world out there. At a fundamental level, they are seeing the world around them from a perspective of dependence. They see their employment contract as one where they suppress themselves in exchange for a promised future. The problem is that this is no longer a realistic view of the employment relationship.

We all know that it is no longer possible for any organization to offer a promised future to anyone. Instead, people have to see themselves as businesses of one. They have to find their security not in what their employer has to offer but in their own capabilities. The new employment contract is then based on individuals bringing forward their commitment to create value in exchange for being given the opportunity to develop their capabilities.

This new employment contract points to the need to ensure that our management approach promotes and facilitates self-initiative. We could put all of the learning programs that we want on Clarica Connects, but if people are not functioning on the basis of self-initiative, they will not take advantage of what it has to offer. Individuals have to be in ownership of their performance, first and foremost. They need to assume ownership of their learning in order to develop the capabilities they need to perform up to ever-increasing expectations. Finally, they need to exercise ownership over their careers to harvest the benefits of their investment in their performance and their learning. If this value chain is not clear to them, it is unlikely that they will bring themselves forward to take advantage of the knowledge and learning tools we put at their disposal. On this basis, I don't believe that a successful knowledge strategy can be put in place where people are still stuck in the entitlement mode. There is no knowledge strategy possible without that shift to self-initiative. My sense is that many organizations launch knowledge strategies without taking this into account.

The shift from a narrow self-centered perspective to interdependence and the ability to partner is the other dimension of the cultural change required for knowledge. Someone who is in entitlement and dependence will be unable to actually be in strong partnership. Those who are dependent will believe that when they are collaborative they are making themselves dispensable. People can best partner when they are self-initiated and confident.

The question that most often comes up in this context is how an organization provides incentives to its people to exchange knowledge and to build on one another's ideas. The most meaningful step an organization can make in this regard is to foster an organizational culture that engenders self-initiative. The second step is to help individuals realize that knowledge has value. If they hoard knowledge, they in fact destroy value for themselves and the organization. Whereas, if I share knowledge, I build value for the organization, I become a relevant node in the overall system, and I keep my knowledge up to date. The third step is to emphasize the importance of inserting knowledge processes in the way work gets done. It's a matter of how we work in this organization. If you don't work this way, you've dealt yourself out of the framework of how we are getting work done in the company. For instance, when we formed these teams in the context of the acquisition of the Canadian operations of MetLife, there was really no choice for team members: Either you became an active participant in knowledge transactions, or you dealt yourself out of the game by refusing to take part. In such a context, if someone chooses not to participate, it is the end of their ability to contribute to the work of the team.

It has become an accepted practice at Clarica to start the work of a team by creating a knowledge database that contains the objectives of the team, the roles of its members, and the project outline and milestones. Whenever we get engaged in a major project in the organization, the first thing is to put together a knowledge database that connects all those who work on the project.

JC: *How do you accomplish the necessary values realignments, and what indicators do you look for in that transition?*

HS-O: Many organizations have done values work, but very few have been able to make it a meaningful exercise. Here again, the approach taken to do this work is key to achieving the objectives. The first and most important step is to define the values of the members of the organization. We identified the values of all organization members through a questionnaire designed for this purpose. Having compiled the results, we went back to our members to report the results. We described the values of all our members and explained how we were thinking of aggregating these values into three major themes to form the core values of the organization.

Through extensive debriefs with members of the organization, we refined the definition of three core values, which we have identified as stewardship, partnership, and innovation. *Innovation* is a composite of knowledge, learning, and innovation. *Stewardship* is about utilizing our resources and those of our customers and leveraging those resources to the best extent possible. *Partnering* is working internally in teams, working with our customers as partners, and working with all of our business partners through mutual respect.

This work on values is at the heart of our knowledge strategy. Knowledge is not possible without relationships. And relationships are only possible if there is a minimum level of congruence based on values. Healthy, collaborative partnering relationships will form the bases for the free flow of knowledge within an organization. There is a distinction between knowledge and knowing. *Knowledge* is the stock, the content. *Knowing* is the process of turning this content into action, of inserting it into one's practice. By definition, knowing has to be embedded in how we do our work and create value. Knowing is only possible in the context of well-functioning relationships where there is trust.

We used this approach to values identification in the context of the integration of the people from MetLife who joined our company. Once they filled out the values instrument, we were able to compare their results with the results of Clarica members. We were then able to discuss the two sets of values and what we needed to do to bridge those values in order to work together effectively. This exercise turned out to be a key element of our integration strategy. The people who were joining from MetLife reacted very positively to having their values taken into account in the process of shaping new organizational units.

We are using the work we have done on values to move the organizational culture away from dependence and entitlement toward self-initiative. The values instrument we use is also a measurement tool. We know that at Clarica, on the average, our people are just on the cusp between entitlement and self-initiative.

We are putting in place a measurement process that allows us to survey a random sample of our population on a quarterly basis. This will allow us to identify how the values of the organization are evolving, to evaluate the extent of the development we have achieved, and to identify the developmental challenges we are encountering. This ongoing monitoring will help us design the interventions that will accelerate the culture shift to self-initiative and interdependence.

JC: *How are members of the Clarica community under-standing and accepting these realignments?*
HS-O: We have a clearly laid out set of objectives for organizational change. I agree that we are being quite ambitious in our change agenda. I personally do not believe that you can bring meaningful change to an organization through the baby-steps approach. It is important to present a clear vision for change and to challenge the organization toward achieving significant change. If you don't aim for ambitious targets, you end up treading water or running on the spot.

It is essential that the members of the organization see the connection between the change and better performance. Otherwise, there is no point in going through the necessary grinding of teeth associated with organizational change.

Fortunately, I work with an absolutely outstanding team of very strong members. Has everybody accepted that what I am talking about has to do with knowledge? Clearly, no. But, most of our members recognize that we have transformed how people think about their work in this company through the way we use the technology infrastructure and the communities of practice, the way in which we manage projects, teams, and people in general. Is there resistance? Of course, there is. If we look at the distribution of our people on the spectrum of values-based development, we know that a large segment of our population is deeply anchored in the entitlement mode.

JC: *What outcomes, as far as human capital, structural capital, and customer capital, do you see resulting from the realignment?*

HS-O: I personally believe that we have stronger and more trusting partnerships within the organization. We have a stronger partnership with our agents. Just the fact that we are speaking about them as being members of the organization affirms our collective ownership: Each member is responsible for co-creating the future of our firm. We have made very tangible progress in this collective understanding.

Knowledge as Practice

JC: *What is the difference between knowledge as stock and knowledge as practice in your view?*

HS-O: *Knowledge as stock* is where people put knowledge in a central place for everyone to access. This is explicit knowledge as a rule, and it resides in technology vessels that can be accessed from anywhere in the firm on demand. One example we have at Clarica of knowledge as stock is a multiwindow information system built to support the customer service representatives in our call center. When a customer calls, the service representative has a list of all of the solutions purchased from us by this customer, details on their most recent transactions, the issues that were encountered, and how they were resolved. There is another window that has the answers to any inquiry the customer might have. As customers introduce their questions, the customer service rep zeroes in on the corresponding logic trail to be able to provide the best answer that anyone could give in the company. Instead of training customer service representatives for months, we now only need to help them learn how to travel this application as they interact with the customer.

Knowledge as practice operates through a network of communities of practice. For instance, we have 90 actuaries, who work in different parts of the company. We have brought them to interact together in their own community of practice. Whenever members of the community encounter an issue that they don't know about, they can put forward a productive inquiry: "I have never seen this before. How did you do this?" And then seven or eight others can come in and say, "I've done this before, and this is how you go about it. You look into such-and-such a category on Clarica Connects, you'll find a helpful document in this regard. When I used the information it contained, this is what happened. If I were you, this is how I would go about it." With this approach, you get the full benefit of both the explicit and the tacit knowledge of the members of that community to resolve actual issues as they emerge.

JC: *How do you capture the knowledge of practice? What is your range of ways of capturing that?*

HS-O: The communities of practice function from knowledge databases that need to be constantly cleaned up, kept up to date, and synthesized. Knowledge managers provide this support to communities of practice. They place the accumulated knowledge that has been validated by the community in a virtual library dedicated to this community but accessible to anyone in the firm. The libraries of every community of practice can be accessed through Clarica Connects. It is important to be able to categorize the knowledge and learning that has crystallized in communities of practice in the library to keep the discussion forum from becoming too cluttered. The discussion forum has to be kept for threaded discussions on issues of current relevance to the community.

JC: *How many communities of practice are there at this point?*

HS-O: We probably have as many as 20. Their membership ranges from 10 to 150 people. Some of them have a more formal structure, and some are very informal. For instance, the integration management office is highly formal, with many participants in well-defined roles. But most communities of practice function on a much less formal basis with the support of a knowledge manager. For instance, the senior management team to which I belong uses a knowledge database where all of our reference material is located, including accountabilities, commitments, the minutes of our meetings, records of decisions, and project outlines. This is an example of what we call a community of commitment. Communities of practice have affinities of tasks and learning objectives, while communities of commitment have a common purpose and share in their responsibilities for the achievement of business objectives.

JC: *How do you see these communities of practice evolving?*

HS-O: Communities of practice will be more and more differentiated. They will tend to be widely dispersed on a spectrum from formal to informal.

The more formal communities will be mandated and fully sponsored by the organization with well-defined charters and accountabilities. The more informal ones will be spontaneously set up. They will have less of a formalized mandate, will operate on a more spontaneous basis, and will probably be shorter lived. And in between the two ends of the spectrum, a whole variety of different formats will emerge. We have to be careful not to overly institutionalize and formalize these communities over time. They tend to function best with a strong element of voluntarism. The effectiveness of these communities is ensured by the need for them to address issues and objectives that are seen as relevant by their members.

Key Learning Points

- Intellectual capital is about the management of intangible assets. These represent the largest share of the value of most firms.
- The knowledge strategy of an organization is geared to build the capabilities and the relationships that form the intangible assets of the firm.
- The intellectual capital framework is a representation of the stocks of intangible assets, while knowledge is the electrical current that runs among these assets to grow the human, structural, and customer capital.
- Intangible assets are quite different from tangible assets and need to be managed quite differently, since tangible assets are by definition scare, and intangible assets are by definition abundant.
- There is no point talking about the exchange of knowledge unless the technological infrastructure is in place. Parallel to this are the values that shape the organizational culture in order to align and renew the tacit knowledge of the organization.
- Stories can be the best way to describe specific instances of how the knowledge approach has contributed to the achievement of business objectives.
- The knowledge strategy cannot succeed unless values shift from an entitlement culture characterized by dependence to one based on self-initiative and interdependence, where people begin to see themselves as businesses of one.
- Knowledge is the stock, the content. Knowing is the process of turning this content into action, of inserting it into one's practice. Knowing has to be embedded in how we do our work and create

value. Knowing is only possible in the context of well-functioning relationships where there is trust.

- You cannot bring meaningful change to an organization through the baby-steps approach. It is important to present a clear vision for change and to challenge the organization toward achieving significant change. Otherwise, you end up treading water.

Knowledge Management Is about Change

15

Kent Greenes has made knowledge management work to achieve significant outcomes both as chief knowledge officer and as senior vice president at SAIC, a diverse scientific research and engineering company, and formerly at BP Amoco, where he was head of knowledge management and where he created an internationally recognized knowledge management practice. His role at SAIC is to harness the power of learning across the organization and its subsidiaries and to develop new business opportunities based in the emerging knowledge economy.

This conversation is an opportunity to see how a context for knowledge management and an effective approach can be successfully introduced and implemented in organizations. Knowledge management is a process and an understanding as well as a set of tools and a strategy. Greenes says that, at root, knowledge management is about change, which in turn requires organizational leadership to have a sense of where it wants to go and to be ready to commit the resources and support to enable the organization to get there. At the same time, it is the people throughout the organization who will carry out the knowledge management initiatives. The trick is to weave a top-down and bottom-up approach that aligns and creates the process and performance improvements that will take the organization into its future.

Greenes sees that we are in the second wave of the knowledge era, at a point where people have learned that merely relabeling document management and other information technologies as knowledge management is not the answer. Greenes says this wave is characterized by a growing demand for practitioners with an experience-based track record.

Greenes is a hands-on knowledge management practitioner. He concentrates on how knowledge management will yield a greatly improved performance for an organization. He works to have all stakeholders see direct outcomes that benefit themselves and, by doing so, benefit the organization. Since he views that knowledge is personal, he works to have people involved on an intimate basis, building relationships that are based on trust, which then become as important as the actual knowledge that is generated and shared.

As a result of his work at BP, Greenes was acknowledged by Tom Stewart of *Fortune* as the world's leading money-maker in knowledge management for delivering $260 million to BP's bottom line. Greenes says that most of the benefit came from working with people to apply three simple learning processes to do things better, faster, and cheaper. The gains were not due to fancy technology, but rather from helping people to learn before, during, and after and to apply their learning on the job. He points out that along the way people created a wealth of know-how that the company was able to capture, harvest, and make available to other businesses via web-based knowledge assets. However, as Greenes notes, knowledge capture came second and added even more value as that knowledge was reused and adapted by others across the company.

Greenes has worked internationally in a variety of engineering, management, and technology roles in the science and energy industries. He holds a B.S. in geoscience from Kent State University and an M.S. in geophysics from the University of Arizona.

The Conversation

Project-Focused Knowledge Management

JC: *As a practitioner, how do you look at knowledge management?*
KG: What I would like to share with you is based on my actual experience in delivering knowledge management solutions over the last five years. In every case, this work focused on delivering projects aimed at bottom-line business impact or targeted at strategic growth opportunities. The common theme has been business performance improvement and learning how to

make KM work in the specific culture of the company where it's being applied.

Most of my insights are based on the work originating at British Petroleum in the mid-1990s and are augmented by work in about ten other companies since then. I would say I'm more of a practitioner in KM, as opposed to a theorist. What I hope people take away is that this is real stuff. These are things people can do today. You don't have to have a Ph.D. in epistemology or be an organizational development expert to get it. In fact, those things can get in the way if you try and apply KM without a healthy dose of reality under your belt. People and organizations are all very different, so what you learn in a classroom or apply through some logical thought processes will probably not work the first time on the job. My point is that you do not have to be a rocket scientist to do this. But that does not mean it is easy. In fact, because KM is so dependent on relationships and trust, it can be really hard to make explicit progress.

Challenges in a Flattened Organization

JC: *What were the challenges of heading the knowledge management program at BP? What are your new challenges as the chief knowledge officer at SAIC?*

KG: It turns out the challenges are very similar, although I did not realize that at the beginning. There were really two challenges at BP. The first challenge came from BP reorganizing into a very flat organization when I took on the knowledge management effort. We had decentralized to the point where in an organization of 100,000 people, there were only 300 people in the corporate center, and everyone else was part of 130 business units, which made their own decisions and were accountable for their own profits and losses. Each business unit developed a performance contract with the corporation. The challenge came in dealing with an organization of the future—a federal model—one that no longer had the traditional hierarchical structures or organizational glue to keep people connected.

We all know that hierarchies get in the way, but one good thing a hierarchical organizational structure does is connect the people above and below you in an explicit manner. These connections are channels for information and knowledge flow. Of course, in many organizations, this flow only occurs on a need-to-know basis, which means the open sharing of knowledge does not really occur as freely as the structure implies.

When we flatten an organization, we get rid of those required or obvious linkages. The result is that explicit gaps are created between businesses and people from different business units or teams. Many organizations are just now realizing the need to put formal or informal processes in place to facilitate the sharing and flow of information or know-how to offset these barriers. We often refer to these as *peer processes*.

It is a pretty strange turn of events. Companies flatten to focus performance in profit-and-loss centers, often to create agility at the local level. This agility is supposed to allow these P&L centers to be more proactive and to leverage local market conditions and business opportunities in a way they could not when previously encumbered in their more centralized model. Without realizing the consequences, they sacrifice connectivity and continuity with the collective organizational resources to gain focus and short-term business performance. I actually think this makes a lot of sense, as long as they then put the effort into building back the missing connectivity. They now have the ability to tap the collective intellect of their organization and bring it to bear in their focused business performance. I believe this is why the need for KM has really taken off. It puts the glue back in federal structures and enables these modern organizations to harness the collective power of learning in a very focused manner.

The second challenge was that BP was already a very high performing organization. It was already very successful. It was doing a lot of good things. Most of the business leaders were where they were because they learned how to create radical change. I had a very big challenge in that people were saying, "Why do I need to do anything different?" It turns out that when people become successful, they become very tough to change.

JC: *Did you see the same things at SAIC?*
KG: Yes. SAIC is also a very progressive, entrepreneurial organization with a small corporate center. Everything is paid for by the results we generate. The challenge of a small corporate center, similar to BP, means any corporate initiatives are suspect. Accountability and deliverability are pushed out to the groups and divisions, so initiatives from the center send the wrong message. I found that to be the case in both organizations. KM cannot be mandated in SAIC, nor should it be.

Like BP, SAIC is very successful as well. It has more than 30 years of quarter-by-quarter performance improvement—so many of its associates will need to see how KM can make them even more successful before they adopt new KM practices.

A different challenge at SAIC is that it is basically an external-facing organization, meaning that since everybody in the company sells and delivers services to the external world, there is some internal competition for resources and also for clients. You would expect that in any healthy organization. So, we are also similar to many of the large consultancy companies out there trying to win business. Until they win that business, people inside the company hold a lot to their chest, because they want to make sure their group gets the credit for the win. An upside to SAIC is that we are very open to bringing people in from all over the company and from outside to contribute. In our early internal KM efforts, we had some big successes in internal knowledge sharing and transfer that indicated an openness to sharing that really surprised a lot of people.

JC: *For what reasons were you brought into SAIC?*
KG: Primarily, two reasons. One was to help create a capability to leverage internal know-how across the organization and deliberately channel it to customer projects. The second reason was to establish a KM practice to generate new business and provide a high-road entry into new and existing clients. In both cases, we focus our KM intent and energy not only on delivering continuous performance improvement but on step-change as well.

The approach I have taken to develop our competency in KM is to have our staff work with our experienced KM practitioners on KM projects for internal and external clients. In this way, our KM competencies are developed with real performance objectives, and the people learn what really works. Armed with this new way of working, we cannot help but apply it inside our organization. The results from delivering KM for external clients are making people inside our own organization stand up and take notice. More and more people are saying, "This is good stuff. Let's apply it in our own teams and with our clients!"

But all of this takes time. Since joining the company, I have trained and coached more than 100 people who are now delivering KM practices in client operations. What that means is there are now 100 people who have a built-in preference and level of competency for leveraging know-how inside and outside our company. That's great, but with a company of 40,000 people, it is going to take quite some time to touch all the right people and make this truly a natural behavior in our organization.

Building the Business Case by Example

JC: *What are the ingredients for building a business case for knowledge management? How do you prompt people to understand that they are operating in a knowledge economy?*
KG: The first step is to get the attention of a business leader and her staff. I often do this by sharing a near-market example that really gets them

thinking about the possibilities for step-change in performance enabled by KM. Often it works best to find a powerful story or example where KM has delivered some radical business results outside the client's company, because it's easier for them to see the possibilities. I have learned that many people listen better and learn better from people outside their own company because it is safe to do so. Sadly, in some companies you are supposed to know everything. If you admit that you don't know something, then that may be viewed as an admission you don't have what it takes to be promoted.

Once we've got their attention through some examples, we then ask questions about how might this work in their company. A question I like to ask is: "Where would some fast learning and additional know-how make a big difference to your performance in the next six months?" This usually starts a dialogue about potential areas where KM could impact their existing operational performance or where some strategic learning is required for future success.

We look for repeatable work activities and projects, things that they must do as part of their core business so that we aren't going to end up delivering KM as a nice-to-have project. We also look for opportunities where they know they need to grow but do not yet have experience in that growth opportunity. The U.S. Army calls these *strategic learning opportunities*. This is often something that people wired in a more strategic way hook onto, or if they are wired more operationally then it is the previous hook, that is, "How can it impact existing operational performance?" Just let me say again, examples are key. Showing people real know-how about something they can relate to is critical. Of course, your ability to share real knowledge and demonstrate tangible business results, that is, putting your knowledge where your mouth is, is what distinguishes the very few real KM practitioners from the masses of people who make a lot of KM promises but haven't delivered.

It's a simple question to ask. When someone says they do knowledge management, ask them to show you some of the knowledge they helped to capture. It is amazing how many KM practitioners can't.

JC: *What kind of knowledge do they show you?*
KG: Well, those that really don't get it end up showing you a lot of information. PowerPoint slides, documents, even websites with lists of what they refer to as lessons learned. But this isn't knowledge. You know knowledge when you see it and hear it because it's directly actionable.

When I refer to knowledge, I'm talking about rich collections of insights and experiences, things that made a difference to someone, explained or described in a way that makes you think twice about not using that know-how. I'm talking about things that rock someone, which they tell in the form of a story, using a rich combination of media that makes things stand out.

We created the capability for capturing the rich content of what we might know and refer to it as e-storytelling in BP. We can actually codify stories and experiences in a manner that has real impact on people and is reusable and adaptable. What's amazing to me is we have been using this approach since 1997, and we have openly shared it with the world. But I can count on two hands how many people are actually codifying knowledge in this very rich way. I think there are at least two reasons why people don't. First, it takes a lot of extra work to elicit and distill knowledge to get to the few things that matter versus a lot of stuff. This is human-intensive work. I still think people don't realize the importance of the people side of all this. Video and audio have an impact on people and help personalize the content. We have learned that people are much more inclined to contact the knowledge source if they see a picture or watch a short, sharp video clip of that person.

Second, I think people do not really want to take the time to ask the question, listen to other people, and do it in a way they don't put out their own biased view inside of it. When you harvest know-how from people, it is very difficult not to put your own two cents in. You need to ask very open questions so the people share what they think is important, not what you think is important.

I am from the knowledge management school which says, "Share the few things and harvest the few things that made a difference, and allow people to use their own heads to make a decision," versus the other school, which in a very systematic way tries to codify everything an expert knows and put it into a software system that is rules-based.

Sure, there is a need for both. If you work in a call center at an investment company and you get a million calls a day, you don't really want to offer the customer services people a knowledge asset that helps them think about the right answer for a customer! What you do is codify the most typical answers and have these in a software system that gives you several choices of the right answer quickly for the customer.

That's just not what I'm into. I find in most corporations, people are pretty smart. You don't have to tell them how to do everything. They don't want "the answer" as much as they want something to help them think about their own decisions. But, I realize there is a place for both approaches.

JC: *How do you prompt people to understand that the world has changed, and they are operating in a knowledge economy?*

KG: First of all, who says we are in a knowledge economy? The last time I looked, I still see and feel a lot of the industrial economy around me. But I also see we are on the early edge of the knowledge age.

I think it's simple. You ask questions, you create possibilities, and, if you know how to do it in a constructive manner, you can challenge people. I was in Korea recently as a civilian observer for a major military exercise the U.S. Navy does every year. When it came to presenting my observations to the admiral in charge, I started by asking him a question: "What if you gave your weapons away, how would you win the war?" That sort of question got him thinking. After some reflection, he responded, "What you're asking me is to step out of the box we've put ourselves in because the weapons we have today everyone else will have tomorrow."

Any product or service you currently offer today will be picked up and reinvented or offered by someone else very quickly. Every competitive advantage eventually turns into a commodity. By asking questions, we try to help people to think out of the box. Whatever has led to today's success will probably not be sustainable and lead to success tomorrow. I think we are dealing with second-order derivatives of change now. It is no longer just good enough to do something good and then learn from it. You have to take that learning and apply it to do something else.

The Knowledge Economy

JC: *Is that what you consider the knowledge economy?*
KG: Yes, of course. If you think about it, if everyone else is going to have what you currently have, what else do you have that will continue to add value and create new things other than your own knowledge and the collective know-how of your people, your partners, and your suppliers? We have seen the lion's share of revenue switch from being generated by products to being generated more by services. A *knowledge economy* is one where people realize productivity and performance come more and more from what people know and how they use what they know, more than it comes from selling a piece of software or product.

JC: *Is it the context that makes the difference?*
KG: You bet. When I talk about creating very rich knowledge assets and communities, context is critical. Knowledge conveys context. Context is what allows people to make sense out of something shared. If they understand the context within which something was learned, then they have a much better chance of actually reusing and adapting that knowledge for

their own use. And that's what KM is really about. What value is there in capturing and sharing knowledge if it's not used or adapted?

Knowledge also needs to stay connected with the people who generated and shared it. We never publish know-how without it being accompanied by the person's name, picture, or video. Knowledge is very personal and can be quite suspect when it's not associated with a real person.

Knowledge Management Is Fundamentally about Change

JC: *What does it take to learn fast, and how do you extend the learning successes of your project across organizations?*

KG: Learning fast is important because not having enough time to learn is always a very good and real excuse. And learning opportunities can pop up at any time, so the quicker we can learn from something new we have just tried, the quicker we can do something to make it even better. The key thing is to keep your learning processes very simple. People remember simple things, which means they can always have them in their mind ready for use when the moment arrives. And I think learning in the moment is what really makes a difference. Opportunities come up all the time for learning. If we are armed with some simple tools in our toolset at all times, and they don't create much extra work and time for people to apply, then there's a much better chance they'll get used.

We use three simple processes that are easy to remember for learning before, during, and after any piece of work, project, or activity. But again, it's very important to show where these processes have made a difference before. This goes a long way to get people to even try. If you get some-one in operations to spend 15 minutes at 11 hours 45 minutes into their 12-hour shift to do an action review, they will probably do it again because it will change the outcome of their work the next time they are on the job.

The other critical point many people miss is you must focus those simple learning processes on local learning and impact first. This means people should not be forced to learn to help the corporation. They should do it to help themselves. Answer the "What's in it for me?" question. The next day, when they come back on the job and apply the results of their action review, their performance will go up and hopefully that means their reward goes up with it. Once you get people learning and performing, you can then think about harvesting that knowledge for the good of the cor-poration. In this way, they will have some valuable knowledge to capture that was based on real performance improvement.

In the future, most people are not going to work for a corporation. They are going to work for themselves. Hopefully, they will do the best work they can for that corporation while they are on the job, but they will be working for more than one company. We see this trend already in the work environment. All the more reason to focus on helping people do a better job and improve their own performance. Then whomever they work for will benefit as well.

I see many KM initiatives getting tripped up by focusing on what the corporation needs. If they capture and reuse know-how for their own team's use, meaningful knowledge will be there when you want to capture it for the rest of the company.

Rule number one: Keep it simple. Number two: Show that the work made a difference before, and show some simple examples. Number three: Focus KM on your local learning and impact first. And number four: Harvest—help people do it and help people apply it. Help them the first few times, and make it a safe environment to try.

When it comes to extending the learnings and successes, you can apply the rich knowledge-harvesting processes we talked about earlier. But let's not kid ourselves—you really can't codify much of what people know. Most of what we do is pretty complex. Of course, knowledge repositories and knowledge assets get a lot of attention if they are visible and tangible. And if you are good at it, you can hopefully harvest enough to get others up the learning curve quicker. But the most current knowledge will always be in someone's head. We actually harvest and package knowledge in a rich way to motivate people to reach out and connect with the people who provided the knowledge.

You can also make a difference by being part of other people's learning processes. If a team gets its peers together to learn how to improve its plan for an upcoming project, you can use this opportunity to share your learnings from your own experiences. But the best way to extend the learning is to share it among a community of people who care about it.

Knowledge management is about change. Learning is not new. KM is about helping an organization move from where it is today to somewhere else tomorrow. The size of that change will depend on how ready it is for it, the leadership provided to help it get there, and the resources and support provided to help. Realizing everybody has a day job and they don't have a lot of spare time to do other stuff means they need help to change. Leadership and support are two things you must provide if you want successful change. Any company that has created purposeful change knows this. A good number of KM efforts have failed because they were not resourced for success.

It is critical to have people available to help people change, and KM is no exception. These people will be most effective if they, too, learn on the job and apply the same learning processes to what they are experiencing in KM.

JC: *Is that how you extend the learning successes of the project across the organization—by having these people seeded around?*

KG: Sure, you have to. Part of their job is to capture the successes and package them in the same rich way you present the know-how—using testimonials from the real people impacted. There will always be a need to create awareness and attention on internal successes and to provide resources to help others get started.

The Role of Leadership

JC: *What are the right conditions for building an effective knowledge initiative in an organization?*

KG: Like most change initiatives, leadership is key. Leadership must create the demand for KM from a performance perspective. You need a leader who says, "I think this is important because———." And that "because" is directly related to the company's performance and growth. This is what gives your KM resources the license to operate, to open doors.

The leadership has to put this in the language of the organization, and they have to really believe it, because they are going to be tested along the way when detours come up. For example, leadership must be consistent whether the price of oil rises or falls, or when a pharmaceutical company gets 90% of the way and realizes, "Uh-oh, we've already tried that drug, and it failed." Leadership, at a very senior level, has got to be there to create the demand for continuous and discontinuous performance improvements. It's that radical part—the discontinuous performance improvement—that requires the collective know-how and idea generation for innovations to really occur.

JC: *What does the leadership do to create the demand?*

KG: Leadership shares their aspiration or a vision that requires all people to stretch beyond what they normally think they can do. They will have to operate differently to achieve that aspiration. They also create the demand by setting expectations for performance improvement or for the changed behavior by saying, "I expect that every business will share what it knows with our other businesses trying to do the same thing." Or, as Jack Welch put it, "You don't have a best practice unless some other business unit is using it." That is a tremendous create-the-demand statement. It also involves linking it always to performance. Not linking it to performance is another major reason why most KM initiatives fail.

Let me illustrate that point with a story. I was presenting to a group of admirals and captains at a U.S. Navy business reform meeting. I gave a talk about knowledge management, focusing on results, and so forth and showed them a lot of examples. At the end I said, "Now, do you have some ideas where you could apply knowledge management to make a big difference?"

One of the captains raised his hand and said, "We're about to spend $10 billion on building a combined marine-navy Internet. If we could leverage our know-how on what search engines to select, would that be the right thing?"

I looked at him and said, "I must not have done a good job in making my point about business performance because I don't see how that's going to deliver performance improvement. Who is your customer?" He said, "The warfighters." I then asked, "How is a search engine going to help the warfighters?" Right then, an admiral yelled across the room and asked another captain how long it took to launch a Tomahawk missile in the Gulf War. The captain answered with a time in minutes that seemed awfully long. The admiral then said to me, "Well, Kent, if we could use knowledge management to cut that time in half, would that be the right business focus?" The admiral got it.

The Learning Process Cycle

JC: *How have you integrated the learn before, learn during, and learn after cycle in your knowledge initiatives?*
KG: First of all, we will not take on a piece of work if people do not let us apply the processes to learn before, during, and after whatever work we are asked do.

The way you integrate it is simple. You look for opportunities as you go, where people (1) are about to do something, (2) are in the middle of doing something, or (3) have just finished something. Like I said, this isn't rocket science.

There is often an opportunity to apply learning-before-doing, to use a peer assist to bring insights from people outside the immediate team to a project or activity before it actually begins. In learning-during-doing, we reflect at each stage in a project or activity, modeling the after-action review approach from the U.S. Army. We ask basic questions: What was supposed to happen? What actually happened? Why is there a difference? What can we learn from this? For learning-after-doing, we conduct a retrospect to elicit key learnings after a project is completed. This an inquiry into personal learning, which we hold as part of a team dialogue to help the members reflect and turn their experiences into advice for the next time a similar project is undertaken. The fact that they are simple and fast means that we are able to coach and apply them on the job as we go. And, we walk the talk. We often perform an after-action review with the customer after our first engagement session.

Finally, you build it into the business process or procedure you are working on improving. Ultimately, whatever you are doing should be focused on a business process of some sort, whether it is improving capital productivity, building gas stations faster, getting a drug to market quicker, or getting more customers in your banking environment. Those are business processes, and you can embed the learning processes as activities at each obvious phase gate or milestone/decision point in the process. In the case of BP, it has taken the learning processes and made them part of its common capital productivity and operational excellence processes. It is part of the way it does business.

From Learning to Capturing

JC: *When you use the learn before, during, and after phases, you have made it more dynamic than other people have been doing. Can you explain how you do that?*
KG: I think it's because we put so much emphasis on these learning processes as the primary drivers of value in a KM effort. We live it, walk it, talk it, breathe it, show it, and deliver it ourselves. One of the ways people understand it is to show them what the impact is. So, we share a lot of tangible results from previous projects we've worked on with customers.

People usually see the value in the learn-before and the learn-during right away because they can see what's in it for them right then and there on a project they are working on. When Tom Stewart wrote about me in *Fortune* magazine and said I was the biggest money-maker in the world, the truth was that most of that money we saved was due to people in the businesses using those three simple learning processes. They saved the money, not me. It was not due to fancy technology or anything like that. It was the fact that people learned before, during, and after and applied it on their projects.

Now, along the way, they created a wealth of know-how that we were able to capture, harvest, and thus make available to other businesses via web-based knowledge assets. But that came second and added even more value as the knowledge was leveraged by others across the company.

And the learning processes don't require a lot of investment to get started. A customer will often say, "Oh, yeah. I could try that," because it's not a big deal to spend 15 minutes doing an after-action review during an operation or two days to do peer assist before you start up a $10 million project.

The retrospects are a little tougher, but most people have been trying to do some sort of post-project appraisal process in their companies already. But often their existing approach is unwieldy, or they end up with a three-inch tome of unusable, unexciting, boring, untruthful lectures that you have to sift through for weeks to get at anything useful. Most people were not happy with the results, so they stopped doing them. They have certainly stopped trying to capture the learnings in a meaningful manner. One of the most frequent requests we get is to coach companies on how to capture and codify their learnings quickly.

Many people are looking for a quick and easy way to harvest after a project. So the retrospect is often appealing, since it only takes a half day. Even if it is not captured, harvested, or codified, the people in that room take those lessons with them. The interesting thing about knowledge is that once you hear something, it becomes part of your brain whether you like it or not.

Team-based Process

JC: *You are being rewired?*

KG: Right. An important point about the three learning processes is they are team-based. They are not individual processes. By their nature, they are tapping the collective intellect of a group of people. Not only is the learning richer, but it also has the impact of helping build relationships and trust within the team that goes through it. It is what we call a double whammy tool. It gives you immediate learnings to help you impact your performance, but it also helps build relationship and trust in your team. The really interesting thing is that these tools become knowledge creation processes as well. Often people do not know why they did things and don't know what they know. These processes allow people to build on each other's learnings collectively, so that there are a lot of "ah-ha's." It brings out learnings people had not thought of before because they often don't take the time to stop and reflect on what they just did. The retrospect causes them to pause, gives them a break point for reflection. The team builds on each other's reflections and, often, new knowledge emerges.

If you think about it, in terms of bang for buck, these simple tools effect a lot of change.

Customers' Expectations

JC: *What kind of customers do you have, and what are they expecting to get out of KM?*
KG: The manufacturing and process industries are major customers. And so are government businesses. They do much of the same things over and over, and they know they are frequently reinventing. These industries or sectors are also going through a major loss of experienced people, so knowledge retention is a real issue.

However, high-tech companies are starting to really get into this because they have to move so quickly, and they are often breaking new ground. Which means they are doing some things for the first time and can't possibly think they have all the answers first time around. They need to be able to learn fast and apply their learning quickly to exploit the opportunities they are trying to create.

In fact, I think KM is easiest to sell when you are doing something new because the behavior barrier about having to admit what you don't already know is not there. Things like e-businesses are real big opportunities, and people are more and more starting to merge KM and e-business, because nobody can say they know the answer. If they think they do, they will find out how wrong they are, like many of the new startups already out of business. They are breaking new territory every time, so in many ways I believe KM is a prerequisite for e-business.

Knowledge and E-Business

JC: *How do KM and e-business create a complementary future?*
KG: Well, they both require relationships and trust. To transfer knowledge and to get people to reuse know-how from someone else requires them to trust you. Just because you get some knowledge from someone does not mean you are going to use it. You are only going to use it if it is contextual, if you can make sense out of it, and you trust it. Knowledge is very personal.

As a colleague of mine says, "Business is strictly personal." Just imagine what it takes to really do sustainable electronic business with someone. I am not talking here about buying paper clips from the cheapest supplier on the Internet. To get people to apply know-how and do real, sustainable e-business, such as carrying out a complex business deal among several partners and suppliers, requires real relationships and trust among the parties involved.

I believe KM is a prerequisite for e-business because if you do not know how to manage knowledge or enable knowledge management, then it is going to be hard to learn fast and leverage those learnings at the pace at which e-business requires. If there was ever a case where someone needs to learn quickly from what they have done before, e-business is it. Given the pace of change, our ability to learn fast is paramount. For example, someone starts a new e-business exchange. Among the risks they face is that there are many other exchanges out there doing some trading or something similar in their industry. Their ability to learn from the one or two that they participate in is critical so that they can keep ahead of the pack and be ready when those exchanges consolidate into one or two in a couple of years, or even a week. They will change. None of this is static.

Competing and winning today now require more speed than ever, much more so than perfection. To move quickly means you better be learning from every little thing you do. If you are going to build a portal for a customer, you better be able to deliver it in a month, three months maximum, because things will have changed so much in that time period that what you build will be outdated. You need to build something good enough in three months and use the *versioning* philosophy, so that every time you do it, you do it a little better or you make step-changes. By the time you deliver it, something else in the e-business environment will have changed, so the ability to learn quickly—if, in fact, you have that capability from your KM practice—is critical in e-business.

Your customers know more about your business than you do in many cases. They are posting little yellow stickies on your website that you cannot see that talk about your company, so that anybody else that visits it sees it. The customers want and have more knowledge than ever before. They want their business deal with you to be based on know-how and relationship, much more than they ever have before. That is directly aligned with knowledge management. You have to learn how to harvest and understand what a customer knows and thinks, and vice versa. And, you have to be able to show it and let them know that you are responding. Many people talk about the shift from make-and-sell to sense-and-respond. That is what knowledge management is all about: helping people think, helping them make sense out of things. To me, the complementary nature of these two areas is very high.

I think the simplest way to put it is: point-of-sale data about what your customers are buying is one thing. However, why customers buy products, what they want to buy in the future, and how they want to relate to an e-business organization are very different things, and that is the knowledge question.

When it comes down to it, what separates knowledge from information and data is the why. Understanding and making sense around why people do this or why they did that is what makes knowledge content richer and more interesting to people. The fathers of reengineering will tell you they did not go as far as they could have because they did not ask the why questions. They did not get into the knowledge component. But, that's ok because KM is just another enabler on the never-ending journey of continuous and discontinuous improvement. To me, within the next couple of years, we will not be talking about KM. We will be talking about something else. I think that has to happen, and I will be glad when it does.

I know that does not go down well with people running a knowledge management service company or consultancy practice, but hopefully they will evolve too. The greatest thing about knowledge management is if you share your know-how with people, it forces you to learn something new yourself. It is not a zero sum game. Hopefully, a lot of us have figured that out. When you share your knowledge, it does not take any of the knowledge away from you, but it does force you to start thinking of some new things and getting more knowledge yourself.

Elements of the Knowledge Framework

JC: *What are the elements of your knowledge framework?*
KG: There are three, and possibly four, components. The first is helping people to learn before, during, and after using the simple learning processes I've already mentioned.

The second component recognizes there are always other people who are working and applying a specific set of skills similar to yours, whether you're a drilling engineer or an XML (extensible mark-up language) programmer. They are the people who answer your questions when you are stuck or in a jam. They are practitioners who do the same thing as you do in a certain field, area, or subject versus a community of interest or a community of commitment. A *community of interest* is just like a special interest group on the web where people get together and put things of interest to them on bulletin boards. There are no requirements for participation. They are like clubs or social groups. They don't have any stickiness.

A *community of practice* is a group of people who get together because they want to share experiences and practices, both virtually and face to face. They make requests of and offers to each other. They are driven by the incentive of reciprocity or recognition among their peers. They often represent an untapped wealth of potential in a company.

The third component is what I refer to as a *knowledge asset*. If you are using the learning processes and gaining insights from others, you need a place to store this know-how so you and others can use it when you need it. Sure, as individuals, we have our brains to store all this learning. A knowledge asset is a common repository the community can contribute to and keep alive. In their simplest form, these assets are very rich web-based repositories containing more than data and information. They contain stories, insights, and good practices which are always linked to people and processes. They are always under construction and owned by the community that uses them.

There is actually a fourth component: the technology needed to make codified know-how accessible and visible, as well as the technology to help people connect and communicate. Let's face it. Once you harvest some know-how, there is no better way to make it available for others than deploying some common enabling technology to do that. If people are spending their time fighting the discrepancies and discontinuities among the systems they are using, that gives people a darn good reason not to share, doesn't it?

Conditions for Communities of Practice to Thrive

JC: *What do communities of practice need so that they can thrive?*

KG: I think all communities probably need different things to thrive, but the basic thing is they need people who share a common need and desire to participate. This is why we encourage making the topic of a community as specific as possible. For instance, a community of engineers in your company is way too general and broad. There are reservoir engineers, drilling engineers, project engineers, software engineers, quality engineers, mechanical engineers, and civil engineers. While a community for engineers may be a great place to start sharing anything and everything about engineering, if you are part of that community and you have a day job, you won't spend much of your time in that community. You'd rather spend the precious time you have in a community where you are going to gain something specific and very relevant to your day job, since that's what you are getting paid for.

What we find is: The more general your community, the more time people spend sharing generalities, and they very soon get bored with participating. Usually they start out in a general subject area and evolve or adapt into subcommunities around more specific practice areas. The interactions and knowledge transfers become much more meaningful and valuable to the members.

Second, I feel very strongly that the community members should be very careful about setting specific objectives and targets. They should all have a common purpose and a desire to share, come together, and help each other. But we have found that when they set a specific target or objective to deliver something by a certain time, then, basically they have become a short-term delivery team. That's great, but a team is an organizational structure meant for a different purpose. When you set a specific target, you naturally constrain the thinking and possibilities that would normally come out of a free-flowing exchange of ideas in a community of practice. Instead, people become focused on delivering a specific commitment. I think the value of communities of practice comes from people thinking quite openly, with diverse contexts and perspectives, sharing different ideas about things that they are actually doing, but not forcing themselves toward a specific solution.

The World Bank and Shell have focused their communities of practice around delivering specific objectives and targets. I understand this is because it was difficult to get communities the license to operate by management unless they could show a measurable benefit or business result. If that's what it takes to get communities to be supported by their management, then so be it. I don't want to make out that they are wrong. In fact, they are doing what it takes to meet their company culture where it's at, and I applaud that. These are very smart people, and the ones leading their efforts have been at it for some time. They have found a way to make KM work for their organizations, and they have made remarkable progress in the field. But I want people to understand if they are going to use specific performance targets to drive their community, there are going to be limitations in the free flow of ideas and possibilities. The good news with these delivery-type communities is they usually focus on meeting some specific target for a limited amount of time, then merge back into more of an enabling type of community.

I guess the other thing that stands out for me in communities that thrive is they all have a leader/facilitator who prompts, provokes, and cajoles the membership into participating. In fact, I know of no community or network that lives without a proactive person in that role. Of course, the people serving in that role can change, but someone is always helping to keep the community alive. Usually, this person is a respected practitioner in the subject area of the community. The leader needs some credibility among the membership. The leader is often the one to coordinate the online discussion forums to help the community interact virtually and the occasional face-to-face gatherings so people can renew their relationships and memberships over time.

JC: *Are there better ways to establish communities of practice?*

KG: I do not know if there is a better way because what you want are people who desire to come together and are not forced to be part of it. You want them to form however they can. Meaning, if leadership or management sees it is in their organization's best interest to maintain some core competencies, then that's a good way for them to start because there will be no problem funding people to spend some of their time to participate in a community that's core to the business. In certain organizations, you need someone who is going to support their participation, because it's not part of their day job.

Smart organizations encourage people to commit to involvement in communities in their annual performance objectives. Their local leaders buy in and have them contribute because they think there is something in it for their business group.

Another way is through the existing functional processes and structures in an organization. We shouldn't forget about those things called *networks*, which we all used to know and love. They thrived in many cases because functional leaders supported them. Often we see those functional networks transition into communities of practice as they get more specific and start to evolve with the KM attention in an organization.

There are also communities that start bottom-up in an organization. Sometimes these can be more difficult to sustain because people have to seek a champion for the funding aspects, but in many companies people feel they have the right to create communities on their own by just getting people interested.

JC: *What role have you had in establishing or forming communities of practice at SAIC?*

KG: In SAIC, they have come up through all of the ways I've mentioned: bottom-up, middle-out, and top-down. My role is to help them get started, to organize for success, and to give them the license to operate. I often am called on to just explain what some of the criteria are for their success, such as the need for a leader/facilitator.

We also help coach the leaders/facilitators and members of a community to make requests and offers, to prompt and provoke each other, and to establish their knowledge assets. We are successful when they get to a point where they are starting to say, "Wait a minute, I've answered this question ten times before. How come we don't have a place where people can just go to get that information or know-how, and we can instead put our attention on the latest problems or opportunities we are facing on the job?" So, we help them codify and harvest their insights and good practices for reuse by themselves and others.

I don't provide them with funding, but I help kick-start them by providing some coaching to get them going, until somebody rises from within the community who has the leadership's support and is willing to say, "Hey, you know, if you're going to facilitate this, and if it's important to the company, you probably need to spend 5–20% of your time doing it."

Developing Customer Agreements

JC: *What is your process for working with clients in knowledge initiatives? Who is involved in your agreements, and what are they agreeing to?*

KG: The buy-in starts at the top. Whoever is going to pay for your services is obviously critical, but that is only the first step. You get their buy-in to do something, usually by showing that there is some business value within the area they are interested in. I have a recent case in point with Amerada Hess. I have engaged its executives: the CEO and all of his right-hand people. In our initial two- or three-hour session, their response was: "We want to do this, we don't know where, but we want some of that," based on the results I was able to show them from KM applications in other companies.

After some conversations, they went ahead with an initial contract to go out and identify specific KM pilot projects that would deliver tangible business results. We then went to specific business areas and started talking to the local business leaders. We do these engagements to create alignment at the level of the people who are actually going to use the knowledge that we help them leverage. That may be senior management, if it is a senior management task. If it is on the shop floor, then we have got to get to the shop-floor level.

At the end of the identification step, we develop a matrix that indicates the fit of the KM project against some KM successes that we have seen work in other companies. These criteria are quite simple and robust: business impact, business advocacy, transferability, reach, and, finally, feasibility, both technical and organizational. We also use these criteria to help the end customer see what it is really getting itself into.

We then do some benefits mapping to show what knowledge is needed to deliver specific business impacts. We show the linkage and alignment between those things, indicating the results, desires, what knowledge is needed, and how it will help deliver their performance improvement. Armed with these two things, we create an agreement that basically contains those elements and encompasses a good old-fashioned plan, in terms of who is going to do what, the resources involved, and the co-ownership.

The agreement includes, then, the business target improvement as well as the approach that we will take, the timing, and that sort of thing. We often have some impact by the time we get to this agreement stage. We have probably already taken the customer or some of the customers through some things like an action review, a retrospect, or something similar by that time. In that way, they start to see some results early on, which is one way they justify paying for it.

JC: *How many people does it take to get a sizable firm like Amerada Hess to get a project under way?*

KG: Who knows? The size of the company isn't a factor when you are just starting out. Since our intent is to begin by demonstrating KM results in the short term, we start small. We find some areas where there is a specific performance improvement desired and where we can deliver in three to six months. We are trying to demonstrate a fast-learning approach, walk the talk, and deliver results. Therefore, it does not matter if it is a company of 100,000 people or 30,000 people, because we still limit the scope for these projects. It usually takes a couple of people (a couple of our people and a couple of their people), not full time but maybe half time, to deliver in that sort of time frame. To go into it any further would really depend on the specifics of the situation. It might take a person-year of effort on our part, squeezed into three to six months, and the same with theirs. It also depends on how many sources of knowledge we have and what the scope is for a particular focus.

We just completed a project to get KM going in a workers' compensation insurance company. The focus was on how to get workers with back injury claims back to work happier and quicker. It was quite focused, but it took about six months because of the soft tissue nature of the injury. The doctors, the lawyers, the nurses, the claims adjusters, and the injured workers all have to be taken into account. The focus, though, is the tangible improvement of getting the workers back on the job more quickly when they are really ready for work. It took us about six months total to create KM awareness in the community, harvest the know-how, and help them apply it on the job, which is the critical piece for performance improvement.

Performance-Based Measures

JC: *What kind of measures are you using?*

KG: The first measurement question is: What is the business performance impact that you are expecting or need? In this case, it is how they target a decrease in the time it takes to get an injured worker back to work. The customer had a baseline from its track record, as well as an industry benchmark. Then, there is a series of support measures, or indicators, after that related to the community, knowledge assets impacting use, the learning processes, and so on, taking those things up. So, in reality, the first measure is still an outcome-based measure in terms of "Did this deliver at this impact?" If the goal is to build gas stations faster and cheaper, then how much faster, how much cheaper, and by when? If it is getting a new drug to market, we need to target what you are putting out there and delivering as a measure of the cycle time. We feel strongly that most early KM efforts have to be focused toward solving a real business problem.

We always ask the question: "How will we know if this is successful?" Once we define the business pain and knowledge gain associated with that, then we add the measures around knowledge sharing, communities, and so on, through the framework that we deliver.

What Skills Are Needed?

JC: *What kind of resources do you see as necessary for the different stages of knowledge initiatives in organizations?*

KG: We look at it as a set of skills, competencies, and behaviors. It is not easy to find the right people, to be honest with you. Because knowledge is so personal, it takes people who have a lot of the softer skills of relationship building. The ability to "meet customers where they are at" is probably the most important thing. In other words, you have to deal with whatever culture you are faced with, not with the culture you want it to be.

KM support requires people experienced in change management, as well as having the hard skills of performance focus, business processes, and delivery. I am talking about teamwork skills, reengineering skills, process management skills, hardcore business delivery, as well as all these other soft skills. Additionally, they need to be good communicators, people who can glean nuggets of insights; they have to be real good listeners. Try finding those people. It is not easy.

A lot of people are trying, and I give them a lot of credit, but the truth is that it is not an easy job to be a knowledge management consultant or facilitator. Unfortunately, many consultancies and organizations throw young people at that role, because they are interested and energetic, but they are about the worst people for the job. I know I am going to get a lot of grief over this, but you need to have been through the school of hard knocks and have done some real work to the point where you understand what it takes to really deliver something. It does not matter whether it involves drilling a well, selling a software package, or trying to get a drug to market. Otherwise, you just will not understand what the customers are facing when you try and help them leverage their personal know-how.

That does not mean people with less real world experience cannot be coached and trained. I think probably one of the best uses of time for new graduates or new recruits is coaching them through a knowledge project because they will learn so fast about the content in the area that they are trying to develop their skills in. I can think of no better way to bring people rapidly up the learning curve.

My best people, who can really help people leverage know-how and reuse it, have been around a while. They are at least in their mid-30s, and usually in their mid-40s.

The Second Wave of Knowledge Management

JC: *How many people do you have at this point working with you?*

KG: We have about 100 people trained. Of those, there are probably 25 who are out there doing it who have been coached in the job.

The current demand for people with a track record in KM just keeps growing. Many organizations have gone through the knowledge management game now at least once. Most of them are now coming back to people who have actually done it versus the people who have sold it because they have replaced document management, or IT, with the phrase *knowledge management* in their brochures. They are now looking for people who are actual practitioners. We are firmly in that second wave. There is a lot of need for it. People are seeing where others have been able to leverage the collective intellect of their corporations, of their partners, and suppliers and been able to move very quickly to deliver extraordinary results. Now people are saying, "I want some of this. We've tried it this other way, it didn't work." So, the opportunity is a great one—for everyone out there, not just SAIC. The pace of change has increased. There is just no doubt about the need to learn quickly from every change and new piece of business you are trying to do.

Another element of the second wave involves moving from capturing what we know to creating new knowledge, the knowledge that we are going to need in the future to be successful. This is exciting stuff. Additionally, there are the advances in technology to allow for richer collaboration, the convergence of video, audio, text, and information. Technology enablers are now available that truly help us leverage knowledge at a distance at reasonable costs.

JC: *Considering what you are saying, what are the next steps for knowledge management at SAIC?*
KG: We have started to build KM competency in areas of our business that generate the major levels of revenue and profit for our company. For instance, outsourcing is an area that generates approximately 10–12% of our revenue (we are a $6 billion company). We were able to get people energized around creating a community of outsourcing practitioners and harvesting their know-how into a reusable Web-based knowledge asset that people are tapping into and that we are keeping alive. Now that the concepts and business models for outsourcing are evolving in e-sourcing and other types of sourcing (ASPs [active server pages] and so on), we are leveraging what we know and are learning to create new knowledge in this area. This is knowledge that both we and our customers can use.

As a result, my job is shifting from creating awareness and basic competency to spreading what we are learning and deepening it across the organization.

The Agility Factor

JC: *Will SAIC look any different a year from now or two years from now based on what you are doing?*
KG: That's a tough question. It does a lot of things really well already from a knowledge management standpoint. Every quarter, a thousand people come together face to face at something we call Meetings Week. It is one of the best examples of knowledge management I have seen because people get together to talk and get to know each other. They share their stories. They do presentations. They involve customers. We web-cast these sessions so the rest of our 40,000 employee-owners can participate, even though they are not able to attend in person.

Equally important, SAIC has been capturing its experiences and lessons learned from major procurements for quite some time. It has codified its systems integration and project management experiences into good practices and procedures and brought this into its training and certification processes. So, there are some good KM practices that were part of the corporation long before I got here.

As far as what will look different, I hope what you will see is an agility factor. People will be able to respond much more quickly with more confidence that they have tapped into all of what we know as an organization. A customer will actually see the difference because he will have even more visible, quicker access to the big brain of SAIC.

Key Learning Points

- The first step in building a business case for knowledge management is to get the attention of a business leader and staff, often using a powerful story of how knowledge management greatly improved performance outside their company. The second step is finding out how this might work in their company.
- You know knowledge when you see it and hear it because it is directly actionable.
- Share and harvest the few things that made a difference, and allow people to use their own heads to make a decision. In other words, not everything needs to be codified.
- When creating very rich knowledge assets and communities, context is critical. Knowledge conveys context and context, is what allows people to make sense out of something being shared.
- Learning fast is important because not having enough time to learn is always a very good and real excuse. Keep learning processes very simple.
- People should not be forced to do KM to help the corporation. They should do it to help themselves. Answer the "What's in it for me?" question. Once you get people learning and performing, you can think about harvesting that knowledge for the good of the organization.
- Knowledge management is about change. The size of that change will depend on how ready an organization is for it, the leadership provided to help it get to where it wants to go, and the resources and support provided to help.
- Leadership must create the demand for knowledge management from a performance perspective, for continuous and discontinuous

performance improvements. It is the radical part—the discontinuous performance improvement—that requires the collective know-how and idea generation for innovations to occur.

- Not directly linking knowledge management to performance is a major reason that most knowledge management initiatives fail.
- The first KM question is: Where would some fast learning and knowledge make a difference to your current performance?

Finding "the Hook"

16

Sharon Oriel is the director of the Global Intellectual Capital Management Technology Center of the Dow Chemical Company. She has been with the Dow Chemical Company for 29 years since receiving undergraduate and graduate degrees in biology. Her career with Dow has included experience in central research, plastics technical service and development, plastics marketing, and for the last 11 years, intellectual capital management. Her focus is on aligning, leveraging, and creating intellectual assets and capital for value growth.

Oriel is one of the cofounders of Dow's intellectual capital managers gathering. She serves on the editorial board of the *Intellectual Capital Journal*. In addition, Oriel served on the research and development task force supporting the Brookings IC project, has been featured in *CFO* magazine, and *Business Finance*, and contributed chapters to numerous books. According to Oriel, the future is truly filled with intangible opportunities. Those who navigate these opportunities with wisdom will create a sustainable future. Oriel considers herself a tempered IC radical.

An Evolutionary Journey

JC: *How do you, as a corporate practitioner, apply IC theory?*

SO: One of the things that I really like to point out about Dow is that intellectual capital management, for us, has not been a great "Ah-ha!" It has been very evolutionary. It has been a journey. This is because back in the mid-1950s, when we formed our first strategic business units, the president of the company created a function called patent administration. This hasn't been a fad of the week for us, or a "Gee, we need to go do this." Since we are a science- and technology-based company, we've always said we needed to manage our inventions.

What has changed is that we've gone from managing inventions for R&D to managing and thinking of patents as intangible assets with the potential to create value for the Dow Chemical Company and really getting the businesses to take ownership. Now we are journeying toward the next generation of broadening the practice to include all dimensions of intellectual capital: the people, the processes, our customers, our suppliers, and our external relationships.

From a practitioner's standpoint, we understand the theory, we go to the conferences, and we build on the foundation we have. But a key point in applying intellectual capital theory at Dow has been to find what I call "the hook." I say this to anybody I speak to because, regardless of whether you are in a service company or a bricks-and-mortar company, you need to find out what your business or your business unit is struggling with. Ask where you can show value if the unit manages its intellectual capital. Our hook was cost savings. We made it very clear that the way we were operating was costing us money, and we were not getting the best returns on our intangible assets. That was our hook. A service company can look at employee turnover or training issues—but always find the hook. The hook enables the practitioner to apply the theory. Only now at Dow Chemical are we using the term *intellectual capital* inside the company. That is because only now is the company ready to grapple with its broader meaning.

If we walked in and threw out some of the terminology that we hear at conferences and that we read in books, people would either throw us out of their offices or be very polite and then go about their old ways. So, again, find the hook, translate it into corporate terms, and then pick up the third key: senior management support. We had that initially in the form of Fred Corson. Fred was the corporate vice president for R&D and a member of the board of directors. We had Fred's support to do this. That was key. This support continues today with Rick Gross as the corporate vice president for R&D.

JC: *When did you actually start?*
SO: In terms of intellectual asset management and intellectual capital management, I would put the start date at 1990–1991. The antecedents for that actually go back to the 1950s, as I mentioned.

JC: *Did a lightbulb go on, or was there a convergence of factors prompting the shift from one kind of effort to another?*
SO: Fred Corson was really the lightbulb. I will tell you a personal story. I was a marketing manager in our plastics business. Fred came to me in 1989 and said, "I would like you to consider taking this position in what is called inventions management." I looked at him and said, "Fred, that's where people go to die." He responded, "No, you don't understand, Sharon. We need to change this. You've been in basic research, you've been in technical service and development, and you're now in marketing. You understand how the company works. You're the kind of person I want to start populating this function." Gordon Petrash was also brought in to run the group. Gordon came from our corporate product department, which managed Dow products on a global basis. Fred started populating this invention management function with people with a different skill base and a more business-driven outlook.

JC: *It shifted from a technician, technology perspective to a business perspective?*
SO: Exactly. That was the real key. We had to be able to then translate the value of intangibles into business terms. At about that same time another factor came into play with the formation of the U.S. Court of Appeals for the Federal Circuit for enforcing patents. A third factor in the mix was that patent fees went up. There's usually a monetary driver. Since we were a company with a very large patent portfolio, we also had a large maintenance tax liability over the life of that portfolio.

The fourth thing was that, internally, we started shifting the costs for obtaining and maintaining patents directly to the businesses. Previously, patent costs had been hidden in corporate overhead. That provided us the hook.

A story I like to tell is about a new business director. I went to that new business director and said, "How would you like to save $3 million?" He looked at me and asked, "Is it legal?" I said, "Yes." And he said, "Make it happen." Then he asked, "What did I just authorize you to do?" We had technology we had acquired from Upjohn's chemical division several years before, some of which we were never going to use. But this person's predecessor had the attitude: "Oh, I'm going to keep it just in case." It was obvious the business was never going to leverage it. The new business director understood that, and he also understood there was a cost involved with keeping it on the shelf. That's a very tangible example of what I mean by the hook. That business director didn't have to go read 200 patents and 15 agreements. He knew that I'd done the homework for him and said, "Make it happen." That established the basis with that business director to start managing his business's intangible assets portfolio.

JC: *So you had to have some idea before you walked into his office that you could save him $3 million?*
SO: Absolutely. Another important advantage that Dow has had in managing our intangibles is not only the legacy organization, but we have an inhouse database, which is more than 20 years old. We have had this database electronically, with all of our disclosures of inventions, all of our filed patents, all of our issued patents, and all of our agreements dealing with intellectual property. Many large corporations are only now getting there and establishing such databases. In contrast, we've had a very valuable tool for many years.

A further advantage is that all of our intellectual assets are tied to a business. With a few keystrokes, we can identify what assets belong to what businesses and what products are protected.

JC: *Is that all across the organization?*
SO: Yes.

JC: *Do people know that they have to do that kind of thing?*
SO: Yes. Dow's intellectual capital initiatives today are really the key to our sustainable competitive advantage. They are absolutely essential. I am finding that when a new business platform is established, the person leading that platform asks for someone to manage its intellectual capital—because in many cases, starting out, that is all it has. That's a real change.

Success Is Making Intangible Value Visible

JC: *What prompted that change?*
SO: We have shown the value of managing intangibles. We formed Dupont Dow Elastomers because of the intellectual capital that was involved. This

is one case that has shown the value of intellectual capital management and made it visible throughout the company.

Dupont had the market franchise in elastomers. It owned that marketplace, it had the manufacturing, it had the sales, but its technology was aging. We had new technology and a very small elastomers business. We brought the new technology; Dupont had the infrastructure. Instantly, we created a billion-dollar company. It is a 50-50 partnership. We brought no bricks and mortar to that. It was all intellectual capital.

JC: *That is impressive.*

SO: It's stories of those kinds of successes that make the difference. We have successfully used our intellectual capital in some major litigation. We have created some significant new sales using our intellectual capital. We have found the hook—and it's money. It's that simple. We actually have T-shirts which say, "We show the money."

The Intellectual Capital Network

JC: *How many people are in your intellectual capital network? Is it a formal or informal network?*

SO: We're more than 50 now, located with their businesses. We have a community of practice. From a historical standpoint, when Gordon Petrash and I joined the group, it was a group—all reporting to Fred Corson. Then we were recharged out to the businesses we were working with. As we built our success, we said, "This doesn't make sense. The businesses should own us." So, people became solid lines to their business R&D director and dotted lines into what we call now the Intellectual Capital Tech Center. We completely flipped it. In many corporations, people get into empire building; instead, we got into networking. Now each business has at least one intellectual capital manager, and in some cases they may have five or more.

JC: *Depending upon the size of the business or the dollar volume?*

SO: Exactly. It depends on the size of the intellectual capital portfolio that needs to be managed.

JC: *What kinds of people are they? What kinds of backgrounds do they have?*

SO: Most everyone comes out of an R&D background. They're technically competent, with usually about 10 years of Dow experience. They are chemists or engineers. They've had a good cross section of experiences in fundamental research as well as exposure to business. The other dimensions are very good communication and human relationship skills.

These are now very desirable jobs. When we have an opening, we usually have at least three very qualified candidates whom we have to select from. We now have four levels within the job family, so there really is a career progression. They may enter with a specific focus on doing competitive technical assessment for their business and move up to a director level, guiding the whole IC organization, for their business.

JC: *To what extent can intellectual capital effort succeed in any one area, if that's the only part of the organization that's involved?*
SO: One of the models that works at Dow is when a business has a particular need, that business may take the lead in that issue. When the value of that particular intellectual capital effort for that particular business is demonstrated, word ripples across to the other businesses that also see the value and need. This turns out to become a continuum of the intellectual capital effort, which I think is very appropriate. Because we have some very, very old products on which the company was founded (for example, chlorine and caustic), the new intellectual capital is part of a continuum of an intellectual capital effort across the company. The old products are in what we call the value preservation mode and will have a minimum level of activity, whereas we are just launching several new e-businesses, with a high level of activity.

If there is an effort focused in one area, if it applies to other businesses, it will be quickly replicated, but it may not be in some instances. This very clearly goes back to the business strategy. If a business is preserving its intellectual capital, that's very different than a business that is actively growing its intellectual capital.

Managing Intellectual Capital across Dow

JC: *You mean there is an understanding that all elements of Dow are not the same?*
SO: Exactly. I think that's also been a strength. We have fundamentals for managing intellectual capital, which cross all businesses. But, after that, it's very business-specific.

JC: *What would be the importance of culture to the perception of the relevance of intellectual capital to the organization?*

SO: We look at culture from a corporate basis, a business basis, an industry basis, a national basis, and, since we are global, an international basis. We also look at culture on a function basis. We have a very strong R&D culture and a marketing culture, and sometimes those cultures clash. We have had to create an intellectual capital culture that can cross all those other cultures. I do not care whether we use a large *C* in culture or a small *c* in culture. What is important is building a culture that has a strong linkage between the business strategy and the human element of trust, where both the personal values and the corporate values are involved in creating the financial value. It is complex.

The short answer is that culture is important. The key is recognizing the role intellectual capital plays in the many cultures, and then creating an intellectual capital culture that's crosscutting. Dow is recognizing that we are a science- and technology-based company, by starting with patents. Our culture understood this. We are now able to build to get to what I call the higher level. If we had started at a much higher, more fully integrated level, it wouldn't have worked. We are now growing into that level.

The Fishnet Organization

JC: *How are you tackling that?*
SO: We have our intellectual capital network. We call it our *fishnet organization*, which has expanded so that we are now much more connected with our human resource development people, financial analysts, and knowledge management people.

Since all of the intellectual capital management people are located within the businesses, it would be very easy for them to fall into their business silos and do a wonderful job for engineering plastics, or polyethylene with no one knowing anything about it. We have a Tech Center, which I think of as the group that keeps the fishnet in repair, going out to the various businesses and asking, "What are your best practices for managing intellectual capital?" and then rippling them out through the whole network.

JC: *Is the fishnet something that's intentionally created?*
SO: Yes. And as a fishnet sometimes gets very taut and other times it's very slack, we operate the same way. The other thing is that the people participating in the fishnet know they can tug on it and get a response. If people in one business are being asked to move into a new area or tackle a new problem, they tug on the fishnet and somebody responds and says, "Oh

yes, I solved that problem, that issue. I answered this question," and helps the other node in the fishnet respond.

JC: *Are these lessons learned captured anywhere?*
SO: Yes, one of the responsibilities of the Tech Center is to capture that knowledge.

JC: *What is the Tech Center? How did it come to be?*
What is the vision for it?
SO: The term Tech Center, again, fits in with the Dow culture. We chose that term very deliberately. Each major business in our manufacturing organization has a technology center, which is responsible for keeping up on the competitive technology as well as capturing the Dow technology for manufacturing products. When we go to build a new plant in Thailand, the people in the Tech Center are the ones with all the specs for building that plant. They also say, "We wished we would have done this in our existing plant, so here's the improvements to put into the new plant in Thailand." Dow understands that, so we've applied this model to our intellectual capital management Tech Center. We have a team in the Tech Center made up of *process leaders*. They are partners with the managers in the businesses. They are the ones who make sure that the portfolios are being managed. They know how to use and search our inhouse database. Because they are a smaller group, they can very quickly literally walk down the hall (they are all housed in one location) or go next door to share knowledge, create new knowledge, and capture knowledge. They are the linchpins for rippling out both best practices and continuous improvement. The Tech Center has responsibility for training and educating all of the new managers who come in. Here again, we get consistency.

The Tech Center is focused on intellectual capital management. New managers come in for learning sessions. We stage things sequentially. We may do an introductory session, and then, after they've been in the job for two or three months, we do the next round. Another key part of the Tech Center is to have everyone come to understand that intellectual capital management is not a solo sport; it's a team sport. Therefore, the Tech Center points the managers to the other resources. We make sure that they are well connected with the Intellectual Property Law Group, obviously. We also connect them with people in human resources, if appropriate, in accounting, in licensing, in knowledge management, and so on. We make sure they get connected with the experts they need to do their jobs. That, of course, extends the fishnet.

JC: *So how are you defining intellectual capital at this point, and what do you think people understand throughout Dow about what that is?*

SO: I think it is well accepted that *intellectual capital* is the knowledge that has potential for value and that it includes our people, our processes, and our external relations. We include the customer, our suppliers, and our external collaborations, which has come to mean that we have hybrid relationships all over the map. This understanding is universally accepted throughout the company.

Intellectual Capital as Significant

JC: *How do people at Dow perceive intellectual capital to be significant?*

SO: I will give you two examples on two ends of the spectrum. One is that our business presidents are talking about their intellectual capital in the same way as they talk about their plants, customers, and so on.

On the other end of the spectrum, our scientists and our researchers now ask the question: "What is the value, and how will my invention be used?" Previously, we rewarded our researchers on sheer numbers of inventions. When I joined the function a decade ago, at the end of the year, a laboratory director would call me and say, "Sharon, would you run a report to tell me how many inventions and issued patents I have for my laboratory?" Then, she would dole out salary increases, with part of the factor being the guy with 10 patents obviously didn't do as good a job as the guy with 100 patents. Now the value proposition is there. They recognize that they are creating intellectual capital. Maybe it doesn't get turned into a patent, maybe it's maintained as a trade secret, maybe they give a talk, maybe they publish a paper, and maybe they do a combination of all of those. We have gone from intellectual property to truly intellectual capital.

Those are two examples of very different functions in the company. It wasn't digital. We did not turn the light switch on or off. Again, it has been a journey. It has been evolutionary.

JC: *Has everyone at Dow, regardless of his geographical location, heard that intellectual capital exists and that it has significance in the organization?*

SO: Yes. When Mike Parker, our president and CEO, does his quarterly communication, either knowledge management or intellectual capital is always portrayed as important. When Rick Gross, our current vice president for R&D, does his global broadcasts, he also talks about the value of IC.

JC: *What is the role of corporate leadership in nurturing the IC effort? How has it evolved from where it started ten years ago?*

SO: Having the CEO talking about it, not just R&D, is a major step. The leadership understands the value of their intellectual capital. Going back to our science and technology roots, we recognize that we have good intellectual capital, but we also recognize that we have to renew our capital, both from a human standpoint and from a technology standpoint, if we're going to remain competitive. We must both renew and grow it. That has very clearly been recognized at the top.

Recasting Dow as a Knowledge Enterprise

JC: *Would you say that Dow is recasting itself along the lines of knowledge or intellectual capital?*

SO: Dow is a knowledge company. Our mission is to constantly improve what is essential to human progress by mastering science and technology. We are being much more deliberate in managing the human dimension and much more deliberate in managing the technical and the business dimensions. I just responded to an e-mail where we were doing a skills-gap analysis on human capital. Again, an example on the other side is that when a new business platform is established, we do not just look at the market size and the competitors. We ask what the intellectual asset lay of the land is. We are asking the question sooner. I think we are moving to a whole new level.

JC: *Is there a framework in which people have references about what value in intellectual capital is and how it can be communicated to others?*

SO: That is our number one initiative for this year. We have struggled with it. R&D measures are truly only one dimension of intellectual capital measurement. We are now driving ourselves to create an intellectual capital measurement system. When we get that developed, it will be appropriately included in the public report.

JC: *Will there be some intellectual capital currency?*

SO: Yes, beyond what we have now. We can do earnings per patent, earnings per employee, all the pretty standard ones, but we're looking to develop a custom measuring framework for Dow. We're developing it internally as well as making use of external experts. We're looking for the best of the best. We absolutely feel that the time is right now to develop a corporate score card for intellectual capital.

The Culture Factor

JC: *How does your intellectual capital effort work in your global network organization, and how do you extend your framework when Dow is engaged in mergers and acquisitions in North America as well as elsewhere, such as your East German acquisition?*

SO: Again, we come back to culture. It may be even that it goes back to our midwestern roots that there is a real culture of sharing. Because our intellectual capital network is global, it's very easy to get people connected to engage in our acquisitions and our mergers. If one of the businesses is the driver or the beneficiary of a merger or acquisition, then the intellectual capital manager for that business takes the lead in being the missionary to that business or to that acquisition. That manager draws on the Tech Center and the rest of the network to make it happen. For something as big as the German BSL (Buna Saxonian Olefin Works Leuna) site, which touches on many businesses, we have a member of the tech center who is physically based in Europe who has taken the lead in providing the umbrella framework for the BSL sites.

Our person's responsibility is to provide the overall intellectual capital framework, to partner with specific intellectual capital managers, if they have particular needs in Germany. This shows good cultural sensitivity. We wanted someone physically located in Germany and someone fluent in German for that role. We also have intellectual capital managers based in Latin America and in the Pacific. So, on a global basis, we don't just send somebody from the United States to impose corporate rules.

Going back to the fishnet model, because our network has grown so much, we are now encouraging the intellectual capital managers in Europe to get together several times throughout the year to talk about intellectual capital issues that are specific to their locations. That's new, but we feel that's very important in terms of keeping the fishnet in repair.

Another way we keep the network healthy is to have an annual gathering, where as many members of the network as possible get together. That's a real sharing time and learning time. One of the tools we use to share knowledge is poster sessions. Since we had so many new people, we thought about how to get names and faces together as well as get best practices out. We borrowed from the scientific community and decided to do posters.

Every two months, we also have a network meeting. The meeting is physically based in Midland, Michigan, but we use all of the electronic tools to bring in as many people as we can on a global basis. We usually focus on a topic. One part of the meeting is devoted to a topic, such as tools for measurement, and another part of the meeting is devoted to updates on what's happening in the network. Those are examples of ways we keep everyone connected.

JC: *Are the 55 people in the network enough for Dow, which is a company of 40,000 people?*
SO: The right answer will be determined by the businesses. I would be very comfortable if the number dropped back to 20 if that were what the businesses need. It really is determined business by business.

JC: *How did Dow come to expand its areas of concern about intellectual capital to include the social and environmental dimensions as well as the financial or economic, and what difference has it made that you've moved in that direction?*
SO: What I see, reflecting on 29 years as a Dow employee, is that in the past, Dow did not do a lot to publicize what kind of a company we were. We knew we were good technically, we knew we did the right thing environmentally, but we had the attitude that this should be obvious.

When Keith McKennon became president of Dow North America in the early 1990s, he started us on our journey of communicating the social and environmental dimensions very publicly. We have always done this type of work, but it's only been in the last five to eight years that we have chosen to communicate it. The difference it has made, both in accelerating our intellectual capital journey and for the corporation, is that people are starting to perceive us in a different light, and employees are now taking pride in what we have always been doing and feeling a lot more corporate ownership.

JC: *But is there a sense of how intellectual capital weaves into the social and environmental dimensions?*
SO: That is only developing now. It's still more implicit than explicit.

JC: *How has the Internet changed how intellectual capital and intellectual property are maintained and cultivated at Dow?*
SO: There are both pluses and minuses. The Internet has greatly facilitated collaboration in the research community. That can be both a plus and a

minus, because if we have not protected our intellectual capital or educated our people about what they're sharing, we can have loss. On the other hand, we can also gain through accelerated collaborations and that includes the sharing of intellectual capital in the fullest sense. The Internet has also accelerated the movement of human capital among companies, universities, and so on. It has also prompted us to patent our business practices and business models.

Collaboration and the Internet

JC: *Has your business model changed based on the Internet?*
SO: It has changed only in the sense that we're now filing cases on some of our business practices and business models, along with everyone else in the world. That is the most tangible change. It's business by business, but we're encouraging businesses as they develop new business models to consider protecting them. And Dow has e-businesses.

JC: *Dow has made an active effort to extend outside its boundaries to collaborate with other institutions in developing intellectual capital. You have seen this as important for increasing the speed of developing new offerings and cutting the time to market. How do you see this as part of your intellectual capital development effort?*
SO: We see it as a very integral part of our development effort. One of our corporate values is an outside-in focus. Every business looks out to external resources and partnering relationships. We have about 200 external collaboration agreements in place across the company.

We very clearly see these collaborations as part of our intellectual capital development. Two of our businesses have added the phrase "being in charge of managing the external R&D collaborations" to the job descriptions of their intellectual capital managers. Their job is to manage relationships and also make sure that the intellectual capital is captured and leveraged appropriately.

JC: *You have woven that role into the process?*
SO: Absolutely. These external collaborations not only address getting or creating new intellectual property, but also can serve as a recruiting tool. You can see how the human capital dimension is woven into our work.

We have a very flat organization and no executive dining room. Yesterday I was at lunch with two of my colleagues, and Mike Parker, our

CEO, appeared and asked, "May I join you?" Mike was talking about how our external collaborations are so key to keeping us competitive.

JC: *Is this one of the ways Dow will be seen as a cutting-edge, attractive organization that people want to join and stay at?*
SO: That's right. People see what the existing managers are doing, and there is a lot of word-of-mouth. We have people whom we're interviewing say to us, "Wow, this is the most exciting job I've seen."

JC: *Has Dow found that moving forward in its intellectual capital initiatives is a competitive advantage?*
SO: I believe so. Since it is so crosscutting, our initiative allows people to keep up with the technology. We also have the human side involved, both internally and externally. We get very tangible results when a new project or product is successfully launched because of the intellectual capital contribution. It is not the whole thing, but the contribution dimension is there. It's the multidimensionality that I think is so attractive and compelling. We reside within intellectual capital, but we touch on the financial, business, human resources, and technical sides.

A Relationship between Intellectual Capital and Knowledge Management

JC: *What's the relationship between the intellectual capital effort and the knowledge management effort?*
SO: It's one of collaboration and at this point it's very complementary. We have a director of knowledge management who has been very focused on the tool side, setting up the infrastructure to help organizations capture their knowledge and then mine it. I would say they are part of Dow's overall corporate intellectual capital effort, and I think they would agree with that. But the corporation hasn't chosen to be that explicit with this linkage.

When I talk with our chief information officer, he also understands this, but he felt the need to build the infrastructure to support knowledge management. We have continued to build the umbrella of intellectual capital management. Someday, it may all come together. I used to get frustrated and be on a campaign to pull it all together, and then I stepped back and said, "Sharon, that's really dumb. There's nothing broken right now. It's all working. We're all moving in the same direction. Maybe we would go a little faster if it were linked at the top, but it's working."

Trends in Intellectual Capital

JC: *What are the key trends that you see evolving in intellectual capital, in intellectual property, and in knowledge management? What has changed significantly in the past years, and what do you expect to be changing?*

SO: We can say globally that intellectual property value is clearly increasing. That is a trend that will continue. But I'm going to do a flip on you, because I really question, as we go forward, whether patents will continue to be the trading element for intellectual capital. I believe patents are going to become obsolete. I do not think the patent offices around the world can keep up with patenting. We have already seen that demonstrated. They are trying to change, but businesses are not going to wait for patents to issue. They just are not.

We obviously have a lot of things to change but with the speed at which things are moving, whether you are a chemical company or a dot.com, people are not going to wait for patents. Speed to market is the key. Something has to change. What I see in the future is a development, as we have our stock exchange now, of perhaps a shadow exchange called the intellectual capital exchange.

In the future, we will also need to find a way to do what I call forward accounting. Steven Wallman, the former chair of the Securities and Exchange Commission, is a promoter of this. Standard accounting practices have been around for 500 years and have always produced a historical look, like looking in the rearview mirror. One of our efforts in showing value will be to create some type of forward projection to show how the intellectual capital of a corporation will impact on its future earnings and growth.

JC: *Will that be the engine of change?*

SO: That's right. We need to be able to articulate that future so that an investor or analyst for the current stock market (or, in the future, for an intellectual capital exchange) can look at Dow, at Microsoft, or at a dot.com and say, "Oh, I understand its intellectual capital portfolio and its basis, and therefore I'm going to invest based on——"

Corporations, whether they are the dot.coms or the heavy bricks-and-mortar types, will begin to strategically manage their intellectual capital. It just has to be strategic. The winners are going to be the ones that do it because they will have created their sustainable competitive advantage based on their intellectual capital.

JC: *And that's happening at Dow at this point?*

SO: I think we are well on that journey. We manage intellectual capital as a strategic resource. Again, since we're a knowledge company with bricks and mortar, just as we manage our hydrocarbons today, we're going to be managing our intellectual capital as a resource. We're going to know where those resources are, what we need to grow, and when we need to harvest—all aligned with the business purpose and the business strategy. This is sustainability.

Most companies are managing their intellectual capital, but they do not put that label on it. It's when consciousness gets raised that they really start saying, "We can create value, we can become more competitive, and we can maintain that competitive edge." That is Dow today.

Key Learning Points

- Think in terms of managing intellectual capital assets as strategic resources.
- Gradually broaden the intellectual capital perspective to include recognizing the roles of your people, processes, customers, suppliers, and external relationships.
- Find "the hook" that shows the value of managing intellectual capital (time, money, speed) and that helps solve a critical issue your company is struggling with.
- Do your homework before you work with anyone.
- Establish a network of intellectual capital developers attached to the different stakeholder businesses.
- Align the intellectual capital effort with each unit's business strategy.
- Create an intellectual capital culture that cuts across the different cultures of your organization.
- Try using a fishnet structure that can link all of the different businesses and allow critical information and best practices to easily ripple throughout all business units.
- Be pragmatic about the organization of intellectual capital, knowledge management, and information technology. The prime thing is that the relationships work.
- The winners are going to be the ones who have created their sustainable competitive advantage based on their intellectual capital.

The Springboard Story

17

Stephen Denning was a key player in the strategic shift of the World Bank toward becoming a knowledge-based organization. As the lead person for instituting knowledge management at the World Bank, trying the generally accepted approaches to communicating the complex idea of knowledge management with marginal success, he discovered that storytelling was the most effective vehicle for about "knowledge management." This is not storytelling in the entertainment sense, but storytelling in the sense of conveying the kernel of a significant change experience. He has found that storytelling is a vital element for developing a knowledge-sharing culture and a knowledge-based organization. Without it, he feels that the World Bank would not have achieved the change in emphasis to knowledge as a central pillar and resource that it has.

Denning has written about the evolution of storytelling into a powerful tool for organizational change and knowledge management in his book, *The Springboard: How Storytelling Ignites Action in Knowledge-Era Organizations*. In recognition of his knowledge management accomplishments at the World Bank, he was selected as one of the world's most admired knowledge leaders in a study by Teleos and Work Frontiers International.

From 1996 to 2000, Denning was the program director of knowledge management at the World Bank. A lawyer by training, Denning has held various management positions at the World Bank. He now consults and gives workshops with other organizations in the United States, Europe, Asia, and Australia on knowledge management and organizational storytelling.

The Conversation

Beginning a Knowledge Initiative

JC: *What prompted the World Bank to begin its knowledge management initiative? Have the leadership's expectations changed since you began the initiative?*

SD: We began in 1996 to consider what the future of the World Bank was going to be. There was a lot of public discussion about the future of the World Bank. It had been for most of its 55-year life a money-based lending organization. It was becoming apparent by the mid-1990s that the lending function was to some extent being met by the private sector, which was now providing financial flows that were a large multiple of what the World Bank was providing. When the World Bank was founded, this alternative did not exist for most countries.

The bank's future as a purely financial organization was unclear. The cold war was over, and a lot of political events had occurred that also raised questions about why the World Bank continued to exist and what was to be its future.

We started considering information as one of the things that was troubling us. We were drowning in information. But even more important was our idea that knowledge lay at the heart of the whole development process. We had acquired a tremendous amount of know-how as to what works and what does not work in trying to reduce global poverty. So we started to think: Suppose we could share that know-how, not only among the staff, making it easily accessible, but also sharing it with everyone around the world who could make a difference in the fight against poverty? This would be not only the direct clients who were borrowing from the World Bank, but also all the other millions of people who were involved in taking decisions affecting poverty, so that they had better know-how and could have more of an impact. Then we could become a really useful kind of organization for the future. We began talking about this as an idea in early 1996.

I had been asked to look into information, but it seemed to me that if we dealt with this huge volume of information, we would, at best, become a more efficient organization. We would save money, but we would still be basically the same organization. But, if we started to share our know-how in a systematic fashion, we could become a very different, more relevant, and exciting kind of organization for the future.

That was the vision, and I would say it is still. As implementation has gone on, we have learned a great deal. Some things have worked much better than others. And, some things that we had not thought of doing, we have ended up doing a lot of. We have had to innovate as we have proceeded in order to make the vision work. But I would say that the vision is still essentially, in very broad terms, the same vision.

JC: *What did knowledge management mean to the leadership at the beginning? Has that shifted?*
SD: It did not mean anything. In fact, one did not really explain it by explaining the term *knowledge management*. My experience was that when I started trying to define this phrase, it was very difficult to explain. When I tried charts, the way the consultants use charts, I found that they did not really work. People found the charts as puzzling as the term knowledge management. When I tried prose, people did not read it, and that did not work. If I could turn to a dialogue with some people and spend a week with them, I could then get to understand their problems and show how this would respond to their concerns. But this took a week, and typically I did not have a week. I would usually have something like 15 seconds, or 5 minutes, and so I had to move more quickly.

The only thing that worked for us was telling stories or giving examples of how this phenomenon had worked, either inside our organization or elsewhere. And enabling people, then, to co-create the vision of what the organization could become.

JC: *That gave the leadership an idea?*
SD: Those examples enabled them to imagine the vision for themselves in their own words and in their own contexts.

I would tell them, for instance, a story about Zambia, which was one of the stories I told in 1996. I said, "The future is going to be different. How? What will the future look like? It will look like today.

"Let me tell you about something that happened in Zambia just a few months back in June 1995. A health worker in Kamana, Zambia, logged onto the website for the Centers for Disease Control in Atlanta, Georgia, and got the answer to a question on how to treat malaria. And that was June 1995, not June 2015. This was Kamana, 600 kilometers from the capital.

"And, this was Zambia, one of the very poorest countries in the world. The most important part of the picture was that the World Bank was not in it. We didn't have our know-how organized so that we could make it available to all of the people inside and outside the organization so that they could use it in the fight against poverty. Just imagine if they could use that know-how. Just imagine if we had our know-how organized in this way, what an organization we could become."

Telling that kind of a story enabled a number of senior managers and many front line staff not to think so much about Zambia, or health, or Kamana, but to think about their own contexts. They started to think, "I'm in finance, and we could do that in finance. Yes, why not?" Or, "I'm in highways in Latin America. Yes, we could start to get organized. Yes, that might be interesting."

As a result of that process, they started to imagine what the World Bank could become and what their lives in the World Bank could become. In the process, they became very excited about this as an idea. In due course, they persuaded the president that this was an exciting idea, and he snapped it up, to his great credit.

JC: *Is that how it moved from the background to the fore-ground?*
SD: Right. The president was interested in information. He had been talking about the idea that we should be doing something in information, so he was quite interested in this general area. He was a strong and effective leader in encouraging the idea, picking it up, and dramatically announcing it at the annual meeting in 1996. He has stayed the course and has continued since then to champion it in the organization. This shows how important it is to have a leader in an organization who can understand an exciting idea and can support it consistently over time.

Strategic Intent

JC: *What is the relationship between the World Bank's knowledge initiative and its ability to accomplish its strategic intent?*
SD: It has become a central pillar. We have been a lending organization. Now the official strategy is that knowledge is on a par with money. I would say that, over the coming period, we will see knowledge as more important than money. It will become the more important pillar.

JC: *Will knowledge become the currency of the bank?*
SD: In a sense, yes. When we started in 1996, the World Bank did not

have a mission statement. We had been in business 50 years and had no mission statement.

When we were trying to get the knowledge initiative launched, we could not refer to amission statement and say, "This would be a better way of achieving the mission." We had to say, "Imagine if we had a mission statement, what would it be like, if knowledge was a big part of it?" And, that is what happened. The mission statement was finalized in January 1999. One of the reasons that it could be finalized was that by then knowledge had become a big part of our activities.

The dilemma that the management had been struggling to resolve for 50 years was: We are a lending organization, but we have also something to do with poverty. What is the relationship?

Obviously, if we are just a lending organization, we could never hope to achieve a great reduction in global poverty, so there was a significant disconnect. The disconnect was solved when we said, "That's right. Our mission is to fight poverty. And, we have two main arms to do that. One is money, that is, lending, and the other is knowledge."

Once that was in place, we could come to closure on the mission statement. Our mission statement is: Fighting poverty through lending and through sharing knowledge. There are other means, but essentially, those are the two main pillars.

Seven Key Elements

JC: *What have been the key turning points in the development of the knowledge capacity at the World Bank? Are different elements more mature than others at this stage?*

SD: The whole approach is still in motion. At this point, we see ourselves as just over halfway through this journey of transforming the whole organization into a knowledge-sharing organization. We have put in place a number of things. But the impact of those things is still being worked through. For instance, we have put in place a knowledge-sharing strategy, which is part of the official strategy of the organization. It is part of the mission statement. It is in the budget. It is in the work programs. It is explicit that this is something the World Bank has decided to do. You can see the visible trail, the elements of that in the decision making of the organization, and it is disseminated widely throughout the organization.

Second, we have an organization in place, a small team of just a couple of people spearheading the change across the organization and keeping it on track. Along with this is a decentralized implementation, basically with the line managers being responsible for implementation.

Third, we have put in place a budget. Three percent of the administrative budget of the organization is devoted to this. The total administrative budget is $1.5 billion, so 3% is around $50 million. That sounds like a lot, but the major consulting firms are spending somewhere between 6 and 12% of their total revenue, which is even higher in proportion and larger in absolute amount.

Our allocation is not so much for IT but for people in operations and the front line staff so that they have the time to do this as part of their jobs. It is not something they have to do on the weekends or in the evenings. Knowledge sharing is part of their nine-to-five job.

Number four is that we have changed the incentives. We changed the personnel system of the World Bank so that there are only four core behaviors. One of those core behaviors is knowledge sharing and learning. Every manager and staff member, from the president down to the messenger, has an annual review with his manager. In effect, the manager asks, "What did you do to share your knowledge over the last year, and what are you planning to do over the coming year?" That was put in place in early 1998, implemented for the first time in 1999, and implemented a second time in 2000. One can start to see the impact of that over time.

JC: *What impact do you see?*
SD: It took quite a long while to get the decision implemented. Then, on the first go-round, people said that they could not see any impact. But after the second go-round, we started to see that some of the "incorrigibles" of knowledge management, those people we thought would never get it, began asking: "Could you tell me what this knowledge thing is about? I really need to find out. I have just been through my personnel thing. I've just had a budget discussion, and I'd really like to know more about this. Maybe we could discuss what it's about? Maybe you could come and talk to our group?" We started to see after the second round that the incorrigibles started to feel the impact of the change.

So the initial impression that it was not having any impact was incorrect. It takes a while. We heard from other organizations that this change does not appear to have an immediate impact. But what it does over time is scoop up the laggards and those who did not quite get it on the first go-round and encourages them to join the organization and make it part of their work.

The fifth is communities. That has involved supporting communities of practitioners, which we call *thematic groups* in the World Bank, endorsing that as a way of organizing, and stressing that this was how we were going to carry out knowledge sharing in the organization.

The sixth is technology. This has meant putting in place tools. These were often just simple tools, e-mail and web sites, whereby we could start to have communities operating with people scattered around the world and use the web to make know-how available very easily and cheaply across the organization and beyond.

The seventh is measurement. This is putting in place a measurement system that can track what is happening and tell us how much of what we intended to happen had actually happened, as well as finding out what the staff thought about the communities. This is a modest tracking system. It is very simple and provides some basic facts about knowledge sharing in the organization.

We put in place those seven things. Over time, they are continuing to encourage the organization and its managers and staff to get on with implementing the strategy.

JC: *Were they put in place all at the same time, or what was the sequence in which they began?*
SD: We started talking about this early in 1996. The president announced it in October 1996, at the annual meeting of the World Bank. Over the next four months, we incorporated it into the Strategic Compact. This was a formal strategy document of the World Bank, which was unanimously approved by the board of directors in March 1997, and it laid out a game plan in explicit terms. A budget for this was put in place in June 1997. I had been was formally appointed as the program director of knowledge management earlier, in October 1996.

In July 1997, we established a knowledge management board that enabled coordinated decision making across the organization. There were a number of problems in terms of actually getting money to flow from this budget decision. In response, in January 1998, we decided to fund these emerging communities of practice directly. That led to a rapid acceleration of the growth of these communities, which had been just a handful in 1996 and maybe around 25 by mid-1997. By the middle of 1998, there were more than 100 of these communities, thematic groups, covering every aspect of the World Bank's activities.

The personnel change was decided in February 1998. It was implemented for the first time in the personnel annual reviews in April 1999 and for the second time in April 2000.

The technology tools have continually evolved as we have moved along. The tracking system initially focused on inputs, that is, how much money was going into it. We then started to look at both how many communities there were and how active they are. We have steadily shifted focus now to outcomes, asking staff and outsiders: "Is what they are doing useful? Is it working?"

Having external evaluations has also been helpful to us. In April 1999, we had an external evaluation led by Larry Prusak of IBM, which included Bob Hiebeler, head of knowledge management at Arthur Andersen, Tom Davenport of Andersen Consulting, Kent Greenes from BP, Wendy Coles from General Motors, and so on. We used them as a sounding board as to whether we were on the right track. The American Productivity and Quality Center (APQC) benchmarking has also been very helpful to us.

The selection of the World Bank as one of the world's ten Most Admired Knowledge Enterprises was helpful to us in terms of reassuring the management that, although there were many problems, blemishes, and issues still to be sorted out, there had been progress. The selection demonstrated that we were actually doing what many other organizations were still trying to do.

From Knowledge Management to Knowledge Sharing

JC: *Tell me about the change from using the term* knowledge management *to the term* knowledge sharing?
SD: We hesitated a long while about changing from the term knowledge management to knowledge sharing. We thought that knowledge sharing was a more suitable name because people generally found knowledge management a confusing term. To many people, it conveyed the idea that knowledge management was some kind of obscure black box, some kind of brain in the sky, some kind of fad, or some kind of gadget that was not very practical.

We thought that knowledge sharing was much more intuitively understandable and a down-to-earth way of describing it. But we were worried that if we started using a different term it would confuse people, after having used knowledge management for some time.

When we did make the change in January 1999 to call our effort knowledge sharing, most of the managers heaved a sigh of relief and said, "Thank goodness. I wonder why we did not do that earlier." This has been a big plus for us.

JC: *Is it easier to share knowledge than to manage it?*
SD: As Larry Prusak says, you cannot really manage knowledge. Can you manage friendship, or piety, or courage? These are not the kinds of things that you can manage. You can manage the environment, you can manage the people, you can encourage the sharing of knowledge, but you cannot really manage knowledge.

We have tried consistently to use the term knowledge sharing, although there are still a lot of historical remnants of knowledge management as a term around. My title is still program director, knowledge management. We have not gotten around to changing that, but the mission statement is in terms of knowledge sharing, and the strategy documents are now all in terms of knowledge sharing.

Making It Work

JC: *How many people are on your staff?*
SD: There are now four staff members. However, there are hundreds of people involved in the knowledge movement across the organization. We have these 116 thematic groups, which are communities of practice. Each of those groups has between two and five leaders. As a result, we have several hundred people who are leaders of the communities. Then, on average, the 4,000 staff in operations are members of between two and three communities.

Each person in operations typically belongs to two or three communities. In varying degrees, we have a large part of the whole organization involved. We have several hundred for whom this is really quite an important part of their day-to-day work. But it is a highly decentralized organization. In other words, these four people who work for me are not controlling things.

JC: *What does the staff do on a day-to-day basis?*
SD: They do whatever needs to be done. In the early days, it was articulating what it was we were trying to do, communicating that through storytelling, and sorting out any other issues that needed to be sorted out. If the budget was not flowing, we were the people who had to figure out why it was not and what could be done about it. If the personnel system had to be changed, we were the people who had to spark that change, agree on the language, get management support, and push it through.

JC: *Is that primarily how your group relates to the rest of the World Bank organization and its partner organizations?*
SD: Our group was initially in the computer department of the World Bank, what we call the information solutions group. To my mind, it was not the ideal place for us to be.

Over time, it has become part of the operations of the World Bank. It is a way of doing the operations of the World Bank in a more effective and agile way. It is not principally a computer matter. Nevertheless, this was the most congenial home for us at the time, and so that is where we started out in October 1996. We stayed there until the middle of 1999, when the management, particularly after the review with Larry Prusak and his colleagues, became aware that knowledge sharing was an operational idea and a way of doing the business of the World Bank. As a result, they decided we should move into operations. We moved into what is called the operations core services network, which is the crosscutting network that handles organization-wide functions. We have been there since then.

JC: *Is that a good fit for you?*
SD: There is no perfect fit, but because it is in operations, it is certainly closer to where we need to be. I do not think there is any ideal home, but this has proven to be very satisfactory.

JC: *How many people are in the World Bank universe?*
SD: The whole organization is 10,000 people around the world, with 4,000 people in operations. I would say this pattern of small knowledge teams leading the effort, though, is common across organizations that are perceived as doing well in knowledge management.

If you look at the five organizations that were benchmarked by APQC in 1999 in terms of successfully implementing knowledge management (Siemens, Chevron, Xerox, World Bank, and Hewlett Packard), they all have the same arrangement. They all have a tiny, tiny group, somewhere between four and eight people. Some of those organizations are very, very large, but they all have a tiny group leading the knowledge effort.

There have been other organizations which started out with a very large group, and there are still some of them going, but most of those have shifted to this pattern of highly decentralized organization and a tiny, tiny group that puts the responsibility for making this happen with the line managers.

This is something that can only happen with the line management. If you have a large group at the center, it starts to become something different.

Is a small group enough? It is not like a job where you can measure it in terms of numbers of things that you have to do. It is more a question of what is the quality of the interactions, and what kinds of things can you spark, ignite, and catalyze that happen across the organization. For that, I think, a relatively small group probably has an advantage over a big one. It is inevitably something that happens opportunistically. In other words, one waits for opportunities when issues are open for discussion, and then one can make progress. For instance, 1998 was a time when the management was willing to consider changing the personnel system. We took advantage of that and pushed it through. But there were other things that they were not interested in addressing at that particular time.

We focused on the things that could be done in that time frame. A key element in making things happen is sensing the scene, seeing what is possible, and working within the bounds of what is possible. Like politics, it involves the art of the possible.

The Springboard

JC: *What is a springboard story, and how did you come to write your new book,* The Springboard?[1]

SD: I certainly did not set out to use storytelling as a tool. I did not imagine in 1996 that I would be writing a book about storytelling. It was not on my radar.

If somebody had told me, "In a few years' time, you will have written a book on storytelling," I would have said, "That is absurd." If someone had asked me why it was absurd, I would have said, "One thing I know is that knowledge is abstract. Knowledge is solid, abstract, and analytic. That's how we make progress in the world. That's the whole basis of science, that's the basis of the tremendous material progress in the world. Storytelling is something that we have put aside. It's not serious. It's trivial. It's anecdotal. Serious thinking is abstract and analytic." That is what I would have said.

The book is an account of how I learned how wrong I was. It tells how I stumbled upon a different way of understanding what was happening in the world and a different way of using stories, in order to accomplish what I needed to do. It was as much out of desperation as anything else that I ended up in this mode. I simply found that nothing else worked. I tried charts, and they did not work. I tried prose, and no one read it. Dialogue took too long. The only thing that worked was storytelling.

I was barely even realizing what I was doing until about the middle of 1997. People were asking me, "What is happening in the World Bank? Here is a knowledge program that is moving along at this rapid pace in an organization which is notorious for being change-resistant, even hostile to anything fundamental changing. How is it that things are moving along so quickly?"

Then, I would say things like: "The president is leading it." And, they would say, "Yes, but he's leading a lot of other things, and they aren't

---

[1] Stephen Denning, *The Springboard: How Storytelling Ignites Action in Knowledge-Era Organizations* (Boston: Butterworth Heinemann, 2000).

moving along so energetically." Or I said, "It's a good idea." And they said, "A lot of good ideas are not being implemented so energetically."

Then in November 1997, at a conference in North Carolina, I put up a slide in one of my presentations saying, "Maybe it's storytelling. Maybe it has something to do with telling stories?" That resonated with people. Then somebody came up to me after the conference and said, "Why don't you write a book?" I said, "About what?" And they said, "About storytelling." And I said, "That's very interesting, because the sum total of my knowledge of storytelling is in that slide: Maybe it has something to do with storytelling."

Over the next two years, I did in fact learn a great deal more about storytelling. We experimented. We tried out different things. The book is the story of my discovery of the power of storytelling.

JC: *You call it* The Springboard. *What does* springboard *convey that storytelling by itself does not?*

SD: There are many different kinds of stories and many different purposes in telling stories. You can use stories to build community, to communicate knowledge, or to convey tradition. I found myself using stories to spark active and energetic change in an organization. I found that a certain kind of story enabled people to imagine a different kind of future. It served as a springboard from which they could get to the next level, in terms of imagining a different forward prospect, co-creating the future, and imagining a different identity for themselves and for the organization as a result of this.

It became apparent to me that it was working. I might tell a story about one thing, say, Zambia, and the audience in their own minds would invent another story which fit their environments, their languages, and their situations. The first time I became aware of this was when I told the Zambia story to a group of senior managers in April 1996. This was actually a group of managers who were responsible for the change process. Up to this point, I had not really been seeing very much interest on their part in knowledge management. I made this presentation and told the story. Immediately after the presentation, somebody rushed up to me and asked, "What's holding it back? Why aren't we doing it? Why aren't you pushing this harder?"

At that point, I had been pushing as hard as I could. What was striking about this was that they were asking these questions as though it were their idea. It was now *their* idea, and I was the person who was not pushing hard enough on their idea. This was great because I had been trying to get people interested in the idea. Now they had taken it over.

It was not my idea any more. They were now starting to imagine what this different future could be like. The whole meaning of the encounter did not strike me at that time, but it stuck in my mind that this was a strange conversation.

Later on, I started to join the dots and see how these stories were enabling people to imagine a different kind of future.

A Leap in Understanding

JC: *Is that why you called it Springboard?*
SD: A springboard story enables a leap in understanding for people. That was quite unusual. It was something that I had not come across before. In fact, some academics told me it could not happen. Their view was that the mind was a computer; it worked by weighing the evidence pro and con. When the mind has enough reasons for doing something else, then it eventually changes direction and decides to do something else.

What we were seeing here was rather that the mind was changing direction with a snap. A whole new idea was grabbing them. A new gestalt was taking over in a flash, and they were off to the races.

It was of course very fortunate to stumble upon something like that for getting energetic change in a very difficult environment like the World Bank.

JC: *Do you think that people felt powerless, on the one hand, and they now felt powerful enough so that they could radically change their world?*
SD: It was not so much power but the fact that they had suddenly, rapidly, and almost instantaneously become enthusiastic about an idea that just a few minutes before they were unaware of or highly skeptical about.

The interesting thing was that their identities were enmeshed in the idea of the World Bank as a lending organization. Their whole world view was seeing: "I'm a manager in a lending organization, and that's why I'm a significant individual." If someone questioned that, then it was as if they were questioning the person's worth and their sense of identity. But, if they could start to imagine a different future for themselves, they could start to imagine a new identity for themselves. It was not someone doing it to them. They were doing it to themselves. They own it since they created it.

We were not actually asking them to articulate this story. They were imagining it as I spoke. I was talking to them about Zambia, or Pakistan, or Madagascar, and mentally, at the same time they were hearing this story, they were starting to think how things could be different. They were not put on the spot to articulate what this new vision might be. They were under no pressure. They did not have to do it. It was something natural and spontaneous.

JC: *Did you differentiate among different people, different levels, and different kinds of groups, or were the stories equally effective across all boundaries?*

SD: I found that the effective stories worked at all levels inside the World Bank. I did not have different stories for the top management and some for the front line staff. I used the same stories for all groups. Once we found a story that worked, then we found that it worked with all levels. Some of these stories did not work with groups in other organizations because the other organizations did not have the same background. The story did not have the same kind of resonance in their particular settings, as it did in the World Bank.

There were other occasions, such as when I went to Boston and tried to talk to a group about doing research on storytelling, and it did not work. So storytelling is not a panacea. It doesn't work on every occasion. It is a question of finding the story that fits the particular context of the organization. When one finds it, then it works at all levels.

For instance, at the end of 1997, there was a tremendous amount of discord, disarray, and disagreement among people about where things were heading. We had a meeting where we would tell one of these stories, in that case the Yemen story, and suddenly there did not seem to be any more discord. Suddenly, people remembered why we were doing this and how things fitted together. The discord seemed to evaporate.

It was almost a mystery to me that we would be having all of this tension, this difficulty, and then we would go through one of these performances and tell a story, and there would be peace and calm and light for a period. Then more discord would build up, and we would go through a new round of storytelling.

In an organization, the staff's sense of identity is very much tied in with this organizational life story that is in their minds. If we propose change to an organization that is in conflict with the life story of the organization that large numbers of people are carrying around with them, then we are really going to have a lot of problems unless we can get them to co-create a new life story for themselves and for the organization.

JC: *Is this working well with your partner organizations?*

SD: These stories are now working with all of our partner organizations. We just had a series of workshops, one in the United States and then another one in Brighton for European partner organizations. I would say that these stories work uniformly across the organization. In *The Spring-*

board, I tell about a story that didn't work in Bern in 1997. It is possible that I was just a bit early at that time. However, the world has moved on, and these ideas have now become current. People are interested in them. These stories enable them to make the leap, using them as a springboard to a new level of understanding.

Objectives of Storytelling

JC: *What are the objectives of storytelling as you see it? You use a small* s *versus a big* S. *What have you learned from the challenges to this approach? I assume that not everybody is going to swallow this approach whole.*

SD: I used it for the very specific purpose of communicating a complex idea to a large number of people in order to get them into energetic action implementing the idea. That is a very narrow purpose. There are many other purposes for which you can use stories. The stories that I found that worked in that way all had a certain kind of a pattern.

I am not saying that other stories will not have the same effect, but the pattern that worked for me was a story based on a single protagonist, that is, a single hero or heroine, who was in a predicament which was prototypical of the organization. In our case, it happened to be someone in a multidisciplinary team, in a faraway country, facing a client and not having an answer to a problem.

That is a situation that everyone in operations in the World Bank knows, understands, and feels for the protagonist. If we were an oil company, it would probably be about oil drillers. If we were a sales organization, it would be about a salesperson.

The commonality is having someone who is prototypical of the organization, in a predicament that is prototypical of the organization, and then having a story where something unexpected takes place. The unexpected thing occurs, and it happens to be the change idea that I am trying to communicate to the organization.

For example, in the Zambia story, the health worker unexpectedly gets an answer to a problem on how to treat malaria on the spot, by way of the worldwide web. In 1996, that was a surprising turn of events. It caught the imagination of people since this was unexpected. There was a certain strangeness about the story. But, it was also plausible. Yes, the web exists. Yes, it is possible to communicate from Zambia to Atlanta. Yes, the CDC does have a web site. It does have an awful lot of stuff on how to treat malaria. So, yes, this could have happened. This is plausible.

It enables people to start to imagine that the future of the world may not be what they expected. The web enables people to find answers all around the world. People start to think, "So things could be different." It is this kind of a story, with a single protagonist, prototypical in the organization, a certain amount of strangeness, and a certain amount of plausibility that sparks this mental possibility. Most important, the story has to have a happy ending. Hollywood is right. A happy ending is key to the trick.

I had no success at all with telling stories with bad endings. For example, "I know a firm that didn't share its knowledge, and it went down the tubes, went bankrupt, went out of existence." That kind of a story never for me had any success in getting people motivated to do what the firm did not do. It seemed like there was too much of a leap from that negative ending to: "What should they have done?" and then having to think that through.

What did work is telling a story where it was successful, where things ended happily, and where the listener only had to make a tiny leap from the story as I was telling it to their own world, where they could make that leap in reality.

A Non-adversarial Approach

JC: *What have you learned from challenges to your approach?*
That is, when people have not always responded positively.
What kinds of insights have taken you to another place?
SD: Storytelling worked with many, many people across the organization. It did not work with everyone. Simply being patient was part of coping with that. Some of the incorrigibles whom I thought would never get it have finally started to come around and ask me, "Why don't you tell me about it?"

Having a certain amount of patience is part of it, but also storytelling was helpful because it's non-adversarial. If I say to you, "Jay, I want you to implement a knowledge management system. Here are the elements, and I want you to start tomorrow morning," there is an idea—my idea—coming from me to you, almost like a missile. As you see this idea coming at you, your immediate reaction is probably going to be: "Why should I accept this idea coming from outside my world?" And you might be immediately starting to think, "Why should I do this? Why should I adopt his idea in my territory?" which sets up an argument between you and me as to whether you should do this thing.

But if I say, "Jay, let me tell you about something that happened in Zambia a few months ago," it is not threatening; it is not an idea that is coming at you. We are jointly looking at something that happened in Zambia. In fact, it's the very essence of intimacy, not two people facing each other, but rather two people looking at the same thing and sharing the same feelings toward it.

Storytelling is nonadversarial. It is more like dancing, more like collaboration, where we do something together. There are not any winners, and there are not any losers.

If I say you have to do it, that you have to implement a knowledge management scheme tomorrow morning, either you do it or you do not. It is yes-no, that is to say, win-lose. We are both in a situation where there are high stakes. But if I simply say, "Let me tell you about something that happened in another country," then it is up to you to make your own decision to determine whether you are going to get anything out of that or not.

It is much easier and less threatening. The fact of storytelling is: If you do not happen to agree now, you do not make the leap, you do not use it as a springboard, it is not like you have lost or won, or I have lost or won. We are still collaborating. Eventually, you may make that leap or you may not, but the environment does not become as adversarial as when I am trying to push an abstract idea. It was very helpful that, by not having a kind of threatening, adversarial environment, it enabled people to get on board in their own time, in their own pace, in their own language, and in their own context.

Bridging the Narrative and the Analytic

JC: *How do you resolve the dichotomy between the rational, analytic approach and the storytelling, anecdotal approach?*
SD: I see it as a marriage of narrative and analytic modes of thinking. One by itself is not enough. Narrative by itself is obviously not enough, and analysis by itself is not enough. The marriage of the two can be extremely powerful, because the narrative mode of thinking enables one to imagine different kinds of futures. It enables one to think how things could be different. It is basically by stories that we understand how the world can change.

If I tell you a story where there is nothing new, where everything is completely routine, you will tell me that it is not really a story, that you are not interested in it. What attracts us about stories is what is new, some twist, or some angle by which we learn that things are not exactly as we thought they were in the world. Storytelling is tremendously powerful in terms of enabling people to imagine a different future, enabling them to understand and to innovate.

Storytelling is obviously not very good in terms of evaluating regularities. It is not very good in terms of looking at the costs and benefits. For those things, you need analysis. Once you have imagined a different kind of future through narrative, then you need to come back and say, "Ok, suppose we did that, how much would it cost? What would the benefits be, and are the costs worth the benefits?"

If you have understood the idea through a narrative, you are looking at it in a sympathetic way, not in terms of finding fault, or trying to kill the idea even before you understand it. You have gotten inside the idea. Because you are inside it, you have a much more intelligent and sympathetic way of figuring out what would be the costs and the benefits.

In my view, it is this marriage of narrative and abstract analytical thinking which is extremely powerful. I am certainly not saying that it is one or the other. You need both. You need to use both the left side and the right side of the brain.

JC: *How did you arrive at that understanding?*
SD: I started out thinking that narrative had no place, since my whole life had been based on the use of analysis, on abstract thinking, and being a master of analysis and abstract thinking. In my job, I was mainly a left-brain person. I certainly did not think of myself as a storyteller in my work. The story in the book is really about how I found out that the analytical abstract tools could often not get the job done, and out of desperation I reached for other things, things I had no idea whether they could work at all. I learned how to use the right side of my brain in my work.

A Network of Communities

JC: *Do you see the World Bank as an extended organization that is part of a network, and how do you form knowledge partnerships that make up that network?*
SD: Yes, I do see it as part of a network. The nature of that has become apparent over time. When we were talking about this in 1996, we were a very closed organization. We were an organization that had thick cultural walls around it, and the idea that we were going to share our knowl-

edge with the whole world was quite unusual for that organization at that time.

This was somewhat disturbing to some of the managers and did involve quite significant changes to the whole modus operandi of the organization. Nevertheless, we got on with it and started nurturing these communities. We found that the communities started taking in external partners almost naturally, spontaneously, and organically.

There were some things that took a tremendous amount of effort to leverage and to get done, for instance, changing the personnel system in the World Bank. However, the growth of external partners in these communities seemed to happen spontaneously. You can see how it happened because it was a win-win situation. For example, say the highways community of practice in the World Bank suddenly figured out that its members had somehow neglected traffic safety, and they did not know nearly as much about that as they would like to know. However, there is the British Traffic Safety Institute, which knows everything about this. It has spent the last few decades accumulating all that the world knows about this subject, and it is dying to become a member of our community. If we offer the safety institute the opportunity to become a member of our community, it gets access to all of the activities that the World Bank is involved in, and we get access to its knowledge. It is delighted to be part of the community, and we are delighted to have it. We see that kind of win-win situation cropping up all over the world.

These external partnerships seem to have happened magically and spontaneously across the organization. Not in every group, but in most of the groups. In the very successful groups, this has happened on a large scale.

At a certain point, we get to the limits of scale. We have groups now, like the quality of fiscal adjustment group that has 450 members (200 internal members and 250 external members), which probably is almost as large as a community can become, in the sense that people can still know each other.

We started to explore what the next step is, because beyond that, we need to have a wider reach. With the advice of Etienne Wenger, we started to think in terms of fractal communities. Let us think that we have a global community like the fiscal adjustment group. However, in each country, we might have local communities, which would be linked to a global community. We have a global community of highway practitioners, but we also plan to have local networks of communities. That is what the top-level management of the World Bank, in its strategic forum of January 2000, decided that we were going to pilot over the next year or two to try to figure out how to build these networks of communities around the world.

JC: *Are you going to have a role in that?*

SD: That is what we are now doing. I believe that this will lead to a different view of development, where knowledge is the driver. These communities are the crucible, the cradle, and the place where knowledge ideas will emerge. And the funding will eventually become almost secondary to that. The money will support the knowledge-based ideas that emerge out of these communities. That would be a different dynamic from the past where the money has been the driving force and we have to bring in knowledge to make the money effective.

This puts knowledge at the center and brings in the money as needed. It makes knowledge the driving force in the whole process. I believe that this is now inevitable and will happen over the next few years.

Crossing Over

JC: *If you were to start a knowledge initiative afresh in a different organization, how would you proceed?*

SD: I would start talking with the people inside the organization and find out the context of the organization. I would find out what role knowledge plays in the organization, what knowledge is important, how people currently perceive it, whether it is being shared inside, and whether it is being shared outside. Does it have communities, and does it share with outside clients and partners? What is its business strategy? How does it perceive its future? What is it trying to accomplish?

And out of those discussions would come some kind of understanding as to where the organization is, where it might like to be, and how it could get from where it is to where it would like to be.

Many organizations have since come to me with this kind of a question and asked me to come and talk to them. Usually I do not make any recommendations to them about what to do because I, typically, do not know enough about the organization to do that.

I do what I did inside the World Bank, telling them stories about what we did in the World Bank: "We were faced with this situation, and that is what we did. Then we did this, and then we did that."

What happens is that these people, just as the managers in the World Bank did, start to imagine what this might mean for them. They start to think about what a community might be called in their context, what it might do, how it could be useful to their organization, and how it might help them to get to where they want to go.

That process reinforces that they, as the owners of the organization, are the ones who have to reinvent the organization and themselves.

JC: *Do you think it would make any difference to you in working with an old-economy organization versus a new-economy organization, or with a small startup versus a large General Motors?*

SD: The bricks-and-mortar organizations are often older organizations, and they are often set in their ways. They tend to have a vertical hierarchy, and they might be very large. But, they are often also filled with exciting, creative people, and often they have very sharing cultures. So, this thing can take off very rapidly, even in older organizations.

I have also come across startup organizations that have already gotten into nonsharing ways. I do not think that one can assume that startups or dot.coms are in a more sharing mode. Probably the contrary, since they often start out without really thinking very much about the kind of sharing that would be needed to make them sustainable. They are so busy trying to get to some kind of initial viability. They are scrambling around in a somewhat disorganized way. The longer-term picture of what kind of sharing would be needed as the company grows only dawns on them as they have some success and they expand. Then, they suddenly realize, "This isn't what we thought would happen. We don't know what's happening in this organization that once was so tiny that we could know everything. Now we suddenly find that we don't know what's going on any more. We want to get back to the way it was when there were three of us in a garage, talking about what the future was going to be like."

What Knowledge Is Crucial?

JC: *How do people begin to take the time that is necessary to do the knowledge sharing?*

SD: If you are trying to make knowledge sharing happen in an organization, you have to put in place the seven basics.[2] The most important initially are making some strategic decisions about what knowledge you are trying to share, why you are trying to share it, and who you are trying to share it with, and then make a decision that you are going to do it. Then, you put in place a budget that enables people to do this from nine-to-five and don't expect people to do it on evenings and weekends. And next, the rest of the elements—the organization, personnel incentives, the communities, the technology, the measurement system. You are providing whatever

[2] See "The Seven Basics of Knowledge Management" at http://www.stevedenning.com/seven_basics_knowledge_management.html.

support is needed in the organization to make it happen. Deciding to do those things is key.

To some extent, the learning organization people are in a mode of saying, "Let's all learn. Let's learn across the whole organization. Let's learn." But organizations as a whole do not just learn. Learning is only likely to happen in communities where there is trust among the members. This is the infrastructure that is necessary to put in place. Simply saying, "Let us share knowledge," will not be very effective because one needs to make it more precise. What kind of knowledge? And with whom? and why? and how?

In the World Bank, we focused on the know-how of the organization. There were large slabs of knowledge that we said we were not going to focus on. We were not going to focus on knowledge about our customers and clients. We were not going to focus on knowledge about our partners. We were not going to focus on competitive intelligence. We were going to focus on what works and what does not work in development. That is what the knowledge bank was about. Not everyone always respected that. But, by and large, it has been helpful as a kind of compass to keep us on track.

But if we had focused on all the knowledge that is relevant for development, then we would have gotten lost. As it happens, I was at a meeting with some members of the American intelligence community this morning. They, to some extent, are still thinking about the entire universe of knowledge. They are trying to think about how they can get a handle on it. They have not said, "We are going to focus on a certain piece of that knowledge, so that the task becomes manageable." That is what we were able to do at the World Bank, and I think that has been very useful to us.

The Next Stage

JC: *What is your vision for the next stage of the knowledge-sharing initiative at the World Bank?*

SD: Part of it is simply continuing with what we already have: making sure these basics stay in place so that communities continually get stronger and more effective and so that it reaches more and more of the staff of the organization.

The strategic forum, which is composed of the president, the managing directors, the vice presidents, and 40 managers of the organization, each year in January has a session where they think where the organization is heading. The session in January 2000 was a particularly important one because the president had just been reelected for another five years. The focus was: What are the next five years going to look like? What are we going to focus on?

The decisions had more than a one-year time frame. We were looking at the bigger picture. There was a big argument about what the future should look like and how important knowledge should be. The result was that it was decided that it should be very important. It was to be one of the pillars of the future. Piloting these fractal communities was one part of it, and making sure that we were sharing knowledge by way of the web as effectively as we could was another big part of it.

What is known as the global development gateway, sort of a portal of development knowledge, has become a big part of the scene. Yes, a part of our work is just carrying through with what we have already launched and making sure we do not forget that and making sure it carries through. The other part is tackling these new challenges, which are right upon us.

We have covered the basics. For more specifics, I invite people to visit my website at www.stevedenning.com and to pick up a copy of *The Springboard: How Storytelling Ignites Action in Knowledge-Era Organizations*, which goes into these ideas in full.

Key Learning Points

- Springboard stories enable people to co-create the vision of what their organization could become for themselves, in their own words, and in their own contexts.
- Put in place seven key elements:
    - a knowledge-sharing strategy, which is part of the official strategy of the organization,
    - a group (a small team of just a couple of people spearheading the change across the organization and keeping it on track),
    - a budget,
    - changed incentives to reward core behaviors,
    - support for communities of practitioners, stressing that this is how the organization will carry out knowledge sharing,
    - technological tools, and
    - a measurement system that can track what is happening.
- Changing from the term *knowledge management* to *knowledge sharing* can be more suitable because people can find knowledge management a confusing term. Knowledge sharing is much more intuitively understandable and a down-to-earth way of describing it.

- Small knowledge teams leading the effort are common across organizations that are doing well in knowledge management. They can spark, ignite, and catalyze what happens across the organization, inevitably opportunistically when issues are open to discussion.
- Storytelling is not a panacea. It is a question of finding the story that fits the particular context of the organization. When that is found, the story works at all levels of the organization.
- Storytelling is non-adversarial. It is more like dancing, collaboration we do together. There are no winners, and there are no losers.
- There needs to be a marriage between narrative and analytical modes of thinking. Neither is enough by itself. Once you have imagined a different kind of future through narrative, then you need to understand the costs and benefits of moving to such a future.
- At the beginning of a knowledge initiative, find out the context of the organization, what role knowledge plays in the organization, what knowledge is important, how people are currently perceiving it, and whether it is being shared inside and outside.

The Knowledge-Centric Organization

18

Alex Bennet is cofounder of the Mountain Quest Institute, a research and retreat center focused on achieving growth and understanding through quests for knowledge. She served as the chief knowledge officer from 1998 to 2002 for the U.S. Department of the Navy, where she pioneered and led the development of the navy's enterprise-wide knowledge-centric organization (KCO) effort. She also was co-chair of the Federal Knowledge Management Working Group.

In addition to her extensive and diverse career with the U.S. Navy, Bennet has published more than 500 articles, edited several books on knowledge management and e-government, and is co-author of a book on the Department of the Navy's CIO implementation strategy.[1]

Bennet sees that we are moving from the information age into an age of complexity, and knowledge is the best and perhaps the only answer to this complex age. She believes that knowledge, when used in conjunction with strong values, can make a positive difference, can move us forward and promote growth in our chaotic, complex, and uncertain world.

---

[1] Dan Porter, Alex Bennet, Ronald Turner, and David Wennergren, *The Power of Team: The Making of a CIO* (Washington, D.C.: U.S. Department of the Navy, 2002).

The Role of the Chief Knowledge Officer

JC: *What is the role of the chief knowledge officer in the Department of the Navy, and where is that role situated in the infrastructure?*

AB: The role of the chief knowledge officer for the department is situated with the chief information officer (directly reporting to the undersecretary of the navy) and is the responsibility of the deputy chief information officer (DCIO) for enterprise integration. While I was in that position, I also had overall responsibility for policy and guidance in the areas of information management/information technology strategic planning and workforce issues, enterprise licensing, and the communications and outreach program. Situated at the highest level of the secretariat infrastructure, the role was primarily that of a leader and champion, integrator, and change agent.

The Environment

JC: *What kind of model(s) for knowledge management do you see as effective for creating an environment that's conducive to knowledge creation, knowledge sharing, and knowledge value capture for the navy?*

AB: Knowledge creation, knowledge sharing, and value capture are very different things, even though they are all interrelated. We are going to focus on the environment. The Department of the Navy includes the Navy, the Marine Corps, and the Secretariat. It is a large frame of reference. We are the largest navy in the world, with nearly a million people directly connected and an even larger support framework of interconnected people both inside and outside of government. The result is that there is not one specific environment in which we operate.

Imagine the differences that occur across such a large—and geographically dispersed—organization. There is a different environment in undersea warfare than there is in surface warfare, than there is for the Marines who are on the land, than there is for our air community. And that is just one way of dividing it. Then, you have the environments that are differentiated by uniform, civilian, and contractor, and we are all part of the same team.

Yet, there is an integration even among those kinds of things because most of the people who are in our contractor realm actually come out of the service. And most of the people who are civilian employees go on to become contractors. There is a trade there. There is a loop. There are a lot of young people who start in contracting, then go into the service and into a uniform. We have an incredibly fluid movement of people even though we have differentiation among the segments of our population.

We also have incredible geographical dispersion. We are positioned around the world. At the same time, our points are not static. They are continuously moving and fluid. When someone is out there on a ship, he is part of a community that is literally moving, changing its location continuously.

We have a very different environment than any other organization that I know around the world. We are not the same as the other services either, because we have all four types of activities as part of our department.

I would like to discuss those values that are in the environment that perhaps facilitate the creation of knowledge and the sharing of knowledge.

The Importance of Knowledge

AB: First of all, warfare and technology are inextricably related. If we go back and look at who has won wars in the past, we discover that the outcome was very dependent on the technology that was known and used in the process of warfare. Let's go back to the very beginning with the cavemen. When the spear was first developed, a technological development, it gave its possessors a definite advantage over the club. We can go on and on throughout the history of warfare with that same analogy.

Therefore, we recognize the value of technology as it relates to our mission and vision here. That has direct connectivity to the advancement of technology.

Second, we highly value the importance of knowledge because it relates directly to our success in warfare. If we are in the mode to defend, we must have high situational awareness. We must have knowledge of both ourselves and of our opponents. We must have knowledge of the battle space, knowledge of ourselves, and knowledge of the opponent. That is quite easily put but very difficult to do. Further, it is dependent on the information that we get fed and how we connect it up. We have been in the knowledge business since the very beginning of warfare, since the very beginning of the department.

What is different today is that via the Internet everyone has access to everything, and there has been an exponential increase in the amount of data and information. Because everyone is creative and everyone has access to all of this information now, we seem to see more creativity happening in our people, more growth, both internally and externally.

Our environment has the requirement and the demand for Dow Chemical's definition of the "right stuff, right place, and right time." To be successful in our responsibility, we must ensure that we have the best knowledge and that we use it in the best way possible. That means focusing and developing our people. Particularly on the military side, that means we have to have outstanding training programs in which we try to grow our people into decision makers so that they have the ability to use all of this newly available information. You will also find that we have cutting-edge information systems. We are at a different place than most other government organizations because the very success of our business is dependent on all of the things that are part of knowledge management, which are also part of knowledge creation and knowledge sharing.

We highly value innovation. We highly value new ideas. We want to stay on the cutting edge of technology, of processes, of decision making in order to succeed at what our mission in life is. That is number one.

Knowledge Sharing

AB: Let us discuss the sharing piece. We have the same barriers that other government organizations have to sharing—and perhaps external organizations have as well. These include the not-created-here syndrome, the knowledge-is-power issues, and on and on. All of those things are embedded here. What is different about the Department of the Navy is that, side by side with those other things, we have a very high degree of social capital. Our people, particularly in uniform, rotate every two to three years. They move in and out and around the system. We have a flow of people in, out, and around. In addition, once they have been in a situation that can be life-threatening, whether it is a warfare situation or simply being on a ship when there is a problem with the ship, our teams must work together. We have a sense of team that even the other Department of Defense organizations do not have. We have ships out at sea that are staffed by a group of people who are truly a community, in the great sense of the word, and who have to be dependent on each other. There is not one individual on that team who can run that small community or city by herself.

We have learned the value of teams when we are at sea on our ships. That does not always come into the offices, but we do have those learnings there. As a result, we value teams. We recognize that importance, and when we have an emotional experience, when anything goes wrong (and that happens all the time), when we have been through a conflict situation, anyone who is connected with that team or with that unit—before, during, or after—becomes a friend, becomes a part of your network *for life*, for the 20 years of active duty service and beyond that, as a retiree in the naval reserves.

We build relationships and networks that stay in place for the lifetime of an individual that are built on a shared understanding, a shared conflict that was overcome. We have built trust. We have built relationships in a way that is very, very difficult to do for people who are not in those kinds of situations that have the potential of affecting life or limb in some way. As a result, we have a very high social capital and a very fluid, high level of movement in and out, around and about our organizations.

Yes, we have some stovepipes within those communities. Yet, because people go in and out of those communities and because those communities are reliant on each other, they have become very intertwined. The planes are right on the ships and the subs are there protecting both, and we have Marines who ride with all of our battle groups. Because of that intertwining and reliance on each other, we gain a fluid exchange across lines. When people are in clearly interdependent situations, they become closer, which has helped us move fluidly across some of those very natural stovepipes where people are focused very much on one area and not another.

Knowledge Capture

JC: *How do you capture value? Is it through the interactions among people?*

AB: I believe in the development of both nodes and flow. *Nodes* are where we actually have systems that capture some of that information or knowledge and try to provide the context. The concept of a knowledge-centric organization is to have an organization that creates a resource, a node that captures things in balance because we cannot capture everything. We need to really be careful. A big part of achieving that balance is being able to identify knowledge needs at every level of the organization.

Knowledge-Centric Organization

JC: *How is the Department of the Navy knowledge-centric on its knowledge journey?*

AB: Not only do we develop the node, but then we also have to facilitate the flow, and that is through communities. The way that you do that is to do both. It is a balance of both. It is capturing what we need to capture, but then the *flow* is creating porous boundaries, permeable and porous boundaries so that we have people flow in and out, among and about. We have that naturally in our system. Therefore, flow is a very important concept for the Department of the Navy, important to our success in sharing what needs to be shared and in creating new and innovative ideas, which build on other ideas.

The exchange of ideas is very much a social exercise, but we do need the systems to support that social exchange, and we need to do more and more of that virtually. But even in the new virtual world and virtual communications in which we operate, most of those exchanges are built on some sort of relationship. That is why I strongly focus on how those relationships are built.

To accomplish a knowledge-centric organization, we, first of all, put out a tool. We created a community of practice in knowledge management. That community of practice is now about 300 strong. It represents every organizational element around the world in the Department of the Navy. These people truly exchange things and ideas. We have a system that supports that collaboration, and we put everything on it that is available to the department. We share that knowledge continuously and virtually. We also meet four times a year face to face to facilitate that sharing. That is how one element of our knowledge-centric journey takes place and works to cross-communicate and integrate across the department.

The knowledge-centric organization (KCO) was designed for organizations to use as a resource. It is a toolkit for organizations to look at themselves. It enables them to go through a knowledge audit and knowledge mapping so that they can understand what their needs are, what their requirements are, take a look at what they have, at their gaps, and figure out how to connect all that and build the knowledge center. The term that we use, the *knowledge system*, supports a knowledge center that not only has the node development but also facilitates and supports the communities that are needed.

But it is not enough to have the tools. We have to put everything else in place in order for this journey to happen. First of all, we have to get alignment from the top and the leadership.

Shared Vision

JC: *What are the key success factors, and how do you measure your levels of accomplishment?*
AB: We accomplished our journey at the enterprise level by creating a

shared vision, then building the business case, setting limits, sharing new ideas, words, and behaviors, identifying strategic approaches and thrust, developing the infrastructure, providing the tools, measuring, giving incentives for the behaviors, and then visioning an even greater future. That is the gist of the process.

Creating the shared vision has very much to do with leadership. We have to have the leadership support. One of the first things that we did was develop what we thought the future of the Navy and information management/information technology (IM/IT) should look like. The shared vision statement is signed by the Secretary of the Navy, the Chief of Naval Operations, the Commandant of the Marine Corps, and the chief information officers (CIOs) for those three organizations.

We looked at IM/IT and asked; "What is it that we want to do with IM/IT?" We started the vision there and integrated a results-oriented Navy and a Marine Corps team characterized by strategic leadership, ubiquitous communication, and visible technology. We then moved further along to create an effective, flexible, and sustainable Department of the Navy enterprise-wide information and technology environment that enables our people to make and implement efficient and agile decisions in a knowledge-centric culture, where trust and respect facilitate information sharing and organizational learning.

For the Department of the Navy, our entire focus on IM/IT is to get that stuff to the decision maker, which means that what we are really after is focusing on the information itself and connecting that to decision making. We need to have the connection through IT, but IT alone is insufficient. So, we have moved to focusing on doing good information management, but information management alone is insufficient. We have moved to the whole IM/IT arena, getting that information to the decision maker, and knowledge management is an important part of that relationship.

What to Outsource, What to Keep

AB: We have now literally, strategically outsourced our infrastructure. Our entire information technology infrastructure is treated as a service. We no longer own the computers on our desks nor the lines that connect us. That is treated as a service. It was a $76.8 billion contract over five years, won by EDS. It is like a phone service. We have this service, and we have described what that service is in performance terms for everyone. That provides us with the opportunity to focus on what is really important, which is the information, even though we want to stay with the latest technology. This is a part of that infrastructure. It is important to stay right on the front edge and that is part of our agreement, but we do not need to own that technology right here in the department. We also want everyone to have the opportunity for interoperability.

For the ships out at sea that work on satellites we have another program called IT 21. We also have a piece of this embedded in the Marine Corps, and another piece that is on systems abroad. All of these will connect together so the Navy/Marine Corps Internet (NMCI) is focused on the U.S. continent, which we call CONUS.

Goals

AB: The whole plan here, which was submitted to Congress in 1999, has the number one goal of: "Let's build the infrastructure that can be in accord with the architecture and standards of the NMCI." Goal number two is to change the processes simultaneously. We put processes down to a goal level so that we would have objectives and actions that drove to meet this end goal. Goal number three is capital planning, or "How are we going to pay for it?" In sum, the whole plan is written to implement strategies that facilitate the creation and sharing of knowledge to enable effective and agile decision making. That embeds knowledge as a significant definer of the organization.

We have five more goals that were important to have at that level. One is the injection of new technology and information assurance and security. At the Department of Defense, that is absolutely essential. At the top of this list was another very important one: Build IM/IT competencies to shape the workforce of the future. Now this is IM/IT in the workforce, not just the IM/IT workforce, because IM/IT affects all the members of our workforce, no matter where they are located.

Through meeting these goals, we have the ability to touch everyone with what we do here. Another key goal is to foster a technology-enabled information-rich culture.

We said, "It is not enough to say all these things are wonderful, to do all the training, education, and all these related activities." We need to go further. We need to put the rewards and incentives in place, and we need to figure out ways to capture the wonderful social capital that we have and use that to help us change the system itself.

Creating the shared vision started the picture. Then, we created stories that portrayed our concept of NMCI to Congress. Our Undersecretary of the Navy literally took stories of what our organization would be like. And those stories are embedded in the beginning of the KCO model. The stories helped us. We had a lot of leaders behind us. We make a point of capturing our leaders talking about the advantage of what KM can do for us on compact discs, and we spread that word around the world. We share it with everyone. These are some of the ways that we help create the shared vision.

Knowledge Superiority

AB: Then, we build the business case. We tie it directly to what we do on the front line. This is where the concept of knowledge superiority starts coming up. There have been conferences on knowledge superiority. One admiral sponsored a knowledge superiority conference which pulled together 40 or more senior admirals and senior executives to focus on: "What does knowledge superiority mean? What is it that we are going to do on the front line with this new thing called knowledge management? What difference does it make? And how can it help us?"

This vision was a very good fit with our hierarchical, military, structured organization. Now, I wanted to note that because this is from an organization that has a reputation for having preferences on the Myers-Briggs scale of personality framework for mostly STJs (sensing/thinking/judgment) or ISTJ (introversion/sensing/thinking/judgment). Remember, these are people who usually like things very well organized. They like to check the box. They like to have things in place. They like to have a structure they are comfortable with. That is what they are comfortable with, which is a preference. That is not, however, all that they are capable of. This is what they are capable of:

> More than any other nation, more than any other Navy, and more than ever before we rely on the creativity, ingenuity, and intellect of our people. As we cross the threshold of the information age, we intend to realize this awesome potential in every corner of [the] Navy by every person as a highly interactive total team. Transcending even our current advantage in physical firepower, our Navy will be alive with the fire of shared understanding. We will do this because we must, for our Navy's relevance and readiness in this new era, no foe, present or future, will match our knowledge or our ability to apply it, indeed just as global presence has become a way of life for us, so, too, will knowledge superiority become a Navy way of life. (vision statement, Department of the Navy)

Today, we have two planks in our maritime concept. Knowledge superiority has joined the forward presence plank as the second aspect of our maritime concept.

Joint Vision 2020, also from our Joint Chief of Staff, is very embedded in knowledge management and ties directly to all of the things that we are doing here. They use the term *decision superiority*. We use the term *knowledge superiority*.

While they use the term decision superiority, what we are after is the right decisions being made or the best decisions being made. We use the term knowledge superiority because we are focusing more on the people than the decision that is made. Our goal is: "Let's enable the people to be able to make those best decisions." But they are joined hand in hand and are two of the same.

Knowledge Management Is Not on Its Own

AB: Our process is to build a business case and tie it directly to what we do, what the mission/vision is, and how it will assist and benefit what we do. Knowledge management never should be out there on its own. It is not knowledge management for knowledge management's sake. God forbid. Let's keep it a small *k* and a small *m*. It is there to help you do what you do better.

Next, we demonstrate leadership commitment. Donald Rumsfeld, the U.S. Secretary of Defense, talks about what will be new in the world, what may happen really as a result of the interconnections of other things, the emergence of some new characteristics. I very much believe in that. I believe that we are connecting things. As we connect them, continuing down our road, we find that there is the emergence of a lot of new things that we would have never expected. That is very exciting.

Connectedness of Choices

AB: Part of leadership commitment is to have everyone achieve what I call a *connectedness of choices* so that the importance is not in a specific action being the same, a specific decision being the same, because organizations are very different. But the importance is in having that common vision, that shared vision, and being on the path to it, knowing what decisions to make for your organization, your unit, in order to reach that path and achieve that path. In essence, what we are after is a connectedness of choices.

I often talk about past intelligent behavior, which talks about the rise of knowledge management as a discipline. You can think about this as a person, whether it is a child or an adult learning something new, but you can also think about this as the rise of knowledge management as a discipline.

The first thing that happens is we have *discriminative thought*, which means we look at how things are different. A piece of paper, a pen, or whatever, has to have differentiation for you to recognize it. Therefore, the first thing we personally do in our own version of knowledge management is to notice how something is different from other things. At that point, we have discerning thought, which takes our thinking down to the next level. At that level, we look at the relationship of it to other things, and it also brings up the similarities to other things. As we have more knowledge created about all of this, we apply what we are learning, and we have feedback coming back to us that allows us to raise our awareness or consciousness level of what this thing is all about. As we continue receiving this feedback, we are in a position to make the choices and to discern the grand purpose of it all and how it relates to our lives as individuals and our lives as organizations. This is what I call the past intelligent behavior. This is the trek that we are on in knowledge management.

JC: *Do you disseminate this view through your work in building the knowledge-centric organization?*

AB: Yes and broadly. In the models about the knowledge life cycle, we have a picture of someone taking a bite of the apple and we say, "All the things we are doing with the apple are valuable," which are all IT and IM kind of things. But until you take the bite, you chew it, you digest it, and you apply it, it does not count. It still is not knowledge at that point. Knowledge is created within the individual, and knowledge is created in action. Those are basic concepts we need to get across.

We also talk about the essence of knowledge management before we give a definition of what we do. We talk about that essence being a combination of all of the human capital efforts from the past, the present, and the future. It is really important to put that future piece in because you must be a learning organization as well. That means building the capacity. In the end, we value not only people's education and experience, not only their current capability sets, but also their potential capacity for learning in the future. All of that is important.

Then we combine that with social capital, which is the connectivity in the relationships. We take into account all of the cultural issues, the context issues, all of the elements of language, which is basically the sequence of interactions as well. What we are dealing with here is not only the relationships and the interactiveness across those relationships but also how often we relate, the order of the information that is provided back and forth, and the depth of that information.

There is a sequencing and a rhythm that occurs in the exchange in the social capital element. That is a view that has not been developed too much but that we will see more and more. We always tie them together. We look at the way information technology, information management, and knowledge management all relate because they all have the same elements of human capital, social capital, and corporate capital. They are all important and play together.

Those all facilitate understanding. We use models to share them across the enterprise, and we do have a common high-level definition of knowledge management. We look at it as a process for applying all of our intellectual capital directly toward achieving the naval mission. It is not important that other organizations use our definition. If they want something that is a little bit more on the tactical level, that applies a little bit more to exactly what they do, that is fine as long as it is a subset of this higher level.

The Concept of Limits

AB: Another basic model that we use very heavily is the concept of limits. I believe using limits is a valuable tool. It is a tool in our toolkit. When we have something new to address we need to spend some time focusing on it, limiting our focus, limiting our behavior and activity, and thinking so that we can build new ideas and thoughts in that area. If we try to attack everything at once, we do not get the benefit of that.

Let me give you some real examples of the power of limits. First of all, a good example is NMCI. I'm a Mac user. I love my Mac. I want to use it and yet when we went out and we did the NMCI project, the company that won required that we use PCs. I cannot use my Mac. So, I've limited my own behavior. In fact, I have had to sacrifice my Mac. What have I gained? I gained the opportunity to interact with people by setting those limits. I gained interactions with people around the world who are in the Department of the Navy and with that I gained the fluid exchange of ideas and the interoperability concept. Now, I can create more new ideas in areas that I am in.

When I speak to people who are a little bit more theoretical, I usually talk about walking into a large room with a pile of styrofoam balls, all different kinds of colors here, all different sizes. At first I say, "It is just a pile of styrofoam balls," but if I actually walk among them, because of static electricity they start connecting to parts of my body, and if I take a look down at my hand, all of a sudden I start seeing shapes forming, different combinations of colors, and so on. It reminds everyone of things in their tacit knowledge, perhaps some ideas that people are working on, and it leads to new thinking and new ideas coming to the front.

Any time we do that, I think there is an advantage to it, and it is a tool that we need to use. So, we talk about that power of limits.

Setting Self-limits

AB: One of the best ways that I can demonstrate the power of setting self-limits is in the Federal KM Working Group, which I co-chaired for the U.S. government. We pulled together our industry partners, our academic partners, and had five representatives from different government organizations. We initiated a dialogue on what we thought KM was. We found that we had great difficulty in developing common definitions. On the one hand, there are so many different definitions, and at the same time, none of the definitions gave us what we wanted.

Instead, we focused on the questions: "If we sent government workers out to a knowledge management certification course, what are the things we would like those government workers to come back with? What knowledge and what skill sets would we like them to have if we have paid for a certification course?" That allowed us to sort of get around what knowledge management is. We came up with 10 or 12 things initially and eventually, 14 key things working with that group. We now have had these points signed off by the government and we have gotten government learning objectives for KM certification. We started with talking about developing the business groups.

Strategic Approach

AB: The next element is identifying a strategic approach. The approach that we have taken is to use a systems thinking model, derived from Peter Senge's learning organization work. We developed a systems thinking virtual course, with enterprise rights for use by the Department of the Navy. We developed our own archetypes, which are patterns that repeat themselves over and over in decision making, so that we would have our own examples of how this is used in the Department of the Navy. We have that course as part of our CNET program, and it is part of the effort focused on enabling individuals to increase their decision making capabilities.

Our model says that, as our IT investment has increased the available amount of data, information, and knowledge, our decision-making complexity has increased. In the past, we have invested in more IT. We have been in a reinforcing loop. What we have tried to do is put three balancing loops in place. As decision-making complexity goes up, there is a need for workforce cognitive skills. Systems thinking is one of those skills. As a result, we have tried to provide that.

Remember, in our strategic plan, we were able to reach out and touch IM/IT in the workforce. In like fashion, systems thinking is provided to the entire workforce. Last summer, the Master Chief of the Department of the Navy pulled together all of his Master Chiefs and had them take a course in systems thinking. Now we are going to embed it in our enlisted schools starting at the top level and moving all the way down.

Eventually everyone in the Navy will have these skills. Right now, it is available everywhere, and it is starting to permeate throughout the system.

Organizational Knowledge Management

AB: The second approach is for organizations and encompasses the need for organizational knowledge management. We look at knowledge management processes. Those are the things that we are doing with the KCO toolkit. That increases as an organizational decision-making capability, again closing that gap between the capability and complexity.

At the larger enterprise level, we are working on things like NMCI and portals to ensure that we have the availability across the enterprise and, of course, communities. Therefore, our strategic approach is to address every level. We very much believe in Ashby's Law: In order to change a system, you need more things than are in the system that need changing in order to change it. We work very much in a fluid wave-out fashion: always in teams, always trying to share everything broadly so that we not only push from inside the organization and share across, but we also share externally so that our partners—our industry partners and our academic partners—are actually beginning to teach and bring back to our people the same things.

It is very important in our strategy to share not only here in the United States but around the world. Since we are a worldwide organization, we have to have global consciousness raising. We are working at raising the consciousness level so that we are in a position to make choices. Everyone, including all of our partners, is moving along that path with us. We cannot do it alone. In today's world, knowledge management cannot be done by a single organization. It has to be part of something larger. We are, in fact, global.

As a result, we identified our strategic thrust. Those are things like the NMCI and the enterprise portal that we are developing, as well as something called a knowledge wall, which is out on the front. It is a wonderful example of how we use knowledge in conjunction with warfare and people. We have different communities under way. We have distance support. We also have CNET and other information systems that are coming up. At the same time, part of that approach deals with the connectivity first: the nodes and the flow. Our knowledge fairs are a part of that flow.

The Plateau Jump

AB: Event intermediation, an example of which is our knowledge fairs, means that you work, work, work, and eventually you come to a time when you want to make a plateau jump in the organization, where everybody knows what everybody else is doing and they can build on increased efficiencies and increased effectiveness.

When you make that plateau jump, the event is great, and those people who participate are great. Further, what they take back is great, but you want it to continue working, not just be for one day. To accomplish that, we create a compendium, a toolkit for everyone who is involved and for those interested. We capture the leadership's commitment and put that in the compendium. We also video different people talking about their projects. We do that to provide some of the context, not just writing about what the project is, but giving the reasons for it.

Through dialogue we give participants the opportunity to talk about the projects that they have been working on. We capture everything, put it into a compendium, and send that to echelon one, two, and three organizations directly with a note from the CIO himself. Those are the levels of hierarchy, which means that we reach around the world to our organizations that are in different locations. We are reaching not just our high level of management in Washington, D.C., not just our senior leaders, but we try to actually go out to the organizations themselves wherever they are located. We continue to share through the course of the next year.

The compendiums also become useful to our industry partners. They can take a look at what happened, see what some of the Department of the Navy organizations are doing, and offer a product that may be beneficial to the trek that we are going on.

That is the value of intermediation. The next element is to develop the infrastructure. We do that in many ways.

Building the Infrastructure

AB: It is not enough to be a change agent and have a great deal of activity under way. We also have to embed it for the future in the infrastructure. We must actually make very real changes in the structure of our organization. Part of our responsibility at the highest level of the department is, in fact, policy and guidance. But policy and guidance alone cannot make a difference.

We try to work in teams so we can communicate policy and guidance. We have a very expansive outreach strategy to support our communications. We also provide tools so that people have an idea of how to do the kind of things that make a difference, and we provide assistance and consultancy to try to help them move forward.

Those are all part of our strategy. We address the infrastructure itself through our policy and guidance. The very first step of what we did for knowledge management was to issue what we call *governmental guidance*. This gives everyone an idea of the kinds of things that should be done in government and the kinds of things that in fact do not need to be in government.

Continuous Learning and a Workforce Strategic Plan

AB: Another important product is that we issued continuous learning guidance. This has to do with the workforce, IM/IT in the workforce, as well as the IM/IT workforce. We call for 80 hours of continuous learning each year. Using the systems thinking product, the information literacy kit, and the knowledge-centric organization toolkit and participating in things like knowledge fairs count as part of this continuous learning experience. We do not just provide content. We also provide ways of fulfilling our knowledge goals.

We also started looking at changing roles. We created the first government career path guide that actually has all of the knowledge roles in it. We are looking at all of these roles, and we share what we are learning with the rest of government. We try to play this game very much as a partner. It is very important that we all partner together and move forward together.

The knowledge management roles guide is in the workforce virtual CD so that everyone has access to it. It is very extensive. We have really tried to do our homework well and are continuously revising it.

We also put into place a workforce strategic plan. It is the first one ever in the Department of the Navy for the IM/IT workforce. It focuses around knowledge, the creation of knowledge in new jobs, and the kinds of things that need to be done.

Our work is to take all of these pieces and embed them in all of our institutions, so that people in the future will start at a different place than where we began.

That is part of the workforce development infrastructure. Part of that is measuring and providing incentives. We have a team developing the measures that are very important to the Department of the Navy.

The Importance of Metrics

AB: We did an "assist" visit with the space and warfare (SPAWAR) command unit in Charleston, South Carolina, where about 250 people were working on developing a knowledge-centric organization. It was a pilot for our KCO toolkit. We did a survey in conjunction with that in which we asked about the barriers and the things that are hardest to implement. The respondents told us that the hardest things to implement and where we needed to focus were cultural, of course, but, amazingly, metrics was a 17% concern and content stood at 15%. The respondents said that it was more important to understand the metrics that we were going to use than the content we were going to put into the system.

Metrics are that important. They drive behavior. They change behavior. What we needed to do is develop a metrics guide for knowledge management initiatives. This is embedded everywhere.

Then, of course, we began early on an awards program. We have gone through our fifth set of knowledge-sharing awards. We give awards about three to four times a year at major events that are sponsored by the Department of the Navy.

Finally, we are providing the tools. In addition to the KCO and the systems thinking, we also have a workforce CD that has all of the workforce materials on it and an information literacy toolkit, which is meta-information. We have a range of CDs that talk to other aspects of our environment, such as critical infrastructure protection and communities of practice. We have a glossary for IM/IT and other things.

Learning Organization and Knowledge-Centric Organization

AB: I have to make the point very clearly that you cannot be a knowledge-centric organization without being a learning organization. It is absolutely essential that, if you are going to focus on knowledge and be knowledge-centric, you must be a learning organization.

We have come up with a couple of models of the learning organization. One says that as you build more of a barrier around yourself not only do you diminish in size but also you have decreased learning, and as you open up more to become a learner as an individual, you have increased risk and vulnerability.

What is really important is that the same thing is true for an organization, which is that there is a fit between individuals in organizations, and we change, moving along this continuum. When I go into a meeting with a larger organization in the Department of Defense, I very much have to go in with a framework, because we are still a bureaucratic organization and there are still people who have strong opinions. If I went in open, as a learner, I would be troubled and would not be able to affect that meeting at all.

There are times when you need very much to put that structure around you and have some sort of framework protecting you in your environment. There are other times when you go into a learning situation with that frame, and there is absolutely no gain.

It is very important that we look at both organizations and individuals in this particular pattern and understand a relationship so that we recognize the type of thing that we are going into, as well as recognize who we are and what our value is, very much like the Myers-Briggs. We need to know what our preferences are and where we operate on this continuum so that we can prepare ourselves as we go into different situations.

Balancing Knowledge Sharing and Security Needs

JC: *How do you set up your system so people share and also have strategic security in your system?*

AB: We not only need to know what we need to control in the sense of information assurance, in the sense of security, but also in the sense of who you are as an individual. How much do you, as an individual, want to put out there in a particular situation?

Visioning an Even Greater Future

AB: Our vision of what knowledge superiority is for the future, how we would like people to interact can be seen in this story of a young Marine. A young Marine out on the front line is carrying a biological detection device, which starts going off like crazy and moves into its red zone. Noticing that, he immediately gets on his computer and connects to Fort Detrich, Maryland, where he is able to have people there search the extant resources and identify the substance that is setting off his alarm. Simultaneously, he is being connected with experts, no matter where they are in the world, who can give their opinion on what this substance may be and what the best response is. At the same time, leadership has been identified so that troops nearby can be withdrawn and not become casualties. All of this is occurring at the same time, and all are working together so that we can prevent a catastrophe.

Another story that illustrates the power of knowledge superiority involves a young father-to-be who is out on the front. His wife is expected to give birth in six weeks. He's going to be in port in two weeks. All of a sudden, he is notified that there's an emergency cesarean section under way but has no clue what is happening. However, he is told some terms. Armed with that, he goes onto the Internet and starts searching. He connects directly with Bethesda Naval Hospital and is able to dialogue with an assistant of the doctor who, in fact, is in there doing the surgery. Afterward, he is introduced, after a successful birth, to his new daughter right there on the Internet. Talk about the transfer of tacit knowledge. It is one thing for someone to say, "Everything's fine." It is another thing to see your new child and your wife right there on the screen and know that they are fine.

These are the things that show us what we need to be in the future. We understand that we need to move into becoming a knowledge organization, into a knowledge-sharing organization, and that is where we are headed.

Partnering in a Networked Organization

JC: *How do you work with your partners in your networked organization?*
AB: We will never be alone again. No one will ever be alone again. Not only are we networked, but we are networked with a capital *N* and that means people are networked, that means people sharing their thoughts and their learnings, and people trusting and appreciating other people.

The bottom line is that what we are after is a connectedness of choices. The alignment that we need is based, first of all, in the fact that we have common values and a shared vision. The common values allow us to make the right choices to move toward our common vision. Rather than having everything be uniformly the same, alignment in today's world means having a common core set of values and a common shared vision.

Teams in a Knowledge-Centric Organization

JC: *How are you keeping your teams aligned for strategic outcomes and not going off in their own independent directions?*

AB: Teams are still part of knowledge management. People write about communities, but teams are very much an integral part of knowledge management. I talk about flow in three ways. I talk about the flow of data and information. I talk about the flow of people in and out of organizations and segments of organizations, in and out of communities. I talk about flow by Mihaly Csikszentmihalyi as the optimal experience. This is the kind of flow Csikszentmihalyi calls *autotelic work*. That means the kind of work that we are capable of doing but that is just beyond, and it forces us to grow. We gear ourselves to be able to actually accelerate our growth and come to that point.

It is generative. While it is wonderful for an individual to have that, even more often we recognize that kind of flow in a team environment. If you have a group that gets together and develops new ideas and they really get excited about it, that is a team. We can have teams that are exchanging and building on each other. What is occurring is what we used to call *synergy*, which moves us into flow state. This year, we are in a flow state where we are totally open and in a learning situation. We are at one with our environment and that is the focus of everything that has happened. This is a very exciting growth time for us. Teams facilitate that state, and so teams are critically, critically important for us. It is a little harder to get to that state in a community situation.

Managing the Content of a Very Large Organization

JC: *How do you manage all the content in such a huge organization so that it is accessible, reliable, not over-whelming, and usable?*

AB: Those choices have to be made at every level of the organization. Anyone who tries to control the amount of content that we have available is going to fail. There is no single way. The first thing you do is you have to have connectivity. That is what needs to be managed. That is with a small *c* and that means the wires, the units, and the availability on the IT side, the technology side, and on the information management side. That is a hardware connection, a machine and technology issue.

But then you need to connect. That's the capital *C* and that is why we are talking about everyone. That is people to people. And those decisions have to be made at every level of the organization. How much risk are we willing to take to leverage how much knowledge? How much stuff should be kept at a local level? How much should become global? How much is it ok to keep in emails and keep informal? How much do you want to formalize? How much should be tacit, as long as you know where those people are, where those experts are? And how much do you need to make explicit?

That balance issue is critical as we implement. Our intent is not to connect everything up. That is not the answer but, in fact, we have to have that balance. One of the ways that we are trying to facilitate that at an enterprise level is by developing a group of communities in all of our functional areas that will be managed at the enterprise level, in that they are all owned by their functional areas and organizations. These are structures that are very much already created and under way, and we are organizing the nodes and support systems for those functional areas. But we will need to have a very aware, midlevel individual who focuses on nothing but what things should be connected to other functional areas and what would be of value there. So, we would have a team of functional area knowledge managers. Today, we call them *integrators*. We are putting in place these integrators, who will work across the enterprise. We will be using the one portal for every concept, but very tailorable, very available. We want to be sure that everyone across the department, no matter where they move, has the ability to use everything else. It is a huge task.

Recycling Organizational Knowledge over Time

JC: *How do you grab hold of the know-how and know-what of the many people who are rotating from position to position, or leaving the department for retirement or other reasons, so that you can recycle what they know?*

AB: Fifty percent of the federal workforce will, in fact, be leaving it by 2004. The figures for the department are large. The average age of our employees is very high. We know that that is coming down the pike. Of course, the first thing that everybody wants to talk about with us is a system for capturing tacit knowledge. A lot of people have come in and talked to us about it. One of the advantages of being in the Department of the Navy is that people get excited about sharing with us since we are such a large governmental organization. We are able to share what we are doing and affect their behavior, too.

It is wonderful to try to capture that experience and knowledge. But it is very difficult to capture tacit knowledge. Regardless, we are going down that road of trying to decide the things that we can capture. For instance, when we have key decisions made now, our organizations, such as the Naval Sea Systems Command, do video clips of the person talking. We can capture a lot of context that way. We have built some context fields to help in capturing some of that so that we can have an understanding. But beyond that, we are working on a program with the rest of the Department of Defense so that when employees—both military and civilians who have been on board for any length of time and have expertise—leave, they do not just leave. We create porous boundaries and have an agreement for the next 18 months so that we can call on them for consulting purposes for a minimum number of hours.

Rather than have core knowledge walk out the door, what we would like to do is have the ability to stream out and pull that knowledge back in when key questions arise. Because information is a moving target and the rate of change is incredible in everything today, probably 18 months to two years would be the maximum time that anyone would be in a recall position. We are not talking about bringing them back from jobs. We are simply talking about having them available so we can create a dialogue and generate some answers.

JC: *Do you view these retirees as your alumni?*
AB: Absolutely! We are trying to do more and more of that through communities. We are expanding communities, and we are moving to have access to these knowledge resources government-wide as well. We have a number of pilots under way in this area. But also, as we open those communities up to industry partners, we will have more and more of the ability to grab critical knowledge and experiences because people flow in and out from government to industry and from industry to government. In addition, almost all of our military people go into the Reserves as they retire, so it would be fairly easy to keep access to some of the expertise there. We would like to do the same thing with our civilian community.

JC: *What are your key success factors, and how do you know that you are actually getting where you want to go?*
AB: The first thing that comes to my mind is stories. We have a lot of figures, including dollar figures, as well as small projects and larger projects where we can demonstrate efficiencies and have been able to increase effectiveness. We have those metrics. But the stories are the things that have

the largest impact because when you hear people talk about something that they love, that they have passion for, and they share something that has happened and say, "You provided me this or that," and "Do you know what that did for me?" it has an incredible impact for me, personally, and also for our organization at large. We actively share that.

We have a wonderful outreach program. Every couple of weeks, we do a virtual newsletter where we capture the stories and share them across the whole system. That is our push strategy. Then other people come back to us. In addition to that, we include some of our successes in our strategic plan that goes to the U.S. Congress. I do not think that has happened in any other agency or organization.

It has worked, not only to show Congress and our other stakeholders what we are doing, but additionally, we take the time to do this plan over a six-to eight-month period so that we can include a lot of participation and involvement. During that time, people are contributing success stories that they think might work in the strategic plan presentation. By the time the plan is actually published, it is already being implemented.

KM Implementation Is Different

JC: *What is the difference between the way the Department is implementing knowledge management from the way it implemented Total Quality Leadership (TQL)?*
AB: The way that we are implementing knowledge management is very different from how we implemented total quality leadership. TQL immediately had a budget behind it. We formed an office that was separate from the larger organizational environment in which we operated. We did some wonderful things, created some good practices and flows, and mandated people to go to certain courses, participate, and learn. Now, while some of that learning occurred, it was never connected to the real life and the real world of what we were doing. It was an additional burden placed on top of people, a learning burden. Eventually that learning did permeate through and did, in fact, start changing the system somewhat. And, if TQL had not been handled the way it was handled, we would not be doing KM quite as well as we are now because we started at a different point. But, with KM, we've kept a small *k* and a small *m*. We have done it as a team. We have done it across the system and instead of doing it to people, people are participating in the development of KM. So it is emerging everywhere. Once again, we are after that connectedness of choice.

Knowledge in the Age of Complexity

JC: *How would you characterize the role of knowledge in our emerging era?*

AB: In a larger context, we are moving into a world that is far more complex than it has ever been in the past. People say we are moving into a knowledge world. I do not think that is true. I think we are moving from an information age into an age of complexity. The reason that I prefer to look at it that way is I believe knowledge is the answer to the complexity age. I believe that, instead of being the thing we are focused on, knowledge is the thing that can make a difference, make some movement forward, and promote some growth in the somewhat chaotic, complex, and uncertain world that we all find ourselves in.

Key Learning Points

- What is different about the Department of the Navy is the high degree of social capital, since people rotate every two to three years. During these times, they may have been in a situation that is life-threatening and may have worked together for survival. People have to be interdependent to survive. These relationships build networks *for life*. This is the source of the enterprise's very high social capital.
- To build the knowledge-centric organization (KCO), the Department of the Navy developed nodes at the organizational level but is facilitating flow at the enterprise level through connectivity and communities. It is capturing what it needs to capture and then developing porous boundaries so that people and their ideas flow in and out, among and about.
- The Navy undertook its journey at the enterprise level by creating a shared vision; building the business case; setting limits; sharing new ideas, words, and behaviors; identifying the strategic approach; developing the infrastructure; providing the tools; measuring; providing incentives; and continuously visioning an even greater future.
- Stories are used to build an understanding of the shared vision. The Undersecretary of the Navy literally took stories of what the organization would be like to the U.S. Congress. Those stories are embedded in the beginning of the KCO model. Stories are having the largest impact in indicating how the Navy knows it is getting where it wants to go in its KCO efforts.
- The business case for KM is tied directly to front line defense and achieving knowledge superiority. KM is not intended to ever stand

out there on its own. It is knowledge management to help achieve the naval mission. That means keeping a small *k* and a small *m*. KM is there to help connect information and people, and people and people.

- An enterprise's KM effort cannot succeed alone. In today's world, knowledge management cannot be done by a single organization. In fact, it isn't done at all. It is part of something larger, of everything the enterprise does. Rather than having everything uniformly the same, alignment in today's world means having a core set of values and a shared vision, and then collectively moving toward that vision.

- The Navy is creating the first government career path guide that includes knowledge worker roles.

- Anybody who tries to control the content of an organization the size of the Department of the Navy is going to fail. The first step is connectivity and that can be managed at the enterprise level. That is connectivity with a small *c*, meaning the wires, hardware, and software in technology terms and structure, organization, and search capabilities in information terms. Then, content is needed. That is the capital *C*. Fusing these two for effect is why there is the need to talk about knowledge management.

- Balance is critical as we implement. The intent is not to connect everything up, not to capture everything. That cannot be the answer. The Navy is trying to facilitate an understanding of these issues through a group of functional area communities that will be managed at the enterprise level.

Convergence—Toward the Next Stage

Synthesis

While all the contributors to *Knowledge Capital* start out from their own unique perspectives, clusters of ideas, experiences, and capabilities emerged across the sessions, which point the way to a framework for the next generation of the knowledge field. While a number of these capabilities already exist in various stages of development in different organizations today, their power will become reinforced and magnified as they mature and link together to become the basis for how the knowledge-based enterprise does its business.

This epilogue is a synthesis of these areas of convergence. Look at these clusters as elements of a roadmap that will guide you to the next generation of the knowledge-based enterprise. The areas of convergence explored are

- fulfilling the promise,
- knowledge as a factor of production,
- diverse in form but with common principles,
- knowledge as a valued asset,
- market-based adaptive/springboard enterprises,
- knowledge capital strategy,
- values alignment,
- core components in place,

- learning,
- getting the knowledge enterprise off the ground,
- from audit to assessment,
- alliances,
- intellectual assets and intellectual property, and
- future centers.

You can start your journey toward creating a knowledge-based enterprise by mapping the points of convergence to the practices in your own organization. Gauge how your organization is structured and aligned and its recipes for its operations. Note where your obstacles and opportunities are. Then begin, step by step, to build the capabilities that will transform your organization over time into a winning, knowledge-based enterprise.

The Wars of Capabilities

The upcoming enterprise wars will be wars of capabilities, not wars of position. They will be won by knowledge-based enterprises that understand that the future is theirs if they build for it. While financial and physical resources capital will always be important ingredients in any successful business recipe, it will be the ability to leverage usable knowledge capital that will give the knowledge-based enterprise its edge. Enterprises able to engage their workforce, strategic allies, and customers and execute their plans will have the advantage. Absolute size and vast amounts of resources will not be the core factors that determine success. In fact, massive size and immense, but immobile, resources may be detrimental. Instead, it will be the ability to cultivate and mobilize resources in imaginative, intelligent, and unpredictable ways that will make the difference.

Fulfilling the Promise

The next generation will move from the edge of its current practices and insights to fulfill the promise of the knowledge movement. Next-generation knowledge initiatives are more rigorously defined, measured, and have clear sets of benefits. They integrate knowledge value creation, value capture, and the ability to realize that value into a holistic knowledge framework. They also fuse knowledge capabilities with other capacities to produce strategic outcomes.

These enterprises complete the shift from the dominance of the *congealed resources* of the industrial era, where goods and services were characterized by a high proportion of physical resources and a low proportion of knowledge resources, to one emphasizing *congealed knowledge* offerings, where the primary ingredient is intellectual content, either embedded in a physical package or standing alone. In short, the knowledge input of the goods and services will be what differentiates the offerings and provides the prime degree of value to customers. To support the knowledge deployment and incorporation, the enterprise itself will use technologies that provide an increasingly frictionless basis for the exchange of knowledge, allowing knowledge resources to readily flow throughout the extended enterprise and become the lifeblood for renewing the enterprise's network and its offerings.

To support that flow, a next-generation knowledge-based enterprise is characterized by a sound foundation of values, a knowledge strategy, a clear vision with strenuous goals, and the belief that all people in the extended enterprise are autonomous owners of their human capital who freely share it with their colleagues.

Knowledge as a Factor of Production

Next-generation enterprises are knowledge businesses. Knowledge becomes the prominent and recognized factor of production in organizations. The rise of knowledge as a factor of production changes the equation of how the enterprise operates. It causes a rethinking of the very foundations of the dominant business model, based on the scarcity of resources, and reframes it as one based on the abundance of resources. The revolution in the business model is based on the fact that knowledge is an inherently renewable resource that can move without friction and with little or no cost across any boundary. While there is always the reality that knowledge requires contextual understanding and, therefore, will never be completely frictionless, the emphasis on usable knowledge radically lowers the cost of doing business, while at the same time leads to a significant expansion in the network of actors allied with the enterprise.

To take advantage of this shift, the enterprise transitions from being a fortress organization to being a permeable extended enterprise, linking its core functions and leadership with various kinds of staff, strategic partners, and customers.

The next-generation knowledge enterprise differentiates between knowledge, which is its stock and content, and with knowing, which is the process of turning content into action. Knowing is embedded in how all members of the enterprise do their work and create value. And knowing is only possible in a context of well-functioning relationships where there is trust. Trust is the glue that holds the organization together. People will share critical information and knowledge to the extent they trust their collaborators. Access to their essential know-how and key relationships are central to achieving the high levels of responsiveness that differentiate and enable success in the knowledge era. Therefore, a core requirement of the knowledge-based enterprise is that it become a trust-based enterprise as well.

Diverse in Form but with Common Principles

The days of one-size-fits-all formulaic solutions for knowledge-based enterprises are legacies of the past. Knowledge-based enterprises are diverse in form, content, and structure but have compatible characteristics both across industries and sectors. The knowledge enterprise is marked not only by how it shares and grows its knowledge but also by how it builds more and more knowledge into its products and services. Business recipes are used to determine the specific resources needed and how those resources are combined for transformations of tangible and intangible resources into value-added goods and services. The amount of knowledge as well as its intensity changes how an enterprise navigates, the nature of its product offerings, and all of its relationships. The enterprises that make this shift are in a powerful position to transform their industries and reframe how their businesses are conceived.

Knowledge as a Valued Asset

Next-generation knowledge enterprises value their knowledge assets with the same significance that they do their financial and physical assets. This has strong implications in the enterprise for the role of knowledge in its practices, how to account for it, and how to generate it.

One such implication is a stronger and more specific emphasis on learning, risk taking, and innovation in the enterprise. The enterprise structures itself to promote continuous learning, sharing, and leveraging its knowledge throughout its extended network. It operates as an active communications system internally with its own people and externally with its suppliers and customers. At the same time, the enterprise has to make decisions as to what knowledge is available for what purposes and for which actor. This means that the enterprise has an active decision-making process to resolve the contradiction between knowledge that must be accessible and able to flow to produce value and knowledge that needs to be protected for security and privacy reasons. The bases for these decisions on the availability of knowledge hinge on a sensitive understanding of the need for individuals to know.

The knowledge-based enterprise makes sure that it manages its resources to create value not only in the eyes of the company, but for stakeholders, investors, and customers as well. It begins to use a value-accounting capability that captures the totality of value and not just cash resources.

Market-Based Adaptive/Springboard Enterprises

The enterprise operates as a market-based adaptive enterprise, combining what the market asks for directly with what the business is capable of delivering. It recognizes that it needs to operate as a knowledge system and be aware of the kinds of knowledge that are brought in, the channels through which knowledge flows, and how those channels are open or closed to different kinds of knowledge assets. It monitors the different parts of the system to understand where the elements of its system interface with customers and interact internally. The opportunities for significant change are found in these interface areas.

To optimize knowledge flow and responsiveness, the enterprise designs its structure so that it can readily link all of the different operations, allowing critical information and best practices to easily ripple throughout all of the elements of the organizational network. An example of one such design is the fishnet, which allows the reshaping and shifting of resources and communications in response to changing conditions and needs.

A key differentiator for the next knowledge-based enterprise is that its knowledge is actionable. Execution, or the ability to execute a strategy, becomes far more important than the quality of a strategy. Conditions are changing too quickly to allow the time to develop perfect plans. Instead, the priority is for actionable strategies, ones into which updated knowledge inputs are continuously infused. These strategies also feed into the enterprise, reshaping its organizational structures so that it can readily assert its capabilities when, where, and how it needs to in order to achieve its strategic intent.

Knowledge Capital Strategy

Knowledge-based enterprises have a knowledge capital strategy geared to build the capabilities and relationships that form the intangible assets of the organization. These enterprises are known for managing their intellectual capital assets as strategic resources. They have an intellectual capital framework that represents the stock of intangible assets and use the knowledge that flows from those assets to grow the human, structural, and customer capital of the enterprise. The organization's structural capital becomes the springboard for its workforce to leverage its human capital potential, which, in turn, renews and enhances the enterprise's structural capital capability base.

A knowledge-based enterprise accomplishes significant change by presenting a clear vision of that change and challenging the enterprise to achieve it. While the enterprise realizes that taking baby steps only results in treading water, it also pragmatically broadens, as the opportunities arise, its knowledge effort to encompass all of its people, processes, customers, suppliers, and external relationships.

One of the defining elements of the knowledge capital strategy is determining what types of knowledge are relevant to achieving the strategic intent of the enterprise. All areas of knowledge are not equally valuable for accomplishing an outcome. In some enterprises, competitive intelligence may be most critical; in others, it may be technical knowledge or the knowledge of best practices. Targeting core knowledge areas gives a needed focus, a workable definition of relevant knowledge, and the ability to more effectively navigate in achieving enterprise goals.

A knowledge capital strategy can be opportunistic in the sense that knowledge teams search out the knowledge-related "hook" that solves specific, critical issues for an individual, team, or enterprise. Finding the hook is necessary for people to buy in to any specific knowledge initiative since the initiative will live or die on whether it is sufficiently backed by key individuals and teams. If resolving a knowledge issue causes a leap in performance, the knowledge initiative will be greeted warmly and supported. If not, no matter how well intentioned and funded, the knowledge initiative will be a costly and misdirected waste of time, energy, cash, and credibility.

Knowledge-based enterprises establish a network of trained intellectual capital developers, attached to the different stakeholders, to guarantee that knowledge initiatives are targeted correctly and garner strong support. These developers monitor, manage, and implement the knowledge capital strategy, watching to see that it is relevant to individual stakeholders, while simultaneously ensuring that it is linked to achieving the business goals of the enterprise.

Knowledge-based enterprises also look at their operating terrain in a different way. They view their enterprise network as a territory that can be navigated using a topological, contour map perspective to discover where and how to create the minimum energy route to move strategically. They also utilize the topological map to see where it has high intellectual capital utilization and how it can improve low intellectual capital utilization. At the same time, knowledge-based enterprises understand that their environments are more like dynamic seascapes of ever-changing waves than landscapes composed of stationary features. Using this perspective, they are able to determine optimal value-creation paths and how to extract the value that has been created.

Values Alignment

Enterprises understand that their brand is their values promise externalized and brought to the marketplace. The first step in determining the dimensions of the brand is a values alignment process geared to define the mission and vision of the enterprise, what it is trying to accomplish. The configuration of values will differ from one organization to another, but the goal is to align the values with the organization's intent, structures, and practices so that they support the achievement of desired outcomes.

Shared values do not mean homogeneous values. Values are different around the world and from culture to culture. The headquarters of a Silicon Valley, California, global enterprise cannot effectively dictate its values to its business unit in Japan. However, it can both cultivate its values and honor the diversity of values within the context of its overall enterprise values framework. As a result, networked enterprises with multiple centers around the world find that they have to move away from being headquarters-centric and learn how to incorporate the diversity of values as a requirement to achieving meaningful communication and collaboration.

The knowledge-based enterprise must then distill and continuously readjust its overall values framework so that it resonates across the different cultures of its extended enterprise. Only when an enterprise has a vital culture can it deal effectively with issues of technology and globalization and also tackle the very difficult, but important, intangible stuff of national boundaries, cultural differences, and identities, which can easily sink vastly valuable economic combinations.

A fundamental values shift taking place in the next-generation knowledge enterprise is the transition from the values of an entitlement culture, distinguished by dependence, to a culture based on self-initiative and interdependence, where people see themselves as businesses of one. This shift is essential for the enterprise to fully engage the capabilities found in the human capital of its workforce to continually build and rebuild the enterprise. The enterprise can provide the context, the cultural framework, the educational opportunities, and the supporting technologies for people in the workforce, but people must see they are autonomous actors who are working for their own interests while they are simultaneously accomplishing the strategic intent of the enterprise and meeting the customer's interests.

The shift to autonomy goes beyond the traditional notion of empowerment, since the basis of empowerment is that people need to be given power or authority by an organization. In contrast, with autonomy, people, by definition, have the power to begin with, and it is the organization's job to support them in carrying out their individual responsibilities to achieve enterprise goals.

Core Components in Place

A next-generation knowledge-based enterprise needs a robust and resilient knowledge structure in place to be effective. At the core of the knowledge structure is a small leadership team that coordinates the knowledge strategy with groups of colleagues dispersed throughout the enterprise. Large, monolithic, headquarters-based knowledge organizations are not as effective in the rapidly changing and collaborative next-generation world.

A second component of the knowledge effort is a working budget that provides the necessary resources to support the activities. A third component concerns incentives. The enterprise changes and aligns the incentives for all participants to reward core behaviors so that they are in accord with the culture and actions necessary to meet enterprise goals. These incentives reward autonomy, just-in-time learning, and collaboration, while dissuading clannishness and adherence to rigid prescriptions.

Tied to its emphasis on learning and collaboration, the enterprise transitions itself from its current, more vertical structure to become organized as a dynamic set of knowledge communities. These communities understand that they need as members both visionaries, who can map out the larger changing context, and pragmatists, who have their strengths in developing and carrying out operations. Each are needed to make the knowledge enterprise resilient since the knowledge economy will rapidly move from boom to bust and back again. These communities must enable the enterprise to be robust enough to accommodate the rapid development and dispersion of knowledge, short time horizons, production runs, and life cycles that require continuous reinvention. In keeping with the shift toward autonomy, community members themselves gradually transition from seeing themselves as employees to, instead, understanding themselves as collaborating citizens in control of their intellectual capital investments.

Another component is a technological infrastructure that can facilitate the exchange of knowledge. New technologies also enable knowledge to be captured while people are doing their work, allowing the enterprise to much more easily access both tacit and explicit knowledge so that it can evaluate, share, and leverage it.

Finally, the knowledge-based enterprise has a performance-based measurement system for tracking and navigation. Internally, such a system allows senior leaders, middle managers, and front line employees to understand how well their knowledge recipes are working, where corrections need to be made, and how what they do affects and is affected by everything else in the enterprise system. Externally, performance-based measurement allows stakeholders, analysts, and market makers a more transparent understanding of how the organization is operating and thereby gives them a better basis to evaluate a company for investment purposes.

Learning

There is no split between learning and working in the next-generation knowledge enterprise. There is far less of a need to take time off to learn since learning is built into the knowledge process. The knowledge effort is part of a broader and more integrated effort to manage and develop human capability for enhanced business performance. In the extended network, not only is the workforce continuously engaged in a learning process but also all stakeholders are participants, including customers. The sharing of new knowledge is necessary to co-create the goods and services that are increasingly customized and continuously renewed.

This means that the next-generation enterprise fights its wars on the basis of its capabilities and that strategies are based on the ability to hustle, that is, to change as conditions change. Continuous just-in-time learning is a central tenet of operations, where management sets the framework and learning context and individual workers take control of their own learning, which allows them to work more effectively toward the enterprise's goals and objectives, while at the same time building their own personal capabilities. In this new environment, everyone becomes a chief learning officer, responsible for her own learning.

A major implication of this change is in the research and development area, which transitions from being a separate and special unit to being the domain of the entire organization. All members become responsible for contributing their insights and experiences to the knowledge base and to the creation and marketing of new products and services.

Getting the Knowledge-Based Enterprise off the Ground

Springboard Storytelling

Knowledge-based enterprises use stories to describe specific instances of how the knowledge approach has contributed to the achievement of business objectives. Knowledge teams leading the knowledge effort use storytelling and other approaches to spark, ignite, and catalyze what knowledge flows across the enterprise. By highlighting how significant and relevant accomplishments took place, storytelling draws people into co-creating their vision of how they can develop the enterprise with their own initiatives, for themselves, in their own work, and in their own context.

Role of Leadership

A key role for leadership is to create the demand for knowledge initiatives from an enterprise performance perspective. Leadership, by setting up the enterprise knowledge framework, puts themselves at the forefront of their organizations. As they navigate the organization into becoming a knowledge enterprise, they strengthen the best of the organization's own values, its practices for innovation, and the roles that everyone plays. A complementary effect of instituting the knowledge effort is that the enterprise finds it has enhanced its ability for recruitment and retention since the emerging enterprise is seen as a most exciting, attractive place for people to join and stay.

Leadership also requires that the enterprise expand its definition of intangibles management to include social and environmental dimensions. While a number of enterprises have included these relationships in their annual reports for some time, next-generation enterprises distinguish themselves by actively connecting and recasting these efforts as part of their overall intangibles development strategy. This changes how programs are carried out, but equally important, it also changes how stakeholders and the general public perceive what the enterprise is doing and the array of issues it considers critical to its well-being and future. This is part of the ongoing building of the brand of the organization and the strengthening of the relationships in its network. As this takes place, people become more aware of the role the enterprise is taking in the world and take enhanced pride in the enterprise.

Role of Managers

Managers and supervisors function as the enterprise's gatekeepers since they have the greatest awareness of the knowledge-building or -destroying implications of whatever they do. Managers, supervisors, and the people they manage develop core skills in negotiating flexible, customized deals, which are win-win contracts for both the enterprise and those employed. These deals are the operating framework in which people can see the basis for how they receive a high rate of return on the investment of their human capital and where enterprises can see how they gain the capability to rapidly and effectively bring offerings to the market.

Managers and supervisors also take the lead in using the principle of creative abrasion in organizing the work of the enterprise. They deliberately hire people and formulate teams of people who think differently to unleash the creative potential that is latent in a collection of unlike-minded individuals. They have the skills to promote and manage the creative diversity of their teams so that the teams have the requisite variety of responses to the unprecedented, novel situations with which they are charged to deal.

Role of the Workforce

Enterprises engage owners of human capital, who have the abilities and behaviors to allow them to gauge what the market wants, develop an offering quickly, and then get it out to the world. People, in turn, are recognized as the owners and investors of their human capital and are able to move their human capital assets freely from one organization to another if they choose. As part of the deal, enterprises do not force people to learn solely to help the enterprise but to build themselves up and to develop knowledge capacities that are directly actionable.

From Audit to Assessment

The enterprise moves from traditional audits to an intangibles assessment orientation, where enterprise leaders are highly aware of the factors that are driving what is being measured and disclosed. With an understanding of these drivers, leaders can determine what is going wrong in an organization, what is going well, what could go better, and how and where to make improvements. This is a shift away from financial accounting and toward a richer, more contemporary version of management accounting. This assessment in the future may not be called accounting but will use a framework outside the accounting model that provides for a more contextual valuation, recognizing that value is, realistically, derived from the perspectives of the various stakeholders. This transition also deals directly with the notion that innovation in an enterprise is not only about new goods and services but also intimately about the enterprise business model as well, that is, how innovatively leaders manage.

This updated rendition of accounting is called forward accounting. In it, funds provided for building intangibles, such as brand, websites, and other intangible wealth, are recognized as creating value and not accounted for only as expenses.

Underlying this change in accounting in the next generation is a systematic recognition of intangibles that includes the reporting of these intangibles in financial statements. This new information is material in allowing investors and decision makers to compare company to company and sector to sector.

Forward accounting also shows how the intellectual capital of an enterprise will impact on the enterprise's future earnings and growth, giving investors the chance to look at an enterprise and say, "I understand their intellectual capital portfolio and their basis, and therefore I am going to invest based on these, these, and these factors." The result is a more efficient capital allocation and investment environment, and it brings about the establishment of a level playing field for all organizations, regardless of whether they are more bricks-and-mortar intensive or intangible-knowledge intensive.

Alliances

Alliances may become the most important value driver of all for knowledge enterprises. Alliances create the ability to leverage a network or web of commercial contacts to create value. This means that an enterprise can morph into a permeable organization that derives value from alliances, not solely from end-to-end control. This changes the whole dynamic of the enterprise, requiring the use of a different set of principles for navigating in a network environment.

Intellectual Assets and Intellectual Property

One major change that takes place in the next generation of knowledge organizations is that there is less value in protecting information and more value in sharing information. Things move and change too quickly, with too many people needing to have access and be involved in continuously innovative change. Rapid innovation leads to new developments that may make patents obsolete long before the investments are recouped. Yet, obtaining patents continues to be a time-and-money-intensive, as well as uncertain, process. Despite reforms and reengineering, patent offices of the world will not be able to keep up with patenting. Business is not going to wait for them to change and is setting up intellectual capital exchanges, similar to stock exchanges.

Existing intellectual property exchanges already allow intellectual capital portfolio managers to make decisions on which properties have significant value to the enterprise and are worth protecting and which are worth more to the company by being sold on the market. The next generation will go several steps beyond and make the full array of intellectual property accessible in a market environment.

Future Centers

Knowledge-based enterprises need to live in both the present and the future. They realize that they cannot guide the enterprise by the views they get from looking in their rearview mirrors. Instead, they link their short-term actions to what they expect will be the markets of the future. This gives them the chance to create those markets and not just react to them. This perspective makes an enterprise more open to a range of opportunities and interests it might otherwise miss, or for which it would not be prepared.

A future orientation is systematically embedded into all of the enterprise's structures and processes. It sets up future centers, whether its own or as part of a collaborative group, where the enterprise experiments with knowledge-based prototypes of goods and services that might be needed in the future. It looks at the upcoming world from the perspective of the next generation and takes the needs of that generation seriously. Its future context provokes a broader thinking about what capacities need to be developed for future needs and also keeps a keen look on present capacities to see how they can be adaptable for future conditions. Developing a good future orientation can accommodate short-term market expectations while countering tendencies for too myopic a vision and a premature obsolescence of goods and services.

Moving to the Next Generation

The elements discussed here are a number of the dimensions of a next-generation knowledge framework. While there will be new developments and perspectives emerging every year, this group of dimensions provides a baseline opportunity to take a good look at an organization and benchmark its readiness to operate as a knowledge-based enterprise. Anyone in the enterprise, from the leadership to the front line, can today map out how the enterprise looks at knowledge as a factor of production, as an engine for change, and as the basis for building the future. That is an exciting and valuable perspective. It is also a highly participatory perspective.

Be part of the conversation involved in creating the next generation of knowledge-based enterprises. Look at your organization and see how well it is embedding knowledge into its processes, practices, perspectives, and actions. Begin the process by sharing the materials in *Knowledge Capital* with your colleagues. Try out some of the ideas and practices discussed in one of the chapters. Your new experience will stimulate you and your organization to rethink the business recipes you use. In the course of your conversations, you will build the knowledge-based enterprise.

The message is that no one owns the future or the next generation of the knowledge movement. There are also no predetermined winners in the upcoming Wars of Capabilities. Those wars will be won by those who perceive that the world is continually changing, that knowledge is a central ingredient in any business recipe, and that a knowledge-based enterprise will be the best opportunity zone in which to be.

Leading Your Organization into Becoming a Knowledge-Based Enterprise

1. What are examples of how knowledge has grown as a factor of production in your organization?

2. What kinds of knowledge are key inputs in your organization's goods and services offerings?

3. How do you measure and report the value of your knowledge assets (from more directly measurable intellectual property to harder-to-measure intangibles, such as brand, the ability to respond, and so on)? Do these measures help guide organizational decision making and resource allocation?

4. Is your organization moving to become a sense-and-respond enterprise? What is helping your organization move down that path? What is blocking you?

5. What is your knowledge strategy? How was it created, and who is deploying it? How do you measure the effectiveness of your implementation?

6. How do you make sure you include the necessary knowledge inputs in your organizational processes to ensure high levels of performance?

7. What are the core shared values of your organization? How did you determine them? Who is responsible for ensuring that they are aligned with your knowledge strategy and your organizational goals?

8. Who is part of your knowledge enterprise, and how do they link in

your knowledge network (for example, senior leadership, middle management, supervisors, front line workforce, strategic partners/suppliers, customers)?

9. How can you use springboard stories (how people successfully overcame obstacles through using knowledge-based interventions) as catalysts for knowledge sharing?

10. How are you preparing for the future? Who is responsible for anticipating the needs of the next generation of customers and for developing the knowledge for prototyping responses to those needs?

RESOURCES:

Books for Building a
Knowledge-Based Enterprise

Adriessen, Daniel, and Rene Tissen. *Weightless Wealth: Find Your Real Value in a Future of Intangible Assets*. London: Financial Times/Prentice Hall, 2000.

Blair, Margaret M., and Steven M. H. Wallman. *Unseen Wealth: Report of the Brookings Task Force on Intangibles*. Washington, D.C.: Brookings Institution Press, 2001.

Botkin, Jim. *Smart Business: How Knowledge Communities Can Revolutionize Your Company*. New York: Free Press, 1999.

Brooking, Annie. *Intellectual Capital: Core Asset for the Third-Millennium Enterprise*. London: International Thompson Business Press, 1996.

Chatzkel, Jay. *Intellectual Capital*. Oxford: Capstone, 2002.

Collison, Chris, and Geoff Parcell. *Learning to Fly: Practical Lessons from One of the World's Leading Knowledge Companies*. Oxford: Capstone, 2001.

Danish Trade and Industry Development Council. *Intellectual Capital Accounts: Reporting and Managing Intellectual Capital*. Copenhagen: Erhvervsfremme Styrelsen, 1998.

Davenport, Thomas H., and Laurence Prusak. *Working Knowledge: How Organizations Manage What They Know*. Boston: Harvard Business School Press, 1998.

Davenport, Thomas O. *Human Capital: What It Is and Why People Invest It*. San Francisco, Calif.: Jossey-Bass, 1999.

Davis, Julie L., and Suzanne Harrison. *Edison in the Boardroom: How Leading Companies Realize Value from Innovation*. New York: Wiley, 2001.

Davis, Stan, and Christopher Meyer. *Blur: The Speed of Change in the Connected Economy*. New York: Warner, 1998.

Denning, Stephen. *The Springboard: How Storytelling Ignites Action in Knowledge-Era Organizations*. Boston: Butterworth-Heinemann, 2000.

Dixon, Nancy. *Common Knowledge: How Companies Thrive by Sharing What They Know*. Boston: Harvard Business School Press, 2000.

Edvinsson, Leif. *Corporate Longitude: What You Need to Know to Navigate the Knowledge Economy*. London: Financial Times/Prentice Hall, 2002.

Edvinsson, Leif, and Michael S. Malone. *Intellectual Capital: Realizing Your Company's True Value by Finding Its Hidden Brainpower*. New York: Harper-Business, 1997.

Fitz-enz, Jac. *The ROI of Human Capital: Measuring the Economic Value of Employee Performance*. New York: AMACOM, 2000.

Leonard-Barton, Dorothy A. *Wellsprings of Knowledge: Building and Sustaining the Sources of Innovation*. Boston: Harvard Business School Press, 1995.

Leonard, Dorothy A., and Walter C. Swap. *When Sparks Fly: Igniting Creativity in Groups*. Boston: Harvard Business School Press, 1999.

Lev, Baruch. *Intangibles: Management, Measurement, and Reporting*. Washington, D.C.: Brookings Institution Press, 2001.

Low, Jonathan, and Pam Cohen Kalafut. *Invisible Advantage: How Intangibles Are Driving Business Performance*. Boston: Perseus, 2002.

Rumizen, Melissie C. *The Complete Idiot's Guide to Knowledge Management*. Indianapolis, Ind.: Alpha, 2002.

Saint-Onge, Hubert, and Debra Wallace. *Leveraging Communities of Practice for Strategic Advantage*. Boston: Butterworth-Heinemann, 2002.

Stewart, Thomas A. *Intellectual Capital: The New Wealth of Nations*. New York: Currency Doubleday, 1997.

Sullivan, Patrick H. *Value-Driven Intellectual Capital: How to Convert Intangible Corporate Assets into Market Value*. New York: Wiley, 2000.

Sveiby, Karl Erik. *The New Organizational Wealth: Managing and Measuring Knowledge-Based Assets*. San Francisco, Calif.: Berrett-Koehler, 1997.

Teece, David J. *Managing Intellectual Capital: Organizational, Strategic and Policy Dimensions*. New York: Oxford University Press, 2001.

Wenger, Etienne, Richard McDermott, and William Snyder. *Cultivating Communities of Practice: A Guide to Managing Knowledge*. Boston: Harvard Business School Press, 2002.

Wiig, Karl M. *Knowledge Management Foundations: Thinking about Thinking—How People and Organizations Create, Represent, and Use Knowledge*. Arlington, Tex.: Schema, 1993.

———. *Knowledge Management: The Central Management Focus for Intelligent-Acting Organizations*. Arlington, Tex.: Schema, 1994.

———. *Knowledge Management Methods: Practical Approaches to Managing Knowledge*. Arlington, Tex.: Schema, 1995.

INDEX:

natural segmentation approach, 96
Naval Sea Systems Command, 385
navigators. *See* IC navigators
near-death experience, 48–49
"need to know," 150
networked organizations, 146–48, 210, 222, 316, 382
network organizational models, 42–43, 48, 51, 54
networks of communities, 357–59
neural networks, 70–71
new economy organizations, 45–48, 50
　catalysts for, 177–79
　human capital in, 165–66
　IC growth model and, 111–12
　intangibles in, 258, 262–66
　knowledge sharing in, 360
　values alignment in, 219
New York Stock Exchange, 111
NICE (Newly Intellectualized Capital and E-Solutions), 125
Nike sneakers, 42
1980 Census, The (Mitroff, Mason, and Barabba), 130
Nissan Design International, 33
NMCI (Navy/Marine Corps Internet), 371, 375, 377–78
nodes, 368
Nokia, 118
No Limits to Learning (Botkin, Elmandjra, and Malitza), 41
nonalignment of values, 214–15
nondurable manufacturing companies, 249–51
nonfinancial reports, 121, 243–44, 245
Norsk Hydro, 68
Norway, 126, 255
not-for-profit opportunity, 193

Ober, Josiah, 225
OECD (Organization for Economic Cooperation and Development), 257
old economy organizations, 46–48
　IC growth model in, 111–12, 115
　intangibles and, 245–46, 262–64, 266
　knowledge sharing in, 360
Olivetti, 255
Olson, Ken, 47–48

OnStar system, 49, 145–46
opportunity for growth and advancement, 184–85, 187–88, 195
Oracle, 123
order-to-delivery mechanism, 152–53
organizational capital, 87, 125–27
organizational development (OD), 179–80
organizational learning, 57–58
Organization and Employee Research Practice, 182
Organization for Economic Cooperation and Development (OECD), 242
Oriel, Sharon, 15–16, 274–75, 324–39
Outlast Technologies, 41–42
outsourcing, 370–71

paradigm knowledge, 58, *fig. 4.1*
Pareto level, 101
Parker, Mike, 332
partnering, 291
PCMs (phase-change materials), 41–42
peer processes, 300
perceived value, 93, 95–97, 102–6, *fig. 5.5*
performance metrics, 217–18
Perrin, Towers, 182
personal knowledge, 58, 59–60
personal navigators, 123, 127
perspective, 26
　IC, 104–7
　organizational, 66
　systematic, 129
Petrash, Gordon, 326, 328
Piaget, Jean, 185
Pike, Stephen, 103
plateau jumps, 378–79
Polaroid, 46
political entrepreneurship, 118–19
Porras, Jerry I., 179
Porter, Dan, 364
Porter, L. W., 90
Pottruck, Dave, 186, 193
Power of Team (Porter et al.), 364
pragmatists, 44–45
price as value driver, 95, *fig. 5.5*
Prince Henry the Navigator, 9–10, 17
process leaders, 331